Fine
WoodWorking
Design Book Three

Fine WoodWorking
Design Book Three

558 photographs of the best
work in wood
by 540 craftspeople

Selected by the editors
of *Fine Woodworking* magazine

The Taunton Press

Cover photograph:

Tim Donahue–Furniture Designer,
Wilton, Conn.

Sphere Construction; figured gum, walnut veneers; 18 in. dia., 2 lb. Photo by Woody Packard.

"A design exercise made in response to the definition of a vessel. The sphere is hollow and completely closed."

©1983 by The Taunton Press, Inc.

First printing: June 1983
International Standard Book Number 0-918804-18-3
Library of Congress Catalog Card Number 77-79327
Printed in the United States of America

A Fine Woodworking Book

Fine Woodworking® is a trademark of The Taunton Press, Inc., registered in the U.S. Patent and Trademark Office.

The Taunton Press, Inc.
52 Church Hill Road
Box 355
Newtown, Connecticut 06470

Contents

Introduction

Welcome to *Fine Woodworking Design Book Three*, a broad photographic survey of the state of the woodworker's art in the early 1980s, an idea book.

Among all the crafts, woodworking is fundamental, because with wood you can make just about any tool or construction you might need: bowls to buildings. This very ubiquity may be why woodworking in general and furniture making in particular seem the odd men out, isolated from the craftier crafts by woodwork's necessity to function, and situated in the intellectual shadows of industrial design, architecture and sculpture. In our century, the economics of industrial design or mass production, along with the proliferation of uniform synthetic materials, almost eliminated the activity of designing and making wooden furniture. Why its revival now? I have heard various speculations, none persuasive. It's true that the cost of shipping and marketing mass-produced goods has grown so cumbersome that furniture made in small shops is competitive once again, though some people contend that it always was competitive, especially at the high end. It's also true that woodworking is thoroughly absorbing, but other activities offer equal challenge, though few are so enduringly satisfactory when finished. Sometimes I imagine the trees themselves have called out to some druidically receptive individuals.

For whatever reason, increasing numbers of people have taken up woodworking. For most it is a consuming hobby, bu some of them have found ways to make a living at it. Whether done by amateur or professional craftspeople, the work i this book makes it clear that technical mastery is not the problem it was just a few years ago. These people have learne how to make wooden objects that will last. Consequently, analysis of woodworking technique has become less fruitfu and technique is no longer an issue for much critical discussion. At the same time, the academic critics have grudgingly al lowed that antique furniture as the interior expression of architecture is high art, but this merit badge hasn't yet bee passed along to contemporary furniture. Critical discussion has only rarely gone beyond the mere categorization of styles

Consequently, artisan woodworkers and designer-craftspeople working in wood often have a hard time figuring out wha to think about what they do. They have no ready map showing how their work fits in among contemporary art, craft an design. Under the circumstances, it's easy to imagine one's own production to be the field's main line, to regar everything else by anybody else as trivial aberrations. However, as the photographs in this book demonstrate, there ar any number of true paths and no one main line. Post-modernists and eighteenth-century loyalists alike prefer the comfor of forms and details they've seen before.

As you look at the work in this book, remember that to understand a piece of woodworking, before bothering abou styles, you ought to consider what the maker says about his or her intentions, as well as what the object says for itself. On may ask for whom the thing was made, for what purpose, and on what sort of budget? A showpiece of a table built o speculation is a different class of object than a dining table commissioned by a family with children. How was the piec made, in which woods and other materials, and how important were the tools in determining its ultimate appearance What ideas drove the maker, what was he or she trying to do? A seat that intends simply to be sturdy and comfortabl tells a different story than one meant for the ceremonial use of the chairman of the board. Unlike the makers of antiqu furniture, contemporary artisans are available (usually eager) to discuss their concerns in economic, technical and artisti terms. But to those who stop and listen, a successful piece of furniture or sculpture, whether contemporary or antique speaks for itself. Is the chair comfortable, the table inviting? Are the cabinet's proportions harmonious, its hardwar tasty? Does the sculpture touch you, make you think?

Where this book came from—In late 1982, *Fine Woodworking* magazine invited its 250,000 readers to send i photographs of the best work they had done during the previous four years. The ensuing 2,800 manila envelope disgorged about 20,000 photographs. Entrants were offered a directory listing in the back of this book, and thousands c them accepted (p. 193). We loaded the envelopes into a mountainous wall of 30 filing drawers. During the next six week we sifted the mountain down to a single drawerful of photos, which our editorial and production staffs then transforme into this book.

Faced with that mountain of envelopes, we could feel only respect for the people whose work it represented, for the tru those woodworkers had placed in us. A random peek anywhere in the collection was likely to uncover awesomely goo woodworking. Nevertheless, our job was somehow to jury out most of the entries. We had to remind ourselves that w were going to publish a book of photographs. We were not seeing any actual wooden pieces. We were choosin photographs of things designed and made out of wood. The best black-and-white photograph in the world is still a abstract step backward from the real object. Some kinds of woodworking take good photographs, but some, lik marquetry pictures, do not.

Our first step was finding the best photographs—performing triage on the whole set of entries, sorting them into "Yes "No" and "Maybe" piles. The "No" pile, half the set, was for photographs that were too tiny, blurry or greyed-out t print, too cluttered or close-cropped to fit onto a page. The "Yes" pile was for superior photographs that had evoked pleasurable "ahhh" when removed from their envelopes. Everything else was "Maybe." Over the next two weeks, fou rors (myself as editor of *Fine Woodworking* magazine, associate editor Rick Mastelli, contributing editor Tage Frid and Taunton Press design director Roger Barnes, along with Emma Frid, who kept those envelopes smoothly flowing) sifted the "Yes" and "Maybe" entries down to the 558 photographs published here.

We four jurors are all craftspeople ourselves. We know what it takes in skull-sweat, time, skill, materials and pure perseverance to design, make and finish a careful piece of woodworking. Often we could gauge the spirit behind an entry by the way it came to us: an envelope scribbled into the mail by a busy shop accustomed to sending pictures to juries and prospective clients, a package meticulously swaddled to defy postal mishap. Some entries included long letters full of hope for the small spot of celebrity that publication might bring. Others were almost anonymously casual. Most entries, however, revealed a quiet pride in accomplishment—the maker evidently having already received the real satisfaction in designing, building and presenting the real wooden things whose images we now held.

While we might assess design in a photograph, craftsmanship ought to be seen and touched. Even so, we often saw startlingly good design flawed by obviously shoddy craftsmanship, or doomed by cross-grain construction. Some entrants eliminated themselves with their own detail photos: the piece looked great, but the joinery close-up revealed ugly gaps. We saw many sparkling photographs of apparently superb craftsmanship applied to well-known designs. These were as likely to be contemporary as traditional; people enjoy making (and need in their homes) the quiet little cabinets that James Krenov has popularized, as much as they like Early American corner cupboards. Such favorites are most satisfying to make, and so we included good examples of the various types. We enjoyed the juxtapositions of things often seen with new variations, and new ideas.

When we prepared our first design book, in the spring of 1977 (then titled "biennial," since we naively expected to be able to do it every two years), we were astounded by the outpouring of talent, the woodworking exuberance, it revealed. Even so, it was difficult to come up with enough good photos for even a slim volume. *Design Book Two*, in 1979, was a deliberate attempt to survey the breadth of the craft and give some small exposure to as many woodworkers as possible. But we learned that woodworking is too slow and two years too short for design ideas to advance much, so we came to prefer a more selective, more spacious layout. *Design Book Three* follows a four-year pause. We think it documents a vigorously maturing craft and art. I hope you enjoy its pages.

John Kelsey
May 18, 1983

Bowls

John Whitehead, Portland, Oreg.
Bowl; birch; 7 in. x 5.5 in. Tooled finish.
"I like the immediacy and directness of turning. I try to reach the viewer (and toucher) through a combination of discipline and spontaneity."

Francois Lambert, St. Polycarpe, Quebec, Canada

Salad bowl; elm; 7 in. x 14 in. Photo by Andre Bourbonnais.

John Jeno Linek, Brisbane, Queensland, Australia

Open Forms; jacaranda; 6 in. x 6 in.

"Mostly working from the log, incorporating bark, sapwood and defects. I only enhance what is already there."

(Bottom left) **Michael Hosaluk,** Saskatoon, Saskatchewan, Canada

Bowl; Manitoba maple burl; 4 in. x 7.5 in. Photo by Grant Kernan.

John A. Sage, Liberty, Maine

#4 Weed Bowl; spruce burl; 10 in. x 16 in. x 16 in. Photo by Brian Vanden Brink.

Dennis A. Dahl, Phillips, Wis.

Vase; cherry; 5.5 in. x 3.5 in. Photo by R. Bruce Thompson.

Lawrence Judd, Yamhill, Oreg.
Bowls; black walnut and English walnut graft; 7 in. x 10 in., 7 in. x 6.5 in. Green-turned, irregular tops. Photo by Edwin Borgeson.

F. W. Schmidt, Austin, Tex.
Weed Pot; oak; 4.75 in. x 3.5 in.
"Small gouge was used to texture natural defects in this wood. Area of texture flashed with torch."

Ed Taylor, McLean, Va.
Bowl; willow burl; 9 in. x 4 in. Photo by C. M. Robb.

Wendell Smith, Fairport, N.Y.
Hollow Form; curly maple; 8 in. dia.

Peter Winters, Los Angeles, Calif.
Bowl #32; thuya burl; 4.88 in. x 6.5 in., 4 oz.

Felicia Fields, Felton, Calif.
Bowl; Norfolk Island pine; 3.75 in. x 4 in.
Photo by Michael Kirkpatrick.

"Wood is from Hawaii; knots are translucent
red when held up to the light."

Del Stubbs, Chico, Calif.
Tulips; manzanita limbs; tallest, 3 in. high.

Jack Fenwick, Montreal, Quebec, Canada

*Bowl with lid; spalted beech; 4 in. x 5.75 in.
Plate; bird's-eye yellow cedar; 1.25 in. x 6
in. Bowl; spalted beech; 3 in. x 5 in. Photo
by Kennon Cooke.*

A. J. Golichowski, South Bend, Ind.

*Laminated wood jar; mahogany, white ash,
walnut veneer; 7.5 in. x 6.25 in. Photo by
Commercial Photo Service Inc.*

"After a Costa Rican ceramic jar (circa 500
B.C.) in National Gallery of Art."

Francis L. Scott, Gowanda, N.Y.

*Brandy snifters; lignum vitae; 6 in. high.
Photo by John Slaughter.*

"They are not coated or finished with
anything (completely unnecessary)."

Bruce Mitchell, Inverness, Calif.

*Tripoda 1982; bay laurel burl; 4 in. x 13.5 in.
Photo by Richard Allen.*

"I'm exploring the expressive qualities of
wood to fulfill the need for vessels which
transcend traditional functions of utility."

Clead Christiansen, North Ogden, Utah

*Hollow-turned vase; wormy ash; 4 in. x 6 in.
Photo by Peter G. Russell.*

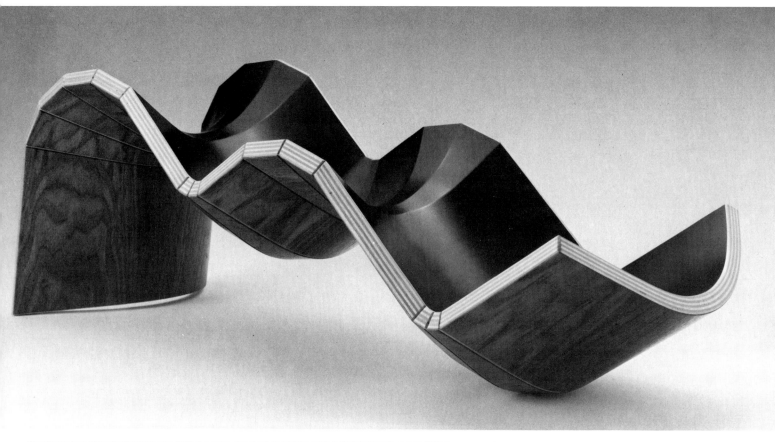

Donald Lloyd McKinley, Mississauga, Ontario, Canada

Segmented Serpentine Double Bowl; walnut face veneer, maple core; 10 in. x 10 in. x 27.5 in. Polyurethane finish (black inside). Photo by Paul Newberry.

"As a salad bowl, inevitable surplus cascades to lower level and allows a different dressing to be used."

Garn Menapace, Spencer, N.Y.
Carved bowl; cherry; 4 in. x 6.5 in. x 8 in.

Robert W. Sheedy, Tacoma, Wash.
Turned container; padauk, Honduras rosewood legs, ebony claws; 24 in. x 10 in. Lid lifts off, revealing 3-in. opening.

"Round forms are life forms."

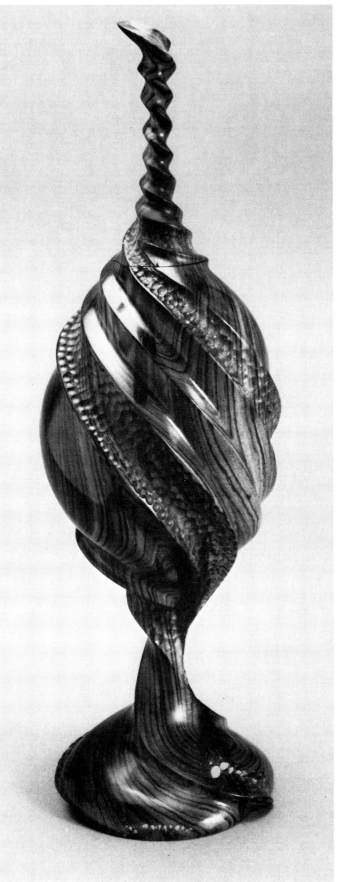

David Groth, Trinidad, Calif.

Salad set; myrtlewood; 9.5 in. x 27 in. x 27 in.

"I attempt to combine function with simplicity of design into the expression of my work."

Todd Hoyer, Bisbee, Ariz.

Homage to Nakashima; Sonoran acacia, ebony; 3 in. x 16 in. Collection of E. Jacobson. Photo by Lutz Studio.

(Bottom left) **Terry L. Evans,** Augusta, Kans.

Confetti Box; maple, cristobal, rosewood, sycamore, locust, pear, moradillo, walnut, purpleheart, kingwood, persimmon, maple veneers; 4.5 in. x 6.5 in. x 5.5 in. Photo by Michael Carlisle.

William Hunter, El Portal, Calif.

Wavelength Urn; kingwood; 12 in. x 4 in. Photo by Bob Barrett.

"Some days I feel like the luckiest guy in the world! I'm able to make a living at something I enjoy so much."

Cabinets

Richard L. Heisey, Winchester, Va.

*Breakfront china cabinet; (solid woods)
Honduras mahogany, yellow pine, maple;
(veneers) mahogany crotch, striped
mahogany; (inlays) plum pudding
mahogany, African cherry, maple burl,
boxwood, ebony, bee's-wing satinwood,
curly maple, Pennsylvania cherry, ivory;
89.5 in. x 72 in. x 20.5 in. Photo by Ed
Holdsworth.*

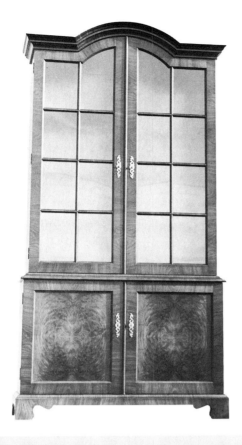

Fred F. Siedow, Jr., Portland, Oreg.

Bookcase; American black walnut, walnut and crotch walnut veneers, glass, brass hardware; 90 in. x 49 in. x 16 in. Made in two separate pieces. Photo by Stacy Wong.

Allan Smith, Pennington, N.J.

Chest of drawers with latticework sides; white oak; 50 in. x 36 in. x 21 in.

"Idea for decorative latticework provided by my client, Dr. P.S. Shenkin."

Silas Kopf, Northampton, Mass.

Telephone Stand; birch plywood (painted black), parquetry door of benin, padauk and three species of mahogany; 30 in. x 16 in. x 16 in. Photo by David L. Ryan.

Béla Foltin, Jr., Athens, Ga.

Dowry Chest; red oak; 40 in. x 22 in. x 32 in. Photo by Susan Snyder.

"The design is in the style of old Hungarian peasant chests."

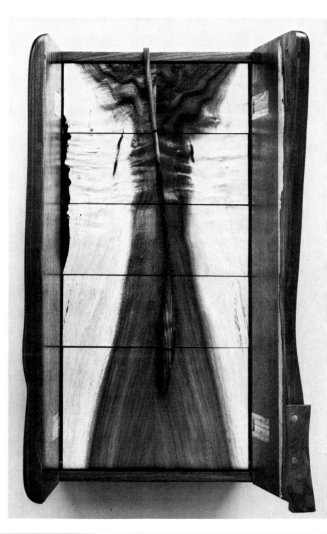

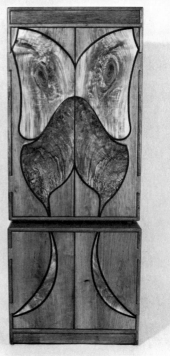

Michael Kranz, Bennington, Vt.
Sideboard; black walnut, padauk; 36 in. x 40 in. x 14 in. Photo by Christie Nevius.

Charles B. Cobb, Santa Rosa, Calif.
Double Image Series #3 (wall-hung cabinet); African padauk, Hawaiian koa, tulipwood hinges. Suede-lined drawers. (Cabinet is shown closed at bottom.) 36 in. x 18 in. x 1⅛ in. Photos by Bill Galloway.

Raymond A. Kelso, Collegeville, Pa.
Secretary; cherry, cottonwood, spalted curly maple, walnut; 86 in. x 35 in. x 21 in. Photo by Bruce A. Blank.

Roger Deatherage, Houston, Tex.
Display Cabinet; walnut, Brazilian rosewood, East Indian rosewood, glass, Plexiglas; 26 in. x 9 in. x 7.5 in.

**William Riemer and Peggy Riemer,
Little Wolf Time Co.,** Ogdensburg, Wis.
*Sunburst Cedar Chest; cherry, aromatic
cedar, birch; 24 in. x 49 in. x 19 in. Photo
by Image Studios.*

Barry R. Yavener, Bethesda, Md.
*Blanket chest; imbuya; 20 in. x 40 in. x 18
in. Photo by Ken Nelson.*

Michael Mocho, Jemez Springs, N. Mex.
*Cabinet; Honduras mahogany; 72 in. x 32 in.
x 15.5 in. Photo by Dick Kent.*

Bix duPont, Glastonbury, Conn.
*Sweater chest; cherry, cedar, oak; 32 in. x 43
in. x 23 in. Photo by Phillip A. Fortune.*

Timothy J. Zikratch, Pocatello, Idaho
*Stereo cabinet; cherry, bird's-eye maple,
black walnut, stained glass, brass hinges; 80
in. x 27 in. x 20 in. Photo by Peter Vincent.*

Doug Courtney, Portland, Oreg.
*Chest-on-chest; rosewood, ebony, brass; 72
in. x 36 in. x 16 in.*

Dimitri Cilione, Tucson, Ariz.
*Butsudan (Buddhist altar); eastern black
walnut, California walnut, gold leaf,
florescent lights; 72 in. x 52 in. x 28 in.
Photo by Dianne Nilsen.*

"This piece was done for a very religious,
sweet Japanese woman."

Jeffrey N. Dale, Petaluma, Calif.

Armoire and lotus chair; (armoire) Andaman padauk; 80 in. x 44 in. x 24 in. (chair) cherry; 36 in. x 25 in. x 22 in. Hoopes collection. Photo by Morrie Camhi.

"I draw upon impressions collected from world travel and contact with other cultures. I bring these to bear upon the processes of design and construction, which I execute simultaneously."

Aesthetic Designs in Hardwood, Vallejo, Calif.

Chest of drawers; Honduras rosewood, red oak, baltic birch; 42 in. x 41 in. x 21 in. Photo by Steve Rugg.

"Book-matched rosewood drawer fronts determined the design and size."

Mike Norby, Dallas, Tex.

Commode; walnut, pecan, purpleheart, teak, tulipwood, red oak; 27 in. x 36 in. x 21 in.

"I greatly enjoyed the challenge of devising new ways to interpret an old form. In some respects, it is more difficult than developing new shapes."

Joel Katzowitz, Marietta, Ga.

Movers Dresser; solid oak and plywood, birch plywood, mahogany, acrylic paint; 39 in. x 58 in. x 18 in.

"The dresser's cratelike look is reinforced by the fact that its only means of support appears to be the two painted movers."

Steven Emrick, Ellensburg, Wash.
Desk; cherry, walnut, ash; 54 in. x 36 in.

David Curry, Heartwood, Boulder, Colo.
Hall Tree; cherry, oak, leaded-glass mirror; 78 in. x 27 in. x 14 in. Photo by Photo Works.

Thomas C. MacMichael, Ellensburg, Wash.
Self-Closing Circular Cabinet; ash, cherry, black walnut; 43 in. dia., 14 in. deep.

"The door rotates at the center on an axle to admit one to any of the eight storage areas. Due to the lack of equal weight in the open-door section, the entire door recloses immediately. This piece was designed for clothing storage in a bedroom area."

Jeffrey Goodman, Jamaica Plain, Mass.

Walnut Tambour Case-Over-Case; walnut, maple, ebony, silver; 79 in. x 50 in. x 25 in. Photo by David Du Busc.

Lanham C. Deal, Scottsville, N.Y.

Odyssey Display Cabinet; curly maple veneer, ebony, holly; 40 in. x 30 in. x 27 in. Photo by Tim Gohrke.

"Stores two-volume set of Chagall lithographs set to Homer's *Odyssey.*"

Tom Butler, Dexter, Mich.

Wine/liquor cabinet; curly maple, curly cherry, etched glass by Laura Butler; 72 in. 24 in. x 10 in. to 14 in. Photo by David Baditoi.

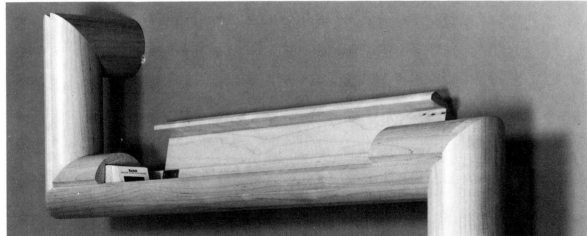

Edward Zucca, Putnam, Conn.

Middleboy 1981; basswood, paint, erector-set parts; 52 in. x 60 in. x 19 in.

"Smaller than a highboy, larger than a lowboy. Painted silver, trompe l'oeil stone."

Jeffrey T. McCaffrey, Portland, Oreg.

Slide cabinet; maple; 60 in. x 36 in. x 7 in. (Detail is shown at right.) Photos by Skot Weidemann.

Don Burkey, Ligonier, Pa.

Goddard blockfront chest of drawers; Honduras mahogany, poplar, maple, brass pulls; 33.75 in. x 38 in. x 20 in. Photo by Chuck Sartoris.

"Top and sides were cut from one piece of mahogany."

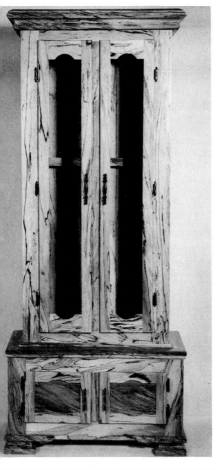

_arry Rogers, Loudonville, Ohio
Gun cabinet; spalted sycamore, glass; 75 in.
_x 32 in. x 12 in._

Roger Joslin, Austin, Tex.
Cupboard with linen-fold doors; cherry,
leaded glass; 84 in. x 42 in. x 20 in. Photo
by Mary Wasnuth.

Joseph H. Twichell, Stow, Mass.
Chippendale three-chest bureau; cherry,
butternut, poplar, aromatic cedar; 53.5 in. x
41 in. x 21.5 in. Photo by David C. Twichell.

"The inspiration for this piece is a bureau
built by Thomas Elfe. The proportions are
redesigned, and the drawer layout and other
details modified to suit my taste."

Theodore A. Bowen, Cottondale, Ala.

Storage cabinet for photographs; black walnut, aromatic cedar, osage orange; 54 in. x 36 in. x 29 in. Photo by Michael P. Smith.

"Prints were destroyed by floods and insects; hence tall stand and cedar drawers."

Stephen Crowley, Aspen, Colo.

Nine-Drawer Dresser; cherry, mahogany, ash, maple; 36 in. x 67 in. x 23 in. Photo by Jim Kahnweiler.

Alan Wilkinson, Sunset Beach, Hawaii

Chest of drawers; curly koa, koa, milo; 64 in. x 40 in. x 20 in. Photo by Jerry Chong.

"Long hours, occasionally a piece you're satisfied with—I'll drink to that."

Richard Barsky, Dovetail Woodworks, Boulder, Colo.

Coopered secretary; claro walnut, bubinga, ebony, brass inlay and leaf; 72 in. x 36 in. x 20 in. Photo by Michael Kitely.

Roger Worldie, Honolulu, Hawaii

Free-standing liquor cabinet; koa-ka, African ebony; 60 in. x 32 in. x 9 in.

"Krenovian in cabinet design, while the delicacy of its base lends a sculptural flair."

Mark Newman, Sherwood, Oreg.

Hutch; Oregon walnut, yew; 64 in. x 28 in. x 12 in. Photo by Harold Wood.

"Oregon black walnut is a wonderful wood. More color variation and a livelier grain than eastern; deep reds, oranges and greens. It's not commercially available so you have to dig it up, but it's worth it. Small local mills sometimes have it or someone may want a tree removed."

Brian Beard, Lakeport, Calif.

*Chest of drawers; ash, pecan; 65 in. x 24 in.
x 13 in.*

"I try to keep the joinery simple and
straightforward. I want to stress the design
and make construction secondary."

John Nicolson, Belgrade, Mont.

*Wall cabinet; Philippine mahogany,
Hawaiian koa; 35 in. x 23.5 in. x 9.63 in.*

"My furniture designs are inspired by the
study and love of architecture."

Frank Nadell, Boston, Mass.

*Lowboy; African rosewood, curly maple,
aromatic cedar, ebony, mother-of-pearl; 30
in. x 36 in. x 18 in.*

Oregon Fine Joinery, Portland, Oreg.
Liquor cabinet; black walnut, ebony, glass; 60 in. x 24 in. x 16 in. Glass fold-down shelf inside. Photo by Joe Feltzman.
"Designed by Michael H. deForest. Cabinet grew around idea to make book-matched doors from piece of figured black walnut."

Eric Hoag, Milford, Conn.
Chest of drawers; bubinga; 35.5 in. x 32 in. x 23 in. Photo by William K. Sacco.

Barrie Graham, Arundel, Quebec, Canada
Chest of drawers; walnut, maple; 32 in. x 42 in. x 23 in.

Robert Fischer, Cherry Hill, N.J.
Silver chest; koa with maple drawers; 36 in. x 24 in. x 12 in.

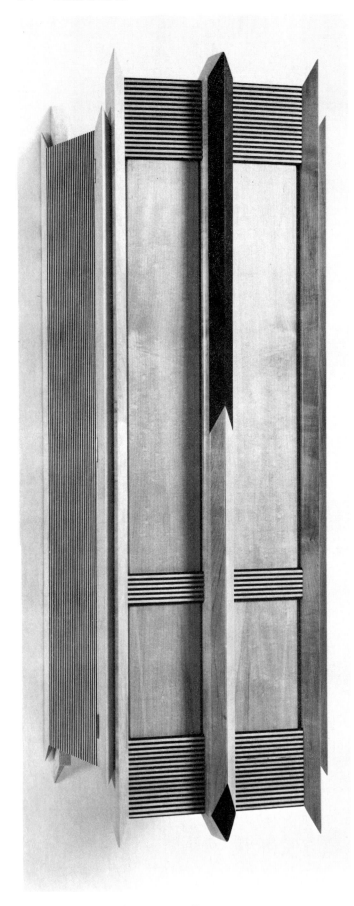

Wendy Stayman, Philadelphia, Pa.
*Wall-hung cabinet; maple, ebony veneer; 41
in. x 12.5 in. x 10 in. Photo by Rick
Echelmeyer.*

**Doug Smith and Morry Nathan, Smith &
Nathan Furnituremakers, Inc.,** Ann
Arbor, Mich.
*China cabinet; black walnut; 78 in. x 41 in.
x 13 in.*

Lewis Buchner, San Francisco, Calif.
*Wall-hung stereo cabinet; paldao, alder
interior; 18 in. x 60 in. x 20 in. Photo by Jo
Schopplein.*

Eric R. Smith, Monrovia, Calif.

Tool chest; Honduras mahogany, Brazilian pau ferro; 41 in. x 30 in. x 19 in.

"I stretched my abilities in the construction, and it is very satisfying to realize you've accomplished something that, at the beginning, was beyond your abilities. It's what it's all about."

Alfred E. Holland, Jr., Orangevale, Calif.

Square Dealer Credenza; padauk; 29 in. x 84 in. x 18 in. Photo by Kurt Fishback.

"Designed and built for a real-estate developer. He makes deals and money. Certainly is square."

Louis Gnida, Montreal, Quebec, Canada

Stereo credenza; quartersawn African padauk, padauk veneers, Indian ebony trim; 26 in. x 66 in. x 20 in. Photo by Paul McCarthy.

"Designed to house high-temperature stereo components. Installed in the plinth is a high air volume, low noise computer-type motor with dust-filtered air-intake port."

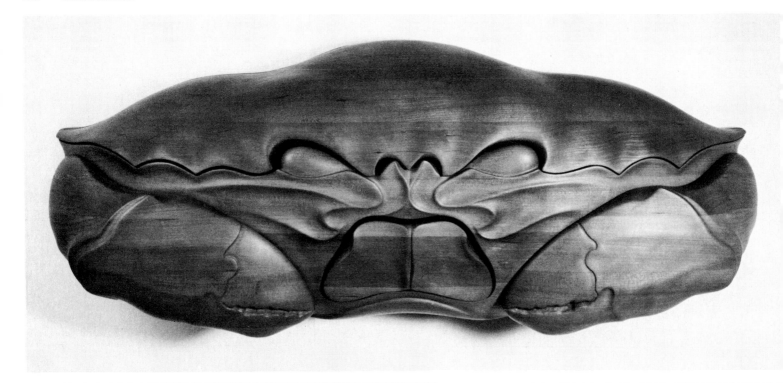

Lottie Kwai Lin Wolff, Madison, Wis.

Crab Cabinet; cherry, brass hinge pins; 9.5 in. x 24.5 in. x 6.25 in. Wall-hung, wood-hinged. Photo by Ted Wolff.

"Lid and claw swing-out shelves."

Jeff Kellar, Portland, Maine

Collector's Display Table; East Indian rosewood, maple, brass; 31 in. x 27 in. x 19 in. (Detail is shown at left.) Photos by Peter MacComber.

Vill Neptune, West Hartford, Conn.

Chippendale lowboy; South American mahogany, red oak, poplar, brass; 30.5 in. x 0 in. x 18.5 in.

"All parts shaped from solid stock. The attern for the knee carving is drawn from everal similar examples of the one symmetrical knee-carving design known in lew England furniture."

Thomas Wood, St. Paul, Minn.

Chippendale cabinet; Honduras mahogany, white oak, sugar pine, Carpathian elm burl veneer, bronze, brass, leather; 30 in. x 32 in. x 18 in. Photo by Jim Gallop.

James Lea, Rockport, Maine

Queen Anne lowboy; mahogany, maple; 32 in. x 33 in. x 20 in.

"Design is my own interpretation of an eighteenth-century Queen Anne lowboy."

Dennis FitzGerald, Greenwich, Conn.
*Chest of drawers; butternut, white oak,
ebony, baltic birch plywood; 60 in. x 32 in.
x 20 in.*

Leo MacNeil, Sydney, Nova Scotia, Canad
*Commode; mahogany; 35 in. x 25 in. x 31.5
in. Drawer pulls carved and gilt.*

Warren A. May, Berea, Ky.
*Bombé chest-on-chest; mahogany, poplar;
in. x 44 in. x 24 in. Photo by Brunner
Studio.*

Gary S. Prater, Marantha Woodmen,
Muncie, Ind.

Highboy; mahogany; 25 in. x 47 in. x 82 in.
Photo by People's Studio.

"Antique highboy form has been reduced in
scale and reshaped to create modern form
that successfully reconciles traditional
aristocratic taste with modern aesthetic
sensibilities. Paul Pitts, Nashville, Tenn.,
carved morning glory vines on front stiles."

Michael Caroff, Santa Monica, Calif.
*Wall unit; walnut, elm burl, inlaid brass; 84
in. x 94 in. x 24 in.*

Douglas Smith, Las Vegas, Nev.
*Dresser; black walnut, bird's-eye maple, East
Indian rosewood; 23 in. x 30 in. x 76 in.
Photo by John Goad.*

"Living at the cutting edge of history, I
synthesize ancient traditions and
proportions."

Tom Brown, Berkeley, Calif.
*Standing cabinet; mahogany, maple, glass;
65 in. x 20 in. x 15 in. Photo by Richard
Sargent.*

Grover W. Floyd II, Knoxville, Tenn.
*Three-drawer table (Hepplewhite style);
Honduras mahogany, pine, walnut, holly,
boxwood, brass; 29.5 in. x 23.75 in. x 15.25
in. Photo by Gordon Hodge.*

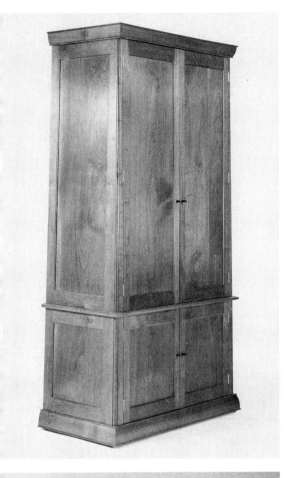

Stephen Bruce Proctor, Leroy, N.Y.

Armoire (gun cabinet); American black walnut, rosewood, ash plywood, red velvet; 76 in. x 44 in. x 18 in. Photo by Andrew J. Olenick.

Don Braden, Oakland, Calif.

Smiles (chest of drawers); hyedua, California walnut; 56 in. x 24 in. x 22 in. Collection of Cal Titus. Photo by Jim LaCunha.

Barry Mills, North Melbourne, Victoria, Australia

Bowl and Tree in Cabinet; huon pine, brass hinges; 60 cm. x 20 cm. x 17 cm.

"A struggle to relate to Australia, my new home, the age and immensity of the landscape, the mystery and power that lies there. I simply pay homage to something infinitely greater than myself."

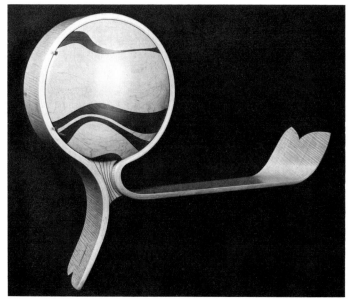

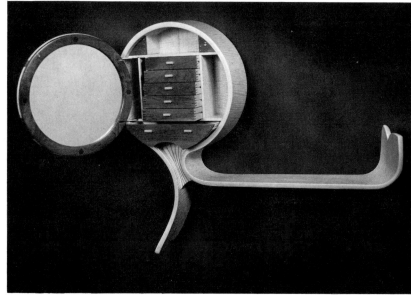

Helmut Lueckenhausen, Surrey Hills,
Victoria, Australia

*Telperion (jewelry case); huon pine; 30 in. x
24 in. x 24 in.*

"Made for Year of the Tree."

Clement S. Ceccarelli, Brooklyn, N.Y.

*Armoire; mahogany, cherry and mahogany
plywood, brass, auto glass. 62 in. x 42 in. x
24 in. Photo by Bob Hanson.*

Tom Kneeland, Penn Yan, N.Y.

*Jewelry cabinet; curly maple, ash, walnut; 36
in. x 48 in. x 11 in. (Cabinet is shown open
at right.) Photos by Niel Sjoblum.*

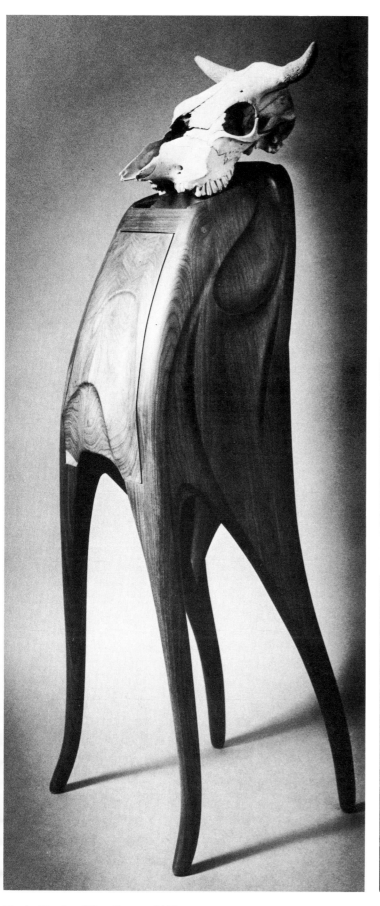

Kevin Kegler, West Seneca, N.Y.
DDSE; walnut, cow's skull; 48 in. x 14 in. x 14 in. Photo by Paul Pasquarello.
"This particular piece is pre-Paz and therefore an important step in the early development of the Paz movement."

Elbert E. 'Skip' Benson, Oakland, Calif.
Container for prehistoric native American pot shards; Honduras mahogany; 29 in. x 19 in. x 21 in. Photo by Richard Sargent.
"The display container was designed to reflect the fact that the shards were found half-buried in the rear of a cave."

Charles Stern, Florence, Mass.
Blanket chest; cherry, maple, cedar; 44 in. x 19 in. x 19 in. Photo by Stan Sherer.

Maurice Fraser, New York, N.Y.

Apartment bookcase; ash, cherry; 48 in. x 27.5 in. x 13 in. Photo by Leonard Lessin.

"Tall books tend to be wider than little books; therefore the differing shelf heights meant to house them dictated their own proper depths, front to back."

Henry Barrow, Glen Echo, Md.

Buffet and Storage Cabinet in Black Lacquer; maple, birch; 36 in. x 52 in. x 20 in. Photo by Dick Duane.

"Interior drawers and shelves for silver, linen and glasses."

Dennis J. Fitzgerald, Hailey, Idaho

Buffet; Honduras mahogany, padauk, East Indian rosewood; 43.5 in. x 48 in. x 17 in. Photo by John Jepson.

Robert Goodman, Wichita, Kans.

Stereo cabinet; African zebrawood; 56 in. x 26 in. x 18 in. Photo by Michael Carlisle.

"Contemporary design based on traditional Victrola; all compartments open by touch latch."

George Gordon, Providence, R.I.

Sideboard (1981); mahogany, teak veneer, bronze; 46 in. x 22 in. x 62 in. Photo by Jessie Marcotte and John Rudiak.

Paul Sturm, New York, N.Y.

Sculptured Display Shelves; bleached white oak; 69 in. x 41 in. x 19 in. Photo by Doug Long.

"Each shelf is made from a single piece ripped lengthwise, notched and reglued around the uprights so that the joint becomes substantially invisible. The question for me is how to make it look just right from all 360 degrees."

Mike Whiteman, Key West, Fla.
Wood Stove Cabinet; walnut, ash, cast-iron door from Home Comfort stove; 30 in. x 44 in. x 20 in.

Hugh 'Huff' Wesler, Springfield, Mass.
1914 Mack Tanker Truck (tool cabinet/bar/crib/???); walnut, cherry, bird's-eye maple, mahogany, spalted birch, glass, brass hardware, bronze screen; 152 in. x 75 in. x 30 in. (Truck is shown closed at top.) Photos by Anita Wesler.

J. Frederick Collins, Hingham, Mass.
Wood Stove; mahogany; 30 in. x 30.5 in. x 14.5 in. Photo by Wayne Lemmon.

C. R. 'Skip' Johnson, Stoughton, Wis.
Mine Car Disaster and Dry Bar; oak, wengé, walnut; 48 in. x 48 in. x 36 in. (Car is shown open at top left.) Photos by H. A. Koshollek.

"Brake handle is door handle exposing shelves, drawer and hanging device for stemware. Bar surface pulls out of undercarriage. Movable wheels, bent axle, a shovel of walnut and oak on left side."

Desks

Bradford S. Walters, Boulder, Colo.
Writing desk; cherry, walnut highlights; 54 in. x 52 in. x 28 in. (Desk is shown on facing page.) Photos by Michael Kiteley.

radford S. Walters, Boulder, Colo.
*Vriting desk. (Detail is shown on facing
age.)*

Alan Lorn, Northampton, Mass.
*Tambour Writing Desk; cherry with
cocobolo drawers; 42 in. x 48 in. x 28 in.
Photo by John Marcy.*

Joseph P. Malsom, Kalamazoo, Mich.
*Office desk and side cabinet; black walnut,
white oak; (desk) 30 in. x 38 in. x 72 in.
(cabinet) 28 in. x 24 in. x 60 in. Photo by
James Riegel.*

Morris J. Sheppard, Venice, Calif.

Desk; zebrawood, ebony inlay, colored lacquers; 72 in. x 34 in. x 30 in.

"Each line of inlay, when viewed from the proper angle, appears as a straight line cutting through all surfaces of the piece."

C. Stuart Welch, Marshall, Calif.

Writing desk; purpleheart, bird's-eye maple. Photo by Donald Eagleston.

David I. Steckler, Plainfield, Vt.

Writing desk; cherry, walnut; 30 in. x 50 in. x 32 in. Photo by David L. Ryan.

"An exercise in cutting decorative dovetails...70, to be exact."

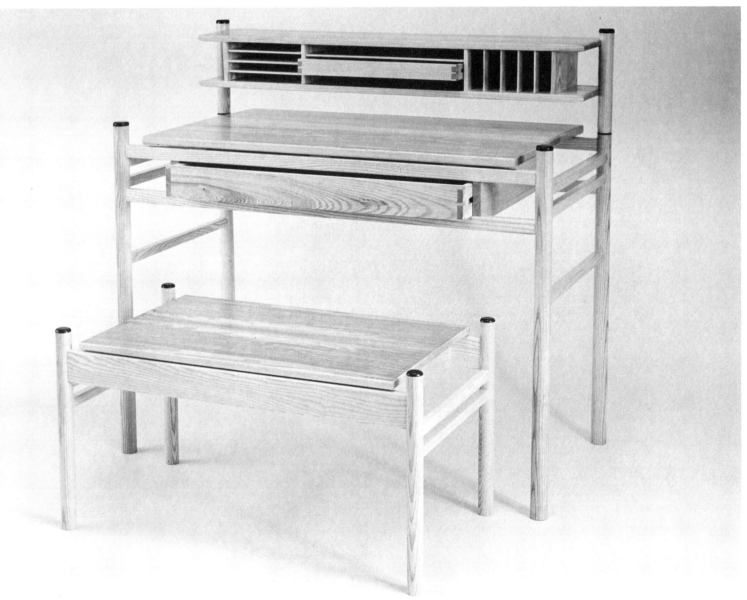

Michael Clark, Boston, Mass.
*Desk; cherry, maple; 29 in. x 78 in. x 31 in.
Photo by David Caras.*

Jerry Lilly, Pittsburgh, Pa.
*Satellite Desk and Bench; ash, ebony, olive
ash veneer, foam, leather; 42 in. x 21 in. x 41
in. Photo by Golomb Photographers Inc.*

"I wanted the piece to appear to have a
floating quality. The bench seat flips over to
reveal a leather cushion."

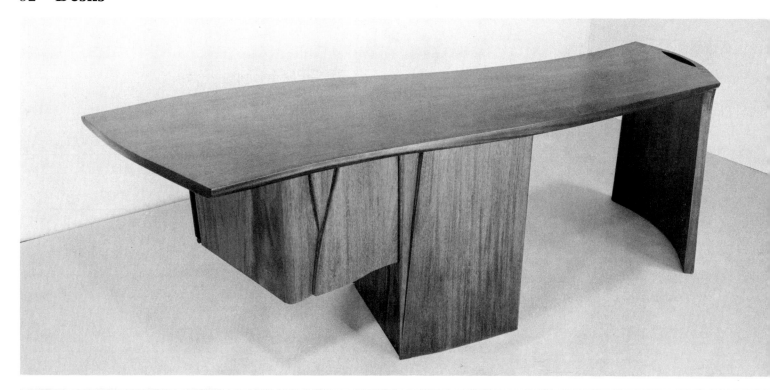

**Ellen Mason and Dudley Hartung,
Raccoon,** Somerville, Mass.

*Ariel Desk; mahogany, maple, leather pencil
holder; 30 in. x 84 in. x 30 in. Photo by
David Caras.*

Nils Falk, Frenchtown, N.J.

*Desk; solid bubinga and veneer, ash,
leather; 29 in. x 60 in. x 28 in. Photo by
Matt Prince.*

Thomas Kohn, North Bennington, Vt.

Occasional typing desk; teak, maple, baltic birch plywood, leather, brass; 30 in. x 48 in. x 28.5 in. Photo by Jeff Curto.

"A piece with knock-down capabilities. Its purpose is for typing/writing, with storage capacity for a typewriter. Burgundy-colored leather provides a comfortable work surface; all visible interior surfaces are candy-apple-red enamel."

Joseph M. Wilson, Pictou, Nova Scotia, Canada

Desk; koa veneer, walnut; 30 in. x 60 in. x 29 in. Walnut bent and laminated for bands. Unit completely disassembles. Photo by Michael Perla.

"When this bent plywood form came out of the jig and stood vertically by itself, it seemed to scream: base, BASE!"

Michael Coffey, Poultney, Vt.

Desk and stool; Mozambique hyedua; 39 in. x 45 in. x 30 in.

"Extreme cantilevers made possible by internal metal reinforcement of joints. Upper doors touch-latch open, then retract on dovetail ways."

Steven M. Lash, West Bloomfield, Mich.

Blockfront desk; Honduras mahogany, chestnut, pine, poplar, brass; 42 in. x 42 in. x 22 in. Photo by Joni T. Strickfaden.

"The desk is designed in the Goddard Townsend style after the desk portion of the John Brown Secretary located in the Garvan Collection at the Yale Art Gallery."

Anthony LaVigne, Troy, Mich.

Bow-front secretary desk; cherry, solid maple and veneer, poplar, brass; 57 in. x 45 in. x 28 in. (Detail is shown at left.) Photos by Bob Long.

Gregory W. Guenther, Savannah, Ga.

Slant-top desk; southern yellow heart pine, brass; 39 in. x 35.75 in. x 18.5 in. Photo by Nancy Heffernan.

"This rare curly heart pine was salvaged from old flooring and paneling. The writing compartment contains six obvious and five hidden drawers."

Edward Nye Gordon, Tucson, Ariz.

Oxbow desk with breast drawer; walnut, oak, ash, brass and bone hardware; 40 in. x 36 in. x 18 in. Photo by Timothy Gordon.

"Desk styled with eighteenth-century traditional details to complement the smaller living areas of the modern-day home or apartment."

Andy Inganni, Washington, Mass.

Fall-front desk; Walnut, maple, cherry, brass; 49.75 in. x 42 in. x 16 in. Photo by Jere De Waters.

"This is my first design work, accomplished while an intern at Leeds Design Workshops. The design was influenced by my woodstove, Japanese furniture and musical instruments."

William C. Oetjen, Ridgewood, N.J.

Desk; red oak; 30 in. x 60 in. x 30 in. Photo by Tory Chisholm.

"The desk top and drawer carcases were designed to create the appearance of floating elements."

Jonathan Cohen, Seattle, Wash.

Asymmetrical Entry Desk; black walnut, Carpathian elm burl, bird's-eye maple; 44 in. x 22 in. x 18 in. Photo by John Switten.

"Piece is designed so that nothing is symmetrical: all curves peak one side of their center point; one stretcher is higher than the other. Left-hand drawer is 6 in. deep; right-hand drawer is 14 in. deep."

James B. Sagui, Bristol, Vt.
Sideboard; curly maple; 36 in. x 18 in. x 72 in.

Michael Williams, Beverly, Mass.
Fall Flap Desk; cherry, maple; 49 in. x 20 in. x 30 in.
"I try to design furniture that is subtle and elegant."

Ford Thomas, Baton Rouge, La.
Desk; walnut, cherry, bronze, brass; 48 in. x 48 in. x 20 in. Photo by Jim Zietz.
"When the top is down, the rule joint is seamless, allowing for a large unobstructed work space."

John Dodd, Rochester, N.Y.

Desk; walnut, tchitola, aluminum; 29.5 in. x 84 in. x 32 in. Photo by Woody Packard.

"The design originated from the concept of incorporating the in and out files into the top."

Joseph Del Nostro, Jr., Los Angeles, Calif.

Corner typewriter desk with beta and file cabinet; walnut, ebony, ash; (desk) 54 in. x 40 in. x 26 in. (cabinets) 24 in. x 40 in. x 18 in. Photo by Don Milici.

"Main typewriter door rides in side-cut grooves on four steel ball bearings and is counterweighted with cable pully and weight running in tube to assist lift and hold."

Tim Donahue–Furniture Designer, Wilton, Conn.

Drafting table; walnut, glass, Plexiglas; 36 in. x 40 in. x 72 in. Photo by Woody Packard.

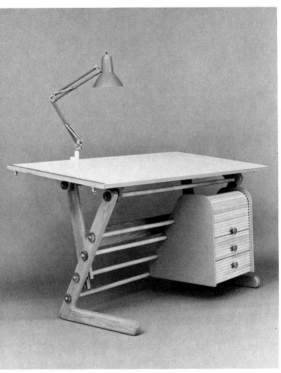

Morgan Rey Benson, El Paso, Tex.

The Lomhurst Drafting Desk/Table; oak, maple, birch, mahogany, pine, vinyl, Formica, aluminum; 30 in. x 58 in. x 30 in. Wooden threads and nuts.

"A combination desk and drafting table designed for graphic artists, the Lomhurst Desk is one of five tables in my line of drafting furniture."

Gordon W. Schaad, Los Angeles, Calif.

System 200™ Modular Desktop Furniture for Microcomputers; red oak; 18.75 in. x 55.125 in x 22.5 in. Photo by Dean Yee.

"Humanize technology with visual and tactile qualities of wood...involve other senses in what can too easily become exclusively cerebral...counterbalance potential sterility of high tech with warmth in design integrating form and function."

Eileen Brogan, South Attleboro, Mass.

Photographer's Light Table; cherry, acrylic, glass; 52 in. x 30 in. x 30 in. Dovetailed. Photo by Bill Gallery.

"Primary design concept was to fabricate a fine piece of furniture, yet one that will withstand the daily hard use of a professional photographer, in lieu of his usual metal light table."

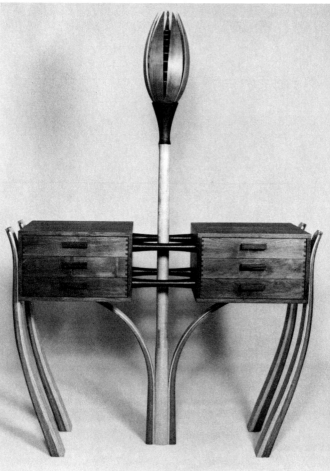

Emmett F. Day, Seattle, Wash.
*Writing desk; Brazilian rosewood, brass,
leather; 30 in. to 38 in. x 60 in. x 36 in. Gold
tooling. Photo by Gregg Krogstad.*

Alan Paine Radebaugh, Albuquerque, N.
Mex.
*Dancer (foyer piece); walnut, ebony, ivory,
brass, mirror, electricity, gold leaf; 44 in. x
27 in. x 22 in. Photo by Ralph Genter.*
"Heels of legs house batteries for bulbs."

Erik Gronborg, Solana Beach, Calif.
*Corner desk; wane, avocado; 69 in. x 22 in. x
23 in.*
"All shaping done on bandsaw. Explicit
joinery and wood hinges, lock, drawer pull."

Ken Fisher, Layton, N.J.
*Swamp Cabinet; walnut, maple, ash,
sassafras, osage orange, white oak, cherry;
72 in. x 52 in. x 16 in. Ebonized oak holds
boxes together. Photo by Reid Baker.*

John E. Carlson, Haines, Alaska

*Rolltop secrétaire (Louis XV style);
mahogany, walnut, rosewood, sapele, other
veneers; 42 in. x 46 in. x 30 in. Tambour
held together with interlocking joint and
steel cable.*

"Most cabinetry involves making containers
of one sort or another. And the way I see it,
if one is going to make containers, make
them superbly."

Tables

Peter Michael Adams, Penland, N.C.
Keel bench/table; walnut; 18.5 in. x 24 in. x 72 in. Photo by Dan Bailey.

"The piece can be used as a bench and/or coffee table."

Robert Kopf, Walnut Cove, N.C.

Triangular coffee table; mahogany, ash, poplar; 16 in. x 48 in. x 42 in. Photo by Dennis Kale.

"My work allows me to explore form, proportion and the relationships of shapes. I also have a lot of fun."

Mark S. Levin, Chicago, Ill.

Lily Pad Table; Honduras mahogany; 28 in. 60 in. x 32 in. Laminated legs tenoned into the top, then sculpted.

Wayne Raab, Waynesville, N.C.

Coffee table; cherry; 32 in. x 48 in. x 17 in.

Richard J. Barrett, Tempe, Ariz.

Pagoda console table; alder, birch, multicoat transparent lacquers, gold leaf; 30 in. x 60 in. x 18 in. Photo by Rick Rusing.

"My design approach involves generating a sense of mystery in the object, of subconscious ties with the past, executed with mechanical precision of the present. From perceptions and stirred memories of creations long ago, or perhaps long ahead."

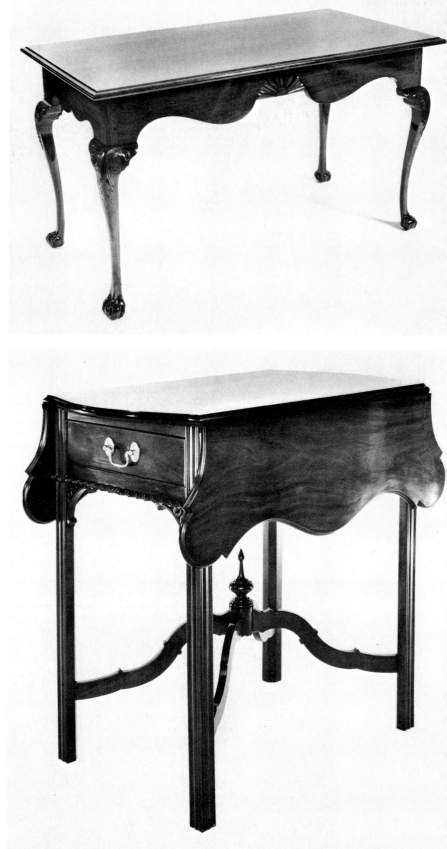

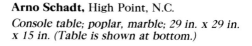

Arno Schadt, High Point, N.C.
Console table; poplar, marble; 29 in. x 29 in.
x 15 in. (Table is shown at bottom.)

Greg Biles, Redwood City, Calif.
Table/desk; Pennsylvania black walnut,
brass fittings; 27 in. x 24 in. x 48 in. Photo
by David Krauss.

"Original design, adapted from museum
photos of American period furniture."

Donald Bradley, Miami, Fla.
Pembroke table; West Indies mahogany,
white oak, poplar; 28 in. x 19.5 in. x 30 in.
Photo by Bill Sanders.

William A. Woodcock, Huntington, N.Y.
*Dressing Table in Style of Late Louis XVI;
Dominican mahogany, sycamore veneer,
cast-brass feet and leg collars, rolled-brass
bead and cove trim; 29 in. x 38.25 in. x 19
in. Photo by Michael Fairchild.*

Gregory J. Landrey, Winterthur, Del.
*Hall table; South American mahogany,
maple, crotch mahogany veneer; 27.5 in. x
24 in. x 15 in. Photo by Herbert L. Crossan.*

Richard B. Crowell, Alexandria, La.
*Sewing table; mahogany, Louisiana cypress,
Louisiana wild cherry; 29.5 in. x 20.75 in. x
15.63 in. Photo by Jack Kohara.*

Clifford J. Rugg and Marc DesLauriers,
Portland, Maine
*Oval table; Honduras mahogany; 29 in. x 38
in. x 68 in. Photo by Macomber Studios.*

David Powell, Leeds Design Workshops,
Easthampton, Mass.

Coffee tables; (front table) walnut; 16 in. x 48 in. x 16 in. (rear table) Maccassar ebony, holly; 18 in. x 60 in. x 16 in. Photo by David Ryan.

Jim Davis, Olympia, Wash.

Coffee table; teak, Nicaraguan walnut, koa, maple, plywood; 16 in. x 82 in. x 32 in.

"There are 87 individual pieces of 1/4-in.-thick teak used in the top of this table, all laminated onto a plywood core. Groups of long, thin tapers are joined to create the illusion of radiating grain patterns."

Michael A. Pereira, Bronxville, N.Y.

Corner table with gargoyle foot and ball; oak, rosewood, walnut, brass; 30 in. high, 1 in. radius. Photo by Rich Jakeway.

"All day, in model making, I make tight-tolerance stuff for designers, but during my lunch hour I make goodies that please me."

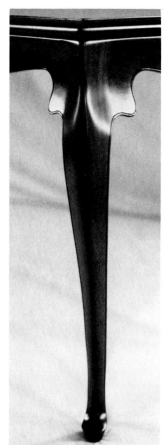

Linda Beck, King of Prussia, Pa.
*Sofa table; mahogany; 30 in. x 21 in. x 60 in.
(Detail is shown at right.)*

Douglas Oliver, Toronto, Ontario, Canada
*Coffee table; bird's-eye maple, Indonesian
rosewood; 14.5 in. x 22 in. x 41 in. Photo by
Paul Orenstein.*

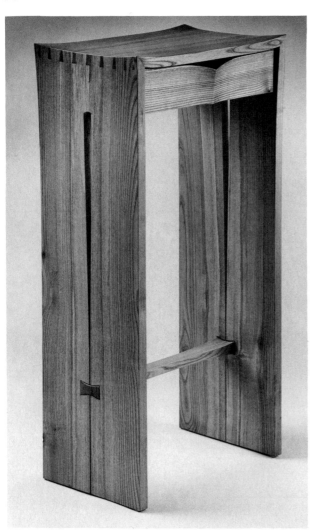

Michael Fortune, Toronto, Ontario, Canada

Hall table with drawers; white ash; 32 in. x 17 in. x 11 in.

Warren S. Fenzi, Scottsdale, Ariz.

Cocktail table; rosewood, bleached ash, ebony; 17.5 in. x 53 in. x 24 in. Photo by John Hall.

"I enjoy a visual illusion, playing with structural competence...it works."

Norman H. Ridenour, San Diego, Calif.

Stereo cabinet; koa; 26 in. x 60 in. x 26 in. Photo by NKS Ltd.

Gail Fredell Smith, Berkeley, Calif.

Coffee table; cherry, oak; 27 in. x 50 in. x 1 in.

"I wanted to give this piece the appearance of being in a state of erosion and change."

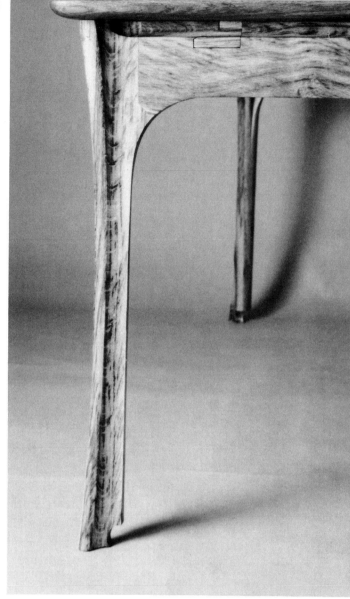

John Kennedy, Philadelphia, Pa.
*End table; walnut, flickering walnut veneer,
rosewood inlay; 32 in. x 36 in. x 24 in. Photo
by Joe Painter.*

Craig Marks, Albion, Calif.
*Coffee table; Honduras rosewood, ebony
inlay; 55 in. x 24 in. x 16 in. Photo by
Gillette Studio.*

Anthony Giachetti, East Boothbay, Maine
*Dining table (expanding); English brown
oak; 29.5 in. x 66 in. x 44 in. Expands to 102
in. wide. (Detail is shown at top.) Photos by
Stephen Rubicam.*

Rocky Cross, Santa Ysabel, Calif.

Spiral table; birch plywood, glass; 17 in. high, 24 in. dia. Photo by Jeanna Kreytak.

"The design was inspired by the art of M.C. Escher. Horizontal wood grain focuses intense energy and movement within the form. What's most remarkable are the changes in form when viewed from different angles."

JAKonicek, Madison, Wis.

Falling Below; walnut, glass; 34.5 in. x 48 in. x 75 in. Photo by Chris Christianson.

"Conceptually began with an inverted, skydiving free-fall maneuver. Human form was abstracted to achieve outstretched, fluid vitality. Glass tops cantilevered, implying tenuous energy in the base."

Roger Bell and George Breck, Sebastopo Calif.

End Table #1; wengé, maple, purpleheart, black plate glass, glass jewel, stainless steel. 28 in. x 18 in. x 22 in. Knocks down.

Leo G. Doyle, San Bernardino, Calif.

Spindle table; bird's-eye maple, Gaboon ebony, beveled plate glass; 15 in. x 35 in. x 15 in. Photo by Thomas Ruvolo.

Ken Hosale, Mequon, Wis.

Table; sugar pine, quartersawn redwood, bird's-eye pine; 36 in. x 31 in. x 36 in. Photo by Chet Worzella.

"I wanted to emphasize the surrealistic function of the legs and to bring old and new together."

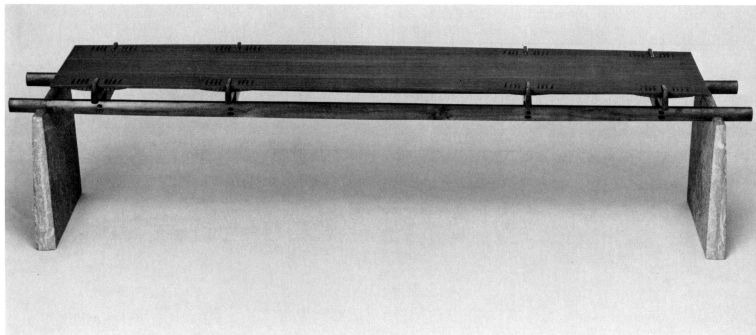

Mark Ruddy, New Auburn, Wis.

*Slab Table #4; black walnut; 17 in. x 24 in.
x 60 in.*

"Turned a wide, albeit badly warped, slab
inside out to get a usable thickness. Ripped
the slab, surfaced the pieces and partially
joined the two former outside edges
together."

Thomas Hucker, Boston, Mass.

*Low table; beefwood, ebony, Kentucky
limestone, waxed linen thread; 16 in. x 72
in. x 18 in.*

Glenn Gordon, Chicago, Ill.

*Feast (dining table); myrtle, ebony
butterflies, maple; 45 in. x 74 in.*

Robert L. DeFrances, Delray Beach, Fla.

*Low table; quartersawn white oak,
zebrawood; 15 in. x 71 in. x 17 in. Photo by
Tom McKay.*

John Michael Pierson, San Diego, Calif.
*Table; California pepper, Bouquet Canyon
stone; 14 in. x 38 in. x 15 in.*

Robert D. Sorrels, Brazil, Ind.
*The Bullet Train Desk; spalted mahogany,
elm, persimmon, glass; 30 in. x 60 in. x 31
in. (Detail is shown at left.) Photos by
Adkins-Burnham Studios Inc.*

Phillip R. Tennant, Indianapolis, Ind.

Stick table; pine, paint, glass (not shown); 16 in. x 16 in. x 16 in.

D.D. Doernberg, New York, N.Y.

Pyramid Table (©1981); walnut, glass; 20 in. x 20 in. x 20 in. Photo by Ken Riemer.

"A threaded rod runs from the point, through the bronze glass and is bolted under the base. All four sides have alternating rings of heartwood and sapwood end grain. The geometric design was my reaction to organic stack-laminated forms."

Robert A. Diemert and Evelyn Diemert, Toronto, Ontario, Canada

End table with shelf and magazine storage; ebonized maple, purpleheart veneer, Baltic birch, black opaque glass; 53 cm. x 61 cm. x 53 cm.

"The result of a collaboration between Evelyn Diemert (a visual artist) and myself.'

David Carlson, Pittsburgh, Pa.
*Coffee table; red oak; 36 in. x 36 in. x 13 in.
Photo by Marty Schilling.*

Michael Pearce, San Francisco, Calif.

*Puppy Love (occasional table); narra,
walnut; 18 in. x 38 in. x 52 in.*

"Each leg mortised into bottom and
reinforced with screws, which are covered
with end-grain inlays sliced off match-
laminated legs, so they appear to extend
through to top of table. Parts bandsawn and
woven before tops laminated."

Peter M. Kenney, Kennett Square, Pa.
Coffee table; maple; 13 in. x 36 in. x 16.5 in.

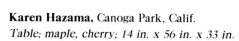

Karen Hazama, Canoga Park, Calif.
Table; maple, cherry; 14 in. x 56 in. x 33 in.

Peter Tao, San Diego, Calif.
Table; birch, jatoba; 16 in. x 22 in. x 55 in.
Photo by C. Quinton Kimball.

Stephen Levitt, Brampton, Ontario, Canada
Coffee table; cherry; 16 in. x 22 in. x 46 in.
"The center section of the top lifts off to
function as a serving tray."

Michael Hurwitz, Cambridge, Mass.
Hall table; walnut; 38 in. x 20 in. x 12 in.
Photo by Tim McClelland.

Frank Weisman, Covelo, Calif.

Love Desk; California black walnut; 30 in. x 36 in. x 84 in. Photo by Tom Liden.

"This desk was designed for two people to work together comfortably."

Kathryn W. Schackner and James Kelly Conklin, Foley-Waite Associates, Montclair, N.J.

Table; Central American mahogany, East Indian rosewood; 29 in. x 48 in. x 16 in. Photo by Marita Sturken.

Richard Tannen, Medford, Mass.

Coffee table; walnut, maple; 18 in. x 22 in. x 48 in.

Diane E.H. Gaudreau, North Wiltshire,
Prince Edward Island, Canada

*Entrance table and mirror; black walnut;
(table) 29 in. x 32 in. x 17 in. (mirror) 28 in.
x 14 in. Photo by Camera Art.*

Patrick Graney, Northridge, Calif.

*Game table; maple, curly maple veneer,
teak; 29 in. x 42 in. x 42 in. Photo by Mike
Levasheff.*

John Tierney, Leeds Design Workshops,
Easthampton, Mass.

*Table for Two; cherry, leather; 29 in. x 44
in. x 31 in. Photo by David Ryan.*

Glenn de Gruy Woodworks, Mobile, Ala.

*Table; pine, mahogany; 48 in. x 48 in. Photo
by Thigpen Photography.*

"A very satisfying occupation. My wife
works with me, and our children spend
afternoons and summers here."

Robert E. Hannan, Natick, Mass.

Writing table desk; ash, clear pine, pine plywood, leather; 30 in. x 28 in. x 48 in. Photo by Sam Gray.

"I love the clean geometry of Art Deco against the lively grain of ash."

Martha Collins, Kalamazoo, Mich.

Gaming Table; cherry, Brazilian rosewood, dyed veneers; 18.5 in. x 20.5 in. x 32.5 in. (Table is shown closed at center right.)

"The chessboard is bordered by a double line of bright green veneer. The playing pieces are inlaid with an alternating pattern of light grey, dark grey, light blue and purple veneers."

Jay McDougall, Fergus Falls, Minn.

Writing table; walnut with maple drawer, smoked plate glass; 29 in. x 42 in. x 19 in. Photo by Doug Giossi.

"Shaded-glass panels were placed in the base to help conceal the drawer contents from most angles of view."

Peter Allen, North Westport, Mass.

Conference table; solid bubinga and veneer; 28 in. x 84 in. x 312 in. Photo by Douglas Dalton.

"Commissioned by the National Fire Protection Association, Quincy, Mass."

John Wall and Michael Goldfinger, Union Woodworks, Northfield, Vt.

Cylinder-base coffee table; solid American walnut and veneer, bird's-eye maple; 16 in. x 29 in. x 48 in.

"Veneer cylinders with removable carved lids. This table is the first of a series of architectonic pieces."

Mike Darlow, Chippendale, New South Wales, Australia

The Elephant Table; Australian red cedar. Photo by Peter Johnson Studios.

Douglas B. Prickett, Rochester, N.Y.

Coffee table; cherry; 18 in. x 24 in. x 44 in.
Photo by Sue Welsler.

John Grew-Sheridan and Carolyn Grew-Sheridan, San Francisco, Calif.

Mensa Series Conference Table; cherry; 29.5
in. x 54 in. x 110 in.

"Designed to seat eight around a dramatic,
simple form. Shape of the base was crucial—
table can be seen down a 100-ft. hallway."

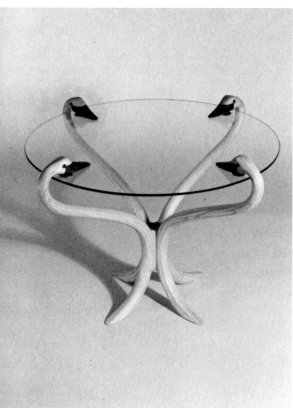

Gary Rogowski, Milwaukie, Oreg.

Altar; Honduras mahogany, rosewood wedges; 40 in. x 62 in. x 30 in. (Detail is shown at top.) Photos by Harold Wood.

"Commissioned by the Lotus Temple of Hermetic Yoga. The lions face the horizons and symbolize the passage of time."

Maggie Coffin, Schenectady, N.Y.

Swan Table; white ash, walnut, plate glass; 16 in. x 30 in.

(Top left and right) **David P. Barresi,** Wilton, Maine

Ostrich Table; black cherry; 26 in. x 24 in. x 39 in., 12 in. wide with leaf dropped. (Table is shown with leaf open at right.) Photos by Roger William.

Bruce Decker, Riverside, Calif.

Western Shirt Table; ash body, East Indian rosewood yoke and cuffs, purpleheart arrow, real snaps; 18 in. x 22 in. x 30 in.

"Cuff and pocket slits (with arrow points) are inlaid."

Jay B. Stanger, Boston, Mass.

Coffee table; ash; 15.5 in. x 60 in. x 21 in.

Stephen Temple, Erie, Pa.

Small Table at Room's Center; native Pennsylvania black walnut; 19 in. x 42 in. x 20 in. Photo by Dennis Marsico.

"The hierarchy of surface supports definition as table; the form supports the surface."

Mitchell Ryerson, Cambridge, Mass.

Folding table; maple, brass; 30 in. x 25 in. x 25 in., expands to 30 in. x 35 in. x 70 in. (Table is shown open at top right.) Photos by David Caras.

"I wanted to make a table that expanded geometrically/biologically (mitosis!), incorporating leaves into the basic structure. Invites you to open and play with it as a kind of life-size puzzle."

James L. Henkle, Norman, Okla.

Coffee table with storage; teak; 14 in. x 41 in. x 15.5 in. (Table is shown open at center right.) Photos by Andrew Stout.

Jonathan R. Wright, Cambridge, Mass.

Extension dining table with three leaves; bubinga, maple, brass catches; 28 in. x 48 in. Photo by Rameshwar Das.

"Closed dimension 48 in. seating six; extended dimension 73 in. seating ten. Rack for three leaves is either freestanding or may be hung."

Mark K. Parrish, Pflugerville, Tex.

Four Elements (writing desk); American black walnut, ebony; 29 in. x 55 in. x 23 in. Photo by Daniel Schaefer.

"Designed around its four elements of leg construction: the top represents the floating dream state; the legs signify logic, standing firmly on the ground; the ebony wedge a link between the two, with the small ebony wedge locking them firmly into reality."

Ronnie J. Ferguson, Portsmouth, Va.

Drop-leaf dining table; zebrawood, brass; 29.5 in. x 38 in. x 66 in. Photo by Dennis A. Mook.

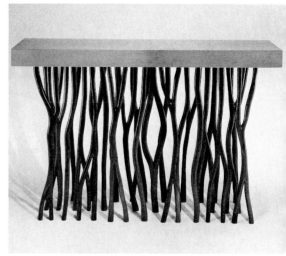

Diedrich Dasenbrock, Alsea, Oreg.

Coffee table; black walnut; 16 in. x 60 in. x 30 in. (Detail is shown at top.) Photos by Jeff Goldner.

"The shape of the table was inspired by the grain pattern of the book-matched planks, the most beautiful wood I've worked with."

Robert Whitley, Solebury, Bucks County, Pa.

Forest console table; hard maple, American black walnut; 36.5 in. x 59 in. x 16 in.

Marek Lisowski, Rosendale, N.Y.
*Table; black locust; 20 in. x 28 in. x 28 in.
Photo by John Eastcott.*

Michael J. Hanley, Cedarburg, Wis.

*Walnut Crotch Table; American black
walnut; 16 in. x 20 in. x 36 in. Photo by
Richard Brodzeller.*

"The front edge of the top has a barklike
appearance. This is, in fact, an inner edge of
the tree where it was split by lightning. The
delicate figure and color of the crotch
section contrasted against the scar tissue
make a rare and beautiful piece of wood."

Steve Heller, Heller's Fabulous Furniture,
Boiceville, N.Y.

*End table; spalted maple, glass; 26 in. x 24
in. x 24 in. Photo by Image Photography.*

"I love the difference between the smooth,
featureless glass, and the roughness of the
wood. The inside curve is sanded smooth;
outside was picked clean and just sanded
lightly."

Chairs

David Van Nostrand, Atlanta, Ga.

Armchair; white oak; 39 in. x 28 in. x 26 in.

"A comfortable seat must first be found
within the huge mass of material before the
sculptural reaction to the remaining mass
can be made. The design becomes a reaction
to the singularities of each individual piece
of wood."

Robert J. Chehayl, Westfield, N.J.

Rocking chair; maple; 27 in. x 69 in. x 26 in. Photo by David Levelie.

Greg Harkins, Jackson, Miss.

Nannie Rocker; oak, hickory, imported maple chair cane; 46 in. x 62 in. x 18 in., 65 lb. Photo by Tom Joynt.

"The Nannie Rocker allows the mother the use of both hands while rocking the baby. Very popular as a sewing chair also."

Steven Caldwell, Seattle, Wash.

Rocker with Fish; walnut, zebrawood, ebony, leather upholstery; 42 in. x 24 in. x 39 in. Photo by Susan Keatts.

John Dunnigan, West Kingston, R.I.

Upholstered bedroom chair; black walnut, ash, cotton velvet upholstery; 30 in. x 30 in. x 30 in. Photo by Rick Mastelli.

Richard Scott Newman, Rochester, N.Y.

Fluted Chair; Swiss pear, 24K-gold-plated bronze, Indian silk; 36 in. x 19 in. x 19 in. Photo by Northlight Studios.

"This is a Neo²Classical piece, that is, a new Neoclassicism. I'm just picking up a tradition we misplaced somewhere."

Normand P. Jussaume, Lowell, Mass.

Side chair; Honduras mahogany; 34 in. x 17 in. x 18 in. Photo by Georges of Lowell.

"A Sheraton-influenced reproduction of original pre-Civil War period."

Peter Spadone, Kennebunk, Maine

Chair, 1982; maple, lavender slip seat; 32 in. x 18 in. x 17.5 in.

Blake C. Tovin, Philadelphia, Pa.
Pull-Up Chair; walnut, wool upholstery.
Photo by Ed Marco.

Michael Strong, Bellingham, Wash.
Pauline armchair with adjustable backrest;
black walnut, wool and cotton fabric by
DesignTex; 38 in. x 28 in. x 33 in. Photo by
David Scherrer.

Alan Marks, Pacific Grove, Calif.
Executive Chair; Honduras rosewood,
ebony, leather; 30 in. x 25 in. x 24 in. Photo
by Carl Anka.

"Chairs always fascinate me because they
change shape as you circumnavigate them."

Bob Ingram, Philadelphia, Pa.
Three-legged chair; walnut, curly maple,
leather; 27 in. x 22 in. x 18 in. Photo by
Rick Echelmeyer.

William Doub, Fort Point Cabinet Makers, Boston, Mass.

Dining chair; cherry, maple, leather; 37 in. x 18 in. x 18 in. Photo by Dean Rock.

"A contemporary design derived from traditional proportions and techniques. One of a set of twelve."

Rex D. White, San Francisco, Calif.

Side chair; walnut, velvet; 38 in. x 18 in. x 18 in. (Detail is shown at bottom.)

Fred A. Roth, Elsinore, Utah
*Étude for Mortise and Tenon; American
walnut, leather; 38 in. x 18.5 in. x 20.5 in.
Photo by Arthur F. Roth.*

Curtis Erpelding, Seattle, Wash.
*Three-legged stacking chair; ash, leather; 34
in. x 18 in. x 18 in. Bent laminated, knock
down. Photo by Joseph Feltzman.*

Don Hennick, Seattle, Wash.
*Knock-down couch; western maple, brass
fastenings; 30 in. x 80 in. x 30 in.*

Jim Fawcett, Esopus, N.Y.

Wheelbarrow Chair; maple, ebony, neoprene, leather, rawhide, needle bearings; 36 in. x 33 in. x 66 in. Photo by Bob Hanson.

William Tickel, Denver, Colo.

Chair; walnut, zebrawood and walnut inlay; 53 in. x 27 in. x 27 in. Photo by Mark Archer.

"I wish to prompt a touch, to stir a feeling of excitement. Pulse."

Joseph Farell, St. Louis, Mo.

Lauren's Rocker; black walnut, bird's-eye maple; 25.5 in. x 14 in. x 25.5 in. Photo by Norman Throgmorton.

"I wanted to design a chair that would be a comfortable and friendly playmate. I must have succeeded—yesterday Lauren, age one and a half, tried to feed her friend a cookie."

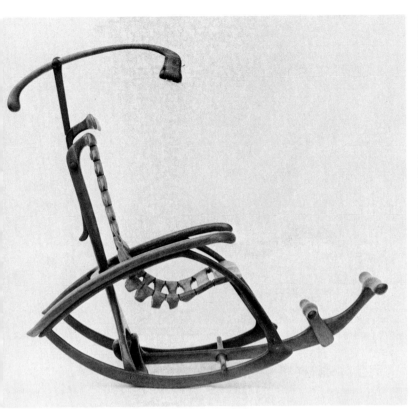

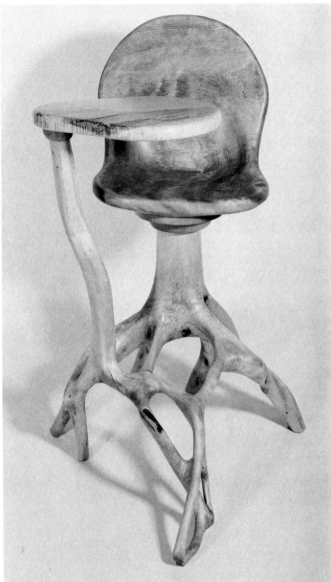

Stephen Tone-Heckeroth, Albion, Calif.

Cable-Back Rocker; madrone, tan oak, aircraft cable, leather; 48 in. x 23 in. x 53 in.

"Reclining angle is adjustable. The integral ottoman rises when the chair rocks back and adjusts for people of different statures, as does the headrest. Reading light is optional. Chair back is patterned after the backbone, complete with leather discs."

(Bottom left and right) **Tom Eckert,** Tempe, Ariz.

MM 342; maple; 37 in. x 35 in. x 32 in.

"A fully functional chair."

David Holzapfel, Marlboro, Vt.

Writing Chair; yellow birch, spalted curly maple, maple, maple burl, chair swivel, brass, nylon; 42 in. x 29 in. x 34 in. Photo by Peter Mauss.

"Seat carved from hollow yellow birch log. Base carved from single yellow birch root system. Table swivel (360°) made of brass and nylon by my father-in-law, J.B. Chassé."

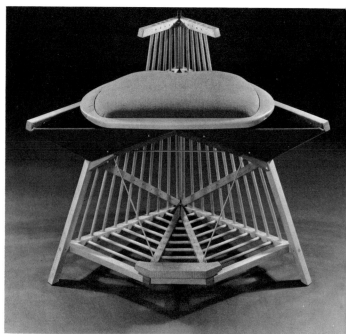

David Shewell, Stoke Newington, London, England

Dining chair (prototype for small batch production); ash, fiddleback sycamore veneer, reinforced calfskin; 110 cm. x 46 cm. x 56 cm. Photo by Tim Imrie and Maggie Ellis.

"A cleaner realization of the basic idea: the interplay of surface and edge."

John Marcoux, Providence, R.I.

Weaver's bench; maple, lignum vitae, brass, cotton; 31 in. x 22.5 in. x 36 in. Photo by Bert Beaver.

"Uses the triangular form and introduces some powerful techniques used by carriage makers."

Stephen Turino, Charlestown, R.I.

Side chair; cherry, poplar plywood, suede, muslin, webbing; 42 in. x 18.75 in. x 18 in.

Robert March, Worcester, Mass.
Couch; padauk, fabric by Heather March; 40 in. x 96 in. x 36 in. Photo by Jack Russell.

William Hammersley, Richmond, Va.
Saddle-spring structure; bleached ash; 60 in. x 60 in. x 30 in.

"I was interested in a strong but flexible whole without the structural or form rigidity of traditional chairs."

Stewart Wurtz, Boston, Mass.
Chair; beefwood, maple, hand-woven wool upholstery; 45.5 in. x 21 in. x 19 in. Photo by Andrew Dean Powell.

Ray Pirello, North Miami, Fla.

Bar stool; cherry, purpleheart, Naugahyde upholstery; 40 in. x 18 in. x 19 in. Photo ©1982 John Zillioux.

"From set of five. Bar in matching woods was also made."

Dan Rodriguez, Comer, Ga.

Stool; East Indian rosewood; 24 in. x 24 in. x 24 in.

James M. McEver, Port Townsend, Wash.

Stool; teak, bubinga; 13.5 in. x 18.5 in. x 15. in. Photo by Paul Boyer.

"Legs splayed all around so one can step onto stool at any point and not tip it over. Crossed, unconnected rails add element of play and allow top to come and go."

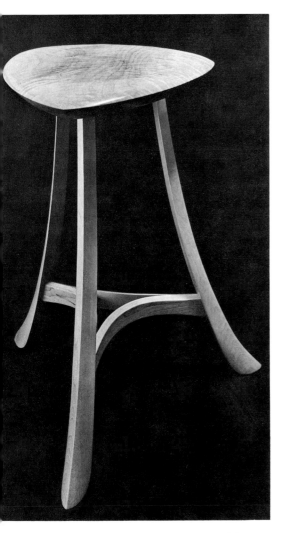

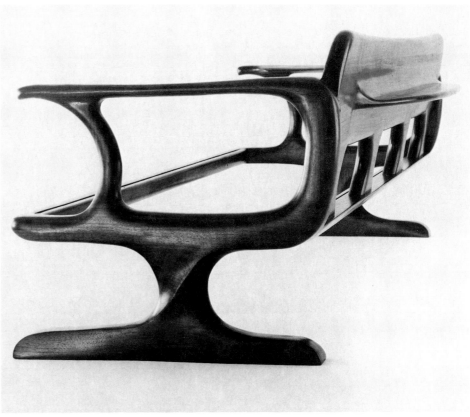

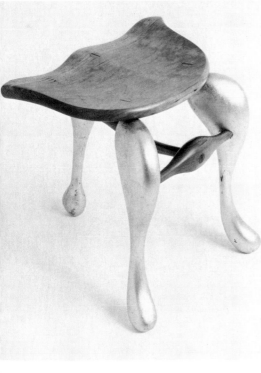

Mark J. Burhans, Athens, Ohio
*Stool; maple; 24 in. high. Photo by Jon
Conklin.*

Ron Curtis, Bloomfield, Conn.
*Fantasy Stool; cherry, maple, gold leaf; 18
in. x 16 in. x 16 in. Photo by Pat Pollard.*

Elliott Grey, Junction City, Oreg.
*Walnut couch; Oregon black walnut; 26 in.
x 34 in. x 72 in. Photo by Hugh Barton.*

John Behm, Lanarkshire, Scotland
*Straw-backed love seat; elm burl, hand-cut
oats straw bound with sisal; 22 in. x 42 in. x
24 in. Photo by John Cumming.*
"I'm in furniture making because it offers
the values of traditional rural self-reliance."

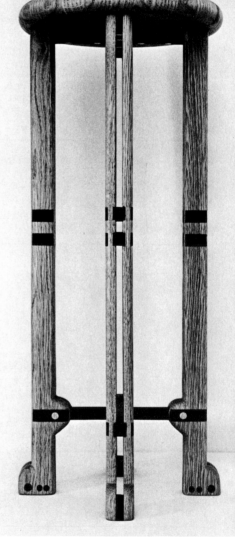

Rick Pohlers, Bloomington, Calif.

Bench; koa, ebony square pegs; 16 in. x 18 in. x 48 in. Photo by John P. Ryan.

"Designed for the foot of the bed, negative areas at each end function as handholds for ease of moving."

(Top left and right) **Carter Jason Sio,** North Bennington, Vt.

Chair; walnut, holly veneer, fiberboard, Plexiglas; 23 in. x 25 in. x 22 in. Photos by Dave Turner.

"The seat is lacquered with a deep green auto lacquer, and all frame inner faces are veneered with holly. Seat and back are removable; inner frames suspended on Plexiglas rod, which supports the back."

Michael Schmitt, Louisville, Ky.

Wood stool; red oak, ebony; 25 in. high, 1 in. dia.

"The inspiration for this design came from dance classes I attend. Being intrigued by the foot and how it supports the body and meets the ground, I attempted to abstract this idea into the support for a stool."

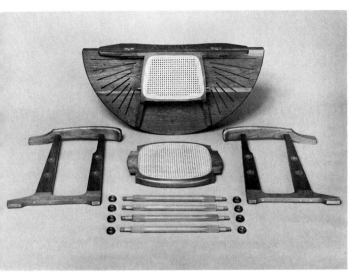

Gordon Kyle, Waterford, Conn.

Queen Bee (table/chair); cherry, walnut, cane, brass hinges; 34 in. x 44 in. x 27 in. (Piece is shown assembled at bottom.) Photos by Tom Hahn.

"Nut-and-strut construction, a no-tool knock down."

Michael Patrick Reilly, Bridgehampton, N.Y.

Piano bench; maple; 19.5 in. x 36 in. x 15 in. Photo by David Preston.

"Bench seat rests on four pivoting dowels in cradles routed into top of each leg. Top opens from either direction, with one central restraining tether."

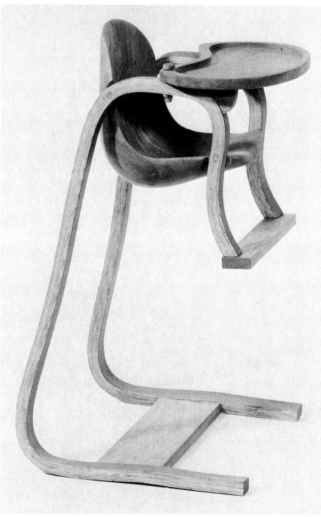

Jack L. Voss, Laguna Niguel, Calif.
*Child's high chair; pine, ash; 56 in. x 30 in. x
16 in. Photo by Bill Janes.*

Keith Cook, Grande Prairie, Alberta,
Canada
*Child's high chair; red oak, Honduras
mahogany; 36 in. x 18 in. x 18 in. Photo by
Paul Pervere.*

Jim Borgford-Parnell, Seattle, Wash.
*Rocking dragon; sugar pine, brass, leather;
27 in. x 15 in. x 48 in. Photo by Dana
Drake.*

"Designed to rock on its fat stomach rather
than rockers."

Douglas Yule, Conway, N.H.
*Rocking horse; maple; 16 in. x 37 in. x 40 in.
Photo by J.B. Mitchell III.*

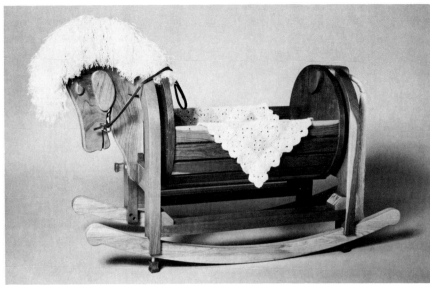

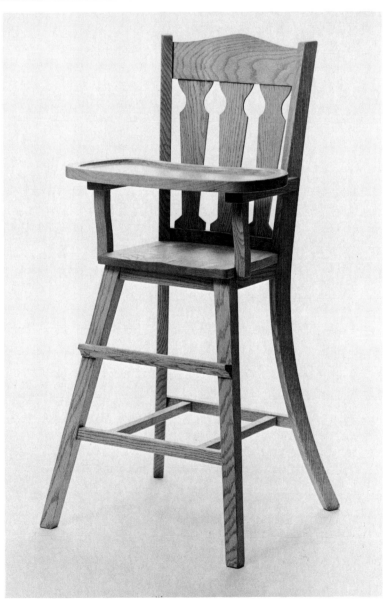

David Delthony, Berlin, West Germany

Rocking object (Schaukelobjekt); pine plywood; 160 cm. x 85 cm. x 90 cm.

"Users can sit facing each other while rocking."

Lanny Mitchell, San Jose, Calif.

Rocking horse; birch, oak, rosewood; 27 in. x 11.25 in. x 48 in. Photo by Richard Mitchell.

(Top left and right) **Ralph B. Schroeder,** Holland, Mich.

Rocking horse/cradle; cherry, ash, polyester, leather; 38 in. x 18 in. x 52 in.

Joseph A. Scannell, Novato, Calif.

Child's high chair; red oak, metal tray hardware; 38 in. x 14 in. x 12 in. Photo by Michael Scannell.

"This is one of two identical chairs of oak for my two children. Each has her name and birthdate carved into the underside of the seat, with plenty of room for the next generation."

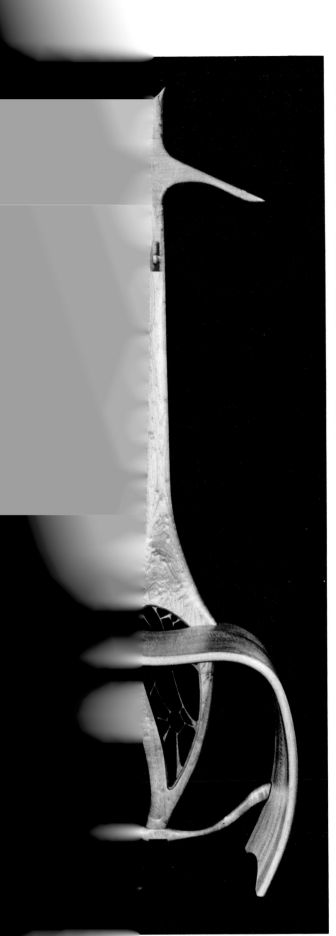

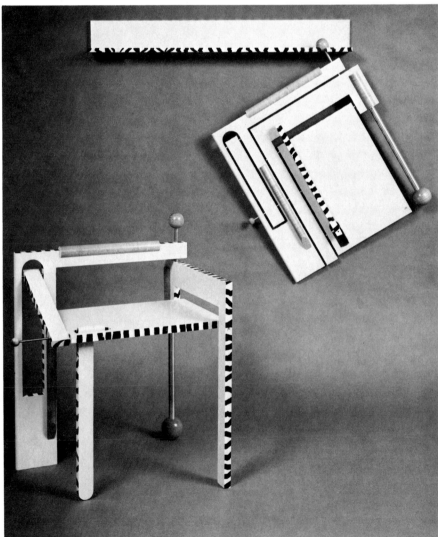

s Gatos, Calif.

; curly maple; 60 in. x

ing for fun."

Sara Jaffe, Berkeley, Calif.

Benucci side chairs; walnut, Honduras mahogany, Honduras rosewood, aluminum, upholstered seat; 33 in. x 18 in. x 18 in. Photo by Richard Sargent.

Thomas Loeser, Cambridge, Mass.

Pair of folding chairs; Baltic birch plywood, maple, stainless steel, aluminum, enamel paint; (open) 28 in. x 27 in. x 20 in. (folded) 28 in. x 27 in. x 3 in. Photo by David Caras.

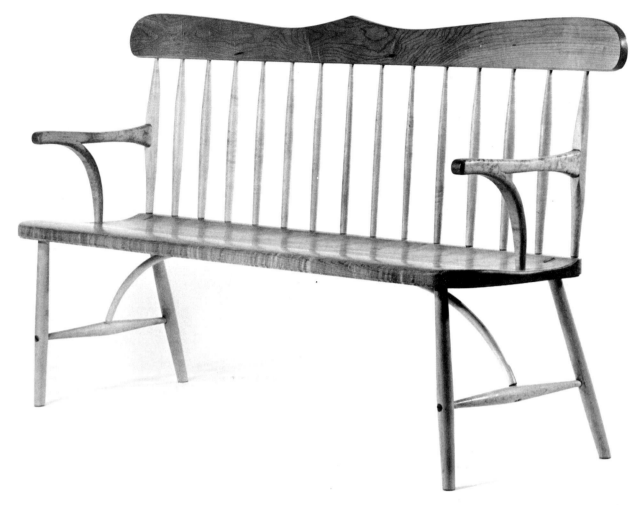

**Custom Woodworking, (M.D. 'Mac'
Campbell),** Harvey Station, New
Brunswick, Canada

*Deacon's bench; hard maple, bird's-eye
maple, walnut wedges; 31 in. x 60 in. x 17
in. Photo by Don Johnson.*

Scott Wynn, San Francisco, Calif.

*Valet Chair; padauk, bird's-eye maple; 40 in.
x 22 in. x 18 in.*

Kirk D. Wonner, Cardiff, Calif.

*Armchair; Baltic birch plywood, birch
dowels; 30.5 in. x 27 in. x 30.5 in.*

Dan Mosheim, Arlington, Vt.
Comb-back Windsor chair; pine, hickory, maple; 45 in. x 23 in. x 20 in. Photo by Cook Neilson.

James Gentry, Madison, Wis.
Side chair; slippery elm, Japanese cloth seat; 38 in. x 21 in. x 21 in.

"Slippery elm is my favorite chair wood. It bends rather than breaks, cuts nicely, takes a beautiful finish and has strong lines."

M. L. Pallischeck, Penn Yan, N.Y.
Captain's chair; red oak, natural cane; 22.5 in. x 21 in. x 20.5 in.

Gerald D. Otis, Albuquerque, N. Mex.

Armchair; American walnut, ebony; 35.5 in. x 24 in. x 27 in. Photo by Dick Kent.

"Legs and arms of glued-up laminations pre-bent in bathtub with riser sections. Ebony laminations outline forms. Based on methods to make composite archery bows."

Scott C. Smith, Pittsburgh, Pa.

Rocking chair; mahogany, ash; 45 in. x 27 in. x 35 in. Photo by Barbara Katzenberg.

Stephen B. Crump, Memphis, Tenn.

Armchair; pecan; 52 in. x 40 in. x 23 in. Photo by Frederick Toma.

"Four chairs were commissioned by the National Hardwood Lumber Association for its new headquarters in Memphis."

Kevin J. Regan, Wappingers Falls, N.Y.

Neo Klismos Rocking Chair; beech, brass; 35 in. x 21.75 in. x 35 in. Photo by Thom Murcko.

Robert Scaffe, Knoxville, Tenn.

Queen Anne side chair; walnut; 41 in. x 20 in. x 21 in. Photo by Steve Anderson.

"I try to avoid strict reproductions, preferring instead to produce original pieces while working within guidelines set by a particular period or style."

John C. Holtslander, Flint, Mich.

Chippendale ladder-back armchair; mahogany, fabric.

"If you want to learn how to make a chair, try this one."

Reginald E. Bushnell, East Dennis, Mass.

Half-round (or corner) chair; Honduras mahogany, pine, webbing, horsehair, needlepoint; 30 in. high, (seat) 19 in. square.

John W. Snead, Newport News, Va.

Chippendale corner chair; Honduras mahogany, cherry slip-seat frame and blocks; 32.5 in. x 27 in. x 23 in. Photo by John B. Warters.

"In my research on corner chairs, I counted only three with spooned and shaped splats. Count this number four. I do not build copies."

Donald Van Sinderen, West Lebanon, Maine

George I armchair and Chippendale pie crust table; (chair) 40 in. x 20 in. x 18 in. Photo by Jack Bingham.

A.B. Acker, Amherst, Mass.

Four Queen Anne chairs (after Langdon); walnut, brocade seat; 40 in. x 20 in. x 20 in. Photo by Mitchell Koldy.

"The originals of these chairs were destroyed, and I commissioned to build their replacements. I had only an oblique photo and overall size to work from. The patron said they were exact replacements."

Mario Rodriguez, Brooklyn, N.Y.

Sack-back Windsor armchair; pine, oak, maple; 37 in. x 23 in. Photo by David Arky.

"Eighteenth-century methods, within same time constraints (two days)."

Bruce Joseph Kunkel, Henryville, Pa.

Windsor-style chair of original design; poplar, hickory, red oak, cherry, walnut; 36 in. x 24 in. (seat) 19 in. high. Photo by Helen E. Kunkel.

William H. James Company, North Conway, N.H.

Comb-back Windsor courting bench; maple, pine; 47 in. x 48 in. x 17 in. Photo by Dick Smith.

Randall K. Fields, Amesville, Ohio

Crest-back Windsor settee; poplar, ash; 41 in. x 21 in. x 42 in. Photo by Chris Eaton.

"My delight is the back, which I found hiding in the middle of a 10-ft. plank."

Susan M. Patterson, Crawfordsville, Iowa
Sack-back Windsor chair; maple, pine, hackberry, milk paint; 39.25 in. x 28 in. x 21 in., 9 lb.

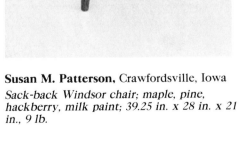

B. Randolph Wilkinson, Richmond, Va.
Windsor high chair; hard maple legs, poplar seat, white oak spindles; 41 in. x 15 in. Removable tray, steam-bent back. Photo by Melissa Kimmel.

John Bickel, Ossining, N.Y.
Dining chair; walnut; 46 in. x 18 in. x 20 in.

Beds

James Adams, Leverett, Mass.
Egg-shaped cradle; maple; 36 in. x 24 in. x 24 in. Photo by Edward Judice.

"I glue up a series of slabs from which I bandsaw concentric circles. The specific diameter and table angle for each cut are determined by direct measurements from a full-scale drawing. The outer ring from each slab is then glued, screwed and clamped in order to form the egg."

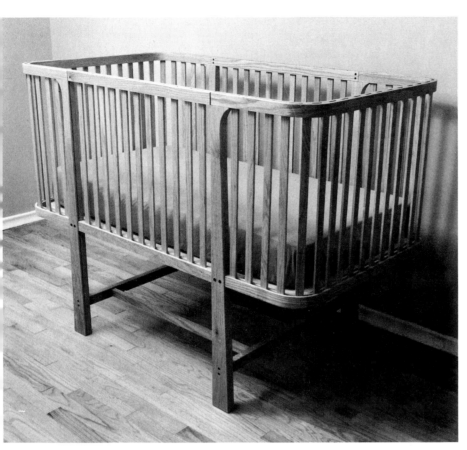

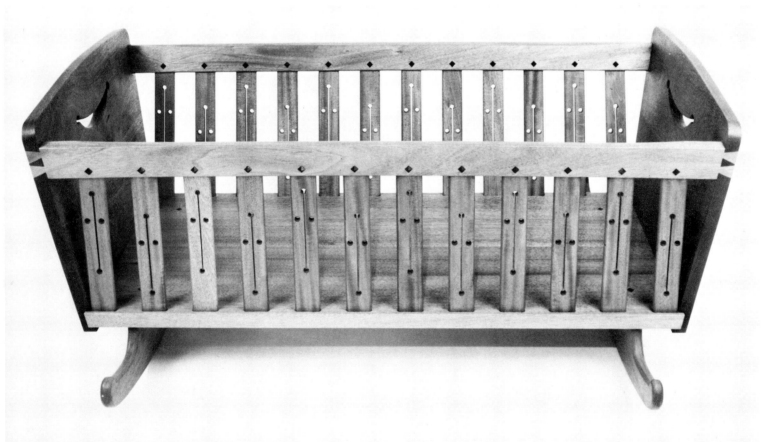

Lawrence A. Moniz, Seattle, Wash.

Crib for standard 28-in. x 52-in. mattress with bumpers; red oak; 32 in. x 56 in. x 42 in. Photo by Jim Ball.

Scott S. Page, Berkeley, Calif.

Cradle; mahogany, ebony pegs; 18 in. x 22 in. x 36 in. Photo by Exposure.

Margaret E. Bigelow, Victoria, British Columbia, Canada

Baby's First Bed; American black cherry, white oak; 52 in. x 30 in. x 21.75 in. Photo by Eugene D. Rubin.

"Combines the feelings that new parents have in wanting something special for their first child, and those that experienced parents have in thinking it's okay for their fifth-born to sleep in a drawer."

Marc Antony Kunkel, Hackettstown, N.J.

*Cradle; black walnut; 48 in. x 48 in. x 24 in.
Photo by Jeff Kunkel.*

"I believe in an honest day's work for a
day's pay."

Donald H. Bailey, Afton, Va.

*Baby cradle; walnut, sea grass, roller-bearing
suspension; 48 in. x 40 in. x 24 in. Photo by
Caston Studio.*

Clark Twining, Glen Gardner, N.J.

*Cradle for Christopher; cherry, curly maple;
54 in. x 42 in. x 30 in. Photo by Minassian
Studios.*

"When I learned there'd be a new addition,
I took a few weeks off from building
kitchens to do something with heart."

Gert Becker, Marysville, Wash.

*Cradle; white oak; 38 in. x 20 in. x 27 in.
Relief carving. Photo by Lloyd Weller.*

: Jeff Justis, Jr., Memphis, Tenn.

Four-Poster Bed, Primitive Style; cherry; 83 in. x 62 in. x 86.5 in. Photo by Rod Phillips.

"Rope-holding knobs on each of the four rails will support rope springs and a feather mattress if one desires not only an authentic look but an authentic feel."

Woodesign, dba Wildwood, Phoenix, Ariz.

Bedroom Set; walnut, bird's-eye maple, bronze mirror; 60 in. x 168 in. x 84 in. Photo by Mark Herring.

"Designers: Larry Langhurst and Bernie Becker. Craftsmen: Bernie Becker and Don Pearse."

John Economaki, Portland, Oreg.

Bed; walnut; 54 in. x 60 in. x 80 in. Photo by Louis Bencze.

James Schriber, New Milford, Conn.

King-size bed; Bolivian rosewood; 28 in. x 78 in. x 82 in. Photo by Doug Long.

Rick Gentile, New York, N.Y.

The Heavenly Attendants (queen-size bed); mahogany, ivory inlay; 51 in. x 66 in. x 87 in. Photo by Steve Chimento.

"Adapted from a Buddhist myth. Design by Joan Columbus."

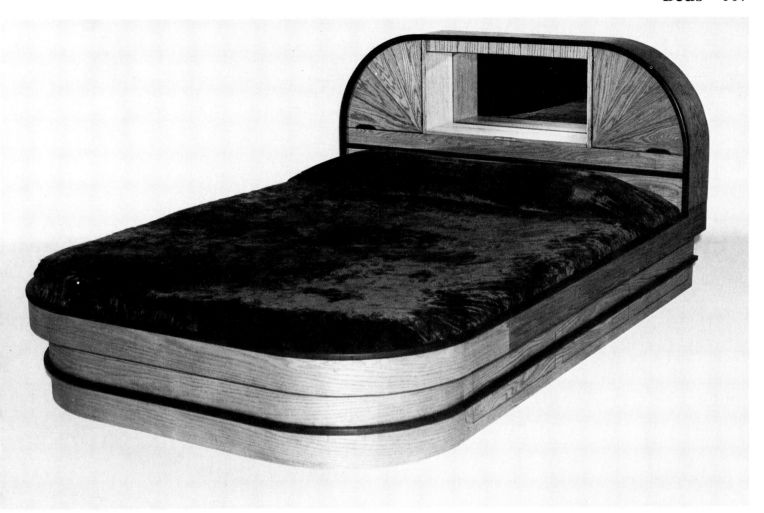

Clark Hicks and Don Carter, Kirkland, Wash.

Platform bed; red oak with Nicaraguan walnut trim. Photo by Christophoto.

"The headboard has a fan-shaped door on each side, a jewelry box with lift-up lid in the middle, and a reading light hidden behind the fascia board. The frame rests on a six-drawer pedestal."

Timothy Sutherland, Sutherland Studios, Atlanta, Ga.

Half-canopy bed; ribbon-striped African mahogany, Carpathian elm burl; 120 in. x 108 in. x 108 in.

"Forty hand-carved sculptures adorn the structure; 50 ft. of hand-carved molding accent the canopy, headboard, sideboard, and footboard. This project took four fine craftsmen five months to build."

Susan LosCalzo, New Orleans, La.

Sunrise Bed; walnut; 54 in. x 68 in. x 86 in. Photo by Judy Cooper.

Tools and Toys

Naomi Stibbe, Tel Aviv, Israel
*Chess set; rosewood, hornbeam, lead, felt; 50
mm. to 100 mm. high, 30 mm. average dia.
Turned and carved. Photo by Yona
Zaloscer.*

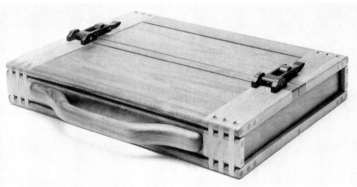

Vincent E. Kershaw, M.D., Omaha, Nebr.

Chessboard; walnut, maple, synthetic rubber; 21 in. x 21 in. x 4.25 in. Photo by Walter Griffith, Jr.

"Elevation of playing field is consistent with the status of the game."

Takeo Omuro, Kahului, Maui, Hawaii

Corporate Abacus; eucalyptus, brass rods, Corian countertop; 4.5 in. x 7.5 in. x 34 in.

(Bottom left and right) **Christian Brisepierre,** Las Vegas, Nev.

Box for a Close-Up Magician; walnut, cherry, rosewood, red velvet; 4 in. x 24 in. x 14 in. Rosewood locks, wooden hinges. (Box is shown open at right.) Photo by John Goad.

"When my friend opens his box and a little red velvet stage appears, the spectators know there will be magic."

Steven Gray, Bozeman, Mont.

Terrestrial telescope; spalted maple burl, desert ironwood burl; 25 in. x 3.25 in. Focal length 20 in., objective 2.5 in. Photo by Robert P. Abbott.

David J. Marks, Custom Wood Working, Santa Rosa, Calif.

My portfolio cover; olive burl, koa, Burmese padauk hinge, leather, brass; 13 in. x 11 in. x 2 in. Photo by Don Russel.

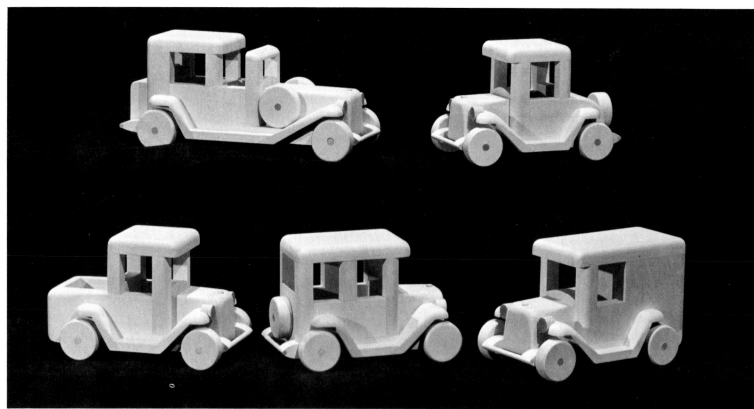

Jon Bricker, Kensington, Md.

Twin Toys for Twin Boys; walnut, cherry, Brazilian rosewood, bubinga, holly veneer, brass, copper screen, silver solder, acrylic; 3 in. x 4.75 in. x 10.5 in. Photo by Edward Owen.

Jim Christo, Jamestown, N.Y.

18-Wheeler Toy; cedar, oak, maple, walnut; (trailer) 9.25 in. x 6.75 in. x 16 in. (cab) 9.25 in. x 6.75 in. x 13.5 in.

Robert H. DeWalt, Independence, Mo.

Toy cars; bass, birch; (car at top left) 14.125 in. long, (others) 10 in. long. Photo by Stephen DeWalt.

"These are prototypes of wooden toys which I have designed, and I sell full-size plans and patterns of same."

Kenneth Vliet, Oldwick, N.J.

Fire engine; 35 exotic and common hardwoods, steel, brass; 10 in. x 8 in. x 30 in.

Peter Dawson, St. John's, Newfoundland, Canada

Toy car; oak, birch, walnut; 4.75 in. x 4.25 in. x 12 in. Photo by Jack Martin.

Bill Stankus, Bayside, Wis.

Alicia's Castle; baltic birch plywood, ebony, maple, cherry, brass hardware; 54 in. overall dia.; (wall) 8 in. high, (large tower) 14 in. x 20 in.

Bill Henderson, Abbotsford, British Columbia, Canada

Front-end loader; western red cedar, alder, mahogany; 8 in. x 15 in. x 8 in.

Kent Bailey, Escondido, Calif.

Single-seater sport plane; oak, walnut, cherry, jacaranda, East Indian rosewood, koa, Brazilian hardwoods, brass, sterling silver, 18K gold, electronic components.

"Sterling silver rear-view mirror, windshield wiper and stereo antenna with 18K gold knob. Wiper doubles as switch for flashing red LED under plane. Runway contains 88 working neon bulbs for night landings."

Richard Schneider, Kalamazoo, Mich.
Helical Mosaic Bracelet and Slave Set; 14 domestic and foreign hardwoods, as many colors of dyed maple; (bracelet) 80 mm. O.D. (slave) 95 mm. O.D. Photo by Dennis Crawford.
"Slave bracelet is flat, main is sculptured."

Seth Stem, Marblehead, Mass.
Serving table; cherry, bicycle wheels; 72 in. x 26 in. x 39 in.

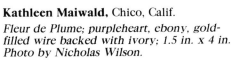

Manuel Albert Gomez, Oakland, Calif.

Natural Comb; purpleheart, tulipwood; 11.38 in. x 3.63 in. x 1.5 in.

Kathleen Maiwald, Chico, Calif.
Fleur de Plume; purpleheart, ebony, gold-filled wire backed with ivory; 1.5 in. x 4 in. Photo by Nicholas Wilson.

Byron Hansen, Wilkie, Saskatchewan, Canada
Velocipede; red oak, walnut, brass; 24 in. x 24 in. x 48 in. Photo by Frank Sudol.

John Nelson, Santa Fe, N. Mex.
Royal Dolphin Cradle; cherry, maple; 45 in. x 22.5 in. x 54 in. Photo by Herb Lotz.

Joe L. Nevius, Kennewick, Wash.
Child's sled; hickory, brass screws; 8 in. x 14 in. x 26 in.

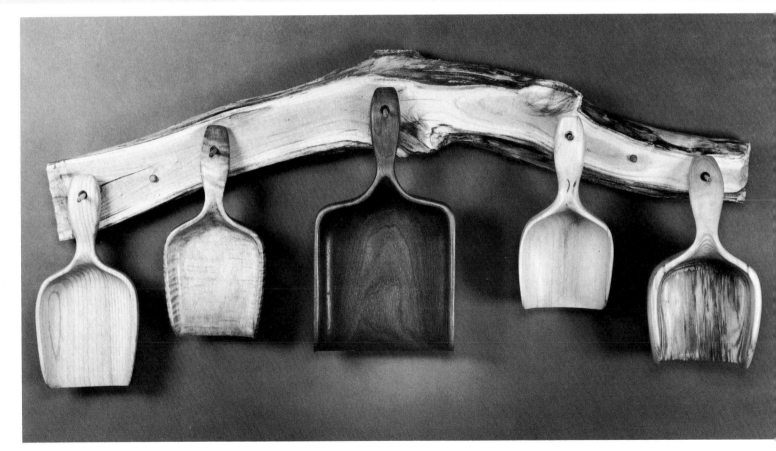

Jude Binder and Norm Sartorius, Big Bend, W. Va. and Parkersburg, W. Va.

Autumn Hare; plum; 15.5 in. long. Hand-carved. Collection of the West Virginia Department of Culture and History. Photo by Rick Lee.

Joe Hogan, Lynn, Mass.

Locust rack with scoops; (left to right) ash, curly maple, walnut, poplar, eastern pine. Photo by Gainsboro Studio.

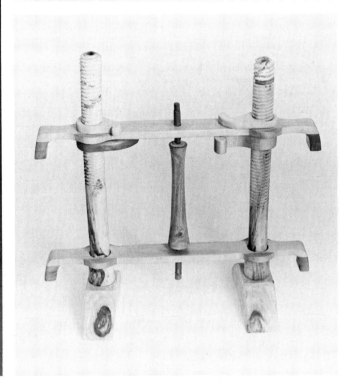

Dean A. Slindee, Prairie Designs, La Crosse, Wis.

Variable height extensions; maple, hardware; 27 in. to 40 in. high, 20 in. to 36 in. wide. Photo by James W. Taylor.

"Made in different widths (4-in. increments) so they stack when not in use."

West Lowe, Missoula, Mont.

Tool chest; oak, walnut; (open) 36 in. x 40 in. x 18 in.

E.J. Lang, Lincoln, Nebr.

Churn and tankard for Norwegian rosemaling; pine and willow saplings; (churn) 9 in. x 34 in. (tankards) 9 in. x 12 in., 9 in. x 14 in. Photo by Paul N. Heiman.

Clement Konzem, Van Nuys, Calif.

Egyptian wood-turning lathe; carob, birch; 28 in. x 28 in. Photo by Fay Irene Konzem.

"Replica of an Egyptian lathe (circa 1500 B.C.), reproduced from a tomb drawing."

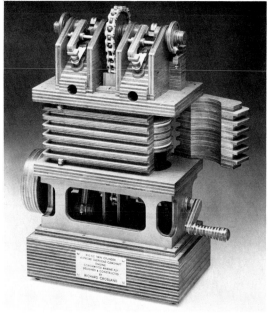

Richard Crosland, Chippendale, New South Wales, Australia

800cc Twin Cylinder 4-Stroke Overhead Camshaft Internal Combustion Engine; coachwood marine plywood, Tasmanian oak, pine, ramin, brass; 20 in. x 16 in. x 8 in. Photo by Kurt Vollner.

"Techniques: calculation, broken and chewed fingernails, trial and error (mostly error), hair loss, a minor degree of success."

Robert M. Davenport, Huntsville, Ala.

Stage piece for rock group AC/DC; western cedar, oak, white pine; 60 in. high. Photo by Roy Simmons.

"Pictured for scale: Tom DeWille, president of Luna Tech Inc., which engineered 16-shot flash/smoke device for which piece was built. Dimensions of U.S. 24-pounder howitzer were followed, but not intended as accurate copy of any historic gun."

Ron Keyes, Wilmington, N.Y.

Wooden Animation; cherry, oak, eastern red cedar, white cedar, Plexiglas; 15.63 in. x 11 in. x 14 in. Photo by McVicker Photography.

"Pulling forward on the handle approximately one-third turn releases one gumball properly upon the perch."

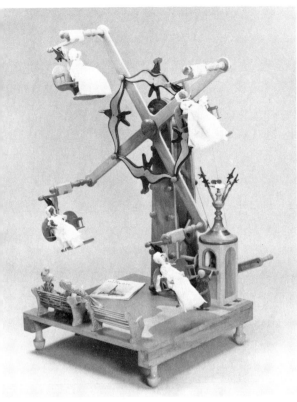

Dick Showalter, McKenzie Bridge, Oreg.

Ferris Wheel; white oak, madrone, cherry, plum, big leaf maple, leather, lacquers; 72 in. x 36 in. x 36 in. Photo by Mike Dean.

"Waterfall effect of cascading hearts and bluebirds is apparent to the discerning eye."

Larry Cada, Newport, Wash.

Ceiling Fan (©1982); maple, white oak, imbuya, bubinga, shedua; 52 in. x 34 in. Runs at 45 to 250 rpm. Photo by Jon Nelson.

(Bottom left) **Dana D. Warwick,** Irvine, Calif.

Sculpture in Time; koa, red oak, East Indian rosewood; 144 in. x 108 in., 1100 lb. Photo by Stuart Naideth.

"Gear movement and slowly oscillating balance beam make a quietly dynamic piece of kinetic clock sculpture. Clock winds itself by means of electric motor that senses when winding is required."

David M. Gillespie, Novato, Calif.

Saturn II Hyperion/Stereo Turntable; American black walnut, 6061 T6 aluminum, 303 stainless steel, antiphon, noiseless steel motor plate, two 300-rpm synchronous motors; 5.5 in. x 19.25 in. x 15.25 in. Photo by T. Collins.

Delbert E. Short, Eugene, Oreg.

Wooden Mechanical Machine; alder, maple; 24 in. x 18 in. x 12 in. Photo by Ron G. Short.

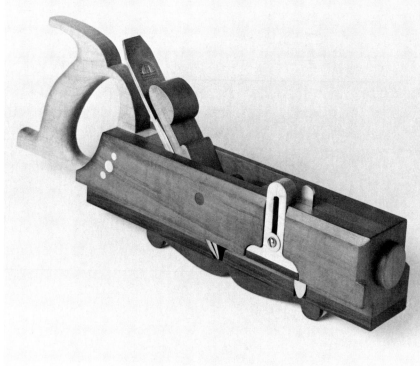

Arthur E. Dameron, Galesburg, Ill.
Spinning wheel; walnut, white oak, osage orange, brass, steel, leather, glue, screws; 38.5 in. x 14 in. x 36 in. (wheel) 21.5 in. dia. Photo by Bruce Janssen.

Thomas J. Duffy, Ogdensburg, N.Y.
Bookbinding press (laying press and plough); cherry, bronze; 38 in. x 33 in. x 33 in. Photo by Allen Burns.

Grey Doffin, Fargo, N. Dak.
Susie's Loom (41-in., 4-harness jack loom); hard maple, a bit of Honduras mahogany, steel, string; 51 in. x 54 in. x 38 in. Photo by Wayne Gudmundson.

Donald Kahn, Hackensack, N.J.
Moving fillister; Swiss pear, lignum vitae, maple, brass hardware, steel spur, iron; 15 in. long, 1.25-in. iron. Photo by Louis Mervar.

Harry Wilhelm, Groton, N.Y.

View camera; curly maple, burl maple, walnut, goatskin bellows, brass; 19.5 in. x 14.5 in. x 12 in.

"Seeing firsthand the vibrant, crystalline quality of Ansel Adams' prints interested me in large-format photography. Since I couldn't afford a camera, I decided to make one."

J.R. Beall, J & J Beall Woodworking, Newark, Ohio

Leica Cabinet Clock; figured maple, black walnut, glass; 13 in. x 26 in. x 11 in. Photo by Bill Cost, Jr.

"Pressing the shutter release unlocks the doors. I like building pieces that are one of a kind with a whimsical twist."

Adrian Searle, Ottawa, Ontario, Canada

8x10 view camera (monorail type); oak, birch, hickory, maple, rosewood, mahogany, brass, glass, neoprene, plastic, spring steel; 26 in. x 20 in. x 36 in.

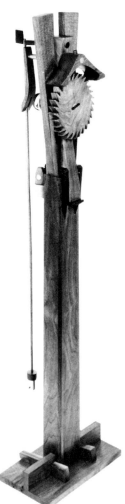

Rick Stoner, Longmont, Colo.
Grandfather with table clock; walnut, oak; (grandfather) 79 in. x 28 in. x 16 in. (table clock) 15 in. x 10 in. x 7 in. German movements. Photo by Mike Signorella.

Barrie Faulkner, Gadshill, Ontario, Canada
Hanging clock; cherry, black walnut; 18 in. x 8 in. x 9 in. Photo by Pirak Studios.

James L. Misner, Jefferson, Md.
4-1/2 Minute Run; black walnut, ebony, brass rods; 47 in. x 12 in. x 7.5 in. Photo by Edward E. Hennemann.

"As its name implies, this piece runs for four and one-half minutes and is a study for future clocks."

Wesley P. Glewwe, West St. Paul, Minn.
Antique wooden-gear wall clock; 145 species of wood; 38 in. x 18 in. x 8 in. Photo by Blumenfeld Photography.

"Gears appear to mesh, but are driven by hidden motor. Time, pendulum and chimes produced by quartz movement."

J. Michael Johnson, Bath, Ohio
Long Drop Octagon Regulator; curly maple; 17 in. x 31 in. Photo by K. E. Johnson.

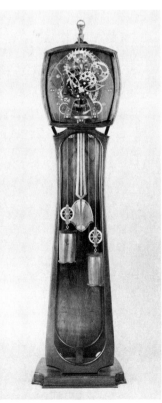

D.C. Story, Pleasantville, N.Y.

The Lobby Clock; oak, particleboard, aluminum, glass; 28 in. dia., 5 in. deep. Tongue-and-groove frame, steam-bent oak case. Photo by Marian Hughes.

Harry M. Myer, Rosemead, Calif.

Clock; walnut, oak, ash, padauk, ebony, tulipwood, birch, mahogany, Circassian walnut; 76 in. x 18 in. x 14 in. Photo by Don El Monte.

Steve Voorheis, Missoula, Mont.

Ceremonial Timepiece; walnut, bird's-eye maple, Maccassar ebony, brass details, rusted steel pedestal; 78 in. x 12 in. x 10 in.

Reid H. Leonard, Pensacola, Fla.

Clock; rosewood veneer, cocobolo; 23 in. x 17 in. x 1.5 in. Photo by Frank Hardy.

"Loo pattern from successive veneer sheets. Time marks are streaks of sapwood."

William Parks, Minneapolis, Minn.

Tallcase clock; cherry; 72 in. x 17 in. x 10 in. Mirrored back.

"Reproduction in the style of tallcase Regulator clocks."

Craig Tinker, Fort Dodge, Iowa

Tinkerville (wall hanging); pine, basswood, plywood, balsa, glass, Formica; 21 in. x 53 in. Photo by Brent Isenberger.

Jon E. Jenett, Santa Barbara, Calif.

Frances; walnut, cherry, birch, ash, rosewood, teak, brass; 17 in. x 6 in. x 16 in. Plank-on-frame construction.

"Design is of catboat, working boat popular in Northeast U.S. late 1800s, early 1900s."

Ron Roush, Harbor City, Calif.

Bottled House, Victorian; walnut, basswood, fir, mahogany, birch, oak, glass, modeling clay, paint, cloth; 16 in. x 9 in.

Herbert A. Consor, Chagrin Falls, Ohio

Circa 1800 Furniture Factory; pine, poplar, maple, sheet metal, wire; 14 in. x 18 in. Photo by Richard Wallace. Courtesy of Little World Limited.

"Replica of 1800 shop in 1/12 scale."

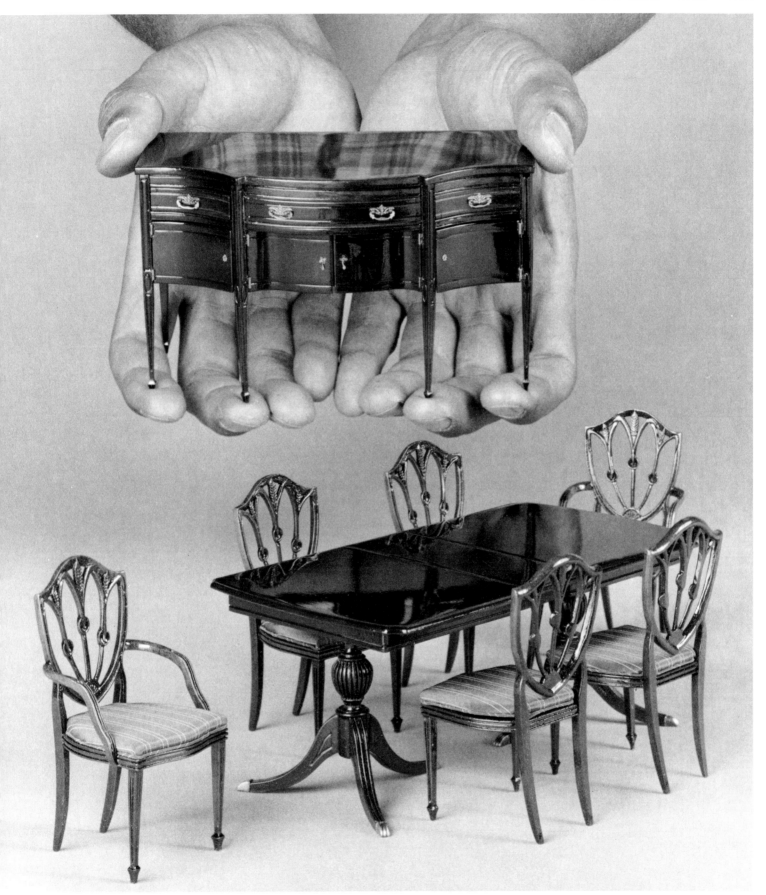

Ferd Sobol, Carpinteria, Calif.

Authentically replicated furniture in miniature dimension; bottlebrush, birch, walnut, tiny brass hardware. Photo by Arthur Montes De Oca.

Musical Instruments

On the instrument:

SOLÍ
DEO
GLORÍA

AVDÍ
VÍDE ⋅ ET ⋅ TACE
SÍ ⋅ VÍS ⋅ VÍVERE ⋅ ÍN ⋅ PACE

Steven W. Sørli, Carlisle, Mass.
*Flemish double-manual harpsichord;
basswood, white spruce, beech, pear, ebony,
maple, white oak, bone, iron, brass, cast-
lead rose, sheepskin; 10 in. x 91 in. x 37 in.
Photo by Carl Garufo.*

"Built entirely from scratch, solid-wood
construction, steam-bent parts, hand-plane
finishes, painted *faux marbre*, block-printed
paper, soundboard painting."

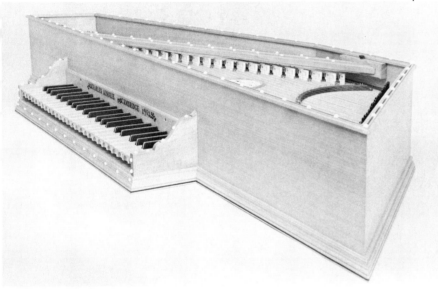

Danyel Clouse, Española, N. Mex.

Ancient Inspirations (Tapo drum); rosewood, moradilla, black walnut; 8 in. x 10 in. x 18 in. Photo by Richard Faller.

(Center and bottom left) **Charles Ainslie,** Cambridge, Mass.

Italian pentagonal spinet; Italian cypress, boxwood, ebony, walnut, Sitka spruce, basswood, poplar, maple, bone, parchment, plastic jacks; 7.25 in. x 56.5 in. x 18.25 in. Photos by Nancy Mattila.

"Copy of spinet made in 1684 by Johannes de Perticis of Florence. Rose made of layers of parchment cut and glued together."

Sal Palombino, Volant, Pa.

Five-string viola with case, cutaway and seven sympathetic strings; Sitka spruce, Pennsylvania cherry, pear and poplar purfling, maple bridge, rosewood pegs, Alaskan cedar linings, ebony fingerboard and tailpiece, fossil walrus, ivory inlays and end pin. Photo by Rob Chambers.

"Designed and built for Fred Mayer, Juneau, Alaska...full range of violin and viola."

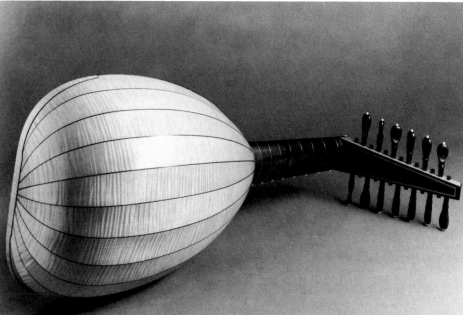

Robert Meadow, Saugerties, N.Y.

Baroque lute; ebony, holly, spruce; 36 in. x 14 in. x 5.5 in. Photo by Richard Starr.

"The challenge in my work is to produce an instrument which, by virtue of both the sound it makes and the ease with which it is played, inspires the musician. It is this pursuit which, in turn, inspires me."

(Top right) **Charles Tauber,** Dundas, Ontario, Canada

Lute; European silver spruce top, English curly sycamore body, Indian ebony rib spacers, fingerboard, tuning pegs and veneers, Sitka spruce neck core, ivory nut; 30 in. x 12 in. x 8 in. Photo by William Knetsch.

"Based on lute by Giovani Hieber, circa 1600. This style weighs about 2 lb."

Don Polifka, Rapidan, Va.

Musical instruments; rosewood, walnut, cherry, spruce, ebony, western red cedar, curly maple, holly, brass, mother-of-pearl, abalone, ivory, bone. Photo by Steve Griffin.

"All instruments are built to be played a long time."

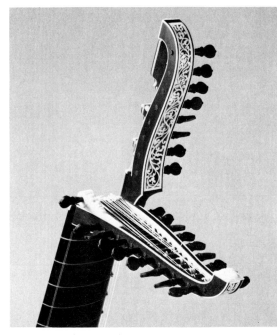

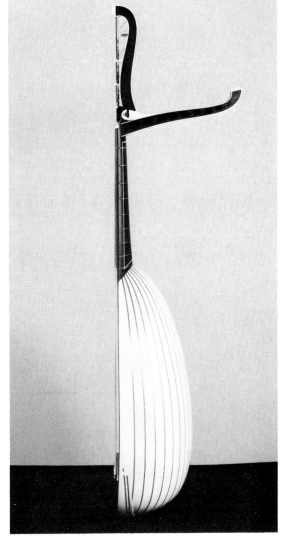

Tom Fellenbaum, Black Mountain, N.C.

Bowed psaltry; walnut, cherry, birch, chrome-plated hardware, brass bridge top; 20 in. x 7 in. x 1.25 in. Photo by Warner Photography.

Rion Dudley, Seattle, Wash.

Mandolin; Sitka spruce top, eastern curly maple back, sides and neck, rosewood inlay, ebony and bone bridge, zebrawood fretboard; 10 in. x 22 in. x 2.5 in. Photo by Mark Lyon.

Richard Berg, Ottawa, Ontario, Canada

14-course baroque lute; European spruce, poplar, ebony, beech, plum, Swiss pear, ivory; 47 cm. x 33 cm. x 14.7 cm., string length 68 cm. (Detail is shown at top.)

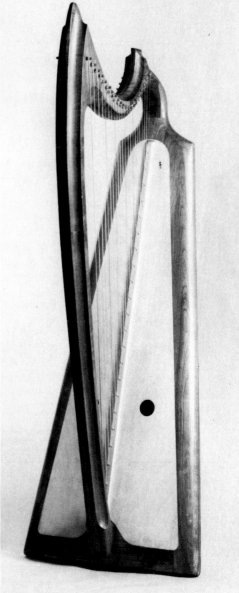

Charles M. Ruggles, Olmsted Falls, Ohio

Pipe organ; black walnut casework and carvings, grenadilla and cow bone manual keys, oak pedal keys, ash bass pipes, poplar, sugar pine, Honduras mahogany, maple, beech, inside pipes, aluminum, brass, steel, tin and lead alloys; 95 in. x 68 in. x 25.5 in. (Detail is shown at bottom right.)

"Roger Hornung made the case and bench, Herschel Westbrook carved pipe shades."

Norman R. Stoecker, Chesterfield, Mo.

Gothic harp; walnut; 40 in. high. Photo by Robert Stoecker.

"A design adapted from the harp shown in the Renaissance painting *Garden of Earthly Delights* by Hieronymus Bosch."

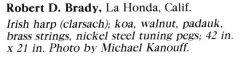

Robert D. Brady, La Honda, Calif.

Irish harp (clarsach); koa, walnut, padauk, brass strings, nickel steel tuning pegs; 42 in. x 21 in. Photo by Michael Kanouff.

Peter D. Kempster, Scott Creek, South Australia

Dital harp; Queensland maple, spruce, brass, steel tuning pins, gut strings; 53 in. x 28 in. x 14 in. Photo by Philip Kempster.

(Top right) **Gabor Schoffer,** Hayfork, Calif.

Psalmist harp; wengé plywood, birch inner pillar, Alaskan spruce soundboard. Photo by Jim Keller.

"The shape is my own design. The hollow solid-front pillar acts also as a sound box, strung with solid-brass and brass-wound strings. It produces pristine cascades of harmony."

Jim Jones, Bedford, Va.

Instruments; (left to right) (mountain dulcimer) walnut; 37 in. x 7 in. x 2.5 in. (hammer dulcimer) cherry plywood; 38 in. x 16 in. x 2 in. (hammer dulcimer) Brazilian mahogany; 38 in. x 16 in. x 2 in. (hammer dulcimer) baltic birch plywood; 38 in. x 16 in. x 2 in. (eight-tone drum) padauk, ash; 20 in. x 8 in. x 8 in. (aeolian harp) curly maple; 28 in. x 5.5 in. x 3 in. (mountain dulcimer) bubinga; 37 in. x 7 in. x 2.5 in. Photo by Toby Hunt.

Jody Nishman, Easthampton, Mass.

Marimba; padauk, bird's-eye maple, cherry, rosewood; 32 in. x 34 in. x 25 in. Photo by D. Randolph Foulds.

Mark Wescott, Somers Point, N.J.

Steel-string guitar; Sitka spruce, Indian rosewood, Honduras mahogany, ebony, holly, brass; 40.5 in. x 15 in. x 4.5 in. (Guitar is shown at left.)

"Sound hole is brass in blackened epoxy."

Per O. Walthinsen, Portland, Oreg.

Clavichord; ash, fir, cherry, bocote, teak, red oak, basswood, maple, Sitka spruce, ebony, brass, steel strings; (closed) 7 in. x 71 in. x 22 in. Photo by Åke Lundberg.

Brahm Friedlander, Kaministiquia, Ontario, Canada

Guitar; Sitka spruce, Honduras mahogany, ebony, bone; 39 in. x 13 in. x 5 in. Photo by Doug Martin.

Craig Woodward, Spring Valley, Calif.

Harpsichord; cherry, spruce, maple, poplar, walnut, rosewood; 36 in. x 40 in. x 90 in. Photo by Jon Woodward.

Abraham Wechter, Paw Paw, Mich.

Thirteen-string guitar; Canadian red cedar, East Indian rosewood, curly maple, curly ebony, poplar, maple, ivory inlaid with mother-of-pearl. Photo by Dennis Crawford.
"Built to order for John McLaughlin."

David Hodge, Sunnyvale, Calif.

Wooden drum; white oak; 32 in. high, 11.75 in. dia.
"Stave construction, steam-bent, then turned on lathe."

Michael Darnton, Atlantic Mine, Mich.

Custom dreadnaught guitar; Indian rosewood, bird's-eye maple, ebony, mahogany, spruce, pearl, abalone, gold-plated tuners; 40.5 in. x 15.75 in. x 5 in. (Guitar is shown at top right.) Photos by Michael Darnton.

(Top left and right) **John Pruitt,** Alpine, Calif.

Acoustic guitar; East Indian rosewood, ebony, spruce, mahogany, olive, abalone, mother-of-pearl, gold pearl, ivory; 41 in. x 16 in. x 5 in. Photos by Chuck Barber.

"Special appreciation must be given for technical assistance to Bob Taylor, Steve Schemmer and Kurt Listug."

Eric C. Thiele, Greenville, N.C.

Nile Music (dulcimer); purpleheart, ash, redwood, brass; 50 in. x 24 in. x 14 in. Coopering and boatbuilding techniques, laminating.

Dick Boak, Church of Art, Nazareth, Pa.

Family of Guitars, 1982; African ebony, Maccassar ebony, East Indian rosewood, Alpine spruce, Amazon mahogany, abalone and mother-of-pearl inlays by David Nichols; (guitar at far left) 41 in. x 15 in. x 4.5 in. Photo by Peters and Kidney.

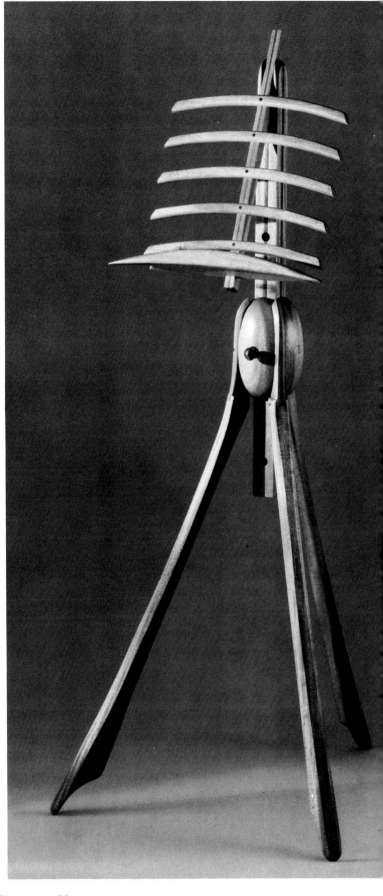

Paula Cooperrider, Tempe, Ariz.

Bryan's Beast; walnut, zebrawood, tulipwood, ash, oak, vermilion, mahogany, honey locust, cherry; 60 in. x 22 in. x 24 in.

"Represents the personal fantasies of the young owner."

Kristina W. Madsen, Easthampton, Mass.

Music stands; walnut, brass hardware; adjustable from 32 in. to 52 in. high. Photo by David Ryan.

Chris Becksvoort, New Gloucester, Maine

Music stand; black walnut, ash, brass hardware; 36 in. to 48 in. x 22 in. x 20 in.

Aspy J. Khambatta, Daly City, Calif.

Music stand; Honduras mahogany, black walnut inlay; adjustable to 43 in., 53 in. or 63 in. high. Collection of Nadya Tichman. Photo by Richard Sargent.

"The form of an object is not arrived upon accidentally, but is a product of contemplation and concentration."

Furnishings

Ross Matuja, Richmond, Mich.
Fireplace mantel; red and white oak; 42 in.
x 84 in. x 14 in. Photo by John Phelan.

Ben Bacon, London, England

Rococo girandole; Baltic pine, lime, brass, materials for water gilding (gesso, red and yellow bole, gold); 37 in. x 19 in. x 4.5 in. Photo by Robert Aberman.

"Frame, bird and figures are carved, then covered with gesso. After ten coats, gesso is recut to restore the original sharpness. Copy of Plate 178, Chippendale's *Director.* Mirror plates intended to reflect the candles."

Joseph Tracy, Mount Desert, Maine

Floor lamp; teak, granite, silk; 70 in. x 26 in. x 13 in.

"A tall lamp with a small base. This piece gains its stability from the weight of the removable beach stone."

John J. Demar, Santa Fe, N. Mex.

Welcome (entryway doors); red alder, brass; 84 in. x 72 in. x 2 in.

"The client requested a design that welcomed the visitor and focused attention on the entry in an otherwise bland exterior. The carving required exquisitely sharp tools, and a grid system to precisely locate each carved scallop."

Steve Davidson and Elon Yurwit, Elk, Calif.

The Fireplace; redwood slab mantels, redwood rails, tiger-stripe redwood panels; 240 in. x 240 in. x 36 in. Photo by Nicholas Wilson.

"Property of McDowell Cellars. Motif for the tasting room based on the grapevines and oak trees surrounding the winery and visible through large picture windows."

Paul Pyzyna, Free Union, Va.

Folding shoji-style screen; Honduras mahogany, rice paper; 92 in. x 108 in. Photo by Susan Mortell.

"The mood of a room is often controlled by its lighting. A soft and beautiful light condition is obtained by back-lighting these screens."

Earl Engelman, The Joiners, Sun Valley, Idaho
Staircase; cherry, white oak; 116 in. x 40 in. x 168 in. Photo by Larry Hill.

Howard Hastings, Barre, Mass.
Bathroom interior; cherry, bird's-eye maple, maple. Photo by Chuck Kidd.

Ed Clay, Napa, Calif.
Screen; California walnut; 76 in. x 66 in. Photo by Balfour Walker.

David L. Trapp, Boulder, Colo.
Screens and matching butterfly table; tiger maple, padauk; (screens) 56 in. x 76 in. (butterfly table) 14 in. x 48 in. x 32 in. Photo by Bill Farrell.

"Art is not doing something special, it is a special way of doing things, anything."

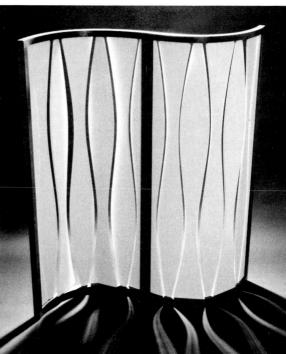

Alois Von Matt, Gladwin, Mich.

Coat hanger; maple, olive ash, tigerwood, silk; 16 in. x 36 in. Photo by Paul A. Duso Gladwin.

Samuel Dickinson, Scottsville, N.Y.

Room divider; cherry, basswood, brass; 66.5 in. x 60 in. x 1.5 in. Photo by Ken Riemer.

"Based on room divider by Eileen Gray that included small panels allowed to pivot to let varying amounts of light come through."

Marianne Bond, Mercer Island, Wash.

Iris, Calla Lily Screen; North Idaho white pine; 72 in. x 58 in. Photo by Kim Brun.

Ed Dadey, Marquette, Nebr.

Magazine rack; wengé; 86 in. x 77 in. x 43 in.

Jeremy Foster, El Jebel, Colo.
*Entry door; black walnut; 36 in. x 80 in. x
1.75 in.*

Jamie Robertson, Cambridge, Mass.
*Interior door; cherry, ebony, brass; 80 in. x
32 in.*
"Curved-shoulder double mortise-and-tenon
joints with ebony diamond through-pins;
dovetailed jamb."

Rodger Reid, New Preston, Conn.
*Living room entrance doors; butternut;
(each door) 80 in. x 24 in. Photo by William
Seitz.*

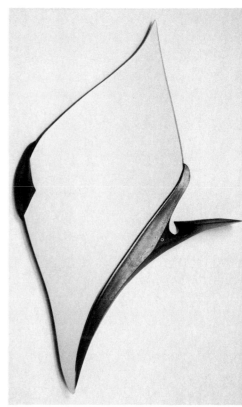

Greg FryeWeaver, Albuquerque, N. Mex.

*For the Clouds (wall mirror with shelf);
bird's-eye maple, maple, walnut, red gum,
pau ferro; 16.5 in. x 28 in. x 3.5 in. Photo by
Robert Reck.*

Martin Linder, Birmingham, Mich.

Candleholder; walnut; 12 in. x 7 in. x 7 in.

Aleida Ijzerman, Mississauga, Ontario,
Canada

*Organic Wall-Hung Mirror; mahogany;
(mirror) 36 in. x 27 in. (shelf) 3 in. wide.
Photo by Peter Hogan.*

Nicolai Klimaszewski, Cincinnati, Ohio

*Freestanding tabletop mirror; poplar,
walnut, etched glass; 34 in. x 40 in.*

"Diamond mirror within larger, clear-glass
diamond."

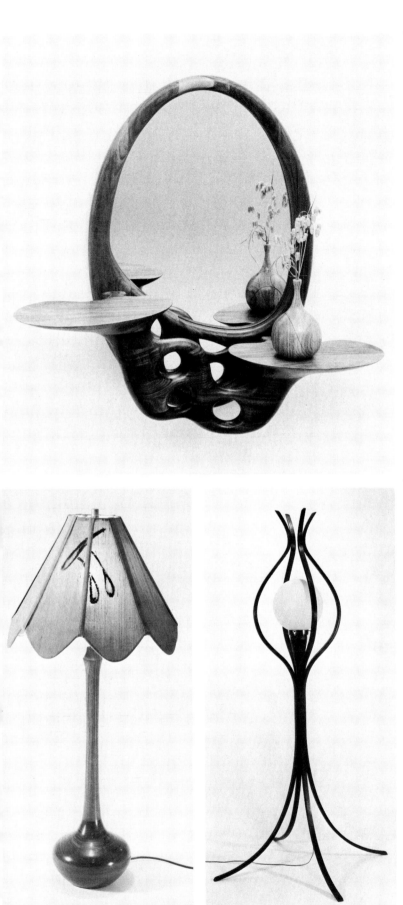

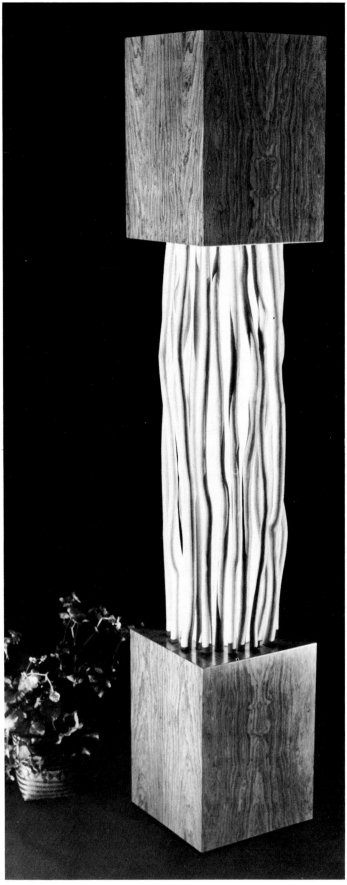

Craig Lauterbach, Monterey, Calif.

Mirror; walnut, glass; 30 in. x 24 in. x 15 in. Photo by Pat Pagnella.

Newell L. White, Rochester, N.Y.

Torchère; Chingchan veneer, mixed hardwood saplings, gonçalo alves, plycores; 81 in. x 14.5 in. x 14.5 in. Photo by Rameshwar Das.

"Wood as element of the biosphere, contrasted with wood to express human wants; energy flowing between matched polar terminals. Bundle of saplings radiate light from center. Four mini flood lamps."

Brian Cullen, Seattle, Wash.

Walnut lamp; walnut, hand-painted silk shade by Linda Baker; 22 in. x 6 in. Photo by John Switten.

Donald Carl Bjorkman, Flagstaff, Ariz.

Bud lamp; Peruvian walnut, glass, metal; 71 in. x 27 in. x 27 in.

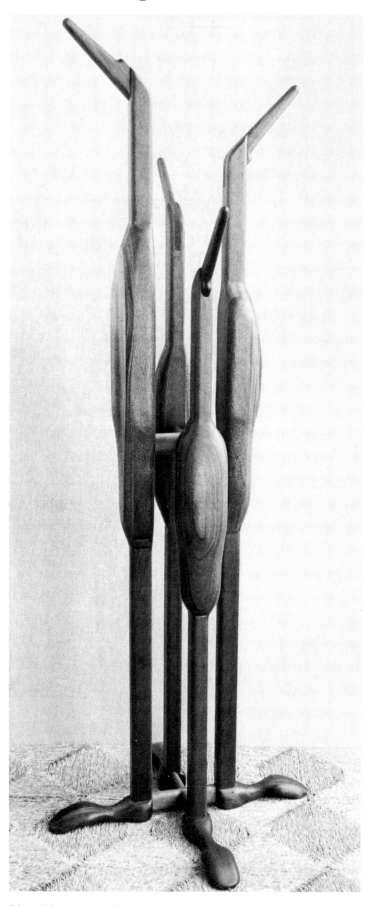

Marc Richardson, Montreal, Quebec, Canada

The Birds (coat rack); walnut, mahogany, cherry; 72 in. high.

Norbert Marklin, St. Louis, Mo.

Bird cage; basswood, glass; 66 in. x 41.5 in. x 26 in. Photo by Keith Miller.

"Krenov style. Interior is two compartments separated by removable center glass panel; with glass removed, becomes a single cage."

Thomas Jensen Fannon, Alexandria, Va.

Pulpit; red oak, purpleheart; 36 in. to top horizontal member. Lift mechanism adds 4 in. to lecturn. Photo by Budd Gray.

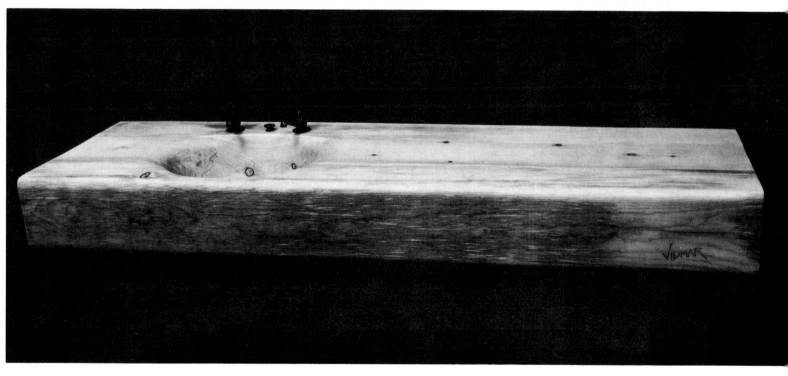

Bert Lustig, Berkeley Springs, W. Va.

Table lamp; Douglas fir; 15 in. x 9 in. Photo by Jean Pierre Hsu.

"The fir is finished by charring and wire-brushing."

Dennis W. Vidmar, Seattle, Wash.

Sink/Counter; one piece of ponderosa pine; 8 in. x 20 in. x 72 in. Impervious finish designed for wooden boatbuilding. Photo by Gregory Minaker.

Jim Boesel, Vancouver, Wash.

Bird cage; cherry, birch, mahogany veneer, brass; 60 in. x 42 in. x 24 in. Photo by J.T. Dvorak.

"Who could refuse a chance to build an exotic bird cage? Designed for two lovebirds. A nesting box in the main cage and a swinging perch in the tower. Unfortunately, the birds died before I was finished."

James B. Rolfe, Fort Bragg, Calif.

Entry doors; white oak, Belgian Art Nouveau glass; 110 in. x 66 in. Photo by Helen Van Gelder.

"It is much easier to make the door first and fit the glasswork to it. If building the door around the glass, allow time and materials for the inevitable near-fits."

(Bottom left) **David Morton, The American Woodworks Co.,** Syracuse, N.Y.

Bar and back bar; quartersawn white oak, stained and sandblasted glass by Joan Riccardi; 120 in. x 288 in. Photo by David Broda.

Tom Gannon, Duluth, Minn.

Cabinetry for ice cream parlor; oak, marble, glass; 90 in. x 108 in. Photo by Bruce Ojard.

"Built for use in museum exhibit area. Design based loosely on cabinetry in an ice cream parlor here in Duluth around 1910."

Kerry Gordon, Arcosanti, Ariz.

Doors; white oak, ash, walnut, antique glasswork by Carol Lorenz; (each door) 80 in. x 28.88 in. x 1.5 in. Photo by Jon Gipe.

Miles Karpilow, Emeryville, Calif.

Double doors; walnut, stained glass; 84 in. x 60 in. Hand-carved joints. Photo by Nick Lawrence.

"Part of my love affair with Art Nouveau, the design is result of absorption rather than direct copy. Glass was done by Lien-Paul Studios, Lafayette, Calif., to my design."

John Gibbons, Hurley, Wis.

*Door; red oak, laminated safety glass; 80 in.
x 36 in. x 1.75 in.*

"All are separate panes of glass. This door is
three days' work, including finishing time."

Pete Bruce, Johannesburg, Calif.

*Door; oak. Photo by Sierra Photography
and Video.*

"Door is recycled railroad boxcar floor.
Made for courtyard, has stained-glass insert
for winter and a screen insert for summer."

Michael P. McDunn, Greenville, S.C.
*Door; padauk, figured redwood, copper,
stained glass, lacquer, DPS wood stabilizer;
80 in. x 32 in. x 1.75 in. Photo by Dave Kay.*
"The stained-glass work and concept by
Lorn Marshall of Fanglasstic & Friends,
Greenville, S.C. Peened copper panel at the
bottom of the door."

Bill Irwin, Pahoa, Hawaii
*Door; oak frame, curly koa panels with ash
laminations, vermilion; 36 in. x 80 in. x 1.75
in.*

David Knobel, Olympia, Wash.

Entryway doors; Honduras mahogany, leaded glass; 80 in. x 60 in. Photo by Woody Hirzel.

"I wanted the grain to follow the curve of the arches, so I laminated eighteen 1/8-in.-thick segments over a particleboard mold with plastic resin glue. The stiles are made of two 1/4-in.-thick plates glued over a lumbercore center."

Joe Mathis and Bill Drawbaugh, Fleetwood, Inc., Austin, Tex.

Video production console; red oak, Honduras mahogany, leather armrest, steel chassis; 48 in. x 168 in. x 48 in. Photo by Michael Lyon.

"Provides a luxurious work environment that reflects the attention given to all phases of every project of third coast video...and Fleetwood, Inc."

Kelly O. Barker, Newport, Oreg.

His and Hers Bathroom Doors; oak, rosewood, black walnut, cherry, madrone, redwood, myrtlewood, kavula, purpleheart, vermilion, bloodwood; 80 in. x 34 in. x 1.2. in.

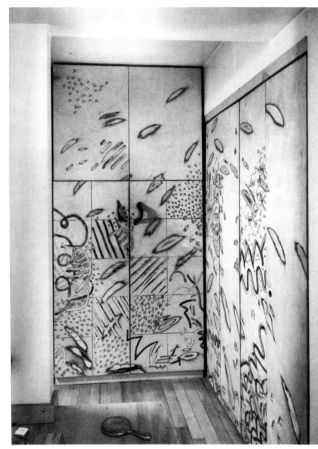

Daniel Bloomer, Waterville, Maine
Kitchen for Manhattan town house; solid cherry and plywood, ash, maple, brass hardware, Formica. Photo by Garry Geer.

Michael R. O'Connor, Milwaukee, Wis.
Mandolin booths; walnut, oak, cherry; 72 in. x 144 in. x 78 in. Photo by Michael Rebholz.
"Intact after three years of heavy use."

Ron Murphree, New York, N.Y.
Bathroom closet drawer unit; birch plywood, cherry, aluminum; 108 in. x 48 in. x 13 in. Collection of Amy Baker Sandback, executive publisher for Artforum magazine. (Unit is shown closed at top.) Photos by Scott Hyde.

Mike Livingston, Hutchinson, Kans.

Pair of chairs for a church; Kansas walnut, bronze, leather; 42 in. x 24 in. x 28 in. Photo by Frank Huntsman.

"The two finials on each chair are made of cast bronze from my foundry. The quotations on the back refer to the carved designs above them."

Bruce Gowdy, Elkhart, Ind.

Iconostasis for St. Michael's Ukrainian Catholic Church; red oak, brass hardware; 128 in. x 276 in. x 8 in. Photo by Robert Lindahl.

Noah Roselander, Parchment, Mich.

Torah Ark; solid cherry and plywood, walnut; 94 in. x 72 in. x 25 in. Photo by Nick Graetz.

"Although not as portable as the original Ark of the Covenant, this ark was designed to be moved about within the temple."

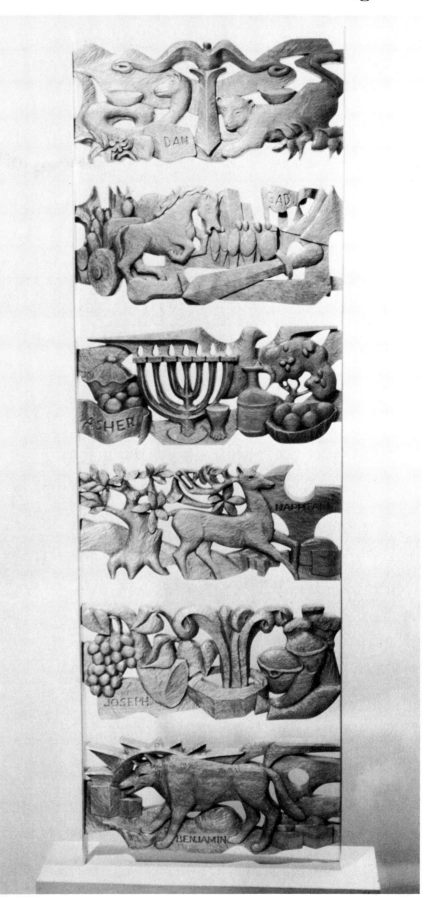

Rudolph Vargas, Los Angeles, Calif.

*Mary Help of Christians (Maria Auxiliadora);
jelutong; 21 in. x 35 in. x 5.5 in. Photo by
Ken von Essen.*

Siegfried Klotsche, Edmonton, Alberta,
Canada

*Canadian coat of arms; various veneers; 51
in. x 42 in. Photo by Kurt Wiatrowski.*
"Average picture takes eight to ten hours,
some half an hour—this was 450 hours."

Jerry L. Caplan, Pittsburgh, Pa.

*The Twelve Tribes of Israel (lower section);
birch; (each unit) 8 in. x 18 in. x 1.5 in. Units
mounted between aluminum strips.*

Ross Craig and Paul Vicente, Berkeley,
Calif.

*Master-bedroom wall cabinets; walnut; 96
in. x 156 in. x 16 in.*

"The entry doors pivot on their outside
ends and float in the opening, forming a
screen. This gave a more open feel to this
suite of rooms than a solid closing door
would have."

Sam Bush, Portland, Oreg.

*Painted bookcase (one of a pair); eastern
maple, particleboard, brass hardware; 108 in.
x 192 in. x 144 in. Photo by Harold Wood.*

"Assisted in construction by Walter Huber.
Custom moldings."

Charles Yinkey and Michael Carner,
Washington, D.C.

*Museum store sales counter; solid white oak
and plywood, simulated leather Formica; 42
in. x 96 in. x 96 in. Photo by Naval
Photographic Center.*

"The design reiterates both the semicircular
plan and the detail of a restored Spanish-
American War-era pilot house, which the
museum has incorporated into its store."

Mark Duginske, Wausau, Wis.
*Skylight grille; oak plywood; (each grille) 64
in. x 30.5 in., curved to a radius of 105.25 in.
Photo by Bill Stankus.*

"Design by Frank Lloyd Wright for his
children's playroom."

Boxes

Ken Walker, Booneville, Ky.

Jewelry box; Andaman padauk, Indian rosewood, suede lining; 4.5 in. x 8.25 in. x 11 in. (Box is shown on facing page, at bottom left.) Photos by Peter Zook.

"My work is influenced by Jim Krenov's elegant simplicity. Through tenons on the frame-and-panel lid are held with rosewood wedges, beveled to match the protruding dovetails."

Fred Maier, Peoria, Ill.
*Jewelry box; walnut; 2 in. x 16 in. x 4 in.
Photo by Lee Roten.*

Ken Walker, Booneville, Ky.
*Jewelry box. (Detail is shown on facing
page.)*

John D. Griffith, Langley, Wash.
*One for Robben (jewelry box); vermilion,
Indian rosewood, maple, brass; 3.5 in. x 13
in. x 10 in.*

Kathy Blair, Sunnyvale, Calif.
*Box; spalted maple, ebony hinges; 3 in. x 7
in. x 11 in. (Box is shown closed at bottom
left.) Photos by Mark Tuschman.*

"I found the spalted maple in the scrap bin
at a local lumberyard—just enough to make
this box. My specialty is what I call
'through-lay.' The technique looks like inlay
at first, but the designs go all the way
through the wood."

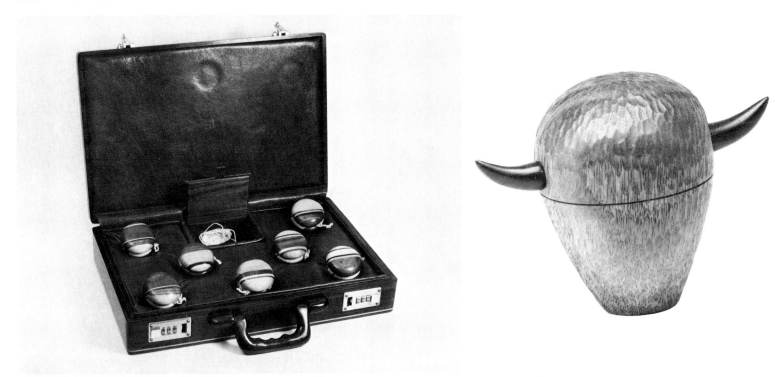

Joe Casey, Minneapolis, Minn.
*Rosewood Attaché Case with Yo-Yos; (case)
rosewood; 12 in. x 18 in. x 3.5 in. (yo-yos)
laminated maple, walnut, ebony, padauk,
oak. Photo by Jerry O'Dair.*

"Designed for use in a board of directors
meeting by those bored of directors."

David Riome, Saskatoon, Saskatchewan,
Canada
*Bison Container; walnut, ebony; 2.5 in. high
Photo by Paul Riome.*

Bruce A. Erdman, Mt. Horeb, Wis.
Sphere boxes; oak; 11 in. dia., 6 in. dia.

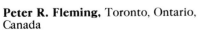

Peter R. Fleming, Toronto, Ontario, Canada

Pyramidal Box #6; curly maple, cherry, African blackwood; (pyramid) 7 in. x 7 in. x 7 in. (legs) 3 in. high.

"Allowing whimsy and spontaneity to fill the hole craftsmanship alone leaves empty."

Stephen N. Bradshaw, Indianapolis, Ind.

Briefcase; American black walnut; 15 in. x 16 in. x 4 in.

(Bottom left) **Kenneth J. Stone,** Arlington, Mass.

Portfolio case; padauk, Douglas fir, brass, leather, cork; 20 in. x 24 in. x 3.25 in. Photo by Jeffrey Collidge.

Mark Zarn, Conifer, Colo.

Otto; zebrawood, padauk; 12 in. x 5 in. x 6 in. Bandsawn.

Bill McDowell and Tom Cunningham,
Syracuse, N.Y.

*Drop-front jewelry chests, boxes and
desktop organizers; black walnut, mixed
hardwoods, beveled glass mirrors, velvet;
(tall chest) 15 in. x 12 in. x 6 in. Photo by
Tom Samara Photograpy.*

"Containers exclude as well as contain
space. Our boxes attempt a synthesis of
these two functions."

(Bottom left and right) **Stefan Smeja,**
Mississauga, Ontario, Canada

*Jewelry box; imbuya, curly maple, mirror,
brass; 10 in. x 9.25 in.*

"Mirror with integrated storage."

David Paul Eck, North Bend, Wash.

*Jewelry case; tulipwood, ebony, silver; 8 in.
x 17 in. Courtesy of Valdis and Jeri
Petersens.*

"Function need not be immediately obvious
to be truly useful."

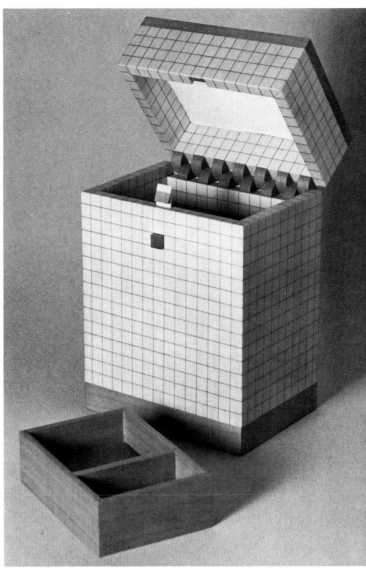

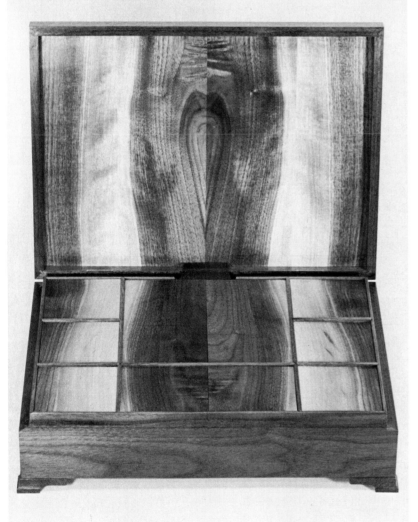

Peter W. Waxter, Rock Hall, Md.

Hexagonal box with mirror tray and gems; rosewood, maple, bird's-eye maple, padauk, ebony, cherry, walnut, osage orange, amaranth, tourmalines, garnets, opals, silver, brass, peach mirror, glass, ink, gesso, pearl lacquer, aniline dyes, gold and silver leaf; 12 in. x 10.5 in. x 5.5 in. Photo by Julia B. Waxter.

"Artwork and design by Rhonda Bigonet."

(Bottom left) **Ray Prince,** Toronto, Ontario, Canada

Face of the Nocturnal Forest I (jewelry box); black walnut, brass hinges, cut screws, leather lid restraint; 3.38 in. x 13.25 in. x 9.75 in. Photo by Henk Visser.

"Center four compartment covers are doors hinged on dowels. Slight pressure pops doors open. Box has two secret compartments."

Bliss Kolb, Seattle, Wash.

Jewelry box; Alaskan yellow cedar, pear, ivory, fabric; 6.5 in. x 4.25 in. x 3 in. Photo by Nancy Roger.

Eric Dewdney, Cambridge, Ontario, Canada

Jewelry box; rosewood, maple, beech; 15 in. x 20 in. x 7 in. Photo by Henry Vanderdraay.

"Special hiding places for special treasures."

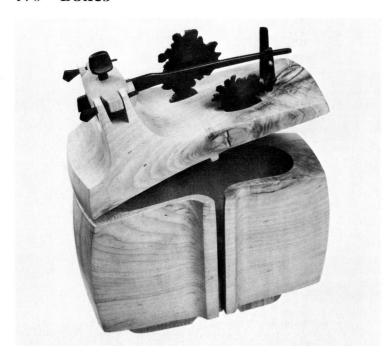

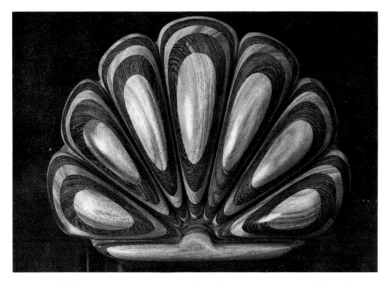

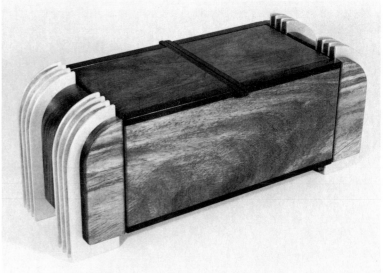

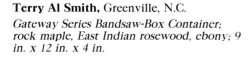

Terry Al Smith, Greenville, N.C.

*Gateway Series Bandsaw-Box Container;
rock maple, East Indian rosewood, ebony; 9
in. x 12 in. x 4 in.*

Ken Bennett and Pat Bennett, Toronto,
Ontario, Canada

*Shell (jewelry box); Honduras rosewood,
Andaman padauk; 4.5 in. x 9 in. x 7 in.
Photos by Lorraine C. Parow and Janet
Dwyer.*

Tom Rauschke and Kaaren Wiken,
Waukesha, Wis.

*Dragon's Castle; black walnut, osage orange,
plum, fiber embroidery, chain, crystal ball;
19 in. high.*

"Miniature fiber paintings by Kaaren
Wiken."

Michael S. Chinn, Ames, Iowa

*VRS-1000; Andaman padauk, Indian ebony,
aluminum; 7 in. x 12 in. x 5 in.*

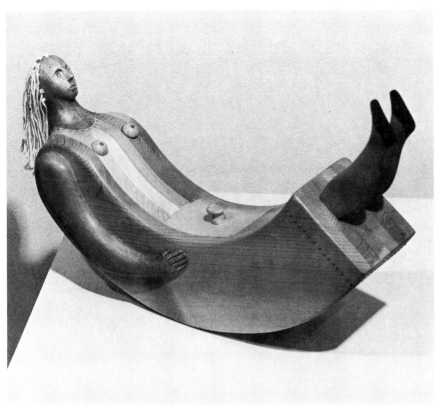

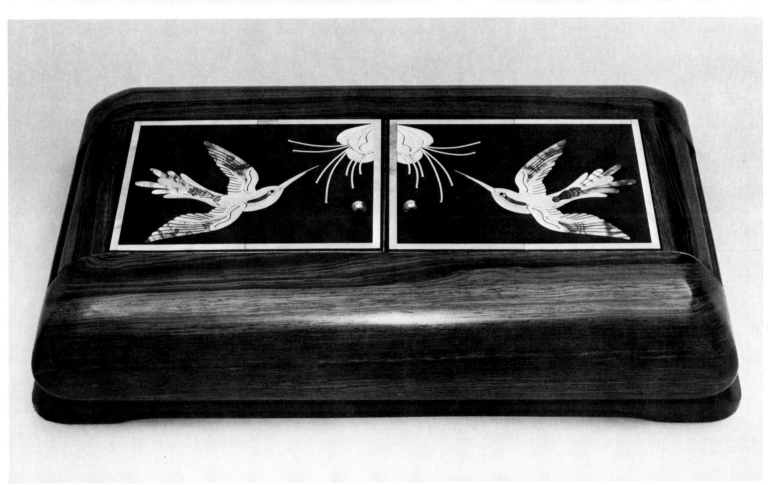

Dee J. Lafon, Ada, Okla.

Rocking Woman (sound and jewelry box); white pine, brass, string; 10 in. x 18 in. x 6 in. Photo by J. Don Cook.

"The piece gently rocks when pushed. A sound device responsive to the rocking motion emits a soft gong. The lid encloses a functional storage space."

Lawrence W. Pillot, Solon, Ohio

Box; Honduras mahogany, East Indian rosewood; 3 in. x 4 in. x 5.88 in. Photo by William Pappas.

Robin Danziger, Kingston, N.Y.

Birds Box; ebony, cocobolo, bird's-eye maple, yellow and rose 14K gold, abalone, gold and white mother-of-pearl, ivory; 18 in. x 10 in. x 3 in. Photo by Bill Sill.

Sculpture and Carving

Constance M. Starr, Albuquerque, N. Mex.
*Bear Fetish; ebony, teak, tortoise shell,
kingman turquoise; 8.5 in. x 3.25 in. x 15 in.
Hi-shi, spear and bear attached by steel
dowels, turquoise eyes set in ebony. Photo
by Dick Kent.*

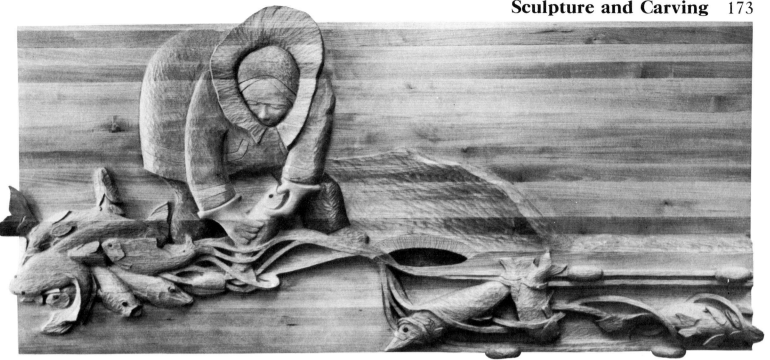

Sandy Stolle, Selawik, Alaska

Niulan (sculptural mural); basswood; 80 in. x 36 in. x 5.5 in.

"Commissioned for the court building in Kotzebue, Alaska. A friend of mine, Niulan, checks her fishnet which has been set under the ice. Niulan wears rubber household gloves for protection from winter's chill and the wind's bite (some Eskimo elders use only their bare hands)."

Connie McColley and Tom McColley, Chloe, W. Va.

Staff of the Elfin Herb Gatherer; white oak, apple, walnut; 27 in. x 9 in. x 9 in. Hand-split white oak, carved handle. Photo by John Erwin.

John Boomer, Navajo, N. Mex.

Two Women; walnut; 28 in. x 8 in. x 4 in. Photo by Peter L. Bloomer.

Thomas H. Williams, Atlanta, Ga.

Untitled Sculpture; teak, zebrawood, rosewood, oak, mahogany, black walnut; 60 in. x 72 in.

"By carving pieces first and then assembling them, you can accomplish sculpture more akin to metal sculpture, yet in wood."

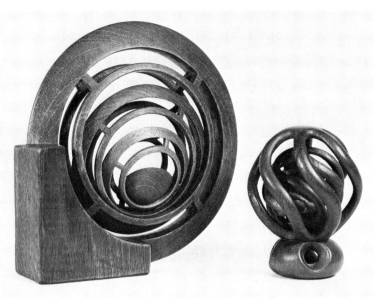

Patricia W. Freeman, Lincoln, Nebr.

Adult Rattles—for the smile and younger feeling felt when shaken; Honduras mahogany; (large rattle) 6 in. x 7.5 in. x 1.5 in. Photo by Cliff Lemen.

"Rattle carving is great fun when I'm in the field collecting biological data for research."

Doug Ayers, Little River, Calif.

Standing Sculpture; black walnut, ramin; 21 in. x 18 in. x 3 in.

(Top right) **Jeffrey Wind,** Barrie, Ontario, Canada

Interpenetrant Twins (crystal structure); African padauk, ebony, ash, pine.

"Book-matched padauk is laminated to pine torsion box with truncated corners. Ebony veneer on ash details the corner."

Ron Vellucci, Hampton, N.H.

Solar Disc (relief wall sculpture); padauk, brass; 18 in. dia., 3 in. deep.

Alan Wilson, Ringwood, Victoria, Australia

Variable Form of Six Warped Planes Hinged Together; Australian blackwood, brass pins; 25 cm. high, 48 cm. long. Photo by Schopplein Studio.

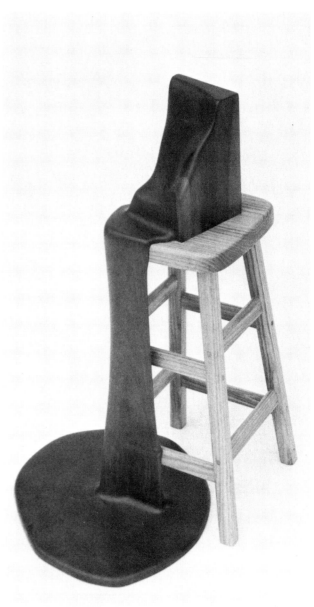

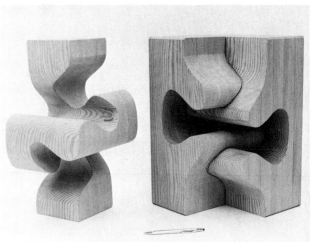

Karlin Wong, Los Angeles, Calif.
Fourth Circle; alder, mulberry, river rock;
46 in. x 20 in. x 28 in.

Carl Johnson, El Cajon, Calif.
Melt 2 and Stool; walnut, oak; 48 in. high.

Stephen L. Casey, Northridge, Calif.
Puzzle Sculpture (©1981); fir; 10.5 in. x 10.5
in. x 16 in.

"Puzzle starts out as a square and can be
reassembled into an endless combination of
forms. When reassembled one way, actually
becomes inverse of itself. One of the four
pieces is separated from the square here."

Michael J. Cooper, Sebastopol, Calif.

Split Personality; western Australian jarrah; 30 in. x 60 in. x 72 in. Photo ©1982 The Art Gallery of Western Australia.

Chris Schneider, Mt. Shasta, Calif.

Memories of an Oriental Evening; Port Orford cedar, incense cedar, stone; 20 in. x 36 in. x 10 in. Photo by Don Brandon.

"The idea is to absorb, translate and manifest a quality of emotional value."

Charles E. Lewis, Altadena, Calif.

Shrine #6; African vermilion padauk, koa, Honduras mahogany, walnut, East Indian rosewood; 65 in. x 18 in. x 15.5 in.

"Along the roadsides in Greece there were many shrines to help the traveler reach his destination safely. Years later, I needed to make a shrine—my daughter was having a hard time getting through her teenage years. I feel we all need a shrine, at times."

(Top right) **Jon Barnes,** Harrogate, North Yorkshire, England

Carved Cloth (wall hanging); Brazilian mahogany; 23 in. x 21 in. x 2 in.

Bruce Guttin, Davis, Calif.

Woman's Shoe; sugar pine; 2.5 in. x 10 in. x 4 in.

Jeffrey Briggs, Newburyport, Mass.

Day Lilies; poplar, mahogany, walnut, maple; 40 in. x 38 in. x 26 in. Photo by Alan I. Teger.

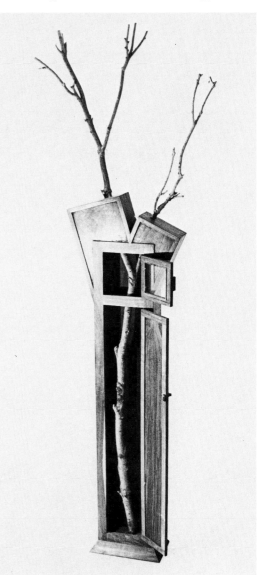

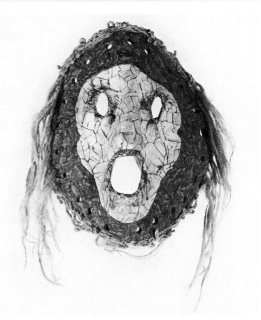

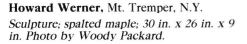

Howard Werner, Mt. Tremper, N.Y.
*Sculpture; spalted maple; 30 in. x 26 in. x 9
in. Photo by Woody Packard.*

Michelle S. Holzapfel, Marlboro, Vt.
*Pumpkin #2; yellow birch burl, cherry burl,
bittersweet, maple; 18 in. x 25 in. x 14 in.
Collection of Patricia Brennan. Photo by
Peter Mauss.*
"I turn, therefore I am."

Michael Bauermeister, Kansas City, Mo.
*Stick Cabinet; walnut, maple splines, glass,
stick; 96 in. x 24 in. x 9 in.*

Deborah Jones, Trumansburg, N.Y.
*Bark Mask #5; pressed wood, acanthus,
birch bark, flax fiber; 10 in. x 8 in. x 3 in.
Photo by Elizabeth Laquer.*

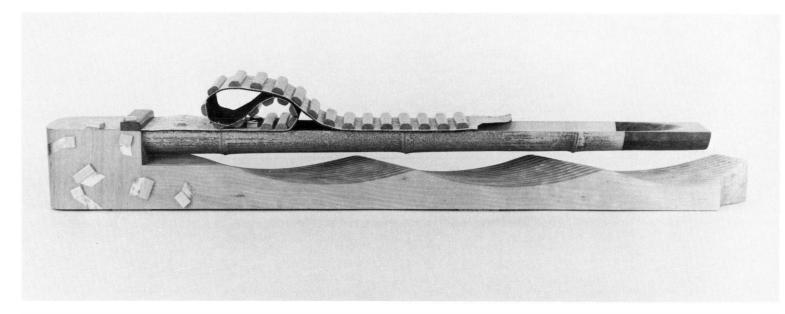

Dennis M. Morinaka, Oakland, Calif.
*Japanese Sun Over Oakland (cantilevered
container); sesame seed bamboo, birch,
redwood burl, Japanese silk, copper leaf.*

Christopher Weiland, Penn Run, Pa.
*Rough and Tough; red oak; 36 in. x 24 in. x
192 in.*
"Part of ongoing playful (Tinker Toy) series.
Mechanical in nature, interlocking."

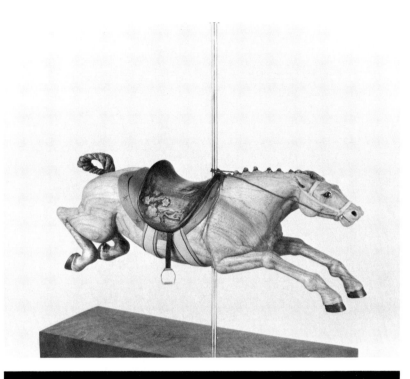

Colleen Chaffee Succi, Newfields, N.H.

Clotho; butternut, Japan and Sturbridge colors, brass, leather, fabric cording; 9 in. x 3 in. x 13 in. Photo by Charles Carswell.

"Carved, burned tail appears hand-braided."

Tom D'Onofrio, Bolinas, Calif.

Dancing Dragon with Crystal Ball; Honduras rosewood, vermilion, ebony, recycled ivory, gold-plated wire, garnets; 17 in. x 8 in. x 8 in. Photo by Kevin Kelly.

Myles Hougen, Samuels, Idaho

Blue Heron; Utah juniper, North Idaho black walnut; 18 in. x 14 in. Photo by Dann Hall.

John W. Mudd, M.D., Kentfield, Calif.

Rocking Rabbit; madrone stump, pau Brazil paw pads, ash teeth, wool buffing pad tail; 40 in. x 35 in. x 42 in.

"Shaping base so my 25-lb. daughter could rock this 250-lb. rabbit was no easy matter."

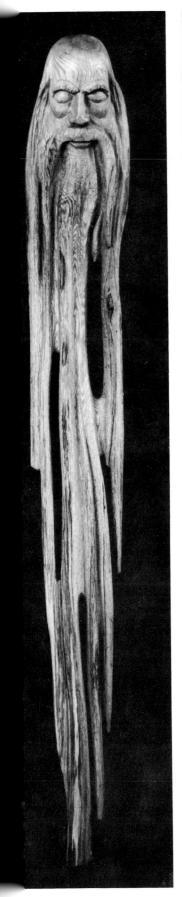

Tom Larkin, Ft. Collins, Colo.
Old Man of the Wood; red oak; 84 in. x 14 in. x 18 in. Photo by Art Directions.

Roland Shick, Bethlehem, N.H.
Untitled; European walnut; 8.5 in. x 5 in. Photo by Sue Garvin.

"I used to draw quite a bit. But not since I picked up a chisel. If I could just figure out how to get these things to breathe...."

James Pritchard, Peterborough, N.H.
Plenty; eastern white pine, paint, shellac; 66.5 in. x 21 in. x 26 in. Photo by Laurel Pritchard.

Dean Butler, Decatur, Ind.
Dance of the Clarinets; walnut; 25 in. x 11.5 in. Photo by Watters Studio.

"I came up with this design to work around the defects in the log."

Mary Shelley, West Denby, N.Y.
North Wind; white pine, acrylics; 36 in. x 40 in. x 1 in. Courtesy of Jay Johnson, America's Folk Heritage Gallery, New York, N.Y. Photo by Courtney Frisse.

Frank C. Grusauskas, Falls Village, Conn.

*Carved hawk; butternut; 11 in. x 9 in. x 5 in.
Photo by George Massey.*

Steve Bomkamp, Pullman, Wash.

*Red-Shouldered Hawk with Snake; maple;
18-in. wingspan, 8.5 in. long. Photo by Jerry
McCollum.*

Floyd Scholz, Hancock, Vt.

*Northwoods Crow; basswood, black walnut,
cedar, copper wire, oil paints; 16 in. x 13 in.
x 24 in. Photo by Richard Robson.*

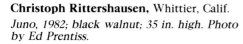

Christoph Rittershausen, Whittier, Calif.

Juno, 1982; black walnut; 35 in. high. Photo by Ed Prentiss.

"Carved cross grain. Block was 18-in. section of 36-in.-dia. trunk, rescued from being split for firewood."

Bill Horgos, Larkspur, Calif.

The Movie Set; boxwood, ebony, ivory; (bed) 3.5 in. x 3 in. x 2.75 in. (bears) 3 in. high. Photo by Lloyd Hryciw.

Mel Schockner and Jan Schockner, Woodacre, Calif.

King and Queen (©1981); Douglas fir, Honduras mahogany, redwood, California black walnut. (Piece is shown at bottom.) 42 in. x 30 in. x 2.5 in.

"Frame is Douglas fir, milled from old house timbers. Background is particleboard. This is our trademark and we're both represented here with some of the tools of our trade."

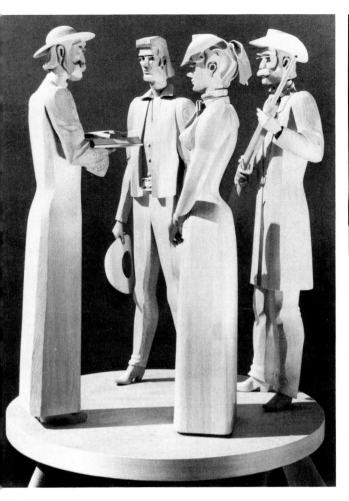

Edwin Fulwider, Bayview, Idaho

*Shotgun Wedding; cedar; 76 cm. x 61 cm.
Lazy-Susan bearing in base. Collection of
Mrs. Caro Lou Bastian.*

Chuck Engberg, Alameda, Calif.

*4 Bums; basswood; 5.25 in. x 10 in. x 3 in.
Finished in oil colors and wax. Photo by
Daniel Photography.*

Charles Shedden, Montclair, N.J.

*Fallen Angel; mahogany with maple wings;
34 in. x 16 in. x 16 in. Photos by Andrew
Rasiej.*

Index

Magazine Staff
Editor: John Kelsey
Associate Editors: Tage Frid, Rick Mastelli
Editorial Assistants: Linda D. Whipkey, Barbara Wills

Book Staff
Editor: Laura Cehanowicz Tringali
Copy Editor: Deborah Cannarella
Layout Artist: C. Heather Brine

Art Staff
Design Director: Roger Barnes
Staff Artist: Kathryn Olsen

Production Staff
Manager of Production Services: Gary Mancini
Production Manager: Mary Galpin
Typesetter: Nancy-Lou Knapp
Darkroom: Annette Hilty, Deborah Mason, Jay Smith

Typeface: Caslon Modified 9 point
Paper: Warrenflo, 65 lb., Neutral pH
Printer: Connecticut Printers, Bloomfield, Connecticut
Binder: The Maple-Vail Book Manufacturing Group,
        York, Pennsylvania

Directory of Woodworkers

When we asked for *Design Book* entries, we also extended an open invitation to be listed in a worldwide directory of woodworkers. The following list represents those shops or individuals that wished to be included.

The directory is organized alphabetically by state, and within each state, alphabetically by city. Where there is more than one listing in a city, the listings are alphabetical by shop or individual. Countries outside the United States are included at the back of the directory. These areas are organized by province or region where appropriate, and then by city and name.

A page reference in parentheses precedes the name of those shops or individuals whose work is included in *Design Book Three*.

Alabama

ATTALLA: **Chris Bailey,** Route 3 Box 107, Attalla, AL 35954. *Period reproductions.*

BIRMINGHAM: **Jack L. Blackwood,** 5540-12 Ave. S., Birmingham, AL 35222 (205)592-7737. *Chests, toys, furniture and accessories.*

Bobby Michelso, RAM Wood, 1321 18th Ave. S. 2, Birmingham, AL 35205 (205)252-4113. *Hardwood furniture and custom woodworking.*

COTTONDALE: **(30) Theodore A. Bowen,** Route 3 Box 585, Cottondale, AL 35453 (205)553-3034. *Custom and original design in woodworking, furniture and timber framing, trim and finish work.*

EUTAW: **Erickson Woodworks,** 158 Myrdledian Ave., Eutaw, AL 35462 (205)372-9727. *Quality handcrafted furniture and cabinets and custom millwork, ranging from traditional reproductions to contemporary.*

GREENSBORO: **Yeager Woodworks,** Route 1 Box 30, Greensboro, AL 36744 (205)624-4263. *Fine furniture.*

HUNTSVILLE: **(126) Robert M. Davenport,** 3106 Crescent Circle S.E., Huntsville, AL 35801.

MOBILE: **(78) Glenn de Gruy Woodworks,** Route 5 Box 246E, Mobile, AL 36609 (205)633-5765. *Lathe, stringed musical instruments, custom furniture, functional designs.*

NORTHPORT: **Craig Nutt Fine Wood Works,** 2014 Fifth St., Northport, AL 35476 (205)752-6535. *Contemporary and period furniture, turning, and carving.*

Alaska

ANCHORAGE: **The Dovetail,** 1820 Toklat St., Anchorage, AK 99504 (907)279-0395. *Custom furniture, cabinets, interiors; design and construction.*

James E. Talley, 4105 Brantley Pl., Anchorage, AK 99504 (907)561-1874. *Custom furniture in solid hardwoods. Sculptural and curved designs, one-off pieces. High-quality cabinetry.*

FAIRBANKS: **Fairbanks Woodcrafting,** 120 Hall St., Fairbanks, AK 99701 (907)452-3630. *Custom furniture and designs, cabinets, doors, leaded glass, display cases, custom stairways and entryways.*

HAINES: **(61) J.E. Carlson Custom Furniture and Cabinetry,** Box 95 (18 Mile Haines Hwy.), Haines, AK 99827 (907)766-2160. *Furniture made to order for all tastes, from the humblest cabin to the governor's mansion.*

JUNEAU: **Newt Cutler Designs,** 226 Highland Dr., Juneau, AK 99801 (907)586-3508. *Small cabinets, jewel boxes, household items, serving boards, game boards.*

SELAWIK: **(173) Sandy Stolle,** Box 101, Selawik, AK 99770. *Multimedia artist.*

Arkansas

EUREKA SPRINGS: **Richard Massey,** Route 2 Box 104, Eureka Springs, AR 72632 (501)253-9094. *Professional quality banjos and mandolins. Also custom furniture.*

FAYETTEVILLE: **Little Wing, c/o Gregory Center,** Spring and West Sts., Fayetteville, AR 72701 (501)521-7666. *Furniture with carved detail or 3-D bas-relief wood carvings to suit customer's desire.*

Bob Winkelman, Fayetteville, AR 72701 (501)521-1309.

HIWASSE: **E.L. Lamps,** Route 1 Box 67, Hiwasse, AR 72739 (501)787-6771. *Turned lamps, also bowls, compotes, music boxes and other specialty items.*

KINGSLAND: **J.M. Langford,** Route 1 Box 143, Kingsland, AR 71652 (501)348-5360. *Traditional woodworking. Dovetailed boxes and benches, cabinetmaking, luthiery, hammered dulcimers, wooden planes and wooden spoons.*

LITTLE ROCK: **David Anhalt,** 310 W. 14th, Little Rock, AR 72202 (501)376-7713. *Original furniture and sculpture.*

Chris Kupper, 2605 S. Tyler St., Little Rock, AR 72204 (501)663-3426. *I design and build in wood and also in stained glass.*

Timothy C. Richardson & David Peterson, 12909 Lorena Ave., Little Rock, AR 72211 (501)225-3935. *Inlays and/or wood-burned hammered dulcimers.*

ROGERS: **French's Custom Woodwork,** 1012 S. Dixieland Rd., Rogers, AR 72756. *Tables, unique joinery, inlay, refinishing, cabinets, carving. Work guaranteed; 17 years experience.*

Arizona

ARCOSANTI: **(154) Kerry Gordon,** Arcosanti Woodworks, Arcosanti, AZ 86333 (602)632-7135. *Custom cabinets, doors, limited run and handcrafted fine furniture.*

BISBEE: **(17) Todd Hoyer,** Box 1451, Bisbee, AZ 85603. *Turned bowls, boxes, custom display cases, jewelry boxes.*

COTTONWOOD: **D.K. Custom Wood, David Keeber,** 715 N. 8th St., Cottonwood, AZ 86326 (602)634-3229. *Will build anything in wood.*

FLAGSTAFF: **(151) Donald Carl Bjorkman,** 4080 N. Zermatt Way, Flagstaff, AZ 86001 (602)526-0584. *One-of-a-kind, limited production and design, prototypes for production.*

William J. Burke, Route 4 Box 720, Flagstaff, AZ 86001 (602)774-3822. *Custom furniture and turning.*

MAYER: **Tim Daulton,** Arcosanti Star Route, Mayer, AZ 86333. *Hard and softwood furniture; one-of-a-kind or limited production.*

MESA: **Harvey Paul Carlton,** Box 4002, Mesa, AZ 85201 (602)969-1023. *I am into containers and specialize in boxes of all types.*

Fincher Executive Furniture, 1238 E. McLellan Rd., Mesa, AZ 85203 (602)962-4998.

Joseph Mayer, Sr., 101 N.E. Hunt Dr., Mesa, AZ 85204 (602)962-1633. *Church furniture.*

Ted Finchen Executive Furniture, 1238 E. McLellan Rd., Mesa, AZ 85203 (602)962-4998.

ORACLE: **Richard Beaman,** Box 476, Oracle, AZ 85623 (602)896-9103. *Functional sculpture.*

PHOENIX: **Bill Baker, Guillarmo's Woodcrafts,** 3062 N. 42nd Lane, Phoenix, AZ 85017 (602)278-6567. *Jewelry boxes of oak with exotic inlays, mesquite vases and specialties, production wholesale items.*

Gene De Haai, 1821 W. Charleston, Phoenix, AZ 85023 (602)863-6041. *Custom handcrafted designed objects out of wood.*

Vern Fetz, 1712 N. 33rd St., Phoenix, AZ 85008 (602)275-5647. *Furniture, turnings and carvings from Arizona woods.*

Doug Forsha, 4304 E. Stanford, Phoenix, AZ 85018 (602)951-9018. *Very high quality bowls, turned and constructed boxes of the finest woods and unique designs.*

R.A. David Enterprises, 7625 W. Avalon Dr., Phoenix, AZ 85033. *Custom furniture construction.*

(115) Woodesign-Wildwood, 115 S. 23rd St., Phoenix, AZ 85034 (602)267-1939. *Designers and manufacturers of fine hardwood furniture, staircases, conference tables, specializing in curves and exotics.*

SCOTTSDALE: **(68) Warren S. Fenzi, Fenzi Design Workshop,** 3140 N. Miller Rd., Scottsdale, AZ 85251 (602)941-5340. *Resident craftsmen: Jeff Kirk, Greg Steen. The design and execution of fine furniture.*

TEMPE: **(63) Barrett Environmental Artworks,** 543 W. 16th St., Tempe, AZ 85281 (602)966-4911. *Original design and execution in all media, and hand-carving, bending, exotic finishes, etc.*

(143) Paula Cooperrider, 1215 E. Del Rio, Tempe, AZ 85282 (602)968-1861. *Functional sculpture, original design.*

(95) Tom Eckert, 1019 Bishop Circle, Tempe, AZ 85282 (602)966-6978. *Wood sculpture, one-of-a-kind furniture commissions.*

Hardy's Custom Furniture, 514 1-2 S. Mill Ave., Tempe, AZ 85281 (602)894-6040. *Custom-made wall units and home furnishings. We also do antique restorations.*

Maggie McClure, 1705 W. University Dr., Tempe, AZ 85281 (602)966-2444.

Paul McClure, Wood World, 1705 W. University Dr., Tempe, AZ 85281 (602)966-2444. *Materials and instruction in cabinetmaking.*

Woodshaping Place, 1843 E. 3rd St. No. 105, Tempe, AZ 85281 (602)894-0175. *Quality work, no particular set items continually produced, everything is generally one-of-a-kind.*

TUCSON: **(22) Dimitri Cilione,** 19 E. Toole Ave., Tucson, AZ 85701 (602)623-2871. *The continual development of fine craftsmanship along with striving for an integral design sense. That's what it's all about.*

(147) Ed Clay, 19 E. Toole Ave., Tucson, AZ 85701 (602)623-2872 (or 5398 Sonoma Hwy., Napa, CA 94558 (707)255-1455). *Custom furniture, one-of-a-kind.*

Concepts in Wood, 3301 E. Camden St., Tucson, AZ 85716 (602)323-8205. *One-of-a-kind items designed to incorporate the customer's needs and tastes.*

David Eisenberg, 316 S. Norris, Tucson, AZ 85719 (602)623-7523 or 623-1851. *Small cases and cabinets, picture frames, furniture repair.*

(55) Edward Nye Gordon, 850 W. Santa Rosa St., Tucson, AZ 85706 (602)294-5005. *Period furniture reproductions and restorations; clock cases.*

Wayne Hausknecht, 418 N. Herbert, Tucson, AZ 85705 (602)624-7179. *Handmade wood doors with 3-in. tenons, custom kitchens, built-ins, furniture.*

Conrad E. Jackson, 11701 Sneller Vista Dr., Tucson, AZ 85715 (602)749-3617. *Colonial, contemporary furniture and toys, made with quality to last for years to come.*

California

ALBION: **(69) Craig Marks,** Box 394, Albion, CA 95410 (707)937-4547. *One-of-a-kind, limited production, contemporary furniture.*

(95) Stephen Tone-Heckeroth, 30151 Navarro Ridge Rd., Albion, CA 95410 (707)937-0338. *Custom rockers, birthing beds and chairs.*

ALHAMBRA: **Ross' Woodshop,** 1845 S. Stoneman Ave., Alhambra, CA 91801 (213)570-6173. *Custom furniture and accessories. Commission work. Small production projects.*

ALPINE: **(142) John Pruitt,** 2049 Star Lane, Alpine, CA 92001 (714)445-2075. *Custom handmade acoustic steel string guitars made by special orders only.*

ALTADENA: **(123) Blue Dolphin Woods, John Nelson,** 256 E. Mendocino, Altadena, CA 91001 (213)798-2529. *Fine wood furnishings for infants and children.*

Scott Cappiello, 316 E. Anna Maria St., Altadena, CA 91001 (213)794-0141. *Design-construct using micrometer close tolerances-small scale productions, one-of-a-kind creations.*

(178) Charles E. Lewis, Sculptor, 2858 Santa Rosa Ave., Altadena, CA 91001 (213)791-4465. *Sculpture, specialty items such as jewelry boxes, shelves for specific areas and uses and unique designs.*

ANAHEIM: **Roger Claassen,** 902 Mohawk, Anaheim, CA 92801 (714)635-6628. *One-of-a-kind woodworking. Commissions accepted.*

Jack Gardner, 644 Camellia, Anaheim, CA 92804 (714)774-4619. *One-of-a-kind wood objects.*

ARCATA: **Anthony Kahn Furniture,** 1250 10th St., Arcata, CA 95521 (707)822-6721. *Large range of furniture, desks, dining and conference tables, chairs, and architectural interiors.*

Leon Geisberg, 413 I St., Arcata, CA 95521 (707)822-2814. *Furniture making with an emphasis on custom desks and other fine office furniture.*

Kevin Miske, 1580 Guintoli Lane, Arcata, CA 95521 (707)822-2336. *Custom woodworking, fine furniture, cabinets.*

W.M. Ulmer Woodworks, 5600 W. End Rd., Arcata, CA 95521 (707)822-7857. *Traditional Windsor chairs created from the log, furniture, sculpted and traditional, cabinetry, sculpted living environments.*

ARNOLD: **Blue Sky Woodcraft, Marty Schlein,** 1440 Oak Circle, Cedar Center, Calaveras County, Arnold, CA 95223 (209)795-1668. *Custom woodworking of all types (from boa constrictor cages to rolltop desks).*

BAKERSFIELD: **Gary Cox,** 257 Los Flores, Bakersfield, CA 93305 (805)325-3603. *Furniture of all styles, turning, doors, cabinets.*

BERKELEY: **(40) Tom Brown,** 2547 8th St., Space K, Berkeley, CA 94710 (415)845-4887. *Furniture and related design.*

Dungaloz Works, Richard Magarian, 2547 8th St., Studio K, Berkeley, CA 94710 (415)845-4887. *Custom furniture and cabinetry designed and fabricated. Limited edition productions. Furniture repairs.*

Sean Finneson, 2138 Derby St., Berkeley, CA 94705.

Charles Gay, 1492 Olympus Ave., Berkeley, CA 94708 (415)841-8494. *Custom tables.*

(104) Sara Jaffe, 2547 8th St., Space K, Berkeley, CA 94710 (415)845-4887. *Design by commission.*

Craig Ganesh Levitt, Open Hand Woodshop, Box 2373, Berkeley, CA 94702 (415)848-3722. *Custom furniture, custom millwork and small production runs.*

(113) Scott Page, Cabinetmaker, Box 5032, Berkeley, CA 94705 (415)655-9595. *Custom-designed furniture and architectural details.*

Constantine Philipides, 1523 Addison, Berkeley, CA 94703 (415)849-1313. *Custom and limited production, traditional, contemporary furniture. Asian design.*

Bill Powning, 2547 8th St. Space K, Berkeley, CA 94707 (415)845-4887. *Custom cabinets and furniture.*

Bill Roberts, 1905 Curtis St., Berkeley, CA 94702 (841)841-8830.

Saydah Furniture, 1411 Fourth St., Berkeley, CA 94710 (415)524-0195. *Unique hardwood furniture designed and constructed. Home-office commissions. Sculptural forms, inlay and carving available.*

Marc Waidelich, 2551 San Pablo Ave., Berkeley, CA 94702 (415)843-8415. *Custom furniture and cabinets for home, office, and commercial work.*

BEVERLY HILLS: **Page Hoeper, The Design Workshop,** 9257 1-4 Burton Way, Beverly Hills, CA 90210 (213)274-4364. *Musical instruments, especially clavichords and virginals. Also wooden planes.*

BIRDS LANDING: **Jim Bartz,** Star Route, Birds Landing, CA 94512.

BLOOMINGTON: **(100) Rick Pohlers,** 915 S. Idyllwild, Bloomington, CA 92316 (714)874-3937. *Chairs, tables, rockers, some cabinets, accessories, custom knives.*

BLUE LAKE: **Lucius M. Upshaw, Sculptor,** Redwood Valley Route, Blue Lake, CA 95525 (707)668-5422.

BOLINAS: **(181) D'Onofrio Fine Woodwork,** Box 326, Bolinas, CA 94924 (415)868-1070. *Hand-carved furniture and sculpture.*

BONITA: **Don Vestal,** 5135 Choc Cliff Dr., Bonita, CA 92002 (619)421-1399.

BUENA PARK: **Daniel F. Demeter,** 6701 Western Ave., Buena Park, CA 90621 (714)739-8136. *Furniture design and manufacture, antique restoration (furniture, architectural and pianos). Quality uncompromised at fair prices.*

BURBANK: **Mike Caldwell,** 4411 Woodland Ave., Burbank, CA 91505 (408)842-5001. *Custom interior woodworking, French doors, leaded glass windows, paneling and mouldings.*

CAMBRIA: **Dick Reynolds,** 481 Plymouth St., Cambria, CA 93428 (805)927-5905. *Walnut furniture. Custom design for each application.*

CAMPBELL: **Randy Canote,** 967 Hacienda Ave., Campbell, CA 95008 (408)379-1366. *Hardwood tables, mirrors, cabinets, inlay, no plumbing.*

CANOGA PARK: **A.G.Y. & Associates,** 6727 Glade St., Canoga Park, CA 91303 (213)883-4970. *Interior and exterior design of furnishings, accessories, and treatments using numerous mediums.*

Don Avila, 20020 Hemmingway St., Canoga Park, CA 91306 (213)882-2560.

Ralph K. Evans, 7352 Owensmouth Ave., Canoga Park, CA 91303 (213)999-6096. *Furniture-sculpture.*

(76) Karen Hazama, 21708 Napa St., Canoga Park, CA 91304. *One-of-a-kind pieces, boxes, gift items.*

Heidi Hillig, 23418 Van Owen St., Canoga Park, CA 91307 (213)999-0240. *Fine woodwork combined with glass. Toys and furniture.*

Bruce Wilkinson, 22216 Tioga Place, Canoga Park, CA 91304 (213)716 6348. *Custom cabinetry and furniture, functional design, inventive engineering, precision joinery, natural oil finishes.*

CAPISTRANO BEACH: **Richard Brassard,** 26125 Victoria Blvd., Capistrano Beach, CA 92624 (714)496-8680. *Yacht interiors, sculptures, household furnishings.*

Yankee Folk Art Co., M.W. Jim Jacobs, Box 2122, Capistrano Beach, CA 92624. *Folk art.*

CARDIFF: **(105) Kirk D. Wonner,** 1009 Hurstdale Ave., Cardiff, CA 92007. *Sculptural furniture.*

Gary E. Young, 1511 Rubenstein Ave., Cardiff, CA 92007 (619)436-1989. *Building, architectural woodwork, custom furniture and cabinets, and musical instruments.*

CARLSBAD: **Ali Aslinejad,** 3008 Segovia Way, Carlsbad, CA 92008 (714)753-9965. *Wooden sculpture and antique furniture reproduction.*

CARMEL VALLEY: **Chris Engle,** 1 Phelps Way, Carmel Valley, CA 93924 (408)549-3818. *Custom kitchens and baths. Also furniture and other specialty wood products.*

CARPINTERIA: **Gary Adkins,** 5550 Casitas Pass Rd., Carpinteria, CA 93013 (805)684-4868. *Cabinetry, furniture, doors and windows.*

(133) The Ferd Sobol Editions, 1375 Santa Monica Rd., Carpinteria, CA 93013 (805)684-4672. *Working from full scale, recreating for discerning collectors, accurately scaled miniature replications.*

CENTRAL VALLEY: **Wood Wise,** 4433 Meade St., Central Valley, CA 96019 (916)275-8012. *Premium cabinets, custom furniture.*

CHICO: **Brotherwood,** 1636 1-2 Laburnum, Chico, CA 95926 (916)345-3368. *Custom furniture.*

(123) Kathleen Maiwald, Box 3915, Chico, CA 95927 (916)345-4616. *Sculpted hardwood jewelry, miniatures.*

Mavis Somers, Box 3986, Chico, CA 95927.

Michael Sterling, Box 4374, Chico, CA 95927 (916)534-5528. *Custom hardwood furniture, residential and commercial. Office suites, entries, architectural woodworking.*

(13) Del Stubbs, 1130 Elmer St., Chico, CA 95926 (916)343-8458.

Western Wood Works, 1591 E. Ave., Chico, CA 95926 (916)893-5329. *Bookcases, hutches, exposed joinery.*

CLAREMONT: **Charles Jacobs,** 672 Rockford, Claremont, CA 91711 (714)624-5425. *Heirloom furniture all hand-carved.*

CLAYTON: **Ripley Custom Furniture,** 8 Whitt Court, Clayton, CA 94517 (415)672-7263. *Individualized design and construction of china and curio cabinets, tables and buffets from quality hardwoods.*

COARSEGOLD: **Out of the Woods,** Box 173, Coarsegold, CA 93614 (209)251-7007. *Creating art objects, turning, etc. Custom furniture.*

CORVALLIS: **Marvell Custom Furniture,** 1740 N.W. Alta Vista, Corvallis, CA 97330 (503)753-6475. *Design and construction of contemporary furniture with stress on line and function.*

COSTA MESA: **Jerry Ernst,** 1061 Visalia Dr., Costa Mesa, CA 92627 (714)557-6609. *Custom woodworking. Furniture and cabinetry.*

J.F. Schroter Antique Arms, Box 10794, Costa Mesa, CA 92627. *Design, building and restoration of antique and modern-antique arms, armor and accoutrements.*

Lannom Cabinetmakers, 2648 Newport Blvd., Costa Mesa, CA 92627 (714)645-3960. *Furniture design, construction and finishing. Traditional mortise-and-tenon and dovetail joinery.*

Montgomery Originals, 126 E. 18th C204, Costa Mesa, CA 92627 (714)642 5412. *Building furniture combining your ideas with our design.*

COVELO: **(77) Frank Weisman, Round Valley Woodwrights,** 76500 Short Creek Rd., Covelo, CA 95428 (707)983-6337. *Expertly crafted kitchens and furnishings for the home and office.*

COVINA: **Daniel's Antiques and Collectibles,** 1152 Lyman, Covina, CA 91724 (213)339-0807. *Buy, sell, trade antique furniture and artifacts.*

CUPERTINO: **Jack Goodman,** 1297 Aster Lane, Cupertino, CA 95014. *Custom design and built contemporary furniture.*

DALY CITY: **(143) Aspy J. Khambatta,** 150 Coronado Ave. 114, Daly City, CA 94015 (415)849-3599. *Fine furniture and accessories.*

DAVIS: **(178) Bruce Guttin,** 1075 Olive Dr. 2, Davis, CA 95616 (916)758-7159.

DEL MAR: **Holger M. Laubmeier,** Box 1217, Del Mar, CA 92014 (619)436-3384.

DESCANO: **Bill Chappelow,** Box 327, Descanso, CA 92016. *Cooking utensils, bowls, wooden scales and balances, toys.*

DIAMOND BAR: **Custom Woodworks, Mark Workman,** 1733 Roundtree Circle, Diamond Bar, CA 91765 (714)861-1140. *Custom interior furnishings and architectural interiors. Marine interiors.*

Hal Metlitzky, The Wood Wizard, 1948 Viento Verano Dr., Diamond Bar, CA 91765 (714)861-7722. *Small articles out of exotic woods, including turning.*

EL CAJON: **J.A. Agostini, dba Pacific S.W. Design,** 331 E. Main, El Cajon, CA 92020 (619)444-2101. *Design consultants, design engineers, efficiency managers.*

(176) Carl Johnson, Ventana Way, El Cajon, CA 92020 (619)448-8542. *Wood sculpture, sculptural doors and leaded glass.*

Woodesigns, 358 Vista Abierta, El Cajon, CA 92021 (619)444-4071. *Custom design and production of wooden objects.*

EL CERRITO: **Jim Campbell,** 499 Colusa, El Cerrito, CA 94703.

ELK: **(146) Tongue and Groove,** Box 1, Elk, CA 95432 (707)895-3610. *Custom cabinets and furniture.*

EL PORTAL: **(17) William Hunter,** Box 321, El Portal, CA 95318 (209)379-2413. *Sculptural lathe work and sculpture in exotic hardwoods, ivories and amber.*

EMERYVILLE: **(155) Miles Karpilow, Cabinet Maker,** 1226 Powell St., Emeryville, CA 94608 (415)655-5272. *Entrances, furniture, carving.*

ESCONDIDO: **(121) Kent Bailey,** Box 780, Escondido, CA 92025. *Sculpture.*

Barbara Boatright, 2250-28 N. Broadway, Escondido, CA 92026 (619)743-2104. *Fine marquetry, unique, original pictures made of exotic hardwoods, wide range of subject. Commissions accepted.*

Curt Carlisle, 710 Aster, Escondido, CA 92027. *Contemporary and modern woodworking.*

Mike Conlen, 945 Vereda Callada, Escondido, CA 92025 (714)746-5198. *Sculpture and one-of-a-kind furniture.*

Handcrafted Woods, 635 Howe Place, Escondido, CA 92025 (619)746-4484. *Hand-carved orginal pieces from avocado and olive wood seasoned and milled by Disparti.*

Patrick G. Warner, 1427 Kenora St., Escondido, CA 92027. *Special lock joinery as applied to case work and framed ware such as tables and chairs.*

Woodware & Treen, 1427 Kenora St., Escondido, CA 92027 (619)747-2623. *All wood case goods, wall assemblies, tables, and custom-fit chairs.*

EUREKA: **Douglas C. Beck,** 116 W. Simpson 2, Eureka, CA 95501 (707)443-2639. *Sculpture in woods of any types, bowl turnings, etc.*

John R. Kelley, 318 Harris, Eureka, CA 95501 (707)442-1189.

Randle Lundberg, 6281 Humboldt Hill Rd., Eureka, CA 95501 (707)1042. *Furniture, woodcarving, sculpture.*

FAIRFAX: **Al Garvey Designs,** 281 Scenic Rd., Fairfax, CA 94930 (415)453-5275. *Sculptured hardwood doors and relief sculpture wall pieces.*

FALLBROOK: **Oakart Originals,** Box 1526, Fallbrook, CA 92028 (619)723-9168.

FELTON: **(13) Felicia Fields,** 6412 Ashley St., Felton, CA 95018 (408)335-3036. *Turned wood bowls and weed pots.*

FONTANA: **Wilson Crider,** 9878 Almeria Ave., Fontana, CA 92335 (714)823-4741. *Small display cabinets and variety of wood-turned items.*

FOREST KNOLLS: **Kirk O'Day,** 70 Montezuma Ave., Forest Knolls, CA 94933 (415)488-4347. *Custom and limited production furniture, accessories and cabinets.*

FORT BRAGG: **(154) James B. Rolfe and Associates,** 890 N. Franklin St., Fort Bragg, CA 95437 (707)964-7893. *Architectural millwork, cabinets, furniture.*

(40) Douglas Smith, 32240 B Ellison Way, Fort Bragg, CA 95437 (707)964-7836. *Solving my client's furniture problems with something of beauty.*

FORTUNA: **Collis Mahan,** 836 15th St., Fortuna, CA 95540 (707)725-2242. *Tables and desks with simple lines.*

FRESNO: **T.J. O'Toole & Co.,** 4586 E. Pine, Fresno, CA 93703 (209)251-0876. *All custom work regarding interiors, some speculations and experimental designs.*

GARDENA: **Creative Wood Concepts,** 18025 Hobart No. C, Gardena, CA 90248 (213)324-7466. *Custom woodworking specializing in wall units, hutches, bar units, vanities, etc.*

GARDEN GROVE: **Specials in Wood,** 11382 Paloma, Garden Grove, CA 92643. *Hand-carving.*

GLENDORA: **Kenneth von Essen,** 403 No. Minnesota St., Glendora, CA 91740 (213)914-1298. *Relief and three-dimensional carving of human form, articulated dolls, doll parts.*

GOLETA: **Tim Balert,** Hookton Cem. Rd., Route 1 Box 50E, Goleta, CA 95551 (707)733-5116. *Classic guitars, instruments.*

GRANADA HILLS: **Raymond Ellis,** 12285 Woodley Ave., Granada Hills, CA 91344.

John Hyde Custom Wood & Glass, 15646 Index St., Granada Hills, CA 91345 (415)366-5754.

John J. Parker, Jr., 12019 Dresden Place, Granada Hills, CA 91344 (213)363-9213. *Wood sculpture and vases.*

Ray Jones Woodcrafts, 17216 Tribune St., Granada Hills, CA 91344 (213)368-6796. *Small, limited production and custom woodcraft items, such as boxes, clocks, bud vases, rolling pins, bracelets, etc.*

Robson Lindsay Splane, Jr., 17514 Horace St., Granada Hills, CA 91344 (213)366-2069. *Industrial design, special projects and packaging design.*

GUALALA: **Larry Lawlor, Furniture Maker,** Box 119, Gualala, CA 95445 (707)785-2170.

HARBOR CITY: **(132) Ron Roush,** 23400 S. Western, Harbor City, CA 90710. *Bottled houses of wood, stone, brick.*

HAWTHORN: **Rick Ouwerkerk,** 5432 W. 142nd St., Hawthorn, CA 90250 (213)973-2385. *Furniture and accessories, cabinetry, laminations, woodturning, bowls, etc. Production runs, unique woods.*

HAYFORK: **(139) Musical Instruments of the Andes,** Box 55, Hayfork, CA 96041 (916)628-4387. *Harps, custom designs, wind instruments, kenas, pan pipes, tree trunk drums, charangos, Andean folk instruments.*

HAYWARD: **(135) Charles Ainslie, Harpsichord Maker,** 1838 Tulip Avenue, Hayward, CA 94545. *Early keyboard instruments and other stringed instruments.*

HOLLYWOOD: **Grand Design, Larry Morgan,** 2011 Vine St., Hollywood, CA 90068 (213)465-4249. *Custom contemporary hardwood furniture. Custom sculptural frames and bases for art pieces.*

HORSE CREEK: **McKinney Creek Woodshop, Tom Garban,** Star Route 2 Box 690, Horse Creek, CA 96045 (916)465-2268.

HUNTINGTON BEACH: **Michael Gandi,** 20622 Goshawk Lane, Huntington Beach, CA 92646 (714)536-8788. *Furniture designing and prototyping.*

Rick Kneale, 18251 Gothard St., Huntington Beach, CA 92648 (714)848-8911.

INVERNESS: **(15) Bruce Mitchell,** Box 308,198 Hawthornden, Inverness, CA 94937 (415)669-7125. *Limited production of one-of-a-kind pieces from predominantly native woods of the Pacific coast. Commissions accepted.*

IRVINE: **Doug Christie,** 4391 Rafael, Irvine, CA 92714 (714)552-5983. *Custom entryways and architectural appointments.*

(127) Dana D. Warwick, 4371 Rafael St., Irvine, CA 92714 (714)551-6877. *Clock sculpture in fine hardwoods. Fine handmade wall and floor clocks with wooden movements, any size. Commissions accepted.*

JOHANNESBURG: **(156) Pete Bruce, The Designers Screw,** 315 Broadway, Johannesburg, CA 93528 (619)374-2236. *Custom furnishings built with craftmanship, patience and care.*

KINGS BEACH: **Royce Furniture,** 8384 Speckled St., Kings Beach, CA 95719 (916)546-3275. *Handmade furniture.*

LA CANADA: **Gordon and Sons Woodcraft,** La Canada, CA 91011 (213) 790-0840.

LA HABRA: **Ben Krieg,** 450 N. Dexter St., La Habra, CA 90631 (213)697-0161. *Furniture and accessory design and execution generally in contemporary themes.*

LA HONDA: **(139) Robert D. Brady, Design Associates,** La Honda, CA 94020 (415)747-0364. *Integrity in design and craftsmanship. Specializing in innovative design solutions for technical or unusual challenges.*

LA MESA: **Larry C. Breedlove,** 4821 Pine St., La Mesa, CA 92041 (619)698-3693. *Custom furniture and turnings.*

LAGUNA BEACH: **Canyon Woodworks Inc.,** 2083 Laguna Canyon Rd., Laguna Beach, CA 92651 (714)497-1346.

Jon Seeman Designs in Wood, 1901 Laguna Canyon Rd. 6, Laguna Beach, CA 92651 (714)494-4746. *Custom contemporary furniture sculptured from exotic hardwoods.*

LAGUNA NIGUEL: **(102) Jack's Wooden Friends, Jack L. Voss,** 31172 Boca Raton Pl., Laguna Niguel, CA 92677 (714)831-6608. *Carving animal chairs, marine sculptures and custom life-size statues designed to client's wishes.*

LaHABRA: **Nok on Wood,** 2301 E. Lambert, Bldg. G, LaHabra, CA 90631 (213)691-3051. *Custom woodworking, wood crafts, furniture repair.*

LAKEPORT: **(32) Brian Beard,** 2699 Scotts Creek Rd., Lakeport, CA 95453 (707)263-6745. *I strive for a sophisticated look yet simplicity in design and construction.*

LANCASTER: **Thomas M. Cromwell,** 1514 Park Somerset Dr., Lancaster, CA 93534 (805)948-9257. *Custom furniture, clock cases, wooden planes by commission.*

LARKSPUR: **(184) Bill Horgos,** Box 677, Larkspur, CA 94939.

Whitney-Chappelle Designers, 405 Elm Ave., Larkspur, CA 94939. *Custom wood furniture and fabrics. Clayton Cook, craftsman, Sandra Cook, designer.*

LAWNDALE: **Cabinet Craft, Bob Bagdasarian,** 4112 W. 166th St., Lawndale, CA 90260 (213)371-8554. *Custom cabinets and woodworking.*

Al Collins, 15409 Roselle, Lawndale, CA 90260 (213)675-1817. *One-of-a-kind pieces.*

LITTLE RIVER: **(175) Doug Ayers,** 5501 Albion-Little River Rd., Little River, CA 95456 (707)937-5634. *Sculpture and weed vases.*

LIVERMORE: **Robert E. Gest, Handcrafts,** 881 El Rancho Dr., Livermore, CA 94550 (415)447-5020. *Carvings, turnings, small furniture.*

John S. Hallam, 842 Los Alamos Ave., Livermore, CA 94550.

Red Hollenbach, 5439 Charlotte Way, Livermore, CA 94550 (415)443-4580. *Woodturning.*

LOMPOC: **Joel Gruenberg,** 1003 E. College Ave., Lompoc, CA 93436 (805)735-4963.

LONG BEACH: **Mark W. Davis,** 3612 Gundry St., Long Beach, CA 90807 (213)424-8321. *Bent laminations, boxes, tables, clocks, most any thing or shape out of wood.*

Halcyon Woodcraft, 1617 E. 10th St., Long Beach, CA 90813 (213)591-7488. *Cabinets, furniture and most anything that can be completed in the shop, not on location. Primarily use solid hardwoods.*

Tom Peck, 254 Argonne Ave., Long Beach, CA 90803 (213)434-1432. *One-of-a-kind furniture.*

Arthur K. Wayman, 7115 Metz St., Long Beach, CA 90808 (213)429-9341. *Tables and cabinets.*

LOS ALAMITOS: **Martin G. Hansen,** 11241 Cherry St., Los Alamitos, CA 90720 (213)493-5161. *Tables, toys, and games.*

Dale R. Leisy, 3171 Oak Knoll Rd., Los Alamitos, CA 90720 (213)431-1995. *Custom design and fabrication. Teak a specialty.*

LOS ALTOS: **Bennett Studio Gallery,** 610 Ranchs Los Altos, Los Altos, CA 94022 (415)948-1676. *Sculpture, furniture, doors, relief carvings, contemporary reproductions.*

LOS ANGELES: **Charles A. Fiedler Design,** 5435 W. 6th St., Los Angeles, CA 90036 (213)933-3779. *Hardwood furniture.*

Custom Woodworking, Lloyd Chain, 4249 Lindblade Dr., Los Angeles, CA 90066 (213)397-5364. *Custom cabinetry, furniture, wood turnings, and special orders.*

(58) Joseph Del Nostro, Jr., 917 Hilldale Ave., Los Angeles, CA 90069 (213)652-7608. *Custom design, freestanding or built-in furniture, solid wood or high-tech finishing materials.*

Francis Woodworker, 1333 No. Sweetzer 2E, Los Angeles, CA 90069 (213)654-2295. *Creative work in wood.*

S.F.G. Co., Sid Garon, 3133 Coolidge Ave., Los Angeles, CA 90066 (213)397-4375. *Custom design, hardwoods, furniture and unique specialties since 1960.*

Elliot Tyson, 3142 Hollycrest Dr., Los Angeles, CA 90068 (213)876-0436.

(161) Vargas Studio, 3661 Whittier Blvd., Los Angeles, CA 90023. *Design, modeling and sculpture.*

(59) Venice Woodworking, 12810 Venice Blvd., Los Angeles, CA 90066 (213)390-4885. *Solid-wood furniture for microcomputers, custom cabinetry, furniture and interiors.*

(13) Peter Winters, Stellar Design and Construction, 2625 Cullen St., Los Angeles, CA 90034 (213)836-7203. *Residential construction remodeling and wood turning.*

(176) Karlin Wong, 2911 Acresite St., Los Angeles, CA 90039 (213)660-0469. *Sculpture, one-of-a-kind furniture, architectural woodwork.*

LOS GATOS: **(104) James Bacigalupi,** Box 74, Los Gatos, CA 95030 (408)354-4583 or 354-4593. *Furniture.*

Roger Heitzman, 21373 Aldercroft Hts. Rd., Los Gatos, CA 95030 (408)353-2464. *Furniture, one-of-a-kind and limited productions, commissioned architectural and cabinetry.*

Joe Kick, 21854 Bear Creek Rd., Los Gatos, CA 95030 (408)395-0207. *Hardwood cradles, woodcarving, custom furniture, wooden toys.*

F.M. Kosheleff, Box 634, Los Gatos, CA 95031 (408)354-5312. *Custom-made string instruments, guitars, packaxes, balalaikas, banduras.*

MANHATTAN BEACH: **John D. Freeman,** 1320 23rd St., Manhattan Beach, CA 90266 (213)546-1320.

MARINA: **Herbert L. Eggleston Jr., Visionary Woods,** 224 Reindollar Ave. Space 133, Marina, CA 93933 (408)384-3037. *Foam-lined hardwood cases for electronic instruments.*

MARSHALL: **(50) C. Stuart Welch, Designer-Craftsman,** 15800 Star Route 1, Marshall, CA 94940 (415)663-1775. *Prototypes, furniture, architectural details.*

McKINLEYVILLE: **Janis Taylor,** 1306 E. Bates, McKinleyville, CA 95521 (707)839-2003. *Custom furniture and ornamental carving.*

MEADOW VISTA: **Ron Riedel,** 2615 Sunrise Dr., Meadow Vista, CA 95722 (916)878-8465.

MENDOCINO: **Crispin B. Hollinshead,** 44890 Gordon Lane, Mendocino, CA 95460 (707)937-0401. *Display cases, fine scale miniatures and models.*

Tom Thompson, Endeavors, Box 1031, Mendocino, CA 95460 (707)937-0449. *Furniture, dominoes, sculpture and functional products.*

Yarman Studio, 604 Ford St., Box 978, Mendocino, CA 95460 (707)937-5553. *Custom-designed furniture, chairs and bar stools.*

MENLO PARK: **Bill Grant Woodcraft,** 115 Hillside Ave., Menlo Park, CA 94025 (415)854-6935. *Period and design furniture pieces.*

Bojan Petek, 125 Pope St., Menlo Park, CA 94025 (415)321-5128. *Custom-made furniture, custom interiors.*

Thomas Keller Designs, 1060 Ringwood Ave., Menlo Park, CA 94025 (415)322-5821. *Commissions, designs for production, steambending.*

MILLBRAE: **Robert Buttler,** Box 771, Millbrae, CA 94030 (415)692-2621. *Custom wooden furniture, design and construction in wood and plastic.*

MODESTO: **Daniel Goodman,** 517 Semple St., Modesto, CA 95354 (209)521-2120.

MOKELUMNE HILL: **Woodworking and Design by Donero,** Main and Highway 26, Mokelumne Hill, CA 95245 (209)286-1543. *Small furniture commissions, built-in china, stereo, library cabinets, kitchens, new and remodel.*

MONTCLAIR: **Hummingbird Woodcraft,** 8971 Rose St., Montclair, CA 91763 (714)624-9485. *Fine cabinetry.*

MONTEREY: **(151) Craig Lauterbach, The Inquisitive Eye,** 820 Airport Rd., Monterey, CA 93940 (408)375-3332. *Stacked lamination and custom furniture.*

MOUNTAIN VIEW: **Robert S. Buchanan,** 206 Jason Way, Mountain View, CA 94040 (415)964-9269. *Specialty: wood body sculptures.*

MOUNT SHASTA: **(177) Chris Schneider, Designer and Craftsman,** 3715 Summit Dr., Mt. Shasta, CA 96067 (916)926-4180. *Design and construction of functional and sculptural work in many media.*

NAPA: **(147) Ed Clay,** 5398 Sonoma Highway, Napa, CA 94558 (707)255-145519 (or E. Toole Ave., Tucson, AZ 85701 (602)623-2872). *Custom furniture, one-of-a-kind.*

NEVADA CITY: **T.J. Crafts, Tony Sauer,** 13705 Bitney Spring Rd., Nevada City, CA 95959 (916)273-6386. *Kitchen and bath cabinets and accessories.*

Tom Banwell Wood Designs, Box 264, Nevada City, CA 95959 (916)265-3765. *Signs, business logos, wall hangings, carved doors, headboards, trims for doors and windows.*

NEWBURY PARK: **Daniel J. Hogan,** 528 Artisan Rd., Newbury Park, CA 91320. *Unique designs made in wood and of heirloom quality.*

NEWPORT BEACH: **J. Rinehart Company,** 1539 Monrovia St. No. 5, Newport Beach, CA 92663 (714)645-9654. *Unusual furniture, accessories.*

N. HIGHLANDS: **Rob Funk,** 7341 32nd St., N. Highlands, CA 95660 (714)334-0953. *Limited production.*

NORTH HOLLYWOOD: **Marley Chung,** 5146 Riverton Ave., North Hollywood, CA 91601. *Toys, accessories and other artistic creations.*

G.S. Brandt Guitars, 11525 Riverside Dr., N. Hollywood, CA 91602 (213)980-9348. *Custom acoustic guitars, both classical and steel string. Commissions and repairs also.*

NORTHRIDGE: **(176) Stephen L. Casey, Designer-Craftsman,** 18606-5 Parthenia St., Northridge, CA 91324 (213)885-7917. *Furniture, sculpture, accessories, original designs to fit customer criteria.*

Christopher's Collectables, 8231 Louise Ave., Northridge, CA 91325 (213)342-7503. *Miniatures, including boxes and carvings.*

(78) Patrick Graney, 8650 Yolanda, Northridge, CA 91324 (213)993-8264. *Simple, unforced, elegant lines, allowing the wood to make its own unique statement.*

NORWALK: **Steve Ankenbauer,** 15613 Bechard Ave., Norwalk, CA 90650 (213)921-7238. *Lathe and sculpture.*

NOVATO: **(127) Dana Design,** 5 Stitt Court, Novato, CA 94947 (415)897-7817.

Ebony Woods, 9F Pamaron Dr., Novato, CA 94947. *Shaper work, trestle tables, occasional tables, buffets, bedrooms, kitchens and a lot of honest hard work!*

(103) Joseph Scannell, 1647 Indian Valley Rd., Novato, CA 94947. *Custom hardwood designs.*

OAKHURST: **Christopher W. Cantwell, Woodworks,** 38033 Highway 41, Oakhurst, CA 93644 (209)683-4281. *Inlaid boxes, furniture made from exotic hardwoods.*

OAKLAND: **Richard Alexander,** 46-37th St., Oakland, CA 94609 (415)654-8095. *Custom furnishings to meet the specific needs of my clients.*

David F. Bai, 411 Hudson St., Oakland, CA 94618 (415)655-1307. *Contemporary hardwood furniture, accessories for business and the home.*

(43) E.E. 'Skip' Benson, 3546 Rhoda Ave., Oakland, CA 94602 (415)531-8081. *Functional designs to satisfy client needs. One-of-a-kind, limited edition commissions.*

(41) Don Braden, Designs, 618 E. 11th St., Oakland, CA 94606 (415)763-1326. *Design and construction of limited edition furniture.*

(123) Manuel Albert Gomez, 536 46th St. 4, Oakland, CA 94609 (415)654-3830.

Jud Peake Construction, 4021 Midvale Ave., Oakland, CA 94602 (415)531-8274. *Homebuilding and commercial tenant remodel. Curved and difficult framing and trim a specialty.*

Donovan Miller, 451B 44th St., Oakland, CA 94609 653-1575. *Wood sculpture.*

(180) Dennis M. Morinaka, 447-25th St., Oakland, CA 94612 (415)832-1423. *Fine art exclusively.*

Tom Mullally, Furnituremaker, 4356 Coliseum Way, Oakland, CA 94605 (415)535-1670. *Custom-designed furniture and cabinets, antique reproductions and furniture made to customer specifications.*

Newhall Wood Design, 1250 57th Ave., Oakland, CA 94621 (415)535-2660. *I am a graduate architect and woodworker building unique furniture, cabinets, and doing architectual problem solving.*

(68) Gail Fredell Smith, 282 2nd St., Oakland, CA 94607 (415)763-8502. *Wood furniture.*

John Weinshel, 1573-A Beach St., Oakland, CA 94608 (415)654-6555. *Hardwood furniture, designed and built by John Weinshel.*

Zacariah Woodworks, 5823 Occidental St., Oakland, CA 94608 (415)655-4101. *I design and build one-of-a-kind objects from domestic and exotic hardwoods.*

OCCIDENTAL: **Marco,** 4615 Timber Lane, Occidental, CA 95465 (707)874-3020. *Custom woodwork.*

OCEANSIDE: **Bill Agles,** 144 Nixon Circle, Oceanside, CA 92056 (619)758-9984.

Sun and Sea Wood Designs, 221 Via El Centro, Oceanside, CA 92054 (619)433-2221. *Furniture, cabinets, doors, windows, solid hardwoods, interior, exterior designs and construction.*

OJAI: **Dennis Fingold,** 16030 Maricopa Highway, Ojai, CA 93023 (805)646-6203. *Specializing in one-of-a-kind design of fine furniture and cabinetry.*

ONTARIO: **Chris Alan Miller,** 1224 N. Baker Ave., Ontario, CA 91764 (714)986-0453. *General woodworking and design.*

ORANGE: **Tim Pellissier,** 536 N. Center St., Orange, CA 92667 (714)639 3933. *Tables, contemporary to modern, hardwoods only. Carvings (impressionist), wall hangings.*

Woodworks, 16402 Heim Ave., Orange, CA 92665 (714)532-5257. *Woodturning, custom furniture, toys, sculpture, prototypes, models, molds and furniture repair.*

ORANGEVALE: **(35) Alfred E. Holland, Jr.,** 7321 Santa Juanita Ave., Orangevale, CA 95662 (916)988-1300. *Aspiring to quiet elegance, I design and build solid hardwood furniture.*

OXNARD: **Michael Sixbey,** 841 Rubens Place, Oxnard, CA 93033 (805)488-6860. *Rocking chairs, dining chairs, custom-made solid hardwood furniture.*

PACIFIC GROVE: **(91) Alan Marks Design,** 1204 Lincoln, Pacific Grove, CA 93950 (408)373-2227. *Chairs individually designed for client's comfort, desks, tables, cabinets, inlay and marquetry, freelance design.*

PALO ALTO: **William Ortiz, Fine Woodwork,** 780 High St., Palo Alto, CA 94301 (415)326-9979. *Original-design furniture.*

PASADENA: **Douglas Heaslet,** 1003 Diamond Ave., S. Pasadena, CA 91030 (213)799-2841. *Furniture/product design. Drawings and prototypes.*

Todd Kendrick, Craftsman in Wood, 3160 E. Foothill Blvd., Pasadena, CA 91107 ((213)795-6627. *Tables, chairs.*

PETALUMA: **Calan Stairwork,** 1323 Scott St., Petaluma, CA 94952 (707)762-0033. *Traditional, housed and wedged, stairways (straight or curved). Spirals a favorite.*

(23) **Jeffrey Dale, Handmade Furniture,** 318 5th St., Petaluma, CA 94952 (707)763-7906. *Harmonious settings of handmade furnishings of original design and Oriental influence.*

Dennis Young, Furnituremaker, 519 1-2 6th St., Petaluma, CA 94952 (707)762-0608. *Handmade furniture of traditional or contemporary design. Specialist in using native California hardwoods.*

PINE GROVE: **William M. Tappe,** Box 1137, Pine Grove, CA 95665 (209)295-1374. *Custom furniture, cabinetry, inlay and marquetry, marquetry wall murals.*

PLACENTIA: **ADG Woodcrafting,** 213 San Miguel, Placentia, CA 92670 (714)524-1946. *Bowl turning, large column turning up to 28 ft. by 3 ft., carving.*

PLEASANTON: **Designs in Wood, Richard Taylor,** 6713 Melody Court, Pleasanton, CA 94566 (415)846-3647. *Furniture and cabinet work.*

POMONA: **Cutshall's Woodworks, Ed Cutshall,** 172 Lincoln, Pomona, CA 91767 (714)620-4168. *Custom work. Something you can't buy in a store.*

McKernon Woodworking, 765 Indigo, Pomona, CA 91765 (714)621-6640.

POWAT: **Louis Shapiro III,** Box 314, Powat, CA 92064 (619)748-2963. *Unique top quality, traditional and old-world style furniture and cabinetry. Work commissioned countrywide.*

RANCHO PALOS VERDES: **Walter A. Donahue,** 29679 Enrose Ave., Rancho Palos Verdes, CA 90732 (213)832-1071. *Custom woodworking and furniture.*

REDLANDS: **DeHoog Constructions,** 10637 Opal Ave., Redlands, CA 92373 (714)794-3960. *We'll try anything.*

Jeanne M. Lane, 423 Phlox Court, Redlands, CA 92373 (714)793-3623. *Lathe-turned plates.*

REDWOOD CITY: (64) **American Masterpiece,** 1743 Hempstead Place, Redwood City, CA 94061 (415)365-7432. *Original designs. American colonial tradition for contemporary living.*

RIVERSIDE: **Jim Cryar,** 6236 Windemere Way, Riverside, CA 92506 (714)686-3583. *Relief-carved, signed and constructed sculptures.*

(83) **Bruce Decker,** 4668 Beacon Way, Riverside, CA 92501 (714)781-4978. *One-of-a-kind and limited editions, personal, household accessories, sculptural functional furniture.*

Robert Leung Wood Studio, 5423 Brittany Ave., Riverside, CA 92506 (714)686-1136. *Custom furnitures and accessories.*

ROHNERT PARK: **Edward Smalarz,** 6468 Meadow Pines Dr., Rohnert Park, CA 94928 (707)585-0967. *General woodworking, photography.*

ROSEMEAD: (131) **Harry M. Myer,** 4631 Fendyke Ave., Rosemead, CA 91770 (213)286-0103.

ROSEVILLE: **Leon W. Jones,** 6933 Folsom Oaks Court, Roseville, CA 95678 (916)791-1547. *Architectural carving as it applies to doors, mantels, walls, bars, furniture and accessories.*

SACRAMENTO: **David C. Mast, Custom Furniture,** 6665 Pocket Rd., Sacramento, CA 95831 (916)393-0386. *Custom hardwood art furniture, desks, shelving, tables, cabinets, cutting boards, boxes and cases.*

Palm Studios, 8115 Eldercreek Rd., Sacramento, CA 95819 (916)386-1160. *Custom wooden stairs, curved rails, turning, furniture, and custom entries and interiors.*

Phillip H. Pfaendler, 6912 Sierra Bonita Way, Sacramento, CA 95831 (916)428-6450.

(35) **Eric R. Smith,** 1600 Wesmead Ct., Sacramento, CA 95822 (916)452-2601. *Quality custom furniture.*

SALINAS: **Michelle Derviss,** 1302 Fairhaven St., Salinas, CA 93905 (408)424-9185. *Contemporary original designs of sculptural utilitarian furniture, cabinets, jewelry boxes and other wooden accessories in life.*

SAN ANSELMO: **Maurice St. Gaudens,** 146 Sequoia Dr., San Anselmo, CA 94960 (415)456-3358.

SAN BERNARDINO: (70) **Leo G. Doyle and Sons,** 378 W. 53rd St., San Bernardino, CA 92407 (714)887-7459. *Design consultant in wood and fabrication of wood products, woodturning a specialty.*

Maderas Finas by Dale W. Vollmer, 1023 Belleview St., San Bernardino, CA 92410 (714)884-9582. *Fine furniture and classic guitars.*

SAN CARLOS: **Joseph Brown,** 1601 Old County Rd., San Carlos, CA 94070 (415)592-9926. *Furniture, architectural woodwork, millwork and case goods.*

Wallsworth Cabinetry, 873 Cordilleras Ave., San Carlos, CA 94070 (415)591-5870. *Space-saving wall-hung cabinetry of traditional design and construction.*

SAN DIEGO: **James T. Ecklar,** San Diego, CA 92107 (714)222-8743. *Special projects only.*

R. Jenuine, 4021 Ingalls St., San Diego, CA 92103 (619)297-8163.

James R. Meyers, 5180 Plainview Rd., San Diego, CA 92110 (619)276-1724. *Custom hardwood furniture, cabinets.*

John Parker, 4456 44th St., San Diego, CA 92115 (714)282-0952. *Design consultant and woodworker sculpture.*

Mark Pearson, SDSU Art Department, San Diego, CA 92182 (619)265-6511.

(73) **John Michael Pierson,** 1255-1/2 Missouri St., San Diego, CA 92109 (619)265-6223.

(68) **Ridenour's Studio,** 11404 Sorrento Valley Rd. 125, San Diego, CA 92121 (619)452-9080. *Highly sculptural style of contemporary furniture for home and office. Chairs, desks, tables and credenzas.*

Westcoast Woodworking, 7235 Arpege Rd., San Diego, CA 92119 (714)464-0760. *Architectural custom construction, general construction. License number B-3809.64.*

SAN DIMAS: **Jim Chilton,** 620 N. San Dimas Ave., San Dimas, CA 91773 (714)599-6245. *Jewelry and reliefs.*

SAN FRANCISCO: **Lani Bader,** 146 Shrader St., San Francisco, CA 94117 (415)386-2121.

(34) **Buchner Design Studio,** 1030 Quesada Ave., San Francisco, CA 94124 (415)822-7300. *Contemporary corporate and residential furniture.*

John Clark, 120 Brannan St., San Francisco, CA 94107 (415)546-9339. *Custom woodworking, design and construction, modern and traditonal designed furniture.*

Victor J. Conti, 586 Monterey Blvd., San Francisco, CA 94127 (415)587-6443.

(185) **Chuck Engberg,** 3960 19th St., San Francisco, CA 94114 (415)865-6933. *Relief carvings, caricatures, whittlings, wood sculptures.*

Mark Graham, 2032 Pierce St., San Francisco, CA 94115 (415)929-0214. *Kitchen cabinets, built in units.*

(81) **Grew-Sheridan Studio,** 500 Treat Ave., San Francisco, CA 94110 (415)824-6161. *Furniture and woodworking classes.*

Karn and Karn, 1254 Taylor St. 10, San Francisco, CA 94108 (415)673-1851. *Custom design woodworking.*

Maxworks, Max Leiber, 3345 17th St., San Francisco, CA 94110 (415)621-6423. *Sculptural furniture design and furniture manufacturing.*

Jeffrey W. Morton, 71 Delano, San Francisco, CA 94112 (415)334-4726. *Restoration of antique furniture reproduction of American tallcase clocks.*

Kukinori Muramoto, 1550-21st Ave., San Francisco, CA 94122 (415)564-4482. *Contemporary design furniture, traditional Japanese tools and technique used.*

Mark Nardone, c/o Robt. Leads, 2565 Third St., San Francisco, CA (415)863-1880. *Custom furniture, cabinetry and fireplace mantels (design and construction).*

(75) **Michael Pearce,** 551 Clipper St., San Francisco, CA 94114 (415)824-4237. *Custom furniture of unique design.*

Pow Her Construction & Cabinetry, 4650 Irving, San Francisco, CA 94122 (415)566-3736. *General construction carpentry, finish carpentry, cabinetry.*

Robert Greenberg Harpsichords, 2325 3rd St. 425, San Francisco, CA 94107 (415)552-1870. *Flemish, French, Italian harpsichords, virginals, clavichords. Brochure available.*

Saul Rosenfield, 128 Precita Ave., San Francisco, CA 94110 (415)648-1339. *Commissioned furniture, cabinetworks, compulsive architectural design and remodeling.*

(92) **Rex D. White,** 260 California St., Suite 405, San Francisco, CA 94111 (415)986-1429.

Wilshire Woodworks, Box 4266, San Francisco, CA 94101 (415)771-1894. *Bowl turning.*

(105) **Scott Wynn,** 120 Brannan St., San Francisco, CA 94107 (415)546-9339. *Furniture, residential design and construction, custom design and woodworking.*

SAN GABRIEL: **Peter Shapiro, Acorn Design,** 303 S. San Marino Ave., San Gabriel, CA 91776 (213)283-2539. *Contemporary furniture design and construction, woodworker's workbenches, custom and limited production.*

SAN JOSE: **Bert Arico Limited Custom Woodwork,** 1897 Foxworthy Ave., San Jose, CA 95124 (408)377-1063. *Jewelry boxes, small furniture items, rocking horses, misc. projects.*

R.T. Woodworking, 14190 Clayton Rd., San Jose, CA 95127 (408)251-6021. *Tables, cabinets and almost anything made of wood.*

(103) **Su-Lan Woodworks,** 1775 S. 1st St. 14, San Jose, CA 95112 (408)297-9663.

SAN JUAN CAPISTRANO: **Michael Levy,** 26472 Evergreen Rd., San Juan Capistrano, CA 92675 (714)495-4189. *Contemporary furniture.*

SAN LUIS OBISPO: **Richard Farwell,** 1551 Palm St., San Luis Obispo, CA 93401.*One-of-a-kind pieces. Cabinets and furniture. Commissions accepted.*

SAN MATEO: **Matt Lambert, Cabinetmaker,** 2185 Palm Ave., San Mateo, CA 94403 (415)573-6377. *Custom furniture. Specialty: wall units.*

SAN PEDRO: **Harold Greene,** 2134 S. Pacific, San Pedro, CA 90731 (213)832-5476. *I do primarily custom furniture but occasionally design kitchens bathrooms, also sculpture.*

SAN RAFAEL: **Amil St. Augustine,** 333 Laurel Place, San Rafael, CA 94901 (415)457-5336. *Commissioned one-of-a-kind articles ranging from small sculptural items through major furniture pieces.*

Rene P. Tatro, 685 Knocknabout Way, San Rafael, CA 94903 (415)472-4430. *Sturdy, functional oak furniture for the particular needs of our family.*

SAND CITY: **Ambrose Pollock Cabinets & Furniture,** 575 F California St., Sand City, CA 93955 (408)394-6272. *Custom woodwork. Tables, chairs, doors, windows, kitchen cabinets and commercial fixtures.*

SANTA ANA: **Jeff L. Gardner, dba Woodesign,** 2520 S. Fairview Unit P, Santa Ana, CA 92704 (714)556-8055. *Individually designed and handcrafted hardwood furniture for residential and commercial interiors.*

G. Martin, Martin Marine Wood Products, 1940 E. McFadden, Santa Ana, CA 92705 (714)541-5010. *Marine cabinetry, louvered doors, caning, production items, specialty items, wide-belt-sanding service, entryway doors.*

Woodshapes Workshop, 1221 S. Cypress Ave., Santa Ana, CA 92707 (714)558-1878. *Custom wood carvings, carousel horses a specialty. Other original designs available or commissions accepted.*

SANTA BARBARA: **Jeremy Carroll, A.T.N. Cabinet Shop,** 716 Bond Ave., Santa Barbara, CA 93103 (805)963-8555. *Custom cabinet work, custom furniture, architectural work.*

John Haskins, 923 St. Vincent Ave., Santa Barbara, CA 93101 (805)965-9752.

(132) **Jon E. Jenett,** Box 5609, Santa Barbara, CA 93108 (805)969-5868. *Ship models.*

Harold Moseley, Cabinet Maker, 517 Laguna St., Santa Barbara, CA 93101 (805)966-4561. *Design and building furniture and cabinets.*

Soboba Wood Company, 15 Anacapa St., Santa Barbara, CA 93101 (805)965-1949. *Sellers of rare and exotic hardwoods.*

SANTA CLARA: **Rihard Bronson,** 2372 Shoreside Court, Santa Clara, CA 95051 (708)988-1375. *Jewelry boxes, turned boxes and bowls, marquetry, clocks and personalized gifts.*

Cabinetics, 5034 Calle De Escuela, Santa Clara, CA 95050 (408)727-6708. *Architectural cabinetry, residential and commercial, contemporary furniture, display fixtures, production wood products, design consultation.*

Sherman Bud Sheppard, 1827 Andrea Place, Santa Clara, CA 95051.

SANTA CRUZ: **Allan Dodd, Live Oak Design,** 2533 Mission St., Santa Cruz, CA 95060 (408)429-8585. *Furniture and residential cabinetry.*

Cliff Friedlander, 316 Fairmount Ave., Santa Cruz, CA 95062 (408)427-2650. *Custom cabinetry, furniture, millwork.*

Joel Herzel, 1211 Laurent St., Santa Cruz, CA 95060 (408)426-0810. *Furniture commissions.*

Martin Rice Woodworking, 575-B 7th Ave., Santa Cruz, CA 95062 (408)475-2900. *Furniture, cabinets, stair moulding, shoji, marine carpentry, etc.*

Sandor Nagyszalanczy, Design & Craftsmanship, 120 Hall St., Santa Cruz, CA 95062 (408)429-8389. *Design and construction of hardwood furniture, cabinets, and custom metal hardware and fittings.*

Bruce Van Allen, Cabinets & Furniture, 1833 Soquel Avenue, Santa Cruz, CA 95062 (408)429-1895. *Custom home and commercial cabinets, original furniture and accessories, doors and windows, jigs and fixtures.*

SANTA MONICA: (40) **Michael Caroff, Design,** 2834 Colorado 29, Santa Monica, CA 90404 (213)828-1500. *Custom-made fine-line furniture and cabinetry.*

Cary Childress, Quiet Roots Woodworking, 1310 1-2 Santa Monica Blvd., Santa Monica, CA 90404 (213)395-1773. *Fine custom cabinets and furniture.*

Robert Ehrlich, 1241 21st St. Apt. D, Santa Monica, CA 90404. *Musical instruments and one-of-a-kind pieces designed and constructed.*

Gerald C. Nash, 364 18th St., Santa Monica, CA 90402 (213)393-7392. *Special commissions only.*

SANTA ROSA: **In Wood, Kevin Hutchinson, Designer-Craftsman,** 3114 Terra Linda Dr., Santa Rosa, CA 95404 (707)528-3097. *Custom design work.*

Joel Levine, Santa Rosa, CA 95401 (707)525-8161.

(119) **David J. Marks, Custom Wood Working,** 2128 Marsh Rd., Santa Rosa, CA 95401 (707)526-2763. *Gallery furniture, exotic woods, one-of-a-kind pieces, ivory, carving, jewelry boxes, hand mirrors.*

SANTA SUSANA: **Bill Coleman,** 6538 Clear Springs, Santa Susana, CA 93063.

SANTA YSABEL: (70) **Rocky Cross,** S.R. 1-24660 Old Julian Hwy., Santa Ysabel, CA 92070 (619)789-4690. *Professional design and fine woodwork.*

SANTEE: **Chuck Stromberg,** 10227 Prospect Ave., Santee, CA 92071 (619)449-7372. *Individually commissioned and/or limited edition wood pieces.*

SARATOGA: **Christopher L. Bostedt,** 12890 Pierce Rd., Saratoga, CA 95070 (408)867-2052. *Jewelry boxes, clocks, small furniture.*

SCOTTS VALLEY: **Michael Simms Sand Dollar Construction,** 2053 W. Rd., Scotts Valley, CA 95066 (408)335-4690. *Custom doors.*

Dave and Anna Weeks, Scotts Valley, CA 95066 (408)438-3648. *Tables, chairs, chests of drawers.*

SEBASTOPOL: (70) **Roger Bell and George Breck,** 433 Vine Ave., Sebastopol, CA 95472 (707)823-1571. *Furniture, custom cabinetry.*

(177) **Michael Cooper,** 11214 Occidental Rd., Sebastopol, CA 95472 (707)823-0499. *Sculpture, primarily in wood.*

SOLANA BEACH: (60) **Erik Gronborg,** 424 Dell Court, Solana Beach, CA 92075 (619)481-9105. *Special commissions with emphasis on sculptural solutions to fit client's needs.*

SOLVANG: **Bud Tullis, Woodworker,** 1703 Ballard Cny. Rd., Solvang, CA 93463 (805)688-3758. *Custom furniture, cabinets.*

SONOMA: **Andrew's Furniture Restoration,** Sonoma, CA (707)938-2373. *Complete restoration, remodeling, repair, parts fabrication, design and construction.*

Robert H. Cannard, 528 3rd St. E., Sonoma, CA 95476 (707)938-2859. *Antique furniture restoration.*

SONORA: **Karpinski Woodworking,** 22600 Meadow Lane, Sonora, CA 95370 (209)532-0218. *Custom-designed wooden objects and furniture.*

SPRING VALLEY: **Balladeer Corp.,** 9248 Olive Dr., Spring Valley, CA 92077 (714)286-3700. *Handcrafted architectural woodwork, custom furniture, libraries, mantels and hand rails.*

Jack Rogers Hopkins, 8651 Lamar St., Spring Valley, CA 92077 (619)466-5149. *One-of-a-kind and limited edition units. Sculpted table bases viewed through glass.*

(141) Craig A. Woodward, 8827 Cara Court, Spring Valley, CA 92077 (619)479-6587. *Custom-designed furniture and kitchen cabinetry.*

STOCKTON: **James Marsh,** 1428 N. Harrison, Stockton, CA 95203 (209)464-1469. *Building and repair of fretted instruments, wooden toys, furniture.*

Patrick Andrew McMaster, 4916 Huntington Lane, Stockton, CA 95207 (209)477-4181. *We design furniture with a person's ideas.*

Valley Clock Repair Shop, Wilbur Earley, 3345 W. Princeton, Stockton, CA 95204 (415)462-0162. *Restoration of old American wood clocks including dials, gears and cabinets, turnings, etc.*

SUNLAND: **Woodware by George,** 9841 Shadow Way, Sunland, CA 91040 (213)353-1932.

SUNNYMEAD: **Anthony W. Groves,** 11070 Davis St., Sunnymead, CA 92388 (714)653-0131. *Original designs, quality construction.*

SUNNYVALE: **(165) Kathy Blair and Jim Frandeen,** 1478 Firebird Way, Sunnyvale, CA 94087. *Custom furniture, small boxes, and portfolios with through-lay designs.*

(141) David Hodge, 889 Rattan Terrace, Sunnyvale, CA 94086 (408)733-9971.

TEMPLE CITY: **Robert J. Palmer,** 9111 E. Olive St., Temple City, CA 91780 (213)285-9588. *Design, construct, hand-carved specialty wood items on commission basis. Limited editions.*

TOPANGA: **Custom Design Woodworking,** 1454 Old Topanga Rd., Topanga, CA 90290 (213)455-1066. *Design and fabrication of objects, cabinets, furniture, etched windows, doors, along with integrated metal and wrought-iron work.*

TOPANGA CANYON: **Alfred W. Brostowicz,** 3352 Tuna Canyon Rd., Topanga Canyon, CA 90290 (213)455-1910. *One-of-a-kind designs and sculptures and custom furniture.*

TORRANCE: **Hoffmann Woodcrafts,** 5321 Carol Dr., Torrance, CA 90505 (213)540-2858. *Most woodworking tools and capabilities for medium-size projects.*

William J. 'Bud' Maley, 4906 Carmelynn St., Torrance, CA 90503 (213)542-1969. *Custom furniture, cabinets, veneering and wood turning.*

TRINIDAD: **Larry Dern,** Box 906, Trinidad, CA 955701 (707)677-3956. *Custom-designed furniture. Fine quality construction and hand-rubbed varnish finish.*

Philip Gerstner, Cabinet & Furniture Maker, Route 1 Box 255, Trinidad, CA 95570 (707)677-0197.

(17) David Groth, Box 803, Trinidad, CA 95570 (707)677-3141. *Hand-carved salad sets which are individually designed.*

TURLOCK: **Linda G. Champion,** 427 Crane Ave., Turlock, CA 95380 (209)632-9772. *Fine furniture designed and built for personal needs.*

UKIAH: **Paul A. Taylor, Jr.,** 8601 Feliz Creek Dr., Ukiah, CA 95482 (707)468-8420. *Furniture, finish carpentry, antique restoration and reproduction.*

UNION CITY: **Quality Woodwork,** 32257 Devonshire Dr., Union City, CA 94587 (415)471-3350. *Custom interior woodwork and furniture design and construction are preferred. Hardwood finish work and wall-unit construction are the most common commissions.*

VALLEJO: **(24) Steve Rugg, Aesthetic Designs in Hardwood,** 73 Parrott St., Vallejo, CA 94590 (707)552-4223. *Custom cabinets and fine furniture.*

Al Tadlock, 10 Laurel, Vallejo, CA 94590 (707)552-2129. *Doll cases and doll furniture.*

VALLEY CENTER: **Valley Center Glass and Wood,** Box 41, Valley Center, CA 92082 (714)749-9727. *Stained glass and doors as of now!*

VAN NUYS: **(125) Clement Konzem,** 6342 Woodman Ave., Van Nuys, CA 91401 (213)782-2692. *Artistry in wood, specializing in innovative wood designs.*

VENICE: **Glen Ernst,** 613 Angelus Place, Venice, CA 90291 (213)827-7040. *Very fine woodwork for yacht or home.*

(50) Morris J. Sheppard Design, 224 Main St., Venice, CA 90291 (213)392-4891. *Furniture of all types, hardwood cabinetry and architectural woodwork on commission.*

VENTURA: **Ken Ballou, Project Secure,** 150 Day Rd., Ventura, CA 93003 (805)642-9012. *Easels and other custom orders.*

Rick D. Ransom, 2869 E. Harbor Blvd., Ventura, CA 93001 (805)642-9255. *Commissioned sculptures.*

Tony Howard Cabinets & Custom Furniture, 2521 Palma Dr. K, Ventura, CA 93003 (805)644-8788. *Individually tailored pieces a specialty.*

VISTA: **John Goff,** 1078 Oak Dr., Vista, CA 92083 (714)724-0638. *Antique copies, contempory furniture, fine woodwork.*

Ted L. Jacox, 230 Neil Terrace, Vista, CA 92083 (619)726-3452. *Wood sculpture and cabinetry.*

WALNUT CREEK: **Frank A. Hiek,** 2330 Buena Vista Ave., Walnut Creek, CA 94596 (415)939-6558. *Small work.*

WESTLAKE VILLAGE: **The Retreat Gallery,** 3865 E. Thousand Oaks Blvd., Westlake Village, CA 91362 (805)496-7615. *Contemporary American craft gallery.*

WESTMINSTER: **Another Design Connection,** 14852 Beach Blvd., Westminster, CA 92683 (714)898-9749. *Creators of casually elegant contemporary furniture.*

WESTWOOD: **Lane B, Lane Buscho,** 20 13 Holmby Ave., Westwood, CA 90025 (213)474-9995. *Large unrepresentational wood sculpture.*

WHITTIER: **Michael Kelley,** 1240 1-2 Pasadena St., Whittier, CA 90601 (213)699-8365. *One-of-a-kind contemporary furniture, limited-production desk accessories, kitchen accessories.*

(184) Christoph Rittershausen, 13102 Philadelphia St., Whittier, CA 90601 (213)696-9474 or 693-4705. *Sculptural commissions, life-size figures, religious carvings, busts, portraits, other traditional woodcarver's work.*

WILLITS: **Lee Davis,** Box 1068, Willits, CA 95490. *Japanese-inspired original boxes.*

WINDSOR: **Philip Nereo Woodworking,** 6851 Starr Rd., Windsor, CA 95492 (707)838-4424. *Furniture, cabinetry, large woodturnings, woodcarving, doors, custom moldings and architectural details. Antique restoration.*

WINTERS: **Cambios Woodworks, Albert Vallecillo,** 8 E. Abbey St., Winters, CA 95694 (916)795-2669. *I am a member of a cooperative shop. We do furniture, cabinetry, architectural and turned woodworking.*

WOODACRE: **(184) Mel & Jan Schockner, Designers,** 16 Sylvan Way, Box 467, Woodacre, CA 94973 (415)488-4054. *Graphic design and wood sculpture (contemporary). Commissions accepted.*

WOODLAND HILLS: **Jack Leland,** 4986 Marmol Dr., Woodland Hills, CA 91364 (916)884-9961. *Contemporary and antique styles, especially country and primitive.*

Betty Babbitt Pfouts, 21228 Lopez St., Woodland Hills, CA 91364 (213)348-8761. *Designs for publications: wooden toys, clocks, trunks, dollhouses and furniture, accessories.*

Michael Shanman, 6125 Manton Ave., Woodland Hills, CA 91367. *Furniture and cabinetmaking.*

WOODSIDE: **John A. Kapel, Designer,** 80 Skywood Way, Woodside, CA 94062. *Prototypes only. One-of-a-kind for custom work.*

Colorado

ANTONITO: **Francis E. Christensen,** RFD Box 167, Antonito, CO 81120 (303)843-5561. *Woodturning, accessories, tableware, box joints, some furniture, staving.*

ARVADA: **Dan Sutton,** 7305 Dudley St., Arvada, CO 80005 (303)423-3850. *Custom furniture and cabinets.*

Tucker Enterprises, 5555 Harlan St., Arvada, CO 80004 (303)423-5535. *Custom only.*

ASPEN: **(30) Stephen Crowley, Furnituremaker,** 630 E. Hyman Ave., Aspen, CO 81611 (Mailing: Box 308, Woody Creek, CO 81656) (303)920-1583. *Furniture, architectural millwork.*

AURORA: **Ken Schroer,** 1984 So. Pitkin St., Aurora, CO 80013 (303)750-0652. *Children's furniture and toys.*

BASALT: **(149) Foster Woodworking Inc.,** 1712 Willits Lane, Basalt, CO 81621 (303)927-4548. Mail inquiries to: Box 517, El Jebel, CO 81628. *Furniture, cabinetry, custom doors. We also sell American hardwoods.*

BOULDER: **Artistry in Wood,** 4733 W. Moorhead Circle, Boulder, CO 80303 (303)499-7153. *One-of-a-kind and limited production furniture and cabinetry. Woodworking for unique situations.*

(30) Richard Barsky, Dovetail Woodworks, 2510 N. 47th St., Boulder, CO 80301 (303)449-7925. *Custom-design furniture and interiors. We have a two-year apprentice program.*

(25) David Curry, Heartwood, 944 Pearl St., Boulder, CO 80302 (303)447-1973. *As a cooperative we're able to offer individually designed furniture at competitive prices.*

J.E. Holloway, 2075 Kohler Dr., Boulder, CO 80303 (303)499-4827. *Original designs.*

John Yoksh Woodworking, 236 Pearl St., Boulder, CO 80302 (303)443-2310.

Tom Luecke, 835 36th St., Boulder, CO 80303 (303)442-5509. *Opening new practice. Single and limited production furniture, turnings.*

Cheryl L. Mitchell, 1708 Quince Ave., Boulder, CO 80302 (303)449-1283. *Abstract sculptures in wood, metals, plastics, stone, glass, and ceramics. Commission inquiries are invited.*

Eric Mouffe, 600 Hawthorne Ave., Boulder, CO 80302 (303)442-5670. *Custom, one-of-a-kind fine furniture.*

Sign of the Times Sign Shoppe, 4565 Moorhead Ave., Boulder, CO 80303 (303)499-5030. *My sign shop specializes in rustic wood signs. I hand-carve or sandblast my custom signs.*

(48, 49) Bradford Walters, Dovetail Woodworks, 2510 N. 47th St., Boulder, CO 80301 (303)449-7925. *Design services, custom woodworking of any kind.*

WCP Wood, 2020 Violet Ave., Boulder, CO 80302 (303)443-0926. *Fine handcrafted solid-hardwood furniture.*

Bruce Woller, 1951 Poplar Lane, Boulder, CO 80302 (303)443-8436. *Furniture, stairways and cabinets.*

COLORADO SPRINGS: **Lowell Bell,** Colorado Springs, CO 80908 (303)495-4754.

Dan Crossey, Lynn Spear, 2001 N. Cascade Ave., Colorado Springs, CO 80907 (303)635-2387. *Custom woodwork, fine furniture. Traditional methods and finish. Simple, clean design.*

Desks & Doors, 1655 Maxwell St., Colorado Springs, CO 80906 (303)392-4351. *Special entry doors, one-of-a-kind desks, framed mirrors.*

Iota Woodworks, C. Scott Taylor, Designer, 2558 Durango Dr., Colorado Springs, CO 80910 (303)390-6200. *Furnishings for home, office. Architectural millwork. Inlay, carving.*

Alfred Maurer, 17810 Woodhaven Dr., Colorado Springs, CO 80908 (303)488-2714. *Design, cabinet work in hardwoods.*

Unique Creations by Julie, 11 Dorchester Dr., Colorado Springs, CO 80906 (303)475-0895. *Custom hardwood furniture and hand-forged ironwork.*

William Jeavons Woodworking, 3805 Sommerset Dr., Colorado Springs, CO 80907 (303)634-5867. *Pieces designed and sculpted to enhance a specific environment. Unusual problems a specialty.*

CONIFER: **Aspen High Woodworking,** 24847 Red Cloud Dr., Conifer, CO 80433 (303)838-4792. *One-of-a-kind.*

(167) Mark Zarn, Woodworker, 13641 Cedar, Conifer, CO 80433 (303)838-2238 and 838-4825. *Fine furniture and kitchen cabinets designed and built on commission.*

CORTEZ: **Wood 'N Waterworks, Joe Millican,** 957 Navajo St., Cortez, CO 81321 (303)565-7945. *Furniture construction, steam work, laminations, chests and family heirlooms.*

CRESTED BUTTE: **The Woodworks, Bill Folger,** Box 262 309 Third, Crested Butte, CO 81224 (303)349-5328. *Toys, turnings, furniture, restoration, gingerbread, carving.*

DENVER: **Artistic Woodworking,** 633 Pearl St., Denver, CO 80203 (303)832-2598.

Dave Boykin, 1422 Fairfax, Denver, CO 80220 (303)388-9502. *Custom woodworking, commissions.*

Anthony R. Brazzale, Woodworker, 149 W. Bayaud Avenue, Denver, CO 80223 (303)733-3569. *Commission work, with emphasis on carving, veneering, bending. Contemporary design, traditional technique, cabinetwork.*

Michael Chariton, 2356 Forest St., Denver, CO 80207 (303)322-7339. *Hardwood furniture and cabinetry.*

Creative Knife, 1430 Race St., Denver, CO 80206. *Fine art woodworking and designs.*

N.M. Jensen, 355 Elati, Denver, CO 80223 (303)534-7592. *Custom woodworking.*

Dennis Lucero, Box 2367, Denver, CO 80201 (303)296-6451.

Morangie Woodwork, Robert M. Ross, 3336 Eliot St., Denver, CO 80211 (303)455-6176. *Interiors, sculpture, cabinetry and design.*

Robert Wood Fine Materials, 547 Kalamath St., Denver, CO 80204 (303)623-5924. *Custom wood and metal working.*

Shane's Woodworks, 327 E. Mexico Apartment 2, Denver, CO 80210. *Cabinet making, designing, woodcarving.*

The Skilled Hand, 1000 S. Franklin St., Denver, CO 80209 (303)778-0613. *One-of-a-kind furniture pieces as functional art forms.*

(94) William Tickel, Box 2367, Denver, CO 80201 (303)296-6451.

Victoriana Construction Co. Inc., 1707 E. 39th, Denver, CO 80205 (303)296-0116. *Custom cabinetry, furniture, millwork.*

ESTES PARK: **Prospect Mountain Crafts,** Box 1027, Estes Park, CO 80517 (303)586-2696. *Wood sculptures, gunstocks, cabinetry, framing, wood and elk antler jewelry and table accessories, stained glass.*

FORT COLLINS: **(182) Tom Larkin, Woodworker,** 216 Wood St., Fort Collins, CO 80521 (303)484-9295. *Woodcarving, chairs, fine cabinetry.*

Nazarene Woodworks, 400 Hemlock, Fort Collins, CO 80524 (303)224-2767. *Working with people to design and construct furniture to meet their specific need.*

Kelvin Packard, 673 Hanna, Fort Collins, CO 80521 (3030 224-4420. *Clocks and waterbeds.*

Solid Wood, 1617 S. County Rd. 5, Fort Collins, CO 80547 (303)493-8418. *Contemporary and traditional designed furniture for functional or decorative purposes.*

GOLDEN: **Craig P. Rupp,** 29838 Ruby Ranch Rd., Golden, CO 80401 (303)526-1164. *Custom woodworking, period furniture and refinishing.*

GRAND LAKE: **Derek S. Davis, Woodworks,** 297 Bloye Dr., Box 42, Grand Lake, CO 80447 (303)627-8248. *Contemporary custom hardwood furniture.*

GREELEY: **K.J. Randich,** 3346 27th St., Greeley, CO 80631 (303)330-0944. *Small objects, by commission only.*

LAKEWOOD: **William Beichley,** 12022 W. Dakota Dr., Lakewood, CO 80228 (303)985-5272. *Custom furniture, architectural woodwork made to be experienced and built to last.*

LAS ANIMAS: **Frank R. Dietrich,** 828 Sixth St., Las Animas, CO 81054 (303)456-1225. *Home furnishings.*

LONGMONT: **Rocking Mountain Chairworks,** 225 So. Price Rd. 40, Longmont, CO 80501 (303)776-3528.

Mark D. Spencer, 10 Birch Court No. 4, Longmont, CO 80501 (303)772-5996. *Furniture, furniture reproduction, toys, cabinets, custom handcrafted woodworking.*

John Rexford Stobbelaar, 7780 Monarch Rd., Longmont, CO 80501 (303)652-2569. *Cabinets and furniture restorations of all types.*

(130) Rick Stoner, 13580 N. 87th St., Longmont, CO 80501 (303)776-1709. *Original designs by commission only.*

John D. Vanman, Box 1724, Longmont, CO 80501 (303)772-0306. *Clocks and cabinets.*

LOVELAND: **Steven R. Anderson,** 4080 Boxelder Dr., Loveland, CO 80537 (303)669-0064. *Custom cabinetry and woodworking, furniture, design, industrial cabinetry.*

MASONVILLE: **Masonville Custom Woodworking,** 6600 Tamarax Court Box 61, Masonville, CO 80541 (303)669-6952. *Custom furniture and cabinetry.*

MONTROSE: **Tormey's Furniture,** 437 N. Mesa Ave., Montrose, CO 81401 (303)249-6875. *Custom woodworking, including furniture, doors mouldings, also repair and restoration.*

MONUMENT: **Zephyr Woodworks, Rick Squires,** Box 1094, Monument, CO 80132. *Fine quality, handmade hardwood and fireplace bellows with brass or turned wood tips and real leather.*

RANGELY: **James D. King,** 321 W. Main, Rangely, CO 81648 (303)675-2328.

RED CLIFF: **Wood Eye Woodworks,** Box 93, Red Cliff, CO 81649 (303)827-5267.

STEAMBOAT SPRINGS: **Contemporary Time,** Star Route 1, Steamboat Springs, CO 80477 (303)879-4124. *Custom and limited edition clockworks and fine furniture in the contmporary style.*

THORTON: **Dave Hicks,** 11597 Milwaukee Court, Thornton, CO 80233 (303)457-3033. *Small wood objects, especially bowls, lamps, etc., and clocks.*

WHEATRIDGE: **Twisted Forest Creations, Daryl L. Cook,** 5250 Quail St., Wheatridge, CO 80033 (303)422-0301. *Burl wood and twisted wood furniture, wooden waterfalls and fine cabinetry.*

John W. Vincent, 2925 Jay St., Wheatridge, CO 80214 (303)233-6061. *Custom design and craftsmanship.*

Connecticut

AVON: **Benson J. Horowitz,** 147 Deercliff Rd., Avon, CT 06001 (203)677-8377. *Design furniture.*

BLOOMFIELD: **(99) Ron Curtis,** 91 Tunxis Ave., Bloomfield, CT 06002. *Custom furniture wood interiors.*

BRANFORD: **Mark W. Leach,** Killam's Point Conference Center, Branford, CT 06405 (203)488-5698.

BRIDGEPORT: **David A. Dietrick,** 78 Bartram Ave., Bridgeport, CT 06605 (203)367-2880. *Furniture, cabinets, beds, houses, sculpture and carving. Designed in collaboration with the buyer.*

Kathy Lewis, 245 Remington St., Bridgeport, CT 06610 (203)335-2217. *Wooden jewelry, miniatures, and wee wooden sculptures.*

CORNWALL BRIDGE: **Homer Page, Country Workshop,** Cornwall Bridge, CT 06754 (203)672-6166. *Specially designed cherry stands and adjustable chairs for musicians.*

DANBURY: **William R. Barlow,** 46 Mabel Ave., Danbury, CT 06810 (203)743-3027. *One-of-a-kind collector items, preferably small, to customer designs or jointly designed on the premises of either.*

Ray Kopp, Looking Glass Interiors, Washington Ave., Danbury, CT 06810. *Specialize in turned objects, both functional and artistic, made from both native and exotic woods.*

Tom Leveille, Danbury, CT 06810 (203)748-3050. *One-of-a-kind accent pieces.*

Richard Valentino, Val's Company, 44 Pleasant St., Danbury, CT 06810 (203)743-6524. *Custom cabinetry and accessories, contemporary furniture, gourmet items, commission work, limited production runs.*

DEEP RIVER: **Richard Gould,** 2 W. Elm St., Deep River, CT 06417 (203)566-2688. *Sculpture and limited editions of furniture. Living atmospheres designed and built.*

FAIRFIELD: **William Kern,** 33 Edge Hill Rd., Fairfield, CT 06430 (203)259-5048. *I make tables and desks to order, filling in with some carpentry and woodcarving.*

Garrett K. Spitzer, 100 Jennie Lane, Fairfield, CT 06430 (203)259-0913. *Main interest in antique reproductions, but open to change. Summer employment only.*

FALLS VILLAGE: **(183) Frank C. Grusauskas,** Sand Rd., Falls Village, CT 06031. *Custom accessories, small cabinets, woodworkingtools,planes,spokeshaves.Also,smallboxesandburl bowls.*

GLASTONBURY: **(21) Interwood Designs,** 141 Pratt St., Glastonbury, CT 06033 (203)633-3766. *One-of-a-kind solidwood furniture.*

HAMDEN: **Charles Zale,** 300 Brooksvale Ave., Hamden, CT 06518.

HARWINTON: **Restorations,** S. Rd., Harwinton, CT 06791 (203)485-9486. *Restore brass artifacts, restore and replace damaged woodcarvings and furniture parts.*

KILLINGWORTH: **William R. Murray,** 50 Bethke Rd., Killingworth, CT 06417 (203)663-2959. *Specializing in antique reproduction, period pieces and raised-panel doors, both plain and carved.*

LAKESIDE: **Contemporary Woodworks, Gendai Mokuchotsu,** Lorenz Studios Box 137, Lakeside, CT 06758 (203)567-4280. *One-of-a-kind furniture and sculpture.*

MILFORD: **(33) Eric Hoag,** 245 First Ave., Milford, CT 06460 (203)874-3819.

MT. CARMEL: **Peter Miller,** 1796 Shepard Ave., Mt. Carmel, CT 06518 (203)288-3855. *Custom-designed hardwood furniture utilizing Shaker concepts and hand joinery.*

NEW MILFORD: **Al McClain, Woodworker,** Paper Mill Farm, Paper Mill Rd., New Milford, CT 06776 (914)832-6352. *Furniture, interiors, spiral stairs.*

Bill Rice, 11 Surrey Lane, New Milford, CT 06776 (203)354-5089. *Decorative bird carvings, both simple and detailed.*

(116) James Schriber, Furniture, 18 S. Main St., New Milford, CT 06776 (203)354-6452. *Furniture, architectural woodware.*

NEW PRESTON: **(149) Wood Interiors,** Kinney Hill Rd., New Preston, CT 06777 (203)868-7706. *Solid-wood frame-and-panel construction, specializing in libraries, paneled rooms.*

NORWICH: **M.P.A. Sculptures,** RFD 3 97 Juniper Lane, Norwich, CT 06360 (203)376-9847. *Abstract and functional art.*

OXFORD: **Peter M. Petrochko,** 370 Quaker Farms Rd., Oxford, CT 06483 (203)888-9835. *Presently equipped to make accessory items; bowls and canisters, some furniture and wood sculpture.*

PUTNAM: **(27) Edward Zucca,** Route 1, Park St., Putnam, CT 06260 (203)928-4380. *Original contemporary functional furniture designed to fill most needs—practical and aesthetic.*

RIDGEFIELD: **Albert Treadwell, Builder,** 130 Bayberry Hill Rd., Ridgefield, CT 06877 (203)431-4501. *Specializing in challenging one-of-a-kind projects, interior/exterior.*

SANDY HOOK: **David Hannah,** Sandy Hook, CT 06482 (203)426-0677. *Contemporary fine furniture, custom-designed and crafted.*

THOMASTON: **Kerry P. Gagne, Cabinetmaker,** 157 Walnut Hill Rd., Thomaston, CT 06787 (203)283-0376. *Creating exceptional pieces of fine furniture in the manner of Early American cabinetmakers.*

TOLLAND: **Gary Mendell,** 22 Garry Rd., Tolland, CT 06084 (203)875-0640. *Unique marquetry and inlaid panels for wall hangings, tabletops, cabinet components and architectural applications.*

WALLINGFORD: **Roberge Custom Furniture & Cabinetry,** 105 S. Elm St., Wallingford, CT 06492 (203)269-6836.

WATERFORD: **(101) Gordon Kyle,** 211 Great Neck Rd., Waterford, CT 06385 (203)442-7621. *Multi-functional knockdown table and chairs.*

WEST HARTFORD: **(37) Will Neptune,** 115 S. Highland St., W. Hartford, CT 06119 (203)232-0432. *Co-op shop with individual specialties. I emphasize custom-made traditional furniture involving carving and/or inlay.*

Larry Sherman, Bebop Wood Shop, 20 Thomson Rd., W. Hartford, CT 06091. *Design and execution of furniture, specialty wood items, architectural projects.*

WESTPORT: **Ian B. Edwards, Cabinetmaker,** 10 Saugatuck Ave., Westport, CT 06880 (203)227-3286. *Antique reproductions, fine furniture, custom work.*

Riverbank Studio, 22 Oak Ridge Park, Westport, CT 06880 (203)227-1422. *Unique furniture and decorative pieces.*

WILTON: **(cover, 58) Tim Donahue, Furniture Designer,** Crossways, 300 Danbury Rd., Wilton, CT 06897 (203)834-1164.

WINDSOR: **Robert L. Southall,** The Loomis Chaffee School, Windsor, CT 06095 (203)688-4934. *Period furniture and antique reproductions.*

WINDSOR LOCKS: **Philip L. Rockey,** 136 Spring St., Windsor Locks, CT 06096. *Furniture repair, reproductions. Custom pieces built to order.*

YANTIC: **Meinleim Company,** Willimantic Rd., Yantic, CT 06389 (203)889-1494. *Design and construct, primarily wood furniture and architectural wall and wall units.*

Delaware

GREENVILLE: **Michael J. Andrews,** Box 4251, Greenville, DE 19807.

MIDDLETOWN: **Carl D. Kingery,** RD 1 Box 189, Middletown, DE 19709 (302)834-7472. *Contemporary furniture design and construction.*

ODESSA: **Kitemark Reproductions,** Box 143, Odessa, DE 19730 (302)834-5115. *Eighteenth-century reproductions.*

WILMINGTON: **Vincent R. Clarke,** 2402 Landon Dr., Chalfonte, Wilmington, DE 19810 (302)478-4473. *Specialty: antique reproductions.*

Jeffrey Hatfield, T-A Mitered Corners, 303 N. Lincoln St., Wilmington, DE 19805 (302)651-3655. *Custom woodworking, traditional and contemporary designs, antique restoration and refinishing.*

R. Burdick and Son, 2 Crestwood Place, Wilmington, DE 19809 (302)762-2046.

Martin A. Smith, Sr., 2418 Marilyn Dr., Wilmington, DE 19810 (302)475-4816.

WINTERTHUR: **(65) Winterthur Museum Cabinetshop,** Route 52, Winterthur, DE 19735 (302)656-8591 (ext. 226). *Furniture conservation, traditional cabinetmaking.*

District of Columbia

Robert G. Fergerson, 3000 Cathedral Ave. N.W., Washington, DC 20008 (202)483-5710. *Sculpture, custom design.*

Eugene M. Geinzer, 1318 36th St. N.W., Washington, DC 20007 (202)337-7443. *Rockers, hinged (wooden) tables and chairs, carved lamination, custom-designed furniture.*

John Goodman, 2402 20th St. N.W., Washington, DC 20009 (202)265-6135. *Decorative joinery, creative solutions to individual problems.*

Thomas Evan Hughes, 1441 Rhode Island Ave., Washington, DC 20005 (202)234-0163. *One-man shop, contemporary designs of the highest quality, widely experienced in executive office furniture.*

David Neigus, 1443 Rhode Island Ave. N.W., Washington, DC 20005 (202)797-8733. *Custom-made hardwood furniture, contemporary designs.*

Pin Oak Design, 1766 Lanier Place N.W., Washington, DC 20009 (202)234-2156. *Custom and limited run (15-30 item run) furniture. Leaded glass.*

Florida

BOCA RATON: **Ron Christensen,** 424 N.E. 6th St., Boca Raton, FL 33432 (305)395-0168.

BOYNTON BEACH: **(72) Robert L. DeFrances,** Boynton Beach, FL 33435 (305)734-6770. *Established one-man general woodcraft shop, tables a specialty. Through galleries and by direct commission.*

CLEARWATER: **Overcashier Wood,** 1211 B Hamlet, Clearwater, FL 33515 (813)821-4780. *Only commissioned work, one piece at a time, solid wood.*

FERNANDINA BEACH: **Marshall Eubanks,** Route 2 Box 251E, Fernandina Beach, FL 32034 (904)261-6753.

Jay C. McLaughlan, Drawer B, Fernandina Beach, FL 32034. *One-off custom work.*

FORT LAUDERDALE: **James Cain,** 3118 S.W. 15th St., Fort Lauderdale, FL 33312 (305)583-0939. *Frame and intarsia panel doors and bar tops.*

Village Wood Shop, 2101 S.W. 2nd Ave., Fort Lauderdale, FL 33315 (305)763-8659. *One-of-a-kind and limited production furniture and cabinetry.*

GAINESVILLE: **Miriam Novack,** 3704 N.W. 40 St., Gainesville, FL 32606 (904)377-6480. *To reflect in wood the sensual beauty and grace found in natural forms.*

JACKSONVILLE: **Judith Gefter,** 1725 Clemson Rd., Jacksonville, FL 32217 (904)733-5498. *Design and crafting of carvings, boxes, frames and sculpture.*

KEY WEST: **Rudy Prazen,** 420 Grinnell St., Key West, FL 33040 ((305)296-4420. *Fine wood cabinets, sculpture and furniture.*

(46) Mike Whiteman, 1114 White St., Key West, FL 33040. *Artist/craftsman in wood. Custom furniture and interior architectural woodworking.*

LAKELAND: **William Longmore,** 7201 E. Rd., Lakeland, FL 33805 (813)858-7374. *Pipe organ builder, wood carvings and furniture.*

LEESBURG: **William C. Kohl,** Route 1 Box 413K, Leesburg, FL 32748 (904)728-2079.

MIAMI: **Architectural Forms, Rob Haskell,** 7206 S.W. 59 Ave., Miami, FL 33143 (305)667-5521. *Custom woodworking, cabinets, etc.*

(64) Donald Bradley Reproductions, 7100 S.W. 60th St., Miami, FL 33143 (305)667-5311. *Seventeenth, eighteenth and nineteenth-century reproductions, woodcarving, sculpture, woodturning and restoration.*

Lucas Custom Cabinets, 831 N.W. 143rd St., Miami, FL 33168 (305)681-5038. *Fine custom-designed furniture in many mediums, including wood, metals and mica.*

Ric Orgaz, 4632 S.W. 10th St., Miami, FL 33134 (305)443-1114. *Specializies in wood turnings and custom handcrafted pieces.*

(98) R.E. Pirello, Woodworking, 2025 N.W. 139th St., Miami, FL 33054 (305)681-2999. *Custom furniture, kitchens and architectural millwork design.*

Richard D.—The Designer, c/o Tom Rowe, 11061 S.W. 57 Terrace, Miami, FL 33173 (305)271-6765. *Custom handcrafted home furnishings and accessories (originals). Designer and fabricator of exhibits, sales office displays, signs and graphics. A Christian enterprise.*

Unique Concepts, Mark E. Krenz, 8816 S.W. 131st, Miami, FL 33176 (305)252-1469. *Custom furniture created from exotic hardwood with quality as a forethought.*

Wood 'n Weave, 6201 SW 112 St., Miami, FL 33156 (305)665-0370. *Specialty turned objects and artistic weaving.*

NAPLES: **Gordon R. Merrick Woodsmith,** 3754 Arnold Ave., Naples, FL 33942 (813)793-1792. *All custom work, furniture and cabinetry, contemporary to traditional.*

Rudy Mafko, 25 Queen Palm Dr., Naples, FL 33942 (813)775-5567. *Wood bowls, vases, wood sculpture.*

ORLANDO: **Manuel D. Correia,** 1826 Inkwood Court, Orlando, FL 32808 (305)295-8396. *All lathe work, specialties include goblets, bowls, cups, mallets.*

The Wee Wood Chuck, 2838 Eastern Parkway, Orlando, FL 32803 (305)629-5271. *Hand-carvings and special custom work.*

OSPREY: **Tom Roberts,** 325 Palmetto Ave., Osprey, FL 33559 (813)966-4849. *One-of-a-kind furniture and hardwood cabinets.*

PANAMA CITY: **Mike Weaber,** 3704 W. 26th Court, Panama City, FL 32405 (904)785-4718. *Sword canes, walking sticks and other one-of-a-kind specialties utilizing black walnut, wild cherry or mahogany.*

PENSACOLA: **Dan B. Henry, DDS,** 4731 N. Davis Highway, Pensacola, FL 32503.

(131) Leonard Furniture Shop, 537 Brent Lane, Pensacola, FL 32503 (904)476-4616. *Hardwood furniture and fine art woodwork.*

H.W. Rundquist, 1302 N. 14th Ave., Pensacola, FL 32503 (904)433-4078. *Toys, utilitarian objects, furniture.*

PLANT CITY: **Heritage Wood Carving,** 1305 N. Lime St., Plant City, FL 33566 (813)752 5902. *Wood signs, decoys (primarily decorative decoys), plaques (relief carvings).*

PLANTATION: **Bruce Whitehead,** Bay D-4, 991 S. State Rd. No. 7, Plantation, FL 33317 (305)581-3880. *Anything unique and challenging in wood.*

PORT ORANGE: **Casey Connelly,** 6020 Hensel Rd., Port Orange, FL 32019 (904)761-8782. *Custom furniture and cabinets (contemporary and eighteenth century).*

PORT ST. LUCIE: **Jim Liccione, Wood Sculptor,** 168 S. W. Selva Court, Port St. Lucie, FL 33452 (305) 878-1608.

QUINCY: **Magnolia Woodworks,** 149 Virgil Way, Quincy, FL 32351 (904) 627-3884. *My designs are created with the customer's ideas and needs in mind.*

RIVIERA BEACH: **Charles H. Nielsen, Jr., dba Nordic Woodworks,** 3682 Industrial Way, Riviera Beach, FL 33404 (305) 848-8595. *Fine furnishings for home, yacht, and office. Custom design and building.*

ST. AUGUSTINE: **Bill Long,** 605 22nd St. N. Beach, St. Augustine, FL 32084 (904) 824-6924. *Small laminated, turned and sculptured bowls, boxes, etc. Furniture by commission. Imported and domestic woods.*

ST. PETERSBURG: **Eugene A. Milin,** 2010 E. Vina Del Mar, St. Petersburg, FL 33706 ((813) 367-3144. *Custom marquetry.*

Overcashier Wood, 2142 3rd Ave. N., St. Petersburg, FL 33713 (813) 821-4780. *Commissioned work, one piece at a time, solid wood.*

SANFORD: **Joe Silvestri,** 210 Melissa Court, Sanford, FL 32771 (305) 855-8341, 324-1405.

SARASOTA: **Antonio V. D'Agostino,** 2557 Arapaho St., Sarasota, FL 33581 (813) 922-1847. *Sculptured wood art objects and fine lathe work.*

John F. Dalton, 4405 17th St., Sarasota, FL 33580 (813) 371-5274. *One-of-a-kind, custom-designed and built pieces.*

Michael Madison, 1792 Northgate Blvd., Sarasota, FL 33580.

Joe Watson, 2411 Webber St., Sarasota, FL 33579 (813) 366-1426. *Custom novelties.*

TALLAHASSEE: **Bullard and Ball Inc.,** 647 McDonnell Dr., Tallahassee, FL 32304 (904) 222-0330. *Furniture, executive desks, furniture-grade architectural millwork, especially entry doors, raised-panel rooms, fireplace mantels.*

Good Vibrations, Jack D. Durbin, 2908 Garfield St., Tallahassee, FL 32301 (904) 878-2260. *Small custom items that other local workers normally turn down, one-of-a-kind items.*

Doug Haydel, Route 3 Box 579A, Tallahassee, FL 32308 (904) 893-1054. *Hand-sculpted forms made from native hardwoods.*

Mark Pelt, 1319 1-2 E. Tennessee St., Tallahassee, FL 32308 (904) 878-2826. *Furniture design and construction, architectural millwork.*

Jane K. Sussman, 1401 Ramble Brook D, Tallahassee, FL 32301 (904) 877-5912.

TAMPA: **Zane Britt,** 4605 S. Matanzas Ave., Tampa, FL 33611 (813) 837-9829. *Exotic hardwood sales, hand methods, private lessons, work with amateurs and do-it-yourselfers.*

J.S. Satterwhite, 4509 Dolphin Dr., Tampa, FL 33617 (813) 988-7098. *Functional sculpture, furniture that incorporates sculptural concepts.*

THONOTASASSA: **Thisse Woodart,** 903 Main St., Thonotosassa, FL 33592 (813) 986-3731. *Tool sharpening, tool making, bandsaw and turning specialties.*

VERO BEACH: **Arnold Banner,** 1106 Sun Villa Dr., Vero Beach, FL 32960. *Contemporary and Mediterranean designs. Functional.*

WEST PALM BEACH: **Wayne Keele,** 4613 Georgia Ave., West Palm Beach, FL 33405 (305) 655-9221.

WINTER PARK: **Robert Entwistle,** 2036 Sussex Rd., Winter Park, FL 32792 (305) 678-6555. *Furniture designer and maker.*

Georgia

ATHENS: **Robert G. Barker,** 147 Mulberry St., Athens, GA 30601 (404) 546-9848. *Appalachian dulcimers, custom construction also hand-carved figures in wood and bone.*

(19) Béla Foltin, Jr., 90 Springdale St., Athens, GA 30605 (404) 548-6752. *Carvings, furniture and carved furniture, especially Hungarian, Eastern European and Oriental.*

ATLANTA: **Carolyn G. Bell,** 341 St. Paul Ave. SE, Atlanta, GA 30312. *Custom lathe work and commissioned pieces.*

Bernier-Bragg, 500 Armour Circle NE, Atlanta, GA 30324 (404) 874-4672. *Original design, commercial and residential furniture.*

Elliott Engineering Inc., 1001 Monroe Dr. N.E., Atlanta, GA 30306 (404) 876-3737. *Antique restoration of furniture and clocks, and antique reproductions.*

George Berry Woodworking, 745 Edgewood Ave. NE, Atlanta, GA 30307 (404) 577-4433. *Custom furniture, cabinetry.*

(117) Sutherland Studios, Box 7086, Atlanta, GA 30357 (404) 688-9089. *Designer builder. A studio of carvers, turners, joiners, working the full gamut of woodworking.*

James Tolmack, 1241 Euclid Ave. NE, Atlanta, GA 30307 (404) 523-0683. *Design and limited production of wooden furniture.*

(88) David Van Nostrand, 1260 Foster St. N.W., Atlanta, GA 30318 (401) 351-2590. *Interpreta Woodworking.*

Jack Warner, 1264 Cumberland Rd. NE, Atlanta, GA 30306 (404) 872-5777. *Wood and ceramic combinations*

(174) Thomas H. Williams, 3502 Cold Spring Lane, Atlanta, GA 30341 (404) 458-3376. *Sculpture, abstract and figures, relief work (doors, kitchens), furniture.*

Wood Design, Paula Vogel Grad, 196 17th St. N.E., Atlanta, GA 30308 (404) 876-8069. *Contemporary custom design.*

CANTON: **Green's Riverbank Furniture,** Route 5 Box 21, Canton, GA 30114 (404) 479-3241.

CLAYTON: **Rabun Laminates,** Route 1, Prime Hill Dr., Clayton, GA 30525.

The Wood Shoppe, Route 1 Box 1275, Warwoman Rd., Clayton, GA 30525.

COMER: **(98) Dan Rodriguez,** 200 S. Ave., Comer, GA 30629 (404) 783-5869. *Functional designs ranging from serving trays to timber-frame structures.*

DECATUR: **Gordon E. Fowler,** 2759 Hutch Dr., Decatur, GA 30034 (404) 284-2482. *Furniture repair, refinishing, touch-up. Custom wood works.*

Ronald A. Lee, 146 Meadowood Square, Decatur, GA 30038 (404) 981-6973. *Custom-made, one-of-a-kind furniture and accessories.*

Michael Torrente, Torrente's Furniture Shop, 799 Densley Dr., Decatur, GA 30030 (404) 320-6876. *Period furniture, reproductions, architectural woodworking, turning, carving, French polishing and antique repair.*

DULUTH: **Rick Morris,** 3976 Heathmoor Court, Duluth, GA 30136 (404) 476-2149. *Small functional wood objects.*

ELBERTON: **Ricky D. Brady,** Route 3 118A, Elberton, GA 30635 (404) 283-8887. *Custom cabinets and furniture.*

MARIETTA: **(24) Joel Katzowitz,** 2398 Worchester Way, Marietta, GA 30062 (404) 973-9631. *Furniture and small accessories with an emphasis on original and functional design.*

Works With Wood, 475 Monteign Court, Marietta, GA 30060 (404) 428-8246. *Originally designed pieces using the finest of woods and traditional joinery techniques.*

MT. AIRY: **Tommy Walker, GA Pine Craftsmen,** Route 1, Mt. Airy, GA 30563 (404) 754-6451. *Early-American-style pine reproductions.*

REIDSVILLE: **Tom Colvin,** Box 1008 Lee St., Reidsville, GA 30453 (812) 557-6333. *My shop is a hobby shop, construct furniture for my home (coffee sets, clocks, tables, etc.).*

RIVERDALE: **John Gorrell Woodworking,** 7188 Whitfield Dr., Riverdale, GA 30296 (404) 996-7596. *Custom woodwork to your specifications. Contemporary and reproduction work.*

ST. SIMONS ISLAND: **Pete Nichol,** 1500 Demere Rd., St. Simons Island, GA 31522 (912) 638-5063. *Custom furniture, wood sculpture.*

SAVANNAH: **(55) Gregory W. Guenther,** 418 E. State St., Savannah, GA 31401 (912) 233-5238. *Furniture and design by commission.*

Hawaii

HAWAII: **R. Tai Lake,** Box 584, Holualoa, Hawaii, HI 96725 (808) 324-1598. *Custom koa furniture. Architectural detailing both in shop and on site.*

Robert Shepherd, Box 166, Honokaa, Hawaii, HI 96727 (808) 775-0075.

Peter A. Lee, 2222 Kalakana Ave. 1216, Honolulu, Hawaii, HI 96815 (808) 922-3355. *Commissions only.*

Grant W. Merritt, dba Sawdust and Mud, 3259 Huelani Dr., Honolulu, Hawaii, HI 96822 (808) 988-7233. *Custom-designed furniture, woodwork and ceramics.*

(31) Roger Worldie, 525 Cummins St., Honolulu, Hawaii, HI 96814 (808) 735-3963 or (808) 537-2642. *Flexible design capabilities utilizing rare Hawaiian woods cut and seasoned by us.*

Bill Zimmerman, 1188 Fort St. Mall, Honolulu, Hawaii, HI 96813 (908) 526-0602. *Interior millwork, cabinetry, doors and furniture.*

(157) Bill Irwin, Solid Arts & Design, Box 1309, Pahoa, Hawaii, HI 96778 (808) 965-8530. *Woodwork and objects featuring laminated designs, architectural crafts, original designs in furniture and interiors.*

MAUI: **Steve Hynson,** 350 Kanoloa Ave., Kahului, Maui, HI 96732 (808) 244-0888. *Custom furniture and accessories.*

(119) Takeo Omuro, 102 Haleakala Hwy., Kahului, Maui, HI 96732 (808) 877-6039. *General woodworking shop. Cabinets, furniture, reproductions, repair, refinishing, wood turning.*

William J. Robertson, Box 88, Kula, Maui, HI 96790 (808) 878-6188. *High-quality handcrafted furniture and accessories of Hawaiian hardwoods.*

OAHU: **Rod Narusaki,** 47-407 Hui Iwa St., Kaneohe, Oahu, HI 96744 (808) 239-6461. *Specializing in fine koa wood furniture of traditional and contemporary design using detailed joinery construction.*

(30) Wilkinson Company, 911 Palm Place, Wahiawa, Oahu, HI 96786 (808) 621-5377. *Catalog and custom furniture, specializing in the use of Hawaiian hardwoods.*

Idaho

BAYVIEW: **(185) Edwin Fulwider,** Lakeview Landing, Bayview, ID 83803. *Wood sculpture (constructions) of all kinds, many religious subjects for churches.*

BOISE: **Charles Eckenrode,** 4414 Freemont, Boise, ID 83706. *Furniture, fireplace mantels, lathe turning, light millwork, finish carpentry.*

Dennis C. Hammond, 3310 McCormick Way, Boise, ID 83709 (208) 362-9324.

Jim Schaffer, 229 1-2 N. Atlantic, Boise, ID 83706 (208) 342-5404. *Bookcases, hutches, desks, chairs, tables and general cabinetry.*

Michael T. Smith, 2160 S. Pond, Boise, ID 83705 (208) 375-0371. *Custom and ornate furniture of all sorts made to order.*

COEUR d'ALENE: **Philip A. Margraff Woodworking,** 923 N. 12th St., Coeur d'Alene, ID 83814. *Interiors, furniture, cabinets in hardwood.*

FRUITVALE: **Kevin Gray, Trail Creek Woodworks,** Box 34, Fruitvale, ID 83620. *Chairs, stools, small tables, carved utensils. Hand-tool oriented.*

HAILEY: **Bradford Custom Woodworking,** Star Route Triumph, Hailey, ID 83333 (208) 788-3727. *Stairway specialties, doors, furniture, finish woodworking.*

(44) Dennis J. Fitzgerald, Box 1291, Hailey, ID 83333 (208) 788-3633. *I integrate all aspects of hardwood interiors (cabinets, furniture, trim), blending wood for accent and detailing.*

IDAHO FALLS: **Hemperly's,** 4270 Greenwillow Lane, Idaho Falls, ID 83401 (208) 523-9866. *Functional art pieces in wood from sculpture to vases.*

Brent Turner, 230 5th St., Idaho Falls, ID 83401 (208) 524-4739. *Custom furniture and cabinets (including kitchens). One-of-a-kind. Your design or mine.*

KELLOGG: **Harry G. Sommers,** Sunshine Star Route, Kellogg, ID 83837 (208) 786-6681. *Specialties are mineral display cases and custom-built items for business establishments.*

MOSCOW: **(183) Steve Bomkamp,** c/o Bill Moore, 812 W. A St., Moscow, ID 83843 (208) 882-0654.

Edward A. Reinstein, 440 E. 8th, Moscow, ID 83843. *Custom-design furniture, furniture restoration.*

POCATELLO: **(22) In the Woods, Tim Zikratch,** 322 E. Whitman, Pocatello, ID 83201 (208) 233-4003.

REXBURG: **Mill Hollow Woodworks,** 310 Mill Hollow Dr., Rexburg, ID 83440 (208) 356-5074. *Wood turning, containers, boxes, one-of-a-kind designs. Domestic and exotic woods.*

Scott Samuelson, 213 E. 200 S., Rexburg, ID 83440 (208) 356-4217.

SAGLE: **Christopher Hecht,** Route 1 Box 213, Sagle, ID 83860 (208) 263-9363. *Furniture, doors, architectural design, millwork, hardwoods.*

SAMUELS: **(181) Myles W. Hougen, Woodcarver,** Route 1 Box 318C, Samuels, ID 83862 (208) 263-1778. *Design and construction sculpture, murals, interiors, exteriors, log homes.*

SUN VALLEY: **(147) The Joiners,** Box 1250, Sun Valley, ID 83353 (208) 726-9742. *General contracting with an emphasis in woodworking excellence.*

TWIN FALLS: **Ronn Phillips,** 353 4th Ave. E, Twin Falls, ID 83301 (208) 734-7382. *Design to fit customers taste and use.*

Richard E. Wilkin, 537 Parkway Circle, Twin Falls, ID 83301 (208) 734-1299. *Custom woodworking (furniture).*

Wilson's Planing Mill & Cabinet Shop, 1623 Eldridge Avenue, Twin Falls, ID 83301 (208) 733-2329. *Custom fine woodwork. Furniture, cabinets, doors, windows, moldings, woodturnings. Custom millwork, furniture restoration.*

VICTOR: **(147) D.L. Trapp, Woodworking & Design,** Box 182, Victor, ID 83455 (208)' 787-2752. *Original, one-of-a-kind pieces, sets and suites in exotic and domestic hardwoods.*

Illinois

ARLINGTON HEIGHTS: **John Bussert,** 725 N. Highland, Arlington Heights, IL 60004. (312) 394-1360. *Custom traditional cabinet work, and furniture.*

Larry D. Olson, 2603 N. Ridge, Arlington Heights, IL 60004. *Clocks, toys, made-to-order requests.*

CARBONDALE: **Michael Meadows,** 605 W. Freeman, Carbondale, IL 62901 (618) 457-2075. *Custom-built unusual acoustic instruments.*

CARPENTERSVILLE: **L.J. Schultz,** 1221 Sacramento, Carpentersville, IL 60110 (312) 428-4857. *Dollhouses, Early American furniture.*

CARY: **Steve Schwartz, Designer Craftsman,** 271 Country Commons Rd., Cary, IL 60013 (312) 639-8989. *Architectural, custom woodwork and purely sculptural forms. Applications requiring unique and creative designs requested.*

CHICAGO: **John A. Baca,** 1414-B W. Sherwin, Chicago, IL 60626. *Custom-designed and built furniture of moderate size.*

Joseph Bagel, 6532 W. Palatine Ave., Chicago, IL 60631 (312) 775-6825. *Free-form carving.*

Edward J. Barry, 1041 W. Oakdale, Chicago, IL 60657 (312) 472-6660. *Animal plant and figurative sculptural and traditional ornamental carving for art, architectural and industrial uses.*

(72) Glenn Gordon, 3523 N. Lincoln Ave., Chicago, IL 60657 (312) 243-3009. *Furniture and sculpture, mainly speculative one-of-a-kind. Commissions accepted.*

John F. Klemundt, 3313 Irving Park Rd., Chicago, IL 60618 (312) 478-1212. *Miniatures, trucks.*

(63) Mark S. Levin, Levin Furniture Design, 3523 Lincoln Ave., Chicago, IL 60657 (312) 883-1151. *The goal of my work is to make beautiful and sensual furniture.*

Joseph Majer, 3238 N. Seminary St., Chicago, IL 60657 (312) 528-6918. *Cabinet work, custom trim and fine woodwork.*

P.C. Baczek Company, 2437 W. Cuyler, Chicago, IL 60618 (312) 583-2368. *Carpenty, remodeling, woodworking.*

Lee Weitzman, 691 N. Sangamon, Chicago, IL 60622 (312) 243-3009. *Wooden objects, furniture and sculpture.*

COAL VALLEY: **Creations in Wood,** 8026 49th St. Ct., Coal Valley, IL 61240 (309) 799-3516. *Hardwood gifts and custom furniture.*

DeKALB: **Douglas Hicks, DeKalb High School,** 1515 S. 4th St., DeKalb, IL 60115 (815) 758-7431. *Lathe-turned bowls, contemporary furniture, furniture repair.*

ELDORADO: **Billy Briddick,** Douglas Ave., Eldorado, IL 62930 (618) 273-5073. *Eighteenth-century-style reproductions.*

EVANSTON: **Kenneth Svenson,** 800 Greenwood, Evanston, IL 60201.

FLOSSMOOR: **G. Russell Clowes,** 1309 Braeburn Rd., Flossmoor, IL 60422 (312) 957-0651. *Solid-wood furniture. Currently making six identical chairs of cherry.*

GALESBURG: **(128) Arthur E. Dameron,** 1248 Beecher, Galesburg, IL 61401 (309) 342-3252. *Small antiques repaired, instruction to those wishing to learn woodworking.*

Tom Wisshack, 1191 Willard St., Galesburg, IL 61401.

GLEN ELLYN: **Fred R. Nauert,** Box 322, Glen Ellyn, IL 60137. *Handcrafted wooden clocks, American hardwoods only, naturally finished to accent the wood grain.*

GRANITE CITY: **Lloyd Miller, Sr.,** 3940 Lake St., Granite City, IL 62040 (618) 931-0561. *Custom woodworking of all types (except for cabinetmaking) and antique furniture restoration. By appointment only.*

HAMILTON: **Alan Curtis, Oakwood Antiques,** 1890 Keokuk St., Hamilton, IL 62341 (217) 847-2648. *Antique furniture restoration, custom-made new furniture.*

HARRISBURG: **Jenner Works,** 410 E. Church St., Harrisburg, IL 62946 (618) 252-4420. *Flitches, billets, handcrafted furniture and home accessories.*

HARVARD: **William Bittner,** 6020 County Line Rd., Harvard, IL 60033 (815) 569-2431.

HIGHLAND PARK: **H.M. Orloff,** 1181 Lincoln So., Highland Park, IL 60035 (312) 432-5956. *Custom, one-of-a-kind contemporary furniture. Marquetry and fine veneers a specialty.*

HINDSBORO: **Stephen Litchfield,** Box 194, Hindsboro, IL 61930 (217) 346-2203.

HUDSON: **David E. Bloom,** 501 S. W. St., Hudson, IL 61748 (309) 726-1257. *Turning, carving, cabinets, laminated free forms.*

LaGRANGE: **Charles Wilkin,** 329 S. 7th Ave., LaGrange, IL 60525 (312) 354-1561.

LOCKPORT: **Jason Failing,** 926 McKinley Court, Lockport, IL 60441 (815) 838-0298. *Wood sculpture, large or small forms.*

Preston Wakeland, 14319 High Rd., Lockport, IL 60441 (815) 838-1285. *Custom solid-wood furniture, cabinets.*

LOMBARD: **James Q. Buffenmyer,** 19 W. 124 Rochdale, Lombard, IL 60148 (312) 627-8444. *Musical instruments, particularly guitars and dulcimers. Also wooden wall hangings.*

METAMORA: **Robert A. Riesselman,** Route 1 Robbinswood, Metamora, IL 61548 (309) 367-2590. *Jewelry, silverware, boxes, game boards.*

MT. VERNON: **James Wielt,** Route 6 Tolle Rd., Mt. Vernon, IL 62864 (618) 242-3628. *Artistic turned bowls, jewelry boxes.*

OAK PARK: **David Orth,** 111 S. Ridgeland, Oak Park, IL 60302 (312) 383-4399. *Freestanding household furniture.*

PARK FOREST: **Rev. William Lankton,** 204 Kentucky, Park Forest, IL 60466 (312) 747-8065.

PARK RIDGE: **Clifford C. Sorensen,** 1805 Glenview Ave., Park Ridge, IL 60068 (312) 825-1840.

PEORIA: **(165) Fred Maier,** 1501 W. Barker, Peoria, IL 61606 (309) 673-0028. *Boxes, furniture, restoration carpentry.*

ROCKFORD: **Thos. A. Moyer, Cabinetmaker,** RR 4 144 Riverside Rd., Rockford, IL 61111 (815) 885-3846. *Cabinets, tables, turnings.*

John L. Roth, 1018 Starview Dr., Rockford, IL 61108 (815) 397-1122. *Custom crafting in native woods, basswood plates and bowls for tole and rosemaling painting.*

ST. CHARLES: **James R. Miles,** 43 W. 370 Foxhill Court, St. Charles, IL 60174 (312) 365-5223. *Furniture, games (chess, backgammon, pente, cribbage, kensington).*

SOUTH HOLLAND: **C.A. Welch,** 15058 Naughton Dr., S. Holland, IL 60473 (312) 331-8354. *Cradles, cabinets, candlesticks made from oak, cherry and walnut.*

SPRINGFIELD: **Aspen Wood Design Inc.,** 1701 S. Seventh St., Springfield, IL 62703 (217) 528-2183. *Custom-designed cabinets, tables and desks.*

Gene Shutt, 24 Circle Dr., Springfield, IL 62703 (217) 529-1457. *Furniture and gift items.*

SYCAMORE: **John R. Beck,** 328 Somonauk, Sycamore, IL 60178 (815) 895-9847.

Der Holtzmacher Ltd., 337 N. Locust, Sycamore, IL 60178 (815) 895-4887. *Originally designed fine wood furniture, specializing in cabinetry, paneling and doors.*

TOLEDO: **George L. Reisner,** Route 1 Box 112, Toledo, IL 62468 (217) 849-3342.

TOLONO: **Jerry Ready,** Route 1, Tolono, IL 61880 (217) 485-5205. *Hand-held mirrors, walnut and cherry slab tables, boxes and chests.*

WHEATON: **Bob Miller,** 1002 Childs, Wheaton, IL 60187 (312) 668-8841. *Lounge chairs, small production items.*

WILMETTE: **William P. Zeh,** 1340 Ashland Ave., Wilmette, IL 60091 (312) 251-7495. *Furniture of original design.*

WOOD DALE: **Otus Woodwork Company,** Box 634, Wood Dale, IL 60191 (312) 766-5722. *Custom furniture (office and residential), light mitre folding.*

Indiana

BLOOMINGDALE: **Glen Summers,** Route 1, Bloomingdale, IN 47832. *Traditional American objects. Hollowing and lathe work.*

BLOOMINGTON: **Clarity Designs,** 4895 Earl Young Rd., Bloomington, IN 47401 (812) 339-6369. *Custom furnishings.*

Landergren Woodworking, 3960 N. Kinser Pike, Bloomington, IN 47401 (812) 339-0467. *Commissioned and limited edition furniture, decorative objects, functional accessories.*

Walter L. Owens, MD, 4531 Sheffield, Bloomington, IN 47401 (812) 332-5119.

BRAZIL: **(73) Renaissance Woodworks,** Route 13 Box 293, Brazil, IN 47834 (317) 344-1766. *Design, one-of-a-kind furniture, residential architecture.*

CARMEL: **David H. Jefferis,** 10505 Fergus Ave., Carmel, IN 46032 (317) 872-4739. *I specialize in custom contemporary hardwood furniture, wood turnings and accessories.*

DECATUR: **(182) Dean Butler,** 128 Harvester Lane, Decatur, IN 46733 (219) 724-4810. *Wood sculpture.*

ELKHART: **(160) Gowdy Woodworks,** 185 Gage Ave., Elkhart, IN 46516 (219) 264-4709. *Custom hardwood furniture, fireplace mantels, and carving for churches, offices and homes.*

ELLETTSVILLE: **Stanford C. Luce,** 815 W. Association St., Ellettsville, IN 47429 (812) 876-4865. *Fine quality handcrafted hardwood furniture by custom order.*

FORT WAYNE: **Gerald Isch,** 2008 Kensington Blvd., Fort Wayne, IN 46805 (219) 422-9025 or 493-3585. *Custom cabinetwork, built-ins and finish carpentry.*

Raymond L. Lauritsen, 5035 Trier Rd., Fort Wayne, IN 46815 (219) 485-2295. *Stereo equipment cabinets, oak bar stools (24 in. and 30 in.), book shelves, etc.*

GOSHEN: **Gene Short,** 315 N. Indiana Ave., Goshen, IN 46526 (219) 533-1566. *Handmade, one-of-a-kind functional and decorative art pieces.*

HOBART: **Rainbow's End Woodworking,** 950 S. Wisconsin St., Hobart, IN 46342 (219) 942-3770. *Custom woodworking, toys, and functional items.*

INDIANAPOLIS: **(167) Stephen Bradshaw,** 3605 N. Central Ave., Indianapolis, IN 46205.

Jack R. Brock, 11325 E. Fall Creek Rd., Indianapolis, IN 46256 (317) 849-1873.

D.W. Smith's Woodworks, 7201 N. Temple Ave., Indianapolis, IN 46240 (317) 251-8399. *Architectural woodworks and carved signage, individual custom pieces.*

Milton F. Johnston, 4359 S. Shelby St., Indianapolis, IN 46227 (317) 783-4207. *Music boxes and toys.*

Kasnak Designs, 5630 E. Washington St., Indianapolis, IN 46219 (317) 357-4936. *Veneering, bent laminates, inlay marquetry, dining chairs, tables, cabinets.*

(74) Phillip Tennant Designs, 439 E. 49th St., Indianapolis, IN 46205 (317) 283-7214.

Stephen W. Tyra, 5416 E. 11th St., Indianapolis, IN 46219 (317) 357-5770. *Toys, jewelry boxes, earring trees.*

LAFAYETTE: **Lawrence F. Duell, Jr.,** 244 Pineview Lane, Lafayette, IN 47905 (317) 447-2235.

Douglas V. Garwood, 2119 Perrine St., Lafayette, IN 47904 (317) 742-5576. *Cabinet making, furniture making, architectural woodworking and small production runs.*

Robert R. Leavitt, 1821 E. 750 S., Lafayette, IN 47905 (317) 538-2917. *Green wood carving, furniture repair.*

W.J. Studden, 140 Knox Dr., W. Lafayette, IN 47906 (317) 463-1947.

MARION: **Alexander Carpentry & Cabinetmaking,** 619 W. 7th St., Marion, IN 46952 (317) 664-8323. *Custom kitchen, vanity, and odd placed cabinets. Commercial teller stands, desks, furniture and banjoes.*

MISHAWAKA: **Daniel W. Locke,** 2304 Trailridge S., Mishawaka, IN 46544 (219) 256-1391. *Custom-designed and built contemporary furniture, antique reproductions, repairs.*

MUNCIE: **(39) Maranatha Woodmen, Gary S. Prater,** Route 6 Box 529, Muncie, IN 47302 (317) 759-6898. *Museum-quality fine furniture from new and original designs influenced by eighteenth-century styles.*

PORTAGE: **Jeff Nixon,** 5974 Marbella, Portage, IN 46368 (219) 762-6044. *Custom furniture and woodworking.*

RICHMOND: **James Sieger,** 1110 Abington Pike, Richmond, IN 47374 (317) 966-3142. *Custom furniture, architectural woodwork, sculpture and painting.*

TERRE HAUTE: **Jeffrey S. Morgan,** Indiana State Univ., Main Technology 206, Terre Haute, IN 47809.

UNIONVILLE: **Michael Evans,** 8787 N. Slippery Elm Shoot Rd., Unionville, IN 47468 (812) 988-7879. *Custom designing and building hardwood furniture and carving.*

Iowa

ALGONA: **J.W. Enterprise,** 1015 N. Minnesota, Algona, IA 50511 (515) 295-2729. *Unique, limited edition, one-of-a-kind custom woodworking. Includes 3-D carvings, furniture, structural, etc.*

AMES: **(170) Michael S. Chinn,** 158 College of Design, Iowa State Univ., Ames, IA 50011 (515) 294-6724. *One-of-a-kind and limited production furniture and accessories.*

Neth Hass, 1401 Georgia, Ames, IA 50010 (515) 292-7970. *Small carved or turned articles, boxes, clocks.*

R. Kirby Poole, 2316 Ferndale Ave., Ames, IA 50010 (515) 232-2654.

CEDAR RAPIDS: **Kim Darrow, Independent Design Assoc.,** 1871 Ellis Blvd. N.W., Cedar Rapids, IA 52405 (319) 363-0537. *Jewelry and custom boxes, sculptured furniture, doors, spiral stairways, cabinets, gunstocks.*

Leon Lueck, Furniture Maker, 4913 Midway Dr. N.W., Cedar Rapids, IA 52405 (319) 396-4494. *Furniture, cabinetry, one-of-a-kind items on a commissioned basis.*

Scott Squires, 2123 Mt. Vernon Rd. S.E., Cedar Rapids, IA 52403 (319) 363-1149. *Wood turning, furniture, carving.*

CRAWFORDSVILLE: **(111) Susan M. Patterson,** Box 45 Route 2, Crawfordsville, IA 52621 (319) 658-2731. *American Chippendale and American Windsor reproductions, select contemporary pieces.*

DAVENPORT: **Dennis Kirby,** 2030 M. Elsie, Davenport, IA 52804 (319) 386-4342. *I do sculpture and custom-designed and crafted jewelry boxes, picture frames, etc.*

Brent J. Starkey, 2930 W. 1st, Davenport, IA 52804 (319) 324-0244.

Vandecar Woodworking, 1232 W. 4th St., Davenport, IA 52802 (319) 323-2303. *Fine furniture and cabinets built to your specifications.*

DECORAH: **Rob Bolson,** Quarry Rd., Decorah, IA 52101. *Containers, sculpture.*

Ken Munkel Woodworking, 1001 Maiden Lane, Decorah, IA 52101 (319) 382-4304. *Custom furniture, cabinetry, wood flooring, wood countertops, and window sash.*

ELGIN: **Don's Woodworking,** 124 Center St., Elgin, IA 52141 (319) 426-5745. *Custom work.*

HAMPTON: **Paul Wullbrandt,** Route 1, Hampton, IA 50441 (515) 456-3580. *Specializes in fine woodwork commissions, etched glass and combinations of the two.*

IOWA CITY: **Communia Woods,** 1515 Broadway St., Iowa City, IA 52240 (319) 338-5748. *A collective shop, builds custom hardwood furniture. Futon furniture is a specialty.*

George Ellis Furniture, 631 S. Van Buren St., Iowa City, IA 52240 (319) 337-6415. *Professional office furniture.*

McGREGOR: **McGregor Woodworks Inc.,** 226 Main St., McGregor, IA 52157 (319) 873-2087. *One-of-a-kind and limited production furniture and case work, lacquer work, design.*

MANNING: **Clarus Heithoff,** Route 1, Manning, IA 51455 (712) 653-2316. *Antique toy cars and trains, candleholders, picture frames, child rockers, spoon racks and silverware chests.*

MUSCATINE: **Bruce A. Strunk,** Route 3 Box 434, Muscatine, IA 52761 (319) 263-5062. *New and original-reproduction long rifles and custom woodworking and chainsaw milling.*

PERRY: **Hickory Barck Shop,** 1720 W. 5th, Perry, IA 50220 (515) 465-2183. *Unique pieces, bending, laminating, antique restoration, sign carving.*

WEST DES MOINES: **Walter Elder, Jr., Elder's Mfg. Co.,** Box 65322, West Des Moines, IA 50265 (515) 223-4653. *Custom-made furniture and cabinets, wood specialties, toys and clock cases.*

Kansas

AUGUSTA: **(17) Terry L. Evans,** Route 2 Box 97, Augusta, KS 67010 (316) 775-5909. *Laminated and inlaid buckles, mirrors, containers, and small liturgical commissions.*

Steve McRae, 1412 Spencer, Augusta, KS 67010 (316) 775-3445. *Bent-wood contemporary designs.*

BURR OAK: **Kelly McNichols,** Route 1, Burr Oak, KS 66936 (913) 587-4727.

DODGE CITY: **Gregory R. Miller,** 707 Hillcrest, Dodge City, KS 67801 (316) 225-4391. *One-of-a-kind furniture.*

HUTCHINSON: **(160) Livingston Foundry and Studio,** 1517 W. 4th, Hutchinson, KS 67501 (316) 663-2947. *Custom furniture usually featuring carving and cast-bronze hardware of my own design.*

IOLA: **Steven A. Sell,** 317 N. Buckeye, Iola, KS 66749 (316) 365-7817.

LENEXA: **H.R. Hommel,** 8417 Meadow Lane, Lenexa, KS 66220 (816) 523-3227. *Reproduction, repair of primitive and Early American furniture. Custom parts, turning, all woods.*

MAIZE: **The Wood Shop,** 1128 W. 53 N., Maize, KS 67101 (316) 722-5539. *Custom-design furniture, products.*

MANHATTAN: **Eugene G. Wendt,** 704 Brierwood Dr., Manhattan, KS 66502 (913) 537-2848. *Jewelry and blanket chests, general case work.*

NATOMA: **John Hachmeister, Sculptor-Craftsman,** Route 1, Natoma, KS 67651 (916) 863-2982. *Sculpture in wood and cast and fabricated metals.*

SALINA: **Herbert F. Morgenthaler, Jr.,** 905 S. 10th, Salina, KS 67401 (913) 825-4908. *Development and expansion of design ideas in conjunction with customers wants and needs.*

SHAWNEE MISSION: **R.C. Williams, Cabinetmaker,** Box 6523, Shawnee Mission, KS 66206 (913) 381-7347. *Open-planed natural finishes, one-of-a-kind and limited production items, special function items.*

TOPEKA: **James 'J.R.' Johnson,** 3109 Bryant, Topeka, KS 66605 (913) 267-5383. *Large figure carving (3 ft. to 20 ft.) and stump, hedge and tree sculpture.*

WICHITA: **Doug Emrich, Wheat Seed Wood Shop,** 4700 S. Greenwood, Wichita, KS 67216 (316) 524-5420. *Traditional reproductions, custom orders, spiral and custom staircases, all hardwood construction.*

(45) Robert Goodman, 1520 E. Fortuna 3, Wichita, KS 67216 (316) 522-3873.

Mark E. Jacobs, 928 N. Doris, Wichita, KS 67212 (316) 945-5659.

Prairiewood Designs, 921 E. Mt. Vernon, Wichita, KS 67211 (316) 264-8498. *Cabinetry, furniture, woodenware.*

Kentucky

BEATTYVILLE: **Wood Creations by Jerry Hollon,** Route 2 Box 157, Beattyville, KY 41311 (606)464-3560. *Contemporary and traditional furniture designs in hardwoods.*

BEREA: **(38) Warren A. May, Woodworker,** 114 Main St., Berea, KY 40403 (606)986-9293. *Fine furniture of classical and original design, also Appalachian mountain dulcimers. Workshop and gallery located on the College Square, Berea, KY.*

BOONEVILLE: **(164, 165) Ken Walker,** c/o Morris Fork Crafts, Route 1 Box 95E4, Booneville, KY 41314 (606)398-2194. *Workshops and classes on basic fine woodwork techniques, use of hand tools.*

BOWLING GREEN: **Ed Craft, The Craft Family Custom Furniture,** Route 2 Box 182, Bowling Green, KY 42101 (502)781-6544. *Custom designing and making of traditional and modern furniture. Designer furniture for shows and exhibitions.*

Frank M. Pittman, Pittman Guitars, 644 Cottonwood Dr., Bowling Green, KY 42101 (502)842-2286. *Handmade acoustic guitars (classical and steel string).*

Reproduction Furniture Heirlooms, 1005 Roselawn Way, Bowling Green, KY 42101 (502)781-5144. *Reproduction furniture and clocks.*

COVINGTON: **Robert Fry,** 1606 Greenup, Covington, KY 41011 (606)291-7053. *Wood sculptor, woodcarving.*

EDMONTON: **James Yule,** Box 77A Route 3, Edmonton, KY 42129. *Individually designed furniture, woodcarving, sculpture, silversmithing, horse gear.*

FRANKFORT: **Ron Brown,** 501 Pawnee Trail, Frankfort, KY 40601 (502)695-3451. *Original handmade hardwood furniture.*

HARRODSBURG: **Calvin M. Shewmaker III,** 606 Cane Run, Harrodsburg, KY 40330 (606)734-9926. *Eighteenth and ninteenth-century century furniture and house joinery by hand.*

KUTTAWA: **M. Russell Parrott,** Box 127, Kuttawa, KY 42055 (502)388-7835. *Realistic and decorative woodcarvings of birds, animals, full-size indians, carousel horses. Full size and smaller.*

LEXINGTON: **Bluegrass Woodworking of Kentucky Inc.,** 1016 Rushwood Court, Lexington, KY 40511 (606)259-0483. *Custom wood and laminate fixtures and furniture. Design services offered for commercial and residential commissions.*

George E. Neel, 709 Sunset Dr., Lexington, KY 40502 (606)269-6780. *Handmade furniture, cabinetry and accessories. Contemporary designs with traditional joinery.*

Ed Sutton, Cowart & Co. Custom Cabinets, 926 National Ave., Lexington, KY 40502 (606)255-3703. *Custom cabinets, fine furniture.*

Lynn B. Sweet, 207 Fine Arts Building, Art Dept., Univ. of Kentucky, Lexington, KY 40506. *Original design contemporary office and residential furniture.*

Lynn Winter, 3436 Simcoe Court, Lexington, KY 40502 (606)269-7489.

Woodgoods, Don Coxe, 936 Manchester St., Lexington, KY 40503 (606)277-1786. *Furniture, architectural specialty work.*

LOUISVILLE: **Benchcraft,** 810 Baxter Ave., Louisville, KY 40204 (502)589-7929. *Contemporary furniture designed and made primarily of solid wood.*

Kinsella Custom Woodworking, 7204 York River Rd., Louisville, KY 40214 (502)366-8707. *Fine handcrafted furniture of walnut and cherry.*

Patrick Lippy, 633 So. 15th St., Louisville, KY 40203 (502)581-9050. *Bent and stack lamenation, butcher block cabinet tops, kitchen cabinets, wall units and commercial furniture.*

(100) Michael Schmitt, 1408 Community Way, Louisville, KY 40222 (502)425-1246.

MONTICELLO: **Hollow Woodworks, Edwin A. Wolf, Jr.,** Box 140 Route 2, Monticello, KY 42633 (606)348-5050.

NICHOLASVILLE: **Douglas V. Marshall,** 205 Ironwood Dr., Nicholasville, KY 40356 (606)885-3919.

PARIS: **Gwilym Adzeware,** Route 3 Box 440, Paris, KY 40361 (606)987-6225. *Hand-carved bowls, spoons and toys, turned bowls, buttermolds, candlesticks, etc.*

VERSAILLES: **Steele Hinton,** 110 Montgomery Ave., Versailles, KY 40383 (606)873-6165. *Dovetailed chests, chests-of-drawers, tables, beds. Frame-and-panel, mortise, tenon, dovetail, joinery.*

Louisiana

BATON ROUGE: **(57) Benchworks by Ford Thomas,** 3057 Zeeland St., Baton Route, LA 70808 (504)344-1026. *Custom-designed, contemporary, hardwood furniture and cabinetry, commerical and residential.*

Rick Brunner Woodcrafts, 8180 Airline Highway, Baton Rouge, LA 70815 (504)923-3011. *Custom-designed contemporary wood furniture and accessories.*

Errol J. Voinche, Cabinet Maker, 1222 Louray Dr., Baton Rouge, LA 70808 (504)766-2257. *Cabinets and furniture.*

BROUSSARD: **David Gent,** 102 E. Main St., Broussard, LA 70518 (318)837-9006. *Repair, restoration of furniture. Specialty is creating contemporary furniture.*

GONZALES: **Three Cedars Cabinet Shop,** Route 1, Bluff Rd., Box 601R, Gonzales, LA 70737 (504)673-4940. *Fine furniture, fine cabinet work, custom kitchen cabinets.*

HAMMOND: **C. Roy Blackwood, Sculptor,** 410 N. Hazel, Hammond, LA 70401 (504)542-4368. *Hand-carved carousel figures, tobacconist figures, figureheads, Americana.*

LAFAYETTE: **Bobby Leonard, Designer Craftsman,** 200 Cameron, Lafayette, LA 70501 (318)237-2967. *Custom-designed quality woodwork.*

NEW ORLEANS: **(117) Lofty Notions, Susan LosCalzo,** 3800 Dryades St., New Orleans, LA 70115 (504)895-4421. *Built-in lofts, bolt-together lofts, beds, wall units, computer furniture, playground equipment, signs and other custom pieces.*

PRAIRIEVILLE: **James Peter Verkaik Fine Wood Work,** Route 4 Box 314-Highway 42, Prairieville, LA 70769. *Commissioned pieces of all types, furniture repair, and interior specialty wood work.*

SHREVEPORT: **M. LaMoyne Batten,** 2021 Dulverton Court, Shreveport, LA 71118 (318)688-4294. *Primarily art-oriented woodworking projects.*

Maine

BANGOR: **Dovetails Plus, Alfred P. Bourgoin,** 19 Frances St., Bangor, ME 04401. *Post-and-beam construction, one-of-a-kind furniture; ceramic tile.*

BIDDEFORD: **James McCarthy,** 5 Amherst St., Biddeford, ME 04005 (207)283-0458. *Originally designed furniture and piano restoration.*

BLUE HILL FALLS: **Jay Peters, Woodworker,** Route 175, Blue Hill Falls, ME 04615 (207)374-2760. *Custom furniture with quiet and refined elegance that slowly reveals subtlety of design and construction.*

BOOTHBAY: **(69) Anthony Giachetti, Cabinetmaker,** Box 504, E. Boothbay, ME 04544 (207)633-3740. *Desks, tables, cabinets designed and made by Anthony Giachetti. Gallery open by appointment.*

BOWDOINHAM: **Eric A. McFarland,** Route 138, Old Post Rd., Bowdoinham, ME 04008 (201)737-2834. *Custom furniture and cabinetry.*

CAPE ELIZABETH: **Norman S. Clark,** 97 Fowler Rd., Cape Elizabeth, ME 04106 (207)799-5651. *Fine custom cabinetry, kitchens and case work, furniture, mirror frames and antique restoration.*

DAMARISCOTTA: **Chretien Woodworks,** Water St., Damariscotta, ME 04543 (207)563-3992. *Custom furniture and woodworking, Chinese domestic, and Queen Anne.*

Malcolm L. Ray, Egypt Rd., Damariscotta, ME 04543 (207)563-3802. *Period reproductions, Shaker and clocks in pine and hardwoods, on order only.*

ELIOT: **Edward E. Houde,** 32 Houde Rd., Eliot, ME 03903 (207)748-3268.

ISLE AU HAUT: **John D. DeWitt,** Isle Au Haut, ME 04645. *Bowls and turnings, free-form stools, benches, tables, carvings.*

KENNEBUNK: **(90) Peter Spadone,** 29 Park St., Kennebunk, ME 04043 (207)985-2152.

KENNEBUNKPORT: **Edward Stone Gallery,** High St., Kennebunkport, ME 04046 (207)967-5916. *Design and build, mostly in hardwoods, mostly formal furniture, on commission.*

KEZAR FALLS: **James M. O'Neil,** RFD 1 Box 191, Kezar Falls, ME 04047 (207)625-8603. *Custom furniture and cabinets.*

LAGRANGE: **R.N. Winters, Cabinetmaker,** Bennoch Rd., Route 16, Lagrange, ME 04453 (207)943-7972. *Custom furniture and cabinetry, special millwork.*

LIBERTY: **(11) Bear Woodworking,** Box 220 Route 1, Liberty, ME 04949 (207)845-2756. *Turning, custom furniture and native wood sales and custom drying.*

MADAWASKA: **Fernand V. Cyr,** Box 447, Madawaska, ME 04756 (207)728-4697.

MT. DESERT: **(145) Joseph Tracy Woodworks,** Route 102, Mt. Desert, ME 04660 (207)244-7360. *Limited production and contemporary commissioned furniture of simple line.*

NEW GLOUCESTER: **(143) C.H. Becksvoort,** Box 12, New Gloucester, ME 04260. *Children's sleighs, sleds, horse-drawn sleighs, custom desks, custom woodwork of all type. Consulting and teaching.*

(97) Stewart Wurtz, Box 532, New Gloucester, ME 04260.

NORTH SULLIVAN: **Pennypacker Wood Design,** Box 75, North Sullivan, ME 04664 (207)422-6895. *Furniture designed for the individual, solid-wood cabinets, interior finish design and construction.*

ORRS ISLAND: **Paul Corriveau, Cabinetmaker,** Route 1 Box 246, Orrs Island, ME 04066 (207)833-6738. *Custom designs of furniture, interior living spaces, architectural pieces.*

PORTLAND: **(65) Marc DesLauriers,** 119 Pine St., Portland, ME 04101 (207)774-4452.

J.E. Flanagan Furniture Makers, 60 York St., Box 7101 DTS, Portland, ME 04101 (207)774-4407. *Furniture and cabinetry made to order. Short runs, wooden boat work.*

Jamie Johnston, 11 Carroll St., Portland, ME 04102 (207)773-5288. *Individually designed and limited production hardwood furniture.*

(36) Jeff Kellar, Box 4770 DTS, Portland, ME 04112 (207)773-6269. *Furniture in domestic and exotic hardwoods. Hours by appointment.*

Portland Millwork Inc., Box 3083, Portland, ME 04104 (207)839-3168. *Custom cabinets, furniture and design.*

(65) Cliff Rugg, Cabinetmaker, 40 Pleasant St., Portland, ME 04101 (207)774-5111. *Custom hardwood furniture, traditional American/English influence, Chinese and contemporary.*

Stephen Ryder, 8 N. St., Portland, ME 04101 (207)774-5299. *Made to order, electric and acoustic guitars and mandolins.*

ROCKPORT: **(37) James Lea, Cabinetmaker,** 9 W. St., Rockport, ME 04856 (207)236-3632. *Eighteenth-century American furniture, totally handcrafted and authentic in design construction and finish.*

SOUTH CHINA: **Scott's Custom Woodworking,** 961 Lakeview Dr., South China, ME 04358 (207)445-4600. *Standard furniture designs, custom orders, repair, restoration, cabinets, kitchens, offices.*

SOUTH HARPSWELL: **Mark R. Murray,** Box 380, South Harpswell, ME 04079 (207)725-7297. *Functional pieces.*

WATERVILLE: **(159) Daniel Bloomer,** c/o Woodworks, 110 Pleasant St., Waterville, ME 04901 (207)873-5865. *Fine hardwood cabinetry, furniture and architectural woodworking.*

WEST LEBANON: **(109) Donald Van Sinderen,** Box 127, West Lebanon, ME 04027 (207)658-9950.

WILTON: **(83) Hardwood Creations,** Box 736, Wilton, ME 04294 (203)645-4657. *Furniture and treen.*

YARMOUTH: **Robert Calcagni,** 4 Ryan Dr., Yarmouth, ME 04096 (207)846-3427.

Maryland

ANNAPOLIS: **Loretta Gibble,** 1424 Millwood Court, Annapolis, MD 21401 (301)757-0261.

Harvey E. Walters, 1505 Circle Dr., Annapolis, MD 21401 (301)974-6655. *Custom furniture, cabinetry, accessories.*

BALTIMORE: **Victor J. Mullan,** 4609 Schenley Rd., Baltimore, MD 21210 (301)243-1399.

Roger Sherman, 2519 Taylor Ave., Baltimore, MD 21234 (301)661-5908. *Custom-designed furniture, inlaid chairs, tables and chests.*

Stuart Sklar, 2904 Taney Rd., Baltimore, MD 21208 (301)764-2193.

James Tabeling, 4608 1-2 Roland Ave., Baltimore, MD 21210 (301)243-5119.

BETHESDA: **(21) Barry R. Yavener,** 8728 Ewing Dr., Bethesda, MD 20817 (301)530-2738.

COLLEGE PARK: **Wood 'n You,** 5827 Swarthmore Dr., College Park, MD 20740 (301)474-0692. *Custom built-ins and free-standing furniture.*

COLUMBIA: **R Wood Design,** 9150 Lambskin Lane, Columbia, MD 21045 (301)997-5026. *Complete custom design and construction of fine furniture and woodwork.*

DARNESTOWN: **Willow Woodworking, Fred Hean,** 14035 Darnestown Rd., Darnestown, MD 20878 (301)258-5273. *Custom-designed furniture and architectural woodwork.*

ELKTON: **Allen L. Romine,** 368 Little Egypt Rd., Elkton, MD 21921 (301)392-3072. *Small custom work.*

FORT WASHINGTON: **Andy Pica,** 13114 Holly Circle, Fort Washington, MD 20744 (301)292-5151. *Creativity, design and execution in meeting contemporary interior design and storage needs.*

FREDERICK: **Stephen Colby, Braddock Design,** 4926 Old National Pike, Frederick, MD 21701 (301)371-5555. *Design and construction of contemporary furniture and fixtures, church furnishings.*

T.F. Foti, 7941 W. 7th St., Frederick, MD 21701 (301)663-3096.

FROSTBURG: **Howard Parnes,** 115 Chestnut, Frostburg, MD 21532 (301)689-2787. *Musical instruments and small furniture designs.*

GLEN ECHO: **(44) Barrow Woodworks,** Glen Echo Park, Glen Echo, MD 20812 (301)229-7710.

JEFFERSON: **(130) James L. Misner,** 3616B Lander Rd., Jefferson, MD 21755 (301)834-7230. *Design and production of contemporary furniture.*

KENSINGTON: **Autumn Woodcraft, Rick Sniffin,** 4512 Saul Rd., Kensington, MD 20895 (301)493-8715. *Licensed general contractors (residential and custom commercial) specializing in high-quality carpentry and cabinetwork.*

(120) Jon Bricker, 10309 Drumm Ave., Kensington, MD 20895 (301)933-7267. *High-quality wood, metal and stained-glass design and construction.*

LAUREL: **Jerry R. Syfert,** 16128 Kenny Rd., Laurel, MD 20707.

LEONARDTOWN: **Barrister Wood Works,** 13 Magee Dr., Leonardtown, MD 20650 (301)475-5117. *Contemporary furniture, clocks, boxes, toys and accessories, and one-of-a-kind commissions.*

MOUNT AIRY: **Stapf-Crafters,** 6 E. Ridgeville Blvd., Mount Airy, MD 21771 (301)831-7339. *New furniture, repair and refinishing, general woodworking.*

NORTH EAST: **Peter Szymkowicz, Heartwood Treenworks,** 489 Hances Pt. Rd., North East, MD 21901 (301)287-5557. *Hand-carved spoons and unique sculptural bowls.*

OAKLAND: **Fine Woodwork by Mike Dehus,** 718 Oak St., Oakland, MD 21550 (301)334-1146. *One-of-a-kind custom furniture, interiors, sculpture and carvings by commission.*

OXON HILL: **Gary L. Schach-de Packh, Milton Schach,** 409 Cedar Ridge Dr., Oxon Hill, MD 20745 (301)839-2376. *Traditional furniture constructions executed in modern style.*

Selene N. Schach-de Packh, 409 Cedar Ridge Dr., Oxon Hill, MD 20745. *Semi-abstract and surrealist sculpture.*

POTOMAC: **Peter M. McMahon,** 9221 Falls Chapel Way, Potomac, MD 20854 (301)340-9476. *Contemporary and traditional custom furniture.*

ROCK HALL: **(169) Peter W. Waxter,** Route 20, Rock Hall, MD 21661 (301)639-7662. *Custom furniture and accessories handcrafted in domestic and imported hardwoods.*

ROCKVILLE: **Amazing Grain Woodworking Inc.,** 742 E. Gude Dr., Rockville, MD 20850 (301)424-4466.

Alan Pechner, The Woodcarvers Tool Chest, 404 Rutgers St., Rockville, MD 20850 (301)424-1688. *Design, carved oceanic style faces, novelties, caricatures. Teach woodcarving, sell hand-carving tools and equipment.*

Phoenix Etc., 210 N. Horners Lane, Rockville, MD 20850 (301)251-9811. *Furniture design, sculpture and carved architectural detailing.*

Ron Rae & Assocs., 649 Southlawn Lane, Rockville, MD 20852 (301)340-8844.

SALISBURY: **Michael Murrell,** 180 Roseberry Ave., Salisbury, MD 21801 (301)749-7786. *Sculptural objects, carved and bent construction, functional and nonfunctional.*

Edward E. Nock, 421 W. College Ave., Salisbury, MD 21801 (301)546-5332. *Furniture, repair and reconstruction of antiques, wood turnings, caning and rushing.*

SILVER SPRING: **Gary M. Katz,** 1920 Chapel Hill Rd., Silver Spring, MD 20906 (301)598-8670. *Custom woodworking designs, cabinetry, furniture-making, and turning.*

John S. Templin, Jr., 15110 Peach Orchard Rd., Silver Spring, MD 20904. *Small furniture pieces.*

STEVENSVILLE: **Darryle F. Inselman, The Woodchip,** 820 Monroe Manor Rd., Stevensville, MD 21666 (301)643-5085. *Nautical woodworking—anything in wood, any kind of wood.*

SYKESVILLE: **Ralph E. Martin III,** 6608 Sweet Air Lane, Sykesville, MD 21784 (301)795-2606. *Early American reproductions.*

TAKOMA PARK: **Michael Billert,** 8510 Barron St., Takoma Park, MD 20912 (301)445-4257. *Small shop for prototypes as well as mass production. Portfolio includes Hyatt Regency and MCI.*

TOWSON: **Brian De Muth,** Towson, MD 21204 (301)296-1597. *Contemporary furniture and accessories.*

LeCompte & Co., 408 E. Joppa Rd., Towson, MD 21204 (301)823-7760. *Chest pieces and looking glasses.*

UPPER MARLBORO: **Steven M. Witchey,** 16616 Clagett Landing Rd., Upper Marlboro, MD 20870. *Woodcarving (high relief and low relief), signs, plaques, frames, furniture, custom pieces and commissions.*

WESTMINSTER: **Michael O'Banion,** 211 Opal Ave., Westminster, MD 21157 (301)857-4469. *Custom design, handcrafting of fine wood furniture and other carved or inlaid pieces.*

Massachusetts

ABINGTON: **James E. Doherty,** 188 Plymouth St., Abington, MA 02351 (617)871-2083. *Traditional furniture and cabinet work for home and business.*

AGAWAM: **Richard J. Milici, Furnituremaker,** 168 Elm St., Agawam, MA 01001 (413)786-3301. *Furniture, furnishings and cabinetry made to order.*

ALLSTON: **Russell H. Riscoe,** 1334 Commonwealth Ave. 35, Allston, MA 02134 (617)232-7762. *Commissioned furniture and wooden accessories including mixed media furniture.*

AMHERST: **Richard B. Lea,** 35 Stagecoach Rd., Amherst, MA 01002 (413)253-3709. *Custom-designed furniture (solid-wood construction), turned lamps and other turned objects.*

R.B. Livington, 161 High St., Amherst, MA 01002 (413)253-5423.

(109) The Yankee Joyner, 53 Henry Steet, Amherst, MA 01002 (413)549-6640. *Formal Chippendale and Queen Anne furniture, fretted string instruments, F-model mandolins.*

ANDOVER: **Bruce H. Reitman,** RFD 1 Foster's Pond Rd., Andover, MA 01810 (617)475-1165. *Clock cases, small boxes and cabinets, wooden tools and instruments.*

ARLINGTON: **(167) Stone Design Associates,** 244 Massachusetts Ave., Arlington, MA 02174 (617)646-0733. *Custom-designed, handcrafted furniture for both home and office.*

BARRE: **(147) Howard Hastings, Woodworker,** Old Stage Rd., Barre, MA 01005 (617)355-2004. *Designing and building custom wood interiors.*

BELMONT: **Lyle D. Lemon,** 226 Beech St., Belmont, MA 02178 (617)489-3674.

BEVERLY: **Jeff Wilkins,** 333 Cabot St., Beverly, MA 01915 (617)922-9422. *Custom furniture, sculpture and cabinetry.*

(57) Michael Williams, 2 Virginia Ave., Beverly, MA 01915 (617)927-9848. *Contemporary furniture.*

BOSTON: **Paul Cusack,** 42 Plympton St., Boston, MA 02118 (617)426-4916.

(92) William Doub, c/o Fort Point Cabinetmakers, 368 Congress St., Boston, MA 02210 (617)338-9497.

Fort Point Cabinetmakers, 368 Congress St., Boston, MA 02109 (617)338-9487. *Custom woodworking, mainly traditional furniture.*

(26) Jeffrey Goodman, 176 Green St., Boston, MA 02130 (617)522-2206. *Furniture design, custom woodworking.*

John Fox Woodworking, 173A Norfolk Ave., Boston, MA 02124 (617)442-3424. *Furniture and accessories on individual commissions.*

Carl Mesrobian, 368 Congress St. 4th floor, Boston, MA 02210 (617)423-5565. *All work made to order. Chairs, cabinets, carving, repairs.*

(32) Frank Nadell, Designer-Craftsman, 53 Hull St., Boston, MA 02113 (617)523-4278.

(83) Jay B. Stanger, 53 Hull St., Boston, MA 02113 (617)523-4278. *Mixed media, casting resin.*

BRIGHTON: **Joan Marian Friedman,** 19 Ransom Rd., Brighton, MA 02135 (617)783-2298. *Custom-designed historic stringed instruments and contemporary furniture, both plain and inlaid available.*

BROOKLINE: **Stephen Beeching,** 118 Mason Terrace, Brookline, MA 02146 (617)566-1724. *Traditional joinery, exclusively handmade furniture of original or traditional design.*

BYFIELD: **William C. Barrow,** 11 Oak Terrace, Byfield, MA 01922 (617)465-5138. *Representations of classical period styling in furniture, mostly case work and occasional pieces.*

CAMBRIDGE: **Jonathan H. Bartels,** 185 Chestnut St., Cambridge, MA 02139 (617)876-8880.

John S. Everdell, 16 Emily St., Cambridge, MA 02139 (617)876-0423. *Furniture and interiors.*

(76) Michael Hurwitz, 16 Emily St., Cambridge, MA 02139 (617)876-0423. *Fine furniture.*

(104) Thomas Loeser, 16 Emily St., Cambridge, MA 02139 (617)661-9836. *One-of-a-kind design.*

Charles Mark, Design, 16 Emily St., Cambridge, MA 02139 (617)661-9836. *One-of-a-kind furniture and sculpture in hardwood.*

(149) Jamie Robertson, 16 Emily St., Cambridge, MA 02139 (617)864-7600. *Fine woodwork and design.*

(84) Mitch Ryerson, 16 Emily St., Cambridge, MA 02139 (617)876-1314.

(85) Jonathan R. Wright, Cabinetmaker, 16 Emily St., Cambridge, MA 02139 (617)876-0423. *Custom cabinets, furniture.*

CARLISLE: **(134) Steven Sørli, Harpsichord Maker,** 1022 Westford St., Carlisle, MA 01741 (617)369-7514. *Historic harpsichords designed with emphasis on a rich, dry, versatile sound. Outstanding decoration by maker.*

CONCORD: **Bill Brace,** 49 Liberty St., Concord, MA 01742 (617)369-1373.

Kenneth S. Ledeen, 95 Coppermine Rd., Concord, MA 01742 (617)371-0223.

CUMMINGTON: **Edward Konieczny,** Nash Rd., Cummington, MA 01026 (413)634-2209. *Commissioned pieces and limited production runs.*

DENNIS: **Scargo Table Co.,** Dr. Lords Rd. S., Dennis, MA 02638 (617)385-3298. *Tables, cabinetry, general millwork, doors, windows, stairs.*

EAST DENNIS: **(108) Reginald E. Bushnell,** Box 26, East Dennis, MA 02641 (617)385-9580. *Any high-style furniture of the Queen Anne, Chippendale or classical periods.*

Ronald C. Ferro Co., Quivett Neck, East Dennis, MA 02641 (617)385-2739. *Authentic post-and-beam homes and additions, unique personal design. Complete building services.*

EASTHAMPTON: **(143) Kristina W. Madsen, Leeds Design Workshops,** 1 Cottage St., Easthampton, MA 01027 (413)527-4952. *Contemporary furniture designed and built to order.*

(66) David Powell, Leeds Design Workshops, One Cottage St., Easthampton, MA 01027 (413)527-4718. *Leeds Design Workshops designs and makes commissioned furniture. LDW also has a full-time two-year training program.*

(78) John Tierney, Leeds Design Workshops, One Cottage St., Easthampton, MA 01027 (413)527-4718. *Leeds Design Workshops designs and makes commissioned furniture. LDW also has a full-time two-year training program.*

David Veleta, Leeds Design Workshops, 1 Cottage St., Easthampton, MA 01027 (413)527-4718.

(140) Wildfawn Woodcrafts, 1 Cottage St., Box 608, Easthampton, MA 01027 (413)527-2127. *Marimbas, jewelry boxes, custom furniture.*

FLORENCE: **Michael Jacobson-Hardy,** 21 Garfield St., Florence, MA 01060.

(43) Charles Stern, 2 Lake, Florence, MA 01060 (413)527-2127. *Custom furniture design and construction.*

GREAT BARRINGTON: **David Goldfarb,** 53 River St., Great Barrington, MA 01230 (413)528-1698. *Custom design and limited production furniture.*

GROTON: **Peter Lavallee,** Box 291, Groton, MA 01450.

HINGHAM: **Dale Broholm,** 200 Central St., Hingham, MA 02043 (617)749-7155. *One-of-a-kind and limited-production furniture.*

(47) J.F. Collins Furnituremakers, 4 Friend St., Hingham, MA 02043 (617)749-7184.

HOLLISTON: **Alexander Marsh, Inc.,** 15 Water St., Holliston, MA 01746 (617)429-5388.

LEVERETT: **(112) James Adams, Cradles to Coffins,** 375 N. Leverett Rd., Leverett, MA 01054 (413)367-2103. *Furniture of all kinds, incorporating unique design, solid hardwoods and tradtional joinery techniques.*

LITTLETON: **Doug Reiner, Woodworker Furniture Maker,** 100 Taylor St. Box 2036, Littleton, MA 01460 (303)486-9295. *Shaker reproduction furniture, fine domestic hardwoods.*

LOWELL: **Alan Bennett,** 23 S. Canton St., Lowell, MA 01851 (617)453-3699. *Custom contemporary and traditional furniture.*

(90) Normand P. Jussaume, Riverby St., Lowell, MA 01850.

MARBLEHEAD: **(122) Seth Stem,** 43 Washington St., Marblehead, MA 01945 (617)631-0125.

MASHPEE: **Sheldon J. Fry, Wood Joiner,** RFD 2 Box 199, 51 Asa Meigs Rd., Mashpee, MA 02649 (617)477-2749. *Custom design and construction. Will consider all projects from furniture to built-in cabinetry.*

MEDFORD: **(77) Richard Tannen,** 574 Boston Ave., Medford, MA 02155 (617)396-8646.

NATICK: **Gary Gilbert,** 7 Clover Lane, Natick, MA 01760 (617)653-7681. *Nonfunctional wood sculpture and commission furniture. All often involve exotic woods.*

(79) Robert E. Hannan, 19 Sawin St., Natick, MA 01760. (617)655-0196.

Albert Weisman, 55 S. St., Natick, MA 01760 (617)245-3366. *Sculptor.*

NEWBURYPORT: **(178) Jeffrey Briggs,** 17 Dalton St., Newburyport, MA 01950 (617)465-5593. *Fantasy and figurative carved wood sculpture.*

Suzi Edwards, 19 Oliva St., Newburyport, MA 01950 (617)462-9916.

Logical Myth Woodworking, 88 Prospect St., Newburyport, MA 01950 (617)462-6459. *Woodcarving, custom furniture, hardwood boxes.*

NEWTON UPPER FALLS: **Gregory Johnson,** 80 Oak St., Newton Upper Falls, MA 02164 (617)244-6220. *Custom finishing and color matching for woodworkers, cabinetmaker, antique restoration.*

NORTHAMPTON: **(19) Silas Kopf, Woodworking,** 20 Stearns Court, Northampton, MA 01060 (413)527-4952. *Marquetry, custom furniture, limited production accessories.*

(49) Alan Lorn, Fine Woodwork and Furniture, Box 1234, Northampton, MA 01060.

NORTHBORO: **David S. Thorpe,** 355 Whitney St., Northboro, MA 01532. *Sculptured jewelry boxes and dishes.*

NORTH WESTPORT: **(80) Peter Allen, Professional Woodworker,** 108 Blossom Rd., North Westport, MA 02790 (617)674-2920. *Design and construction of fine furniture and cabinetry.*

PEABODY: **(124) Dove Tail,** 142 Washington St., Peabody, MA 01960. *Country furniture, post-and-beam homebuilding.*

PRINCETON: **(97) Robert E. March,** 10 Wilson Rd., Princeton, MA 01541 (617)759-3844. *Custom furniture.*

ROCKLAND: **Stephen R. Hanson,** 233 Market St., Rockland, MA 02370 (617)878-9408. *Tables, cabinets, hand joinery.*

ROXBURY: **Philip Wolfson,** 839 Parker St., Roxbury, MA 02120 (617)442-9584. *Custom (commissioned) furniture.*

SAUGUS: **John F. Loverme, Jr.,** 23 Oakland Vale Ave., Saugus, MA 01906. *Custom-built inlaid wood cabinetry.*

SEEKONK: **Lorenzo Freccia,** 8 Dexter Ave., Seekonk, MA 02771 (617)336-7520. *Turnings (lamps in exotic woods, goblets, etc.), custom cabinetry.*

SOMERVILLE: **(51) Michael Clark,** 48 Grove St., Somerville, MA 02144 (617)628-3333.

King Associates, Michael King, 24 Webster Ave., Somerville, MA 02143 (617)628-6600. *Design and construction of fine furnishings.*

Mike Murray, dba Vermont Wood Products, 35 Medford St., Somerville, MA 02143 (617)497-1659. *Commercial and residential custom-designed wood interiors. Japanese style interiors. Custom-designed furniture. Wood houses.*

(52) Raccoon, 20 Vernon St., Somerville, MA 02145 (617)776-9110. *Ellen Mason and Dudley Hartung design and make furniture collaboratively.*

SOUTH ATTLEBORO: **(59) Eileen Brogan,** 440 Robinson Ave., South Attleboro, MA 02703.

SPRINGFIELD: **(46) Hugh 'Huff' Wesler,** 16 Churchill St., Springfield, MA 01108 (413)736-4828. *Whimsical furniture.*

STOW: **(29) Joseph H. Twichell,** Stow, MA, 01775 (617)897-8905. *Custom furniture made mostly of but not limited to traditional styles.*

VINEYARD HAVEN: **John Thayer & Sons Woodworking,** 13A Tashmoo Ave., Box 1670, Vineyard Haven, MA 02568 (617)693-4690.

WALTHAM: **James J. Farrington,** 91 Prospect Hill Rd., Waltham, MA 02154 (617)894-6451. *Custom cabinetry, showcase cabinets, wall systems, shelf units.*

WARWICK: **Michael Humphries Woodworking,** White Rd., Warwick, MA 01364 (617)544-2694. *Commissioned pieces, furniture, cabinets, interior architectural woodwork.*

WASHINGTON: **(56) Andy Inganni,** Middlefield Rd., Washington, MA 01235 (413)623-6677. *Architectural woodworking and furniture; kitchens, stairs, windows, insulated doors, solar design and construction. Instructor with Heartwood Owner-Builder School.*

WINCHESTER: **Wade Holtzman,** 259 Pond St., Winchester, MA 01890 (617)729-2351. *Antique furniture restoration and reproductions, custom interiors (residential and commercial).*

WINTHROP: **Jeffrey Warshafsky and Annamaria Taudel,** 12 Charles St., Winthrop, MA 02152 (617)846-8710. *Contemporary original designs.*

WORCESTER: **Peter McKone Contemporary Furniture Design,** 72 Commercial St., Worcester, MA 01608 (617)752-3844. *Custom-designed one-of-a-kind and limited production pieces in domestic and imported woods.*

WRENTHAM: **Mark L. Swartz,** 65 Desert Brook Rd., Wrentham, MA 02093. *One-of-a-kind or small quantity custom furniture or millwork.*

Michigan

ANN ARBOR: **Dennis Dieckman,** 3382 Chelsea Circle, Ann Arbor, MI 48104 (313)973-8609.

John Rocus, Woodworker, 4875 Ford, Ann Arbor, MI 48105 (313)996-9183. *One-of-a-kind furniture, accessories, sculpture.*

(34) Smith & Nathan Furnituremakers Inc., 403 N. Fifth Ave., Ann Arbor, MI 48104 (313)994-5222. *Custom hardwood furniture and cabinetry for home and office.*

ATLANTIC MINE: **(141) Michael Darnton,** Route 1 Box 80A, Atlantic Mine, MI 49905 (906)482-7716. *Custom steel-string guitars, stringed instrument repairs.*

BAY CITY: **John D. Wright,** 2131 5th Ave., Bay City, MI 48706. *Stools, veneer boxes, salt and pepper shakers, salad services, cutting boards, desks, etc.*

BIRMINGHAM: **(55) A.L. Reproductions and Customizing in Wood,** 615 S. Eton, Birmingham, MI 48008 (313)641-8588. *Custom furniture making with a traditional influence.*

BLOOMFIELD HILLS: **David Burkholder,** 500 Lone Pine Rd., Bloomfield Hills, MI 48013 (313)645-3336. *Architect of homes and custom furniture for the residential environment.*

BOYNE CITY: **The Wood Shop,** 111 E. St., Boyne City, MI 49712 (616)582-9835. *Wooden signs, sculpture and graphics for commercial and architectural applications. Hand-carving, gold-leafing and design.*

CEDAR: **The Underbark, Paul Czamanske,** Star Route, Cedar, MI 49621 (616)334-3753. *London College of Furniture graduate. Custom-design contemporary woodworking, hardwoods, natural finishes. Brochure and references available.*

DEARBORN: **Eric D. Smith,** 2941 Roosevelt, Dearborn, MI 48124 (313)562-5509. *One-of-a-kind and limited-production furniture.*

DETROIT: **Skalski's Woodworking Co.,** 313 Orleans St., Detroit, MI 48207 (313)259-4950. *Specialty, one-of-a-kind, human-scale woodworking providing function utilizing primarily domestic solid hardwoods.*

DeWITT: **Oak Shade,** 10550 Forest Hill Rd., DeWitt, MI 48820 (517)626-6123. *One-of-a-kind. Your design or mine. Furniture and turnings.*

DEXTER: **Neal Little,** 7982 Dexter-Pinckney Rd., Dexter, MI 48130 (313)426-5249.

(26) North Star Woodworking Co., 2730 Baker Rd., Dexter, MI 48130 (313)426-5454. *Designer and builder of fine quality contemporary and Oriental furniture, also architectural woodworking.*

EAST JORDAN: **Andre M. Poineau,** Route 1 Box 488, East Jordan, MI 49727 (616)536-2725. *Custom hardwood doors, furniture and architectural fixtures.*

EAST LANSING: **Paul A. Loeffler,** 1629 Melrose Ave., East Lansing, MI 48823 (517)351-5405. *Original functional fantasy furniture and wood carvings.*

FLINT: **(108) The Wood Plane Studio,** 2417 Fenton Rd., Flint, MI 48507 (313)239-4700. *Original designs, antique reproductions, repair and refinishing and commercial architectural woodwork and carving.*

GLADWIN: **(148) Al's Cabinet Shop,** 1118 W. Cedar, Gladwin, MI 48624 (517)426-2116. *Kitchen cabinets, contemporary custom furniture, marquetry, Formica work.*

GRAND LEDGE: **James V. Thayer,** 11131 Cobble Stone Lane, Grand Ledge, MI 48837 (517)627-6169. *Consignment work in any kind of wood from sketch or photo. Design services available.*

GRAND RAPIDS: **Charles Jerome Cabinetmakers,** 240 Front S.W., Grand Rapids, MI 49504 (616)774-2321. *Louis VI, Charles X, English, late Georgian and Regency. Hand-painted and gilt finishes a specialty.*

Bruce F. Zeeuw, 610 Stanley N.E., Grand Rapids, MI 49503 (616)458-3173. *Commissioned cabinet work, tables, chairs of original design.*

GROSSE POINTE FARMS: **Jeffrey Riddell,** 338 Provencal Rd., Grosse Pointe Farms, MI 48236 (313)884-1177. *Custom furniture design.*

HASLETT: **Thomas E. Young,** 2403 Haslett Rd., Haslett, MI 48823 (517)351-8415. *Custom furniture and woodwork.*

HOLLAND: **Dirk A. De Young,** A 4652 1-2 64th St., Holland, MI 49423 (616)335-6156.

(103) Schroeder Limited, A-6022 138th Ave., Holland, MI 49423 (616)392-5004. *Custom cabinetry, limited production pieces, sculpture.*

Thomas L. Webber, 13897 Van Buren, Holland, MI 49423 (616)399-3547. *Custom cabinets and furniture.*

JEROME: **Eric Sheffield,** 1067 Waldron Rd., Jerome, MI 49249 (517)688-4045. *Custom furniture and accessories.*

KALAMAZOO: **Leonard Beuving,** 214 Creston, Kalamazoo, MI 49001 (616)342-9307. *Tile insetting and tambour design.*

(79) Martha Collins, Furniture Maker, 326 W. Kalamazoo Ave., Kalamazoo, MI 49007 (616)343-7051. *Fine furniture and cabinetry including hardwood kitchens.*

(49) Joseph P. Malsom, 415 Hilbert, Kalamazoo, MI 49007 (616)385-2984. *Custom furniture, cabinetry and architectural woodworking.*

(122) Studio of Richard Schneider, 326 W. Kalamazoo Ave., Kalamazoo, MI 49007 (616)345-8680. *Fine handmade classical guitars of the Kasha sound-board design and wood jewelry.*

LAKE ORION: **R.L. Jackson,** 772 Kimberly, Lake Orion, MI 48035 (313)693-4077. *Small furniture items.*

LANSING: **Stayner Haller,** 1731 Vassar Dr., Lansing, MI 48912 (517)372-3671. *Jewelry boxes, chests and turned objects featuring irregular and figured woods.*

Steven Klein, Dovetail Designs, 1616 W. Mt. Hope, Lansing, MI 48910 (517)372-7796. *Custom furniture and accessories, custom turning, carving, restorations.*

LAURIUM: **Bek Woodcraft,** 436 Hecla St., Laurium, MI 49913 (906)337-2466. *Home accessories and custom work.*

LAWRENCE: **Timothy Cavey, Woodcarver,** Box 311, Lawrence, MI 49064. *Custom wood designs and sculpture.*

Laverne Jewell, Route 2 48th Ave., Lawrence, MI 49064 (616)674-3278. *Custom homes, woodcarvings, sculpture.*

LUDINGTON: **Carl O. Griewahn,** 5747 Riverview Dr., Ludington, MI 49431 (616)845-1116. *Realistic bird carving.*

Frank C. Koehle, 210 W. Tinkham, Ludington, MI 49431.

William J. Sniegowski, 3895 W. Hansen Rd., Ludington, MI 49431 (616)843-8435.

LUTHER: **Custom Clock Shop,** 313 Garfield St. Box 206, Luther, MI 49656 (616)797-5344. *Custom furniture of unique design and materials. Specialty: clocks.*

McBAIN: **Garry Baas,** 7310 S. 8 Mile Rd., Route 2, McBain, MI 49657 (616)826-3338. *Toys, gifts, parts for furniture.*

MARQUETTE: **Ben Niessen,** 724 W. College, Marquette, MI 49855 (906)226-6429. *Custom-designed furniture, period remodeling, saunas, stained-glass windows.*

Taylor Made Furniture, 523 Lake Shore Boulevard, Marquette, MI 49855 (906)226-2641.

MIDLAND: **The Elf's Plane, Roger Szeszulski,** 1149 E. Stewart, Midland, MI 48640 (517)832-2574. *Custom woodworking, furniture, toys, boxes.*

MUNISING: **Northern Sun Woodworks,** Route 1 E., Munising, MI 49862 (906)387-4082. *Custom furniture, spiral stairs and railings.*

NEW BALTIMORE: **Emporium Furniture Workshop, Carol and Russel Hare,** 36461 Green St., New Baltimore, MI 48047 (313)725-2911. *Design and build fine furniture, using solid hardwoods.*

OKEMOS: **Creative Woodcarving, Jack L. Clifford,** 4565 Chippewa Dr., Okemos, MI 48864 (517)349-1611. *Custom-carved signs, sculpture, relief carvings.*

PARCHMENT: **(160) Noah Roselander,** 5410 Collingwood, Parchment, MI 49004. *Professional woodworker.*

PARMA: **Paul Goris, Cabinetmaker,** 5631 N. Parma Rd., Parma, MI 49269 (517)531-3886. *Custom furniture design. Handcrafter of fine Early American furnishings.*

PAW PAW: **(141) Studio of Abraham Wechter,** 34654 32nd St., Paw Paw, MI 49079 (616)657-3479. *Clasical guitars, jazz guitars.*

PENTWATER: **Leprechaun Shop Alan C. Ringquist, Cabinetmaker,** 111 Hancock, Pentwater, MI 49449 (616)869-5919. *Custom contract and residential furniture and accessories.*

RICHMOND: **(144) Artistic Woodworking, Ross Matuja,** 5200 Church Rd., Richmond, MI 48062 (313)727-2411.

Warren Kress & Janice Cole, 4714 Palms Rd., Richmond, MI 48062 (313)727-7913. *Specialties: laminations and free-form, sculpted accessories.*

ROCHESTER: **Leonard Kaczor,** 890 Bloomer Rd., Rochester, MI 48063 (313)652-2937. *Custom-designed furniture, framing of stained-glass windows, metalsmithing, sculpture.*

ROMULUS: **Dale Summers,** 39101 Pennsylvania, Romulus, MI 48174 (313)753-9073. *Small wooden objects, cabinets, antique refinishing and restoration.*

ROSEVILLE: **Majestic Furniture Co., Brian Doslea,** 15238 Common Rd., Roseville, MI 48066 (313)778-9210. *I specialize in woodcarving, veneer and inlay work, and original designs.*

ST. CLAIR SHORES: **Russ Jimison, Jimison Manufacturing Co.,** 20800 Erben, St. Clair Shores, MI 48081 (313)778-1593. *Commission furniture and small giftware, specializing in rare and exotic hardwoods and inlay work.*

ST. JOSEPH: **Klotz Woodworks, John Forney II,** 3515 Lakeshore Dr., St. Joseph, MI 49085 (616)982-0290. *Furniture and architectural woodwork. Range of furniture from traditional to modern, using traditional joinery methods.*

SPRING LAKE: **John C. Druse,** 15705 Pruin, Spring Lake, MI 49456 (616)842-1945. *I design and build hardwood furniture and accessories.*

STERLING HEIGHTS: **Dennis J. Thueme,** 3580 Devonshire, Sterling Heights, MI 48077 (313)264-1681-264-9691. *Master patterns, show models, custom carvings, millwork.*

TRAVERSE CITY: **Richard N. Hill,** 725 S. Maple, Traverse City, MI 49684 ((616)947-5417. *Tables, cabinets, chairs, boxes and mirrors.*

WEST BLOOMFIELD: **(54) Steven M. Lash,** 6177 Orchard Lake Rd., Suite 200, West Bloomfield, MI 48033 (313)851-7272. *Eighteenth-century handmade furniture, none of which is for sale.*

YPSILANTI: **Dane L. Gamble,** 1095 Levona, Ypsilanti, MI 48197 (313)483-1553. *Small tables and desks.*

Minnesota

BEMIDJI: **Kaplan's Creative Woodworking,** Box 544, Bemidji, MN 56601 (218)751-6961. *Wood turnings, round picture frames, custom cabinets, refinishing and repair.*

BRAINERD: **Kampinann Sash and Door Company,** 701 S. 10th St., Brainerd, MN 56401 (218)829-5621. *Custom-designed contemporary and traditional doors, interior finish work and windows.*

COON RAPIDS: **Rich Wilkens,** 10021 Magnolia St. N.W., Coon Rapids, MN 55433 (612)757-4045. *Marquetry.*

DULUTH: **Milton A. Vollmer,** 578 W. Lismore Rd., Duluth, MN 55803 (218)721-3938. *Custom items, large and small.*

FERGUS FALLS: **(79) Jay McDougall,** Box 262, Fergus Falls, MN 56537 (218)739-4264. *Personalized designs and building of fine wooden furnishings.*

GOLDEN VALLEY: **MOCRAFT,** 1831 York Ave. N., Golden Valley, MN 55422 (612)522-5645. *Hand carvings of animals, fish, birds, models of boats and most any designs.*

LAKELAND: **Valley Creek Woodworks,** Box 68, Lakeland, MN 55043 (612)436-5042. *Rolltop desks, hutches, silver chests, wood consulting.*

MANKATO: **William R. Tacheny, Cabinetmaker,** Route 3, Box 46, Mankato, MN 56001 (507)625-7054. *Hardwood furniture and accessories made to order. Some short-runs.*

MINNEAPOLIS: **(166) Joe Casey,** Minneapolis, MN 55423 (612)866-2196.

F.R. Hedding, 10610 40th Ave. N., Minneapolis, MN 55441 (612)544-8231. *My pleasure and satisfaction.*

Michael Mikutowski, 338 24th Ave. N.E., Minneapolis, MN 55418 (612)781-6492. *Custom furniture made of domestic and exotic hardwoods. Cabinetry and commercial woodwork.*

Keith Ostrosky, 604 Ontario S.E., Minneapolis, MN 55414 (612)379-7536. *Custom work.*

(131) William Parks, 2435 Pillsbury Ave. S., Minneapolis, MN 55404 (612)870-0203. *Antique clock reproductions.*

Teke Woodworking, 3100 Snelling Ave. S, Minneapolis, MN 55406 (612)722-8332. *Custom designs-yours or ours. Mixed media (brass, leather, etc.), furniture (many styles), architectural woodworking.*

MINNETONKA: **Randy Guyer,** 2225 Country Lane, Minnetonka, MN 55343 (612)546-9492. *Custom cases and furniture.*

Tom Wolfe, 10100 Hillside Lane, Minnetonka, MN 55343 (612)546-3665. *Furniture and boxes.*

NORTHFIELD: **Holyoke Handmade,** Route 5 Box 202K, Northfield, MN 55057 (507)652-2224. *Handcrafted items of wood, metal, reinforced concrete.*

PALISADE: **Don Mahieu,** Route 2 Box 94A, Palisade, MN 56469. *Hand-carved works in the round and relief.*

PENGILLY: **Marc Jassky,** Route 1 Box 161B, Pengilly, MN 55775 (218)885-3165. *Custom drawing tables, kitchen and bath cabinetry of solid ash.*

ROCHERT: **Bobbe W. Cox,** Cotton Lake, Rochert, MN 56578 (218)847-3872. *Original designs, individual custom designs, accessories and gifts, small furnishings.*

ST. CLOUD: **R.A. Golden, WDWRKR,** 910 So. 10th Ave., St. Cloud, MN 56301 (612)253-1566. *Finding solutions to woodworking problems, whatever they may be.*

ST. PAUL: **John Lunde, dba Taiga Woodworking,** 253 E. 4th St., St. Paul, MN 55101 (612)221-9830. *Thoughtfully designed and carefully made residential and executive furniture in solid domestic hardwoods.*

Doug Miller, 1933 Dodd Rd., St. Paul, MN 55118 (612)454-4769 or (512)657-1210. *Custom furniture.*

Stephen M. Schuweiler, 370 Cherokee Ave., St. Paul, MN 55107 (612)224-6555. *Design and build one-of-a-kind and limited production music boxes and jewelry boxes.*

Visual Grain, 1296 Garden Ave., St. Paul, MN 55113 (612)645-2157. *Complete custom woodworking.*

(37) Thomas Wood, 500 N. Robert 432, St. Paul, MN 55101 (612)224-3745.

SHAKOPEE: **Designs in Hardwood,** 25 1834 Marshall Rd., Shakopee, MN 55379 (612)445-7707. *One-of-a-kind solid hardwood, fine furniture featuring hand-rubbed oil and varnish finishes.*

WATERVILLE: **Backman Cabinet Shop, Jack Backman,** Route 2 Box 64, Waterville, MN 56096 (507)362-4368. *Custom-designed furniture, church sanctuary furniture, altars, etc.*

WEST ST. PAUL: **Milton J. Blumenfeld,** 2035 Shady Oak Dr., West St. Paul, MN 55118.

(130) Wesley P. Glewwe, 906 Oakdale Ave., West St. Paul, MN 55118 (612)457-1107. *Unusual and exotic wooden products. Reproduction of antiques. Wood turning.*

WILLMAR: **Craig Barnes,** 804 W. Litch Ave., Willmar, MN 56201 (612)235-1313. *Woodcarving, restoration, including architectural ornamental design and sculpture. Trained at the Brienz Swiss Carving School.*

Mississippi

BILOXI: **Barry Grishman, Fine Art Woodwork,** 15824 Belmont Dr., Biloxi, MS 39532 (601)392-7346. *Original, one-of-a-kind sculptural vessels, containers with various functions, furniture of several species of tropical and domestic woods.*

JACKSON: **Bill Rusk,** Route 3 Box 314-W, Jackson, MS 39213 (601)856-6227. *Contemporary furniture.*

TOUGALOO: **Fletcher & Carol Cox,** Box 188, Tougaloo, MS 39174 (601)956-2610. *Production and one-off. From utensils and plates to roomfuls. Wholesale, residential, contract.*

VAUGHN: **(89) Greg Harkins, Green Oak Chairmaker Shop,** Opossum Bend Rd., Vaughan, MS (Mailing address: Harkins Woodworks, Box 16165, Jackson, MS 39236) (601)362-4233. *Best known for my plantation rockers, also double rockers, side chairs, baby rockers, stools, benches and tables.*

Missouri

BLUE SPRINGS: **Furniture by Baum,** 1901 W. Walnut, Blue Springs, MO 64015. (816)229-0526.

CHESTERFIELD: **(138) Norman Stoecker, Architect,** 16607 Saddle Creek Rd., Chesterfield, MO 63017 (314)532-3255. *Architecture and woodworking.*

COLUMBIA: **Don Choate,** 801 Alton St., Columbia, MO 65201 (314)443-0083. *Custom furniture nontraditional in nature and cabinetry and sculptural items.*

Tom Cole, 4312 St. Charles Rd., Columbia, MO 65201 (314)449-6667. *One-of-a-kind wooden furniture and small cabinets.*

Columbia Hardwoods, 5166 N. Clearview Rd., Columbia, MO 65202 (314)443-4503. *Retail kiln-dried hardwoods for the hobbyist and professional. Woodworking supplies, literature.*

Elfin Woodworks, 106 Aldeah Ave., Columbia, MO 65201 (314)449-0200. *Funiture, functional sculpture, turnings, kitchen and dining ware, accessories.*

Dan L. Hemmelgarn, 1607 Caniff Circle, Columbia, MO 65201 (314)442-8007. *Fine handmade furniture of original design built to be enjoyed by generation after generation.*

John's Workbench, Route 8, Columbia, MO 65202 (314)445-4027. *Native Missouri hardwood products.*

Paul H. Rawe, 1001 Coats, Columbia, MO 65201 (314)449-8049. *Carpentry and custom woodworking.*

ELDON: **Scott Westbrook,** Route 2 Box 148, Eldon, MO 65026 (314)392-6318. *Contemporary design of handcrafted fine furniture and selected architectural units.*

ELK CREEK: **Wildwood, Charles Lewis & Paul Gross,** Box 33, Elk Creek, MO 65464 (417)932-4056. *Custom-designed furniture out of native hardwoods.*

FLORISSANT: **Ron & Dee Dee Tempel,** 3854 Arbre Lane, Florissant, MO 63034 (314)831-2584. *Heirloom rocking chairs and leg rests, walnut, cherry, oak. Hand-caned, variety of caning designs.*

HANNIBAL: **Donald L. Burroughs, Spiffy Originals,** 3410 W. Ely Rd., Hannibal, MO 63401 (314)221-2064.

INDEPENDENCE: **(120) The Benchcraft Collection,** 3909 Woodbury, Independence, MO 64055 (816)373-2119. *Full-size wooden toy plans and patterns. Catalog $1.*

JOPLIN: **Jack Rouse,** 2431 Tyler, Joplin, MO 64801 (417)623-3251. *Bas-relief pictures of actual places.*

KANSAS CITY: **(179) Michael Bauermeister,** 4242 Holmes, Kansas City, MO 64110. *Wood sculpture, original furniture, handmade kitchen cabinets.*

C.A. Britt, 4223 Oak, Kansas City, MO 64111. *Unique design and construction of sculptural furniture, musical instruments.*

Eclectic Woodworks, Dennis Soden, 3629 Bell St., Kansas City, MO 64111 (816)561-6259. *Custom-designed, one-of-a-kind furniture-sculpture in the Scandinavian tradition.*

R.W. Fox, 5 W. 109th St., Kansas City, MO 64114 (816)942-1801. *Period furniture reproductions principally in Queen Anne and Chippendale styles.*

Jay Johnson, 6512 Linden Rd., Kansas City, MO 64113 (816)444-6615. *Freestanding cabinets, furniture, bowls.*

Kansas City Woodworking, 2030 Grand, Kansas City, MO 64108 (816)474-4618. *Custom furniture and cabinets.*

Wm. Thomas Laux, 8020 Forest, Kansas City, MO 64131 (816)523-4419.

Samurai Woodworks, 3023 Holmes St., Kansas City, MO 64109 (816)931-3050. *Custom softwood furniture from jewelry boxes to porches.*

Clarence A. Teed, 6021 Central, Kansas City, MO 64113 (816)361-3428. *Design and production of handcrafted furniture and wood accessories.*

MANCHESTER: **Robert G. Swanson,** 511 Clayworth Dr., Manchester, MO 63011 (314)527-0415. *Marquetry.*

RUSSELLVILLE: **Sage Wood Products,** Route 2 Box 211, Scrivner Rd., Russellville, MO 65074 (314)782-3448. *Original marquetry, inlay and laminated wood articles, music boxes, game boards, furniture and custom work.*

ST. CHARLES: **Keith M. Silver, dba The Silver Edition,** 11 Mill Bridge Dr., St. Charles, MO 63301 (314)441-1822. *Contemporary woodworking, furniture, cabinets, home accessories, shelves, picture frames and toys.*

ST. LOUIS: **Bernard & Lindenberger Cabinetmakers,** 14 McClure, St. Louis, MO 63119 (314)968-9442. *We design and build custom furniture, cabinetry and millwork, and do antique reproduction and repair.*

Creative Woodworking, 4675 Dewey Ave., St. Louis, MO 63116 (314)353-1411. *Architectural woodwork, custom furniture, commercial bars and restaurant pieces, individualized original designs.*

(94) Joseph Farell, 3444 A Klocke, St. Louis, MO 63118 (314)352-0336.

Forms in Furniture, 1520 N. 13th, St. Louis, MO 63106 (314)231-5088. *Forms in Furniture specializes in design and construction of fine custom-made hardwood furniture.*

Nancy L. Krautmann, 7801 Genesta, St. Louis, MO 63123 (314)352-5654.

Paul E. Krautmann, 7801 Genesta, St. Louis, MO 63123 (314)352-5654. *Toys, furniture, turnings, baskets.*

(152) Norbert Marklin Designs, 4441 Laclede Place, St. Louis, MO 63108 (314)535-3147. *Special one-of-a-kind furniture pieces. Also prototypes of furniture for manufacture.*

SOUTHWEST CITY: **Gerald Sears Woodworking,** Route 1 Box 144, Southwest City, MO 64863 (417)762-3643. *Specialty: western art.*

SPRINGFIELD: **Ramshead Dulcimers, John Horrell,** Box 4612, Springfield, MO 65808. *Custom building of dulcimers.*

STURGEON: **Character Woods,** Route 1 Box 28-C, Sturgeon, MO 65284. *Inlaid wood boxes, chests, countertops and bartops, wall hangings.*

Eddy Fike, Route 1, Sturgeon, MO 65284 (314)875-5814. *Custom construction, cabinets, furniture, gift items.*

WARRENTON: **White Clover Woodworking,** 304 Richmond, Warrenton, MO 63383 (314)456-2675. *Furniture, decorative items. Display, kitchen and bath cabinets.*

Montana

ANACONDA: **Theodore E. Eck and Sons,** 1414 W. Third St., Anaconda, MT 59711 (406)563-7339 or 563-2421. *Residential and commercial cabinetry, showcases, interior finish work, one-of-a-kind and custom furniture.*

BELGRADE: **(32) John Nicolson,** 2600 Amsterdam Rd., Belgrade, MT 59714 (406)388-4730. *Furniture and design by commission, limited editions, interiors.*

BILLINGS: **Dovetail Designs,** 1439 Ave. B, Billings, MT 59102 (406)248-5010. *Custom furniture, traditional joinery.*

The Woodwright, 1916 3rd Ave. N., Billings, MT 59101 (406)248-3393. *Fine furniture of traditional constructions, hand-carving, baroque recorders.*

BOZEMAN: **William E. Almy III,** 326 N. Bozeman, Bozeman, MT 59715 (406)587-3593. *Anything that can be done right, and not in a hurry.*

Arrowleaf Woodwork and Design, 3681 Sawmill Rd., Bozeman, MT 59715 (406)587-3003. *Custom-designed furniture, looms, cabinets.*

(119) Steven J. Gray, Woodwright, 514 E. Davis Box 1884, Bozeman, MT 59715 (406)587-0383. *Custom cabinets, furniture, wood clocks, telescopes, kaleidoscopes, tools and other unique items.*

Woodcrafters of Bozeman, 415 S. Tracy, Bozeman, MT 59715 (406)586-1498. *Custom furniture, repairs on anything. Antique reproductions, store interiors, stripping, refinishing.*

CHESTER: **Custom Woodcraft,** Highway 2 W., Chester, MT 59522 (406)759-5690. *Custom furniture, cabinets and signs.*

CORVALLIS: **Joseph Thompson,** Box 212, Corvallis, MT 59828 (406)961-4591. *Woodwork and carving for problem spaces.*

HELENA: **Scott Walter, Plane and Fantasy,** 2063 Oro Fino Gulch, Helena, MT 59601 (406)442-0277. *Small toys, rocking creatures, commission work, particularly anything different or unusual or requiring design work.*

HIGHWOOD: **Duncan Furniture,** Route 1, Highwood, MT 59450 (406)733-2353. *Creating designs to fit specific purposes and spaces as well as having a pleasing appearance.*

KALISPELL: **Leland Keller,** 563 McMannamy Draw, Kalispell, MT 59901 (406)257-7333. *Custom woodworking concentrating on small items.*

LO LO: **Paul Hellmuth, Expressions in Wood,** 500 Lake Side, Lo Lo, MT 59847 (406)273-6449. *My own modern-designed furniture and custom built-in cabinetry.*

MISSOULA: **David Clamen, Primrose Center,** 401 1-2 W. Railroad, Missoula, MT 59802 ((406)728-5911. *The Primrose Center teaches the crafting of one-of-a-kind or limited production, fine furniture.*

Dovetail Designs, 2008 37th Ave., Missoula, MT 59801 (406)543-8228. *Furniture design, solid hardwoods, period reproductions, architectural woodwork.*

John Hongola, Primrose Center, 401 W. Railroad, Missoula, MT 59802 (406)728-5911.

(125) West Lowe, Primrose Center, 401 W. Railroad St., Missoula, MT 59802 (406)728-5911.

NGL Woodworks, 5545 Skyway Dr., Missoula, MT 59801 (406)251-5672. *Custom fine woodwork.*

Alan Oram, Designer-Craftsman, 401 W. Railroad St., Missoula, MT 59802 (406)728-7380. *Individual pieces done on speculation and commission. Specialties are chairs and seating.*

(131) Primrose Center, Steve Voorheis, 401 W. Railroad St., Missoula, MT 59802 (406)728-5911. *Private academy, teaching furniture design and construction.*

SOMERS: **S K Wood,** Box 342, Somers, MT 59932 (406)857-3816. *Custom-designed hardwood furniture and case work in the Fine Art tradition.*

TROUT CREEK: **Don's Carve Shop, Don M. Hill,** Box 1384, Trout Creek, MT 59874 (406)827-4530. *Woodcarvings, animals and people.*

Nebraska

BEATRICE: **Marvin Camacho-Cook,** 1215 Grant St., Beatrice, NE 68310 (402)228-3751. *Cabinetmaking.*

BELLEVUE: **Stone's Custom Woodturning,** 607 Logan Ave., Bellevue, NE 68005 (402)291-9413. *Turnings.*

FREMONT: **Bobby Alberts,** 1341 N. Hancock, Fremont, NE 68025 (402)721-0077. *Turning, wood collectibles, clocks, toys, special designs.*

GOTHENBURG: **Manncraft Woodworking,** Route 2, Gothenburg, NE 69138 (308)537-3288. *Furniture and various specialty items.*

GRETNA: **Acorn's Wooden Furniture and Design,** 312 Bryan St., Gretna, NE 68028 (402)332-3707. *Custom-made hardwood furniture, refinishing and custom finishes. Antique replacement parts made to order.*

LINCOLN: **(175) Patricia W. Freeman,** 3210 Dudley St., Lincoln, NE 68503 (402)464-7002.

(125) E.J. Lang, 4400 S. 43rd, Lincoln, NE 68516 (402)488-2910. *Norwegian items, country items.*

Jeff McCabe, Luthier-Furniture Maker, 1725 S. 24th St., Lincoln, NE 68502 (402)475-1132. *Guitars, all types, custom furniture, tool building and pattern fabrication.*

Larry Schweitzer, 420 So. 11th St., Lincoln, NE 68502 (402)474-7754. *Furniture design and construction, hardwood toys, boxes, architectural woodwork.*

MARQUETTE: **(148) The Wood Plant,** Route 1 Box 134, Marquette, NE 68854 (402)854-3120. *One-of-a-kind.*

OMAHA: **Carol and Dennis Eby,** 12612 S. 31st St., Omaha, NE 68123 (402)292-3409. *Toys and furniture.*

WALTON: **Stevens Creek Cabinet Shop,** Route 1, Box 82A, Walton, NE 68461 (402)488-8276. *Country furniture in the Shaker style. Mainly case pieces and clocks.*

Nevada

LAS VEGAS: **(119) Christian Brisepierre,** 4295 S. Arville, Las Vegas, NV 89103 (702)871-0722. *French country furniture, armoires, buffets, vaisseliers, contemporary creations, carving, marquetry.*

Paul Haines, Woodworker, 6621 Bristol Way, Las Vegas, NV 89107 (702)878-5037. *Creative containers, cabinets, furniture and accessories.*

Larry D. Huegel, 3401 Sirius No. 10, Las Vegas, NV 89103 (702)873-8746. *Apprentice of John LaBounty. Custom woodworking.*

Philip Poburka, Las Vegas, NV 89108 (702)646-4308. *Custom and original woodwork, furniture and fine carpentry.*

Vegas Cabinets, 3120 So. Highland, Las Vegas, NV 89109 (702)733-7570. *No specialties. Everything and anything built to order.*

RENO: **Kevin L. Schroeder,** 6200 Meadowood Circle 1137 Reno, NV 89502 (702)826-5707. *Cabinets, desks, toys, boxes.*

New Hampshire

ALSTEAD: **Entrances, Donald Pecora,** Route 123, Alstead NH 03602 (603)835-6622. *Custom wood doors, screen door and windows.*

BETHLEHEM: **Broken Tree Woodworks, Michael A. Santomauro,** Box 441, Bethlehem, NH 03574. *Custom furniture interior design.*

CHARLESTON: **Tom Beaudy,** Old Claremont Rd., Charleston, NH 03603. *Shaker-style furniture.*

CLAREMONT: **Fred Puksta,** 6 Elm St., Claremont, NH 03743 (603)542-6317.

CONCORD: **Lawrence Bickford Contemporary Furniture** RFD 4, Box 252, Concord, NH 03301 (603)224-9443. *Functional pieces with clean lines, fine details, careful craftsmanship contemporary design.*

CONWAY: **David R. Higgins,** Box 1355, Conway, NH 03818 (603)447-6778.

Gary Wright, Box 1661 Tasker Hill Rd., Conway, NH 03818 (603)447-2375. *Commission marquetry.*

(102) Douglas Yule, Box 2072, Conway, NH 03818 (603)447-3778. *Traditional and contemporary pieces of sound construction and harmonious line.*

FRANCONIA: **(182) Ironwood Studio,** Box 517, Franconia NH 03580. *Two woodcarvers: Roland Shick and John Serino. Carved signs and custom work.*

GILMANTON: **John Frick,** Box 325, Gilmanton, NH 03237 (603)267-6932.

HAMPTON: **(175) Ron Vellucci, Artist Designer,** 14 Philbrook Terrace, Hampton, NH 03842 (603)926-3502. *Wood relief wall sculptures and contemporary furniture design.*

HANOVER: **Curt Gridley,** Dartmouth College Woodshop Hanover, NH 03755 (603)646-2347.

JAFFREY: **Terry Miller, Craftsman,** 97 Prospect St., Jaffrey, NH 03452 (603)532-7504. *Custom furniture.*

LEBANON: **The Cottage Woodworks, M.T. Ross,** Stony Brook Rd., Lebanon, NH 03766 (603)448-4568. *We reflect simple, functional designs and techniques of the Shakers through reproductions and custom cabinetmaking.*

LEE: **Charles Cox,** Tuckaway Farm, Lee Rd., Route 155, Lee (Dover), NH 03820 (603)868-1822. *Custom design and construction of utilitarian items from spoons, dog sleds, cabinets to houses and barns.*

MANCHESTER: **Kurlansky Furniture Repair,** 35 S. Commercial St., Manchester, NH 03101 (603)668-8059. *Repair, restoration, refinishing of all types of furniture, plus design and construction of fine furniture.*

MERIDEN: **Dana Robes, Wood Craftsman,** Route 120, Meriden, NH 0370 (603)469-3357. *Use hardwoods, mostly in Shaker design.*

MILFORD: **Noon Whistle Woodworks,** 159 Nashua St., Milford, NH 03055 (603)673-7977. *Specializing in design and construction of hardwood furniture and cabinetwork for commercial and residential interiors.*

MONT VERNON: **Daniel Banner,** Salisbury Rd., Mont Vernon, NH 03057 (603)654-6364. *Traditional New England country, native woods, reflecting the Shaker ideal of simplicity, form from function.*

NEWFIELDS: **(181) Plum Blossom Studios,** Otis Rd., Newfields, NH 03856 (603)772-9504. *Animals and figures, decorative art carvings, custom-designed furnishings.*

Frederick A. Wildnauer, Box 105, Newfields, NH 03856 (603)778-1078.

NEWINGTON: **Tom Roy, Designs in Wood,** Fabyan's Point Rd., Newington, NH 03801 (603)436-8962. *Period reproductions and contemporary originals.*

NEW IPSWICH: **Jeff Stubbs,** 96 River Rd., New Ipswich, NH 03071 (603)878-2740. *Cabinets, wood turning, furniture. Repair, custom new construction.*

NEWPORT: **Terry Moore, Cabinet Maker,** 11 Summer St., Newport, NH 03773 (603)863-4795. *Custom kitchens, furniture and custom handmade guitars.*

NORTH CONWAY: **Howard Hatch,** Box 281, North Conway, NH 03860 (603)356-3929. *Design and build to order, residential, office furniture. Priority: fit customer environment.*

(110) William H. James Co., Main St. Box W, North Conway, NH 03860 (603)356-5200. *All handmade, standard line as well as custom work, hand-rubbed finishes.*

NOTTINGHAM: **C.B. Oliver,** Box 204, Nottingham, NH 03290 (603)679-5588. *Shop is quite flexible in capability of design, scale and production methods.*

PETERBORO: **(182) James Pritchard,** RFD 2, Boulder Dr., Peterboro, NH 03444 (603)563-8647. *Figural carvings, accepts commissions for same.*

PORTSMOUTH: **Jeffrey Cooper, Tomorrow's Antiques,** 855 Islington St., Portsmouth, NH 03801 (603)436-7945. *Custom-designed and crafted wood furnishings.*

ROCHESTER: **David R. Foote,** 8 Osborn St., Rochester, NH 03867 (603)335-1105. *Design, drafting techniques. General woodworking, steam-bending, lamination.*

RYE BEACH: **Richard Pascoe,** Box 195, Rye Beach, NH 03871. *Custom furniture, reproductions, turnings, architectural detail work.*

SALEM: **The Dovetailor,** Box 492, Salem, NH 03079 (603)893-2102. *Distinguished eighteenth-century reproductions, custom furniture, antique restoration.*

WEST CHESTERFIELD: **G. Cota,** Old Ferry Rd., West Chesterfield, NH 03466 (603)256-8801. *Highly creative hand-carved signs, other wood products.*

WINCHESTER: **Magic Forest Woodworking,** Route 1, Old Chesterfield Rd., Winchester, NH 03470 (603)239-4837. *Fine furniture, cabinetry carvings, architectural woodworking.*

New Jersey

ALLENTOWN: **The Allentown Feed Co.,** Main St., Allentown, NJ 08501 (609)259-2136.

ASBURY PARK: **William Lee,** 617 2nd Ave., Asbury Park, NJ 07712 (201)775-2987. *Commissioned works include wall murals, sculpture and accessories in wood, metals, etched glass.*

AUGUSTA: **Jim Whitman,** Route 1, Box 716, Augusta, NJ 07822 (201)875-7315. *Custom carving for logos, coat of arms and advertising assignments.*

BARNEGAT: **Lester Smiejan,** 225 Jones Rd., Barnegat, NJ 08005 (609)698-7411.

BARRINGTON: **Richard Feldstein,** 209 Williams Ave., Barrington, NJ 08007 (609)546-8338. *Custom, sculptural furniture, accessories, commercial interiors.*

BLOOMINGDALE: **Heirloom Creations,** 83 Rafkind Rd. Box 64, Bloomingdale, NJ 07403 (201)492-1537. *Custom-designed monogrammed serving trays.*

BRIDGETON: **Robert J. Costa,** Sheppards Mill Rd., RD 2 Box 330, Bridgeton, NJ 08302 (609)455-1715. *Furniture, custom cabinetry, architectural woodworking.*

BRIDGEWATER: **Greg Bodnar,** 1002 Rector Rd., Bridgewater, NJ 08807 (201)526-0179.

Sublimation Woodshop, Charles Mark, 465 Church Rd., Bridgewater, NJ 08807 (201)231-1279. *Original-design furniture made the low-tech way. Woodworking as an outlet for life's frustrations, existential dread, and creative forces. Custom orders only.*

CAPE MAY: **Walter Charles,** 1006 Seashore Rd., Cape May, NJ 08204 (609)884-7143. *For the discriminating.*

CEDAR GROVE: **Glen G. Guarino,** 79 Overlook Rd., Cedar Grove, NJ 07009. *Custom-designed woodworking.*

CHERRY HILL: **(33) Robert Fischer,** 304 Pennsylvania Ave., Cherry Hill, NJ 08002 (609)488-9460 and 795-0520. *Designer and maker.*

CINNAMINSON: **John Potter,** 604 Ivystone Lane, Cinnaminson, NJ 08077 (609)829-8622. *Traditional reproductions, antique restoration and refinishing, wood novelties.*

CLARK: **Keith Naples, Woodworker,** 22 Sunset Dr., Clark, NJ 07066 (201)276-6609. *Furniture, interiors, sculpture.*

CLARKSBORO: **Gary L. Beard,** 120 Timber Lane, Clarksboro, NJ 08020 (609)423-6691. *Unique design, one-of-a-kind.*

CLAYTON: **Lloret Woodworking,** 50 E. High St., Clayton, NJ 08312 (609)881-3698. *Display cabinets.*

COLONIA: **Rick Plesher,** 179 Midfield Rd., Colonia, NJ 07067 (201)388-4171. *Furniture construction.*

COLTS NECK: **Randy Mazur,** 15 Hockhockson Rd. Box 350, Colts Neck, NJ 07722 (201)542-7241. *Custom woodworking done to order; anything in wood.*

EAST HANOVER: **Designit Plus—Woodwork of Distinction,** 30-A Ridgedale Ave., East Hanover, NJ 07936 (201)386-1478. *Design and custom woodwork. Contemporary through period designs of furniture.*

EAST KEANSBURG: **Richard Best,** 69 S. End Ave., East Keansburg, NJ 07734. *One-of-a-kind designs. Customer buys a design and piece not to be repeated by me.*

EDISON: **Curt Fogas,** 69 Schuyler Dr., Edison, NJ 08817. *Reproductions, cabinets and handcrafted novelites.*

FRANKLIN LAKES: **Andrew J. Pitts,** 989 Pines Terrace, Franklin Lakes, NJ 07417 (201)337-7833. *Individually designed furniture pieces, one-of-a-kind.*

FREEHOLD: **Alternative Designs,** 95 Monmouth Ave., Freehold, NJ 07728 (201)780-3947. *Wall units of solid-wood furniture design and construction.*

FRENCHTOWN: **(52) Nils Falk,** 10 Bridge St., Frenchtown, NJ 08825 (201)996-4863. *Design, furniture making, architectural woodwork.*

GLEN GARDNER: **(114) Clark Twining,** Route 1, Glen Gardner, NJ 08826 (201)537-2878. *Single, contemporary design for furniture pieces.*

HACKETTSTOWN: **(114) Puritan Furniture,** 113 Plane St., Hackettstown, NJ 07840 (201)850-8289. *Wall units, period furniture, restoration of fine furniture, custom carving.*

HIGHLAND PARK: **R.H. Karol, Sculptor,** Box 1255, Highland Park, NJ 08904 (201)249-1374. *Realistic and abstract sculpture of the female figure.*

Wood Design by Dennis Oziel, 106 N. 10th Ave., Highland Park, NJ 08904 (201)249-0773. *Wall furniture, tables, bedroom sets, architectural woodwork.*

HOBOKEN: **Willow Woodworking,** 1027 Willow Ave., Hoboken, NJ 07030 (201)798-0143. *Abstract expressionist carvings. Lately moving towards more realistic work.*

JACKSON: **Steve Lambert,** Box 86 RD 3, Jackson, NJ 08527 (201)928-0692. *Original wood sculpture.*

KENDALL PARK: **Steven B. Levine,** 8 Holder Rd., Kendall Park, NJ 08824 (201)297-0131. *Marquetry and inlay.*

LAKE HIAWATHA: **John T. Triolo,** 98-A Dafrack Dr., Lake Hiawatha, NJ 07034.

LAMBERTVILLE: **Peter J. Nelson,** Route 2 Box 8, Lambertville, NJ 08530. *Lathe turnings, antique reproduction chairs.*

LAYTON: **(60) Ken Fisher,** Peters Valley, Layton, NJ 07851 (201)948-5255.

MAPLEWOOD: **William J. Cheve II,** 17 Plymouth Ave., Maplewood, NJ 07040 (201)761-4519.

MAYWOOD: **Daniel Boland,** 455 Latham St., Maywood, NJ 07607 (201)546-1043. *Architectural woodwork, bedroom and dining room furniture.*

MIDLAND PARK: **William J. Moses,** 48 Myrtle Ave., Midland Park, NJ 07432 (201)445-2532. *Furniture that feels good to the eye.*

MILFORD: **Stephen Zdepski,** Route 2 Box 56, Milford, NJ 08848 (201)995-4555. *Mostly reproductions of Early American pieces, mainly in walnut and cherry.*

MONTCLAIR: **(77) Foley-Waite Associates,** 73 N. Willow St., Montclair, NJ 07042 (201)746-2252. *Fine custom furniture and architectural woodworking.*

MOUNT HOLLY: **Edward J. O'Brien,** 8 Oxford Court, Mount Holly, NJ 08060.

MURRAY HILL: **Lawrence E. Lear,** 4 Darby Court, Murray Hill, NJ 07974 (201)464-8312. *One-of-a-kind.*

NORTH BRUNSWICK: **Jeff & Roger Ruppert, Custom Woodworking,** 590 Nassau St., North Brunswick, NJ 08902 (201)247-0551. *All types of woodworking—boats to boxes.*

NUTLEY: **John Russo, Designer-Woodworker,** 396 Prospect St., Nutley, NJ 07110 (201)667-7051. *Custom furniture and cabinetry for interior designing trade and private home clientele.*

OLDWICK: **(120) Kenneth Vliet,** Vliettown Rd., Oldwick, NJ 08858 *Custom cabinetwork, toys.*

PALMYRA: **Thomas More Bujak,** 423 Leconey Ave., Palmyra, NJ 08065 (609)829-3886. *Custom design and construction of functional hardwood woodwork.*

PARAMUS: **George E. Mulhauser,** 545 Clinton Rd., Paramus, NJ 07652 (201)262-2766. *Fine furniture, interiors, boat interiors, sculpture.*

PENNINGTON: **(19) Allan Smith, Cabinetmaker,** RD 1 Box 193A, Pennington, NJ 08534 (609)737-2905 or 466-2039. *Furniture and cabinetwork, designed and built to order. Repairs and restoration.*

PENNSVILLE: **Mulford Custom Woodworking,** 17 Sunset Ave., Pennsville, NJ 08070 (609)678-8189. *Arch woodworking, specializing in veneer work.*

PLAINSBORO: **Henry Schaefer, Cabinetmaker,** 609 Plainsboro Rd., Plainsboro, NJ 08536 (609)799-4175. *Turnings, laminations, jewelry boxes, display cabinets, wall-hung case work and custom furniture. Unusual commissions welcome.*

RANDOLPH: **Joseph W. Pieczynski II,** 44 Center Grove Rd., L Court 28, Randolph, NJ 07869 (201)361-3512. *The design and construction of 3-D puzzle sculptures and fine geometric wood and metal art.*

RIDGEFIELD PARK: **(185) Shedden Sculpture,** 142 Central Ave., Ridgefield Park, NJ 07660 (201)440-6955. *Unique furniture sculpture in wood, metal, stone, fiberglass.*

RIDGEWOOD: **(56) William C. Oetjen,** 302 Pershing Ave., Ridgewood, NJ 07450 (201)445-8646. *Contemporary and traditional custom made furniture for home and office. Commissions accepted.*

RUTHERFORD: **William Calame,** 103 Elliott Place, Rutherford, NJ 07070 (201)933-4195. *All types of handmade toys and crafts. Custom-made to orders.*

Creekside Craftsman, Al Lohrenz, 37 A Ivy Place, Rutherford, NJ 07070 (201)935-3424. *Fine custom woodworking by commission.*

SCHOOLEY'S MOUNTAIN: **(110) Bruce J. Kunkel, Mr. Sawdust Schools of Professional Woodworking,** Box 4, Schooley's Mountain, NJ 07870 (201)879-5899 (Home address: R.D. 1, Box 96, Henryville, PA 18332). *In-depth classes in power tools, hand tools and woodcarving.*

SKILLMAN: **Country Cabinet Shop, Inc., Ned Brown,** Belle Mead Rd., Skillman, NJ 08558. *Self or architect-designed built-in cabinets and one-off furniture pieces.*

SOMERS POINT: **(140) Mark Wescott, Luthier,** 301 W. New York Ave., Somers Point, NJ 08244 (609)927-2486. *Steel-string acoustic guitars.*

SOUTH PLAINFIELD: **Christopher P. Denton,** 102 Garden Dr., South Plainfield, NJ 07080 (201)757-2198.

SPARTA: **David K. Tozier, Custom Fine Woodworker,** 185 Saw Mill Rd., Sparta, NJ 07871 (201)729-7951. *Custom-design pieces in cherry, walnut, other American hardwoods.*

SUMMIT: **Robert Kent,** 81 Woodland Ave., Summit, NJ 07901 (201)273-8830. *One-of-a-kind pieces, with functional and/or sculptural emphasis.*

TITUSVILLE: **Warren Cadwallader, Staub Wood Craft Carpentry,** Box 165 River Dr., Titusville, NJ 08560 (609)737-9531. *Custom pieces. Furniture, cases, cabinets, doors and custom trim.*

VERONA: **Peter S. Given, Jr.,** 41 Howard St., Verona, NJ 07044. *Custom designed furniture and artifacts.*

VINCENTOWN: **Al's Wildlife Carvings,** RR9 Tuckerton Rd., Vincentown, NJ 08088 (609)654-4281. *Wildlife carvings, sculptures.*

William Jackman, RD 4, 23 Foxsparrow Turn, Vincentown, NJ 08088 (609)268-8152. *Wood sculpture.*

WALDWICK: **Wade Thomas, Custom Cabinetry,** Waldwick, NJ 07463 (201)445-2369. *Kitchens, wall units, custom cabinets, furniture, specialty woodworking.*

WEST PATERSON: **Eric Carter,** Weaseldrift Rd., West Paterson, NJ 07424 (201)279-2030. *Custom hardwood furniture, carving inlay.*

WOODBRIDGE: **Perry A. Balog,** 225 Martool Dr., Woodbridge, NJ 07095 (201)634-4435. *The designing and construction of one-of-a-kind, shamanistic pieces and stringed musical instrument construction and repair.*

New Mexico

ALAMOGORDO: **Rob Williams,** 2006 Scenic Dr. C, Alamogordo, NM 88310. *Desk name plates, free-form trinket boxes.*

ALBUQUERQUE: **(150) Greg FryeWeaver,** 1105 Florida N.E., Albuquerque, NM 87110 (505)265-2719. *Specialty and custom work, sculptural design for functional use.*

Harvey Buchalter Sculpture, 1615 Kit Carson S.W., Albuquerque, NM 87104 (505)247-2602. *Unique sculpture in wood and stone. Jewish ceremonial art and objects. Commissions are welcomed.*

Bob R. Henderson, 8836 Harwood NE, Albuquerque, NM 87111 (505)299-9283. *Hand-carved furniture.*

Daniel Phillip Kronberg, 5317 Veronica NE, Albuquerque, NM 87111 (505)294-0237. *Jewelry model maker. Models for emblems, plaques, trophies, medals for casting reproduction. Specialized wood sculpture.*

Mora's Fine Furniture, 1817 Paige Place NE, Albuquerque, NM 8712 (505)292-6608. *Wood sculpture (useful and elegant), home-computer furniture-chests, tables and desks. Also refinishing work.*

(107) Gerald D. Otis, 4605 Compound N. Ct. N.W., Albuquerque, NM 87107 (505)345-7202.

(60) Alan Paine Radebaugh, 125 50th St. N.W., Albuquerque, NM 87105. *Design and manufacture sculptured furniture, sculpture.*

(172) Constance M. Starr, 4605 Compound N. Ct. N.W., Albuquerque, NM 87107 (505)345-7202.

Robert Steffan Sterba, 12000 Prospect N.E., Albuquerque, NM 87112. (505)294-2525. *Turnings, traditional and contemporary, combining art and function. Clean lines, rich finishes.*

Neal Weinberg, 1009 Eighth St. N.W., Albuquerque, NM 87102 (505)765-1544. *One-of-a-kind household and office furnishings. All originally designed.*

CERRILLOS: **J.R. Thomas Fine Furniture,** Box 164, Cerrillos, NM 87010 (505)471-1036. *Custom furniture, cabinets and carving in southwestern styles.*

ESPAÑOLA: **(135) Danyel Clouse, Woodery,** Route 1 Box 388H, Española, NM 87532 (505)753-9575. *Unique, finely handcrafted and precisely strobe-tuned wooden percussion instruments including Tapo drums and marimbas.*

HOLLOMAN AIR FORCE BASE: **George A. Hays,** 2520B San Miguel, Holloman AFB, NM 88330 (505)479-4238.

JEMEZ SPRINGS: **(21) Michael Mocho,** MT Route Box 1-F, Jemez Springs, NM 87025 (505)884-5065. *Furniture, carving, limited production, one-of-a-kind containers and objects, liturgical woodwork, challenges.*

NAVAJO: **(173) John Boomer,** Crystal Trading Post, Navajo, NM 87328 (505)777-2389. *Figures. Walnut, other fine woods.*

PLACITAS: **Dave Cady,** Box 13 TSR, Placitas, NM 87043 (505)867-2100. *Custom woodworking and interiors.*

Rik Martin, Star Route Box 227, Placitas, NM 87043 (505)867-2645. *Small to large individualized works of functional furniture, architectural design in exotic hardwoods.*

QUESTA: **Wabi Woodworks,** Box 743, Questa, NM 87556. *Cabinets, furniture, and doors.*

SANDIA PARK: **Bill Wilmer, Creative Woodworks,** 130 Roberts Rd., Sandia Park, NM 87047 (505)281-2220. *Laminated domestic and exotic woods, turnings, furniture and functional art pieces, rustic and modern design.*

SANTA FE: **Apache Canyon Woodworks,** Route 3 Box 95-I, Santa Fe, NM 87501 (505)983-3049. *Custom furniture, cabinets and sculpture.*

David Samora Woodworks, 1310 Siler Rd., Santa Fe, NM 87501 (505)471-5728. *Architectural millwork, custom doors, carving, cabinetry.*

(146) John J. Demar, Custom Woodcarving, Route 2 Box 266, Santa Fe, NM 87501 (501)473-0032. *Custom woodcarving by commission, traditional and contemporary sculpture, doors, furniture, murals and challenges.*

Kimberly R. Ledford, Route 6 Box 103, Santa Fe, NM 87501 (505)471-4879. *All types of furniture, also some custom cabinetry.*

'Nok on Wood, 2215 Rancho Siringo Rd., Santa Fe, NM 87501 (505)473-1281. *Custom design and construction of contemporary hardwood furniture.*

Norskog & Norskog, Box 5918, Santa Fe, NM 87501 (505)982-1111.

Jeffrey Smith, 822 Gonzales Rd., Santa Fe, NM 87501 (505)988-5951.

TAOS: **JAWAR, James Rannefeld,** Box 1957, Taos, NM 87571 (505)758-8455. *Hardwood furniture, original design, limited production. Doors, sculpture, industrial design, woodworking school planned 1983.*

Don Mikel, Taos Custom Woodworking, Route 1 Box 26, Taos, NM 87571 (505)758-1417. *One-of-a-kind pieces, exotic and standard hardwoods.*

Bruce Peterson, Pilar Route, General Delivery, Taos, NM 87571 (505)758-4086.

Wood, Mud & Sun, Malcolm H. Fleming, Box 2983, Taos, NM 87571 (505)758-8417. *Custom furniture, architectural interiors, cabinetwork.*

TIJERAS: **Leif Gonnsen,** Box 63, Tijeras, NM 87059 ((505)265-5379. *Custom work. Wood, hot forged metal.*

New York

ADDISON: **Purple Island Design,** 3496 Goodhuelake Rd., Addison, NY 14801 (607)359-2731. *Personal desks and clocks. Brochure upon request.*

ALPINE: **Wildwood Flower Woodworking,** Route 228, Alpine, NY 14805 (607)387-9308. *Cabinetmaking, custom furniture and general woodwork.*

ARCRAMDALE: **Woodenworks,** Box 48 Route 3, Arcramdale, NY 12503 (518)329-4107. *Architectural and ornamental woodworking, sculpture.*

ARKPORT: **Stephen N. Marcus,** RD 1 Box 119, Arkport, NY 14807. *Design and construction of individual and/or limited production woodworking.*

BABYLON: **Tom Petry, Woodworker,** 79 Lakeland Ave., Babylon, NY 11702 (516)587-8309. *Furniture design and construction. Custom art framing, boxes, turnings and accessories.*

BOICEVILLE: **(87) Heller's Fabulous Furniture,** Route 28, Boiceville, NY 12412 (914)657-6317. *Free-form woodworking, using the tree as a starting point to further creations.*

BRIDGEHAMPTON: **(101) Michael Reilly, Design,** Box 251, Bridgehampton, NY 11932 (516)726-6584. *Custom furniture designed and built.*

BRONXVILLE: **Phil Marano Inc.,** 78 Palmer Ave., Bronxville, NY 10708 (914)337-1385. *Fine custom furniture, fixtures, store layouts, designs.*

(66) Michael A. Pereira, The Carriage House, 21 Howe Place, Bronxville, NY 10708. *A one-shot deal of anything that spurs my imagination.*

BROOKLYN: **David Benedek,** 134 Dean St., Brooklyn, NY 11201 (212)522-2214. *Interior furnishings and wood objects.*

(42) Clement S. Ceccarelli, 925 Newkirk Ave., Brooklyn, NY 11230 (212)853-6325. *Custom cabinetry and one-of-a-kind or limited editions.*

Edward Devine, 158 Webster Ave., Brooklyn, NY 11230 (212)854-7408. *Dollhouses.*

Jon Elmaleh, 4 Second St., Brooklyn, NY 11231 (212)875-0667.

Chip LaPointe, 419 Grand Ave., Brooklyn, NY 11238 (212)857-8594. *Custom shop recreating details for old houses, cabinets, fireplace mantels, period bars and turnings.*

(159) Ron Murphree, 79 Bridge St., Brooklyn, NY 11201 (212)875-0194. *Commercial and residential work, as well as special design projects.*

(110) Mario Rodriguez, Cabinetmaker, 555 Graham Avenue, Brooklyn, NY 11222 (212)387-6655. *Reproductions, repairs and restorations.*

Water Street Woodworks, 79 Bridge St., Brooklyn, NY 11201 (212)875-7412. *Furniture and architectural woodworks.*

BUFFALO: **David Gilson, Wood Studio Design Dept.,** 1300 Elmwood Ave., Buffalo, NY 14222 (716)878-6032.

Steven E. Kennedy, 303 Summit Ave., Buffalo, NY 14214 (716)833-5080.

Robert Nehin, 22 Starin Ave., Buffalo, NY 14214 (716)836-0027. *Architectural renovation, furniture, work in plastics.*

CARMEL: **Girvan P. Milligan,** RD 9 Daisy Lane, Carmel, NY 10512 (914)277-4905. *Sculptural furniture, accessories and cabinet work.*

CATTARAUGUS: **Pritchard Woodworking,** 43 Leavenworth St., Cattaraugus, NY 14719 (716)257-9286. *Lathe work, furniture making, cabinetmaking, chainsaw sculptures.*

CAZENOVIA: **J. Barrows Carpentry,** Box 259, Cazenovia, NY 13035 (315)655-3254. *Artisanry in building and cabinetry, all kinds of custom building and woodworking.*

CEDARHURST: **Steve Horan, Cabinetmaker,** 362 Washington Ave., Cedarhurst, NY 11516 (516)295-2280. *Anything and everything from rustic to contemporary.*

CHELSEA: **Ric Pomilia,** Box 122 Easter Rd., Chelsea, NY 12512 (914)831-8769. *Cabinetry, furniture pieces by commission, custom stained-glass design and construction.*

CHURCHVILLE: **Auberger and Sons, Scott Auberger,** 1010 Johnson Rd., Churchville, NY 14428 (716)494-1194. *Custom-made wood crafts.*

CLYDE: **William T. Crocca,** 62 W. Genesee St., Clyde, NY 14433 (315)923-7428. *Guitars, occasional custom-made pieces.*

COLD SPRING: **Bruce Donaohue,** Lane Gate Rd., Cold Spring, NY 10516 (914)265-2313.

COLD SPRING HARBOR: **Dick Shanley,** 399 Main St., Cold Spring Harbor, NY 11724 (516)692-6468. *Sculptured furniture and other home furnishings.*

DANSVILLE: **Vince McGavisk,** 18 Clay St., Dansville, NY 14437 (716)335-6623.

DEER PARK: **Norseman Woodcraft, John Gallis,** 112 Brook Ave., Deer Park, NY 11729.

EAST NORTHPORT: **Steven A. Widom,** 523 Third St., East Northport, NY 11731 (516)757-0043. *Fine custom interiors, specializing in architectural woodwork.*

ELLICOTTVILLE: **Joseph King,** 32 Washington St., Ellicottville, NY 14731 (716)699-2169. *Finely crafted woodwork. Limited production, custom pieces and display cases in native hardwoods.*

Gary Mathe, Contemporary Woodwork, Brennan Rd., Ellicottville, NY 14731 (716)699-2557. *Contemporarily sculpted furnishings and fantasy carvings of medium to large sizes.*

ESOPUS: **(94) Jim Fawcett,** Box 65, Esopus, NY 12429 (914)384-6650.

FAIRPORT: **Kevin Mannix Custom Woodworking and Furniture Design,** 254 Watson Rd., Fairport, NY 14450 (716)377-3521.

(12) Wendell Smith, 30 Sandle Dr., Fairport, NY 14450 (716)381-2197. *Turnings.*

FLUSHING: **Philip R. Handy,** 78-05 164th St., Flushing, NY 11366 (212)969-7389. *Scaled-down furniture and miniatures.*

Theo Oosterlinck, 154-43 26th Ave., Flushing, NY 11354 (212)445-0873. *Gothic carvings.*

FRANKLIN SQUARE: **Creative Woodworking,** 61 Madison St., Franklin Square, NY 11010 (212)488-6516. *Boards, bowls, clocks, accessories and furniture.*

FREDONIA: **William R. Bartoo,** 382 Chestnut St., Fredonia, NY 14063 (716)672-6466. *One-of-a-kind pieces.*

FREEPORT: **William Brower,** 55 Frederick Ave., Freeport, NY 11520 (516)378-7026. *Original and traditional furniture, cabinetry, architectural millwork.*

GENESEO: **Jerry Alonzo,** 76 Center St., Geneseo, NY 14454 (716)346-3020.

GLENS FALLS: **John Dunham,** 18 Knight St., Glens Falls, NY 12801 (518)793-4353. *Handmade one-of-a-kind and limited-edition furniture of native hardwoods.*

GOWANDA: **(14) Francis Scott,** W. Becker Rd., Gowanda, NY 14070 (716)532-3818. *Turned and carved objects both functional and nonfunctional.*

GRANVILLE: **Kenneth J. Oriel,** Granville, NY 12832 (518)642-1215. *Custom-made contemporary furniture with the emphasis on simple, quiet design.*

GROTON: **(129) Harry Wilhelm, Designer & Craftsman in Wood,** 254 Luce Rd., Groton, NY 13073 (607)533-7221. *One-of-a-kind furniture and clocks. Finely crafted, gracefully proportioned, solid-wood designs.*

HAWTHORNE: **Lewis Korn Furniture Design,** 253 Commerce St., Hawthorne, NY 10532 (914)747-0848.

HOLLAND: **Denlin Shop,** 241 Canada St., Holland, NY 14080. *Custom furniture.*

ITHACA: **Bosworth Handcrafts,** 132 Indian Creek Rd., Ithaca, NY 14850 (607)272-6716. *Furniture and other objects made of wood designed with the customer for use in daily living.*

B.W. Calnek, 309 Salem Dr., Ithaca, NY 14850 (607)257-4172. *Miscellaneous small woodcrafts including salt and pepper, jewelry and other boxes.*

Glenn Gray, 709 S. Plain St., Ithaca, NY 14850 (607)273-3001. *One-of-a-kind furniture and cabinets, personalized and distinctively made.*

Ken Jupiter, 407 W. Seneca St., Ithaca, NY 14850 (607)272-4902. *One-of-a-kind and limited production furniture, one-of-a-kind and production crafts.*

JAMESTOWN: **(120) Jim Christo,** 608 Charles St., Jamestown, NY 14701. *Original concepts in toys for play or display.*

James F. Dupler, JFD Wood Specialties, 18 Hess St., Jamestown, NY 14701 (716)664-6142. *Cabinetmaking and furniture repair. Personal delivery available.*

Eric Eklum, 117 Beechview Ave., Jamestown, NY 14701 (716)665-5344. *Original designs of Dunlap, Shaker styles, local curly maple, cherry, Windsor chairs, antique restorations.*

Jamestown Community College Artisan Center, Elizabeth Bradbury, Supervisor, 9 Falconer St., Jamestown, NY 14701 (716)484-9920. *College degree and certificate programs in the art of woodworking. Basic and advanced courses.*

JAMESVILLE: **Cherry Valley Furniture Restoration,** 4308 Graham Rd., Jamesville, NY 13078 (315)492-9273. *Restoration, repair and refinishing of fine antiques specializing in L and J.G. Stickley furniture.*

JEFFERSONVILLE: **Roy O'Mara Woodworking,** Sheafer Rd., Jeffersonville, NY 12748 (516)661-5421. *Custom cabinetry, furniture, duplication, restoration, architectural woodworking.*

JOHNSON CITY: **Autumnwood Instruments, Bernd Josef Krause,** RD 2, Box 9 Fredericks Rd., Johnson City, NY 13790 (607)748-2941. *Quality handcrafted string instruments: guitars, dulcimers, mandolins, lutes, etc. Standard or custom. Lifetime guarantee.*

KINGSTON: **(171) Robin Danziger, Designs,** 38 St. James St., Kingston, NY 12401 (914)331-1125. *Custom designs, boxes, desk accessories and objects of art. Also, inlays in precious metals, shell and ivory.*

LAKE GEORGE: **Hally E. Weller,** RD 1 Box 297, Lake George, NY 12845 (518)792-0309. *Small cabinets, boxes and tables.*

LAKE PEEKSKILL: **Renaissance Woodcarving,** Nardin Rd. Box 448, Lake Peekskill, NY 10537 (914)526-3443. *Fine hand-carved signs, screens, mantels, doors and furniture.*

LOCUST VALLEY: **Peter G. De Filippo,** Box 130, Locust Valley, NY 11560 (516)676-5738. *Professional sculptor working in rare woods, marble, bronze, steel.*

LYNBROOK: **William Marsella,** 12 Elm St., Lynbrook, NY 11563 (516)887-1906. *Reconstruct and repair period furniture. Stained glass and fabrication.*

MALDEN BRIDGE: **New Chatham Joiner, Sy Balsen,** Route 66, Malden Bridge, NY 12115 (518)766-2829.

MIDDLE FALLS: **Robert Hargrave,** Box 116, Middle Falls, NY 12848 (518)692-7283. *Laminated and carved plywood furniture, mirrors and accessories.*

MIDDLETOWN: **Lawrence Lamberg,** 16 Adams Ave., Middletown, NY 10940 (914)342-3779. *Custom-designed cabinets and furniture.*

MOUNT KISCO: **Art & Frame Gallery,** 9 S. Moger Ave., Mount Kisco, NY 10549 (914)666-2938. *Wonderful things in wood, small gift items, commissions.*

MOUNT TREMPER: **(179) Howard Werner,** Route 28, Mount Tremper, NY 12457 (914)688-7024. *Sculpture, carved, constructed furniture.*

NAPLES: **Peter Ingle,** RD 1 Hicks Rd., Naples, NY 14512 (716)396-2258. *Handmade and hand-carved items.*

NEW CITY: **Patrick Bremer,** 11 Bonnie Lane, New City, NY 10956 (914)634-3201. *Extensive use of hand-tool technique and traditional joinery utilized in modern forms.*

Paul G. Garber, 30 James St., New City, NY 10956 (914)634-8914. *Design and construction of basic home furnishing, including clocks, tables, cradles, etc. Restoration, refinishing.*

NEWFIELD: **Carl Bass Woodworks,** 58 Cornish Hollow Newfield, NY 14867 (607)272-5977. *Custom furniture, cabinetry, turning, architectural and marine woodwork.*

NEW YORK: **A.W. Pact Woodcarving,** 86 E. Seventh St. No 8, New York, NY 10003 (212)475-3129. *Hand woodcarving architectural, ornamental, residential, figures, portraits, restoration. All designs by Pact.*

Joel Einschlag, 83-10 35th Ave. Jackson Heights, New York NY 11372 (212)651-4427. *Built-ins, custom cabinets and original furniture.*

Donald Fracapane, 25 W. 70th St., 3A, New York, NY 10023 (212)799-7630. *One-of-a-kind as well as architectural (both commercial and residential).*

(116) Rick Gentile, 684 Broadway, New York, NY 10012 (212)677-6637. *Custom furniture and woodcarving.*

Mark Goldberg, Cabinetmaker, 403 Broome St. 4th floor New York, NY 10012 (212)431-7108. *Showcase cabinetry, tables, architectural, interiors, etc.*

(74) Lignum Design Inc., 146 W. 25th St., 12th Floor, New York, NY 10001 (212)242-3493. *Fine woodwork, post-modern furniture design, dependability.*

Bernard Londin, Sculptor, 6200 Spencer Ave., New York NY 10471 (212)796-2926. *Artistic carvings.*

(44) Maurice Fraser Workshop, 153 W. 78th St., New York NY 10024 (212)595-3557. *One-of-a-kind furniture, classical harpsichords, woodworking lessons.*

Eric D. Schlesinger, 255 Centre St. 4th Floor, New York, NY 10013 (212)431-7108. *Custom solid-wood furniture in domestic and imported hardwoods and architectural woodworking.*

Howard Seidel, 364 W. 18th St., New York, NY 10011.

(45) Paul Sturm, 134 Spring St., New York, NY 10012 (212)966-4736. *Designing and building fine freestanding and built-in furniture to order from showroom and portfolio or custom-designed.*

NORTHPORT: **Gerson M. Rapoport,** 7 Jesse Dr., Northport NY 11768 (516)757-3592. *All types of sculptures, specializing in Judaic art, designs combining wood, stained glass and bronze.*

OGDENSBURG: **(128) Thomas J. Duffy, Cabinetmaker,** 23 Commerce St., Ogdensburg, NY 13669 (315)393-1484. *Cabinetry (fine furniture, ships cabinetry), architectural wood working and tool making of first quality.*

Arthur C. Hastings, 705 Pickering St., Ogdensburg, NY 13669

Lou Almasi, Box 512, Orchard Park, NY 14127. *Custom furniture and cabinets.*

OSSINING: **(111) John Bickel,** 6 Grants Lane, Ossining, NY 10562 (914)941-5408. *One-of-a-kind and multiples of my own design.*

PENN YAN: **(42) Tom Kneeland, Designer, Craftsman,** 221 Clinton St., Penn Yan, NY 14527 (315)536-2886. *Contemporary furniture and accessories. Original designs, teaching.*

(106) Pallischeck Bros. Woodworking, 40 Champlin Ave. Penn Yan, NY 14527 (315)536-6961. *Kitchen and office cabinetry, contemporary and period furniture, one-offs to limited production.*

PITTSFORD: **Vincent Barabba,** 522 Stone Rd., Pittsford, NY 14534 (716)385-3657. *Amateur.*

R.J. Harper, 829 Mendon Center Rd., Pittsford, NY 14534 (716)624-2527. *Original furniture, architectural woodwork, staircases.*

PLEASANTVILLE: **(131) D.C. Story & Company,** 30 Willis Place, Pleasantville, NY 10570 (914)769-1722. *Custom-designed and made clocks. Antique restorations.*

POMPEY: **Lee Karkruff, Designer-Cabinetmaker,** Box 132 Pompey, NY 13138. (315)677-9342. *Custom-made cabinetry and fine woodwork.*

PORT JERVIS: **Mortenson & Maher Woodworks,** RD 2 Box 111, Port Jervis, NY 12771 (914)856-1871. *Custom furniture cabinets, made from select domestic, exotic hardwood veneers.*

PORT WASHINGTON: **Northwood Design Inc.,** 80 Shore Rd., Port Washington, NY 11050 (516)883-0101.

POUND RIDGE: **William P. Katz Art Studio,** RD 2 Box 275 Old Stone Hill Rd., Pound Ridge, NY 10576 (914)764-5248. *One thousand sq. ft. studio, fully equipped for working and teaching stone, wood, clay, acrylics, mixed media.*

PRATTSBURG: **Deerlick Woodworks,** RD 2, Prattsburg, NY 14873 (607)522-3212. *Custom woodworking, furniture reproduction and repair.*

PURCHASE: **(38) Dennis FitzGerald,** Visual Arts Dept SUNY at Purchase, Purchase, NY 10577 (914)253-5536. *Custom and commissioned furniture, some architectural millwork.*

PUTNAM VALLEY: **Meyer Weiner,** RD 3 Tinker Hill Rd. Putnam Valley, NY 10579 (914)526-3693. *Turned bowls and one-of-a-kind pieces of furniture.*

RENSSELAER: **Gerald Dwileski,** 50 Sherwood Ave., Rensselaer, NY 12144.

ROCHESTER: **Edgar A. Brown,** 72 Van Bergh Ave., Rochester, NY 14610 (716)482-9027. *Designer-craftsman in wood.*

Ron Callari, 1237 E. Main St., Rochester, NY 14609 (716)482-7233. *Contemporary furniture and accessories.*

(58) John Dodd, 1237 E. Main St., Rochester, NY 14609 (716)482-7233. *Contemporary wooden furniture.*

Jeffrey S. Harrison, 111 Kingsboro Rd., Rochester, NY 14619 (716)235-5917.

David Heyneman, 70 Fifth St., Rochester, NY 14605 (716)423-0128. *Custom electric guitars and basses, furniture, repairs.*

Edward Jacob, 788 University Ave., Rochester, NY 14607 (716)442-8780. *One-of-a-kind contemporary hardwood furniture.*

Richard V. Johnson, 169 St. Paul St., Rochester, NY 14604 (716)454-4395. *Sculptural furniture.*

Steve Loar, c/o College of Fine & Applied Arts, Rochester Institute of Technology, One Lomb Memorial Dr., Rochester, NY 14623. *Designer-craftsman of furniture and turned forms.*

(90) Richard Newman, 66 Frost Ave., Rochester, NY 14608 (716)328-1577. *Custom and art furniture.*

Gregory Olejarski, 653 Winona Blvd., Rochester, NY 14617. *Solid-wood backgammon and chess tables.*

(81) Douglas B. Prickett, 25 Weider St., Rochester, NY 14620 (716)442-0097.

Frederick E. Shroyer, 309 Rosewood Terrace, Rochester, NY 14609 (716)288-3088. *Architectural woodworking, commissioned furniture, sculpture.*

Doug Smith, 86 Devon Rd., Rochester, NY 14619. *Wall cabinets.*

Cynthia Sullivan, 30 Wildmere Rd., Rochester, NY 14617 (716)342-7676.

(151) Newell L. White, Affinity Woodworks Inc., 15 Henrietta St., Rochester, NY 14620 (716)461-2200. *One-of-a-kind handmade furniture, residential and institutional, emphasis on conceptual design.*

Alan D. Winer, 302 N. Goodman St., Rochester, NY 14607 (716)244-5678. *Custom hardwood furniture designed and built.*

W.J. Sloane Woodworking, 145 Westminster Rd., Rochester, NY 14607 (716)442-0549.

ROCKY POINT: **Don Hicks,** 12 Walnut Rd., Rocky Point, NY 11778 (516)744-5502. *Wood and furniture products, interiors.*

ROSENDALE: **(87) Marek Lisowski,** Rosendale, NY 12472 (914)658-9225. *Unusual custom designs in wood.*

SANDS POINT: **Dan Kurshan,** Tibbits Lane, Sands Point, NY 11050. *Abstract carvings in solid and laminated wood.*

SARANAC LAKE: **Michael Welch,** 26 Park Ave., Saranac Lake, NY 12983 (518)891-1867. *Handmade furniture of contemporary design.*

SARATOGA SPRINGS: **Bigelow's Cabinet Shop,** 42 Caroline St., Saratoga Springs, N.Y. 12866 (518)584-8870. *Original designs, made to order, with finest woods and hardware.*

E. Lenz, 8 Third St., Saratoga Springs, NY 12866 (518)584-3595.

SAUGERTIES: **(136) Robert Meadow, The Luthierie,** 2449 W. Saugerties Rd., Saugerties, NY 12477 (914)246-5207. *Japanese hand woodworking, musical instrument making.*

SCHENECTADY: **(82) Maggie Coffin,** 1178 Lowell Rd., Schenectady, NY 12308.

SCOTTSVILLE: **(26) Lanham C. Deal,** 17 Maple St., Scottsville, NY 14546 (716)889-2378. *Fine commissions.*

(41) Stephen Proctor, 18 Maple St., Scottsville, NY 14546 (716)889-2318. *Cabinetmaking.*

Lee Schuette, W.C. Workshop, Scottsville, NY 14576 (716)889-2378. *The fine art of wood work and furniture.*

SEA CLIFF: **John Packard, Cabinetmaker,** 266 Sea Cliff Ave., Sea Cliff, NY 11579 (516)671-1515. *Furniture made to order. Reproductions, original designs. Antique restoration, refinishing.*

SHERMAN: **David Damcott,** Sherman, NY 14781 (716)487-1844. *Custom-made furniture to order.*

SHIRLEY: **Dan Gilhooley Design,** 47 Oakwood Dr., Shirley, NY 11967 (516)281-6345. *Individually designed and handcrafted hardwood furniture.*

SILVER SPRINGS: **Silver Springs Cabinetry,** 5700 Broughton Rd., Silver Springs, NY 14550 (716)493-2172. *General woodworking, specializing in cherry and walnut.*

SMITHTOWN: **Burkco Contracting Co.,** Smithtown, NY 11787 (516)360-9670. *Custom woodworking and interior finish work.*

SPENCER: **(16) Garn Menapace,** Larve Rd., Spencer, NY 14883 (607)589-4326. *Bowls and related objects.*

SPRINGWATER: **Michael James & Son, Craftsmen in Wood,** 7611 County Rd. 37, Springwater, NY 14560 (716)669-2356. *Repair, reproduction commissions, design and production prototypes.*

STATEN ISLAND: **Capt. Jon O. Grondahl,** 83 Champlain Ave., Staten Island, NY 10306 (212)351-4032. *Custom-made furniture. Norwegian rosemaling.*

William Nelson, 101 Cheshire Place, Staten Island, NY 10301 (212)981-6843. *Cabinets and restoration.*

SYRACUSE: **(154) The American Woodworks Co., David Morton,** 2510 Burnet Ave., Syracuse, NY 13206 (315)463-0442. *Primarily commissioned hardwood architectural, cabinet, furniture pieces, bars, mantels, built-ins and design.*

L.P. Lessard, Jr., 103 Merriweather Dr., Syracuse, NY 13219 (315)487-0742. *Specialize primarily in early American reproductions and adaptations.*

Pine Hill Colonials, 420 E. Corey Rd., Syracuse, NY 13219. *Small-run items, wooden toys.*

Michael Quattrociocchi, Syracuse, NY 13206 (315)463-5815. *Custom-designed and hand-built furniture tailored to meet an individual customer's needs.*

(168) Wood Goods, 122 Walton St., Syracuse, NY 13202 (315)475-9565. *Fine hardwood boxes and sheepskin covered wooden toys. Wholesale and retail. Interesting commissions considered.*

TROY: **Robert W. Poppei, Cabinetmaker,** 412 Main Ave., Troy, NY 12180 (518)283-6988. *Fine custom furniture in traditional or modern design, using hand joinery and finishing.*

TRUMANSBURG: **(179) Artemis Woodworking Studio,** Perry City Rd., Trumansburg, NY 14886 (607)387-9603.

UTICA: **Barry J. Wilson,** 5895 Walker Rd., Utica, NY 13502 (315)735-7757. *Woodworking crafts, turnings and boxes. Commission furniture with tambours.*

WALDEN: **James G. Corcoran,** 5 Goldin Blvd., Walden, NY 12586.

WANTAGH: **Anthony Farah, Big Twig Woodworks,** 3722 Hunt Rd., Wantagh, NY 11793 (516)735-1202. *Hardwood furniture and furnishings.*

WAPPINGERS FALLS: **Albert J. Corey,** D11 Carmine Dr., Wappingers Falls, NY 12590 (914)297-1679. *Relief and sculptural carving, also stained glass and crafts.*

(107) Kevin J. Regan, 5 Hamlin Rd., Wappingers Falls, NY 12590. *Commercial and residential custom-designed furniture and interiors, steam-bent designs, spiral staircases. Fifteen years of experience.*

WARWICK: **Richard Cohen,** RD 2 Box 108, Walling Rd., Warwick, NY 10990 (914)986-7475. *Fine furniture and woodworking, custom-designed, handcrafted in variety of finest domestic and imported hardwoods.*

WEBSTER: **Douglas A. Lundy,** 887 DeWitt Rd., Webster, NY 14580 (716)671-7474. *Music boxes, open boxes, puzzles, toys.*

Barry L. Schieven, 617 Bay Rd., Webster, NY 14580 (716)671-5845. *Artist, craftsman.*

WEST ATHENS: **Pisces, Dave Kavner,** Box 151A, West Athens, NY 12015. *Canoe paddles, custom canoes.*

WEST DENBY: **(182) Shelley Signs and Carvings,** Box 94, West Denby, NY 14896 (607)272-5700. *Low-relief carvings, architectural carved panels, custom signs.*

WESTHAMPTON BEACH: **Mullahy Woodworking Design Inc.,** Bldg. 148 Ave. B Suffolk County Airport, Westhampton Beach, NY 11978 (516)288-5155.

WEST SENECA: **(43) Kevin Kegler,** 147 Briarhill Dr., West Seneca, NY 14224.

WHITE PLAINS: **Vincent Bitondo,** 1078 Dobbs Ferry Rd., White Plains, NY 10607 (914)693-8255. *Cabinets, custom turnings including restoration, goblets, boxes. Chip-carving techniques taught.*

Lorenzo Woodworks, 151 S. Broadway, White Plains, NY 10605 (914)428-7693. *Solid-wood cabinetmaking.*

WILTON: **Community Preparation, Woodworking Program,** Wilton Developmental Center, Wilton, NY 12866 (518)584-3110.

North Carolina

APEX: **Woodpecker Enterprises,** Route 2 Box 147B, Apex, NC 27502 (919)362-7073. *Contemporary hardwood furniture, contract design, custom woodworking.*

ASHEVILLE: **Asheville Craftsman Workshop,** 76 N. Lexington Avenue, Asheville, NC 28801 (704)253-1166. *Joinery, design, build and repair. Also our versions of mission oak. Three-man shop.*

Steven Knopp, Cabinetmaker & Joiner, 506 Merrimon Ave., Asheville, NC 28804 (704)258-2586. *Quality period furniture reproductions, period architectural joinery, oriental furniture, ecclesiastical woodworking, carving, sculpture and turning.*

BLACK MOUNTAIN: **(137) Tom Fellenbaum,** 205 W. State St., Black Mountain, NC 28711 (704)669-8950. *Designing and building both traditional and contemporary instruments in the string family.*

BREVARD: **Mountain Forest Studio,** Route 1 Box 3, Brevard, NC 28712 (704)885-2417. *Pottery (functional), raku and porcelain, animals by Mary Murray and drawings and wood sculpture by Tim.*

BYNUM: **Diefendorf & McGinigle Woodworking,** Box 66, Bynum, NC 27228 (919)542-5733. *Custom hardwood furniture, limited-production pieces. Woodworking for special needs.*

CHARLOTTE: **Robert W. Armstrong,** 1916 Sharon Lane, Charlotte, NC 28211 (704)366-8845.

Central Piedmont Community College Woodshop, Elizabeth Ave., Charlotte, NC 28204 (704)373-6651. *Instruction in fine woodwork. Limited custom work.*

Proctor Wood, 4218 Arbor Way, Box 6125-28207, Charlotte, NC 28211 (704)372-0847. *Will make anything unusual or novel in woods.*

CONCORD: **Michael Brown,** Route 8 Box 54, Concord, NC 28025 (704)786-6567. *Cabinetry, lathe turnings, woodcarvings, furniture repair and refinishing.*

DAVIDSON: **Thomas W. Clark,** Box 3023, Davidson, NC 28036 (704)892-0285.

DAVIS: **Pond's,** Box 42, Davis, NC 28524 (704)552-0457. *To make whatever I want, when and like I want.*

FRANKLIN: **Skeenah Woodcraft,** Route 2 Box 835, Franklin, NC 28734.

GREENSBORO: **Harold C. Beaver,** 3003 Trull Ave., Greensboro, NC 27408 (919)288-5322. *Design and construction of jewelry boxes and restoration of antique boxes.*

Paul Sumner, 1709 Holbrook St., Greensboro, NC 27403 (919)852-9870. *Furniture quality tools for handweavers, custom-designed hardwood furniture, quality production craft objects.*

GREENVILLE: **(170) Terry Al Smith,** 309 Summit, Greenville, NC 27834 (919)752-4719.

(142) Eric Thiele, 1306 N. Greene St., Greenville, NC 27834 (919)757-1843. *Wood design service, commercial interiors, cabinets and the artist's studio.*

HAYESVILLE: **Woodcraft Design & Building Arts,** Route 3, Hayesville, NC 28904 (704)389-6428. *We specialize in figure carving, custom furniture, cabinetry, stained-glass windows.*

HICKORY: **Kenneth R. Miller,** 1243 5th Ave. S.W., Hickory, NC 28601. *Custom furniture, beautiful and built to last.*

HIGH POINT: **(64) A. Schadt, Woodcarving and Design,** 1313 Sherman Rd., High Point, NC 27260 (919)883-0051. *Hand-carving and design furniture. Architectural, fine art and sculpture.*

KILL DEVIL HILLS: **R.D. Newberry,** Route 1 Box 596, Kill Devil Hills, NC 27948 (919)441-5904. *Any woodworking challenge accepted here. Waterfowl, cabinetry.*

LEWISVILLE: **Wood-Works by Tom Wilson,** 6091 Shallowford Rd., Lewisville, NC 27023 (919)945-9743. *Custom furniture as well as limited-edition production runs.*

LEXINGTON: **Jim's Cabinet Shop,** Route 11, Box 410, Lexington, NC 27292 (704)869-2720. *Custom furniture, cabinets, lettering, woodcrafts, samples, reproductions.*

Larry C. Rice, 409 Wall St., Lexington, NC 27292 (704)246-5865. *Mountain dulcimers, hammer dulcimers, psalteries.*

MOREHEAD CITY: **W.W. Patrick,** 206 Calico Dr. Box 146, Morehead City, NC 28557. *Custom cabinetmaking in period furniture.*

OTTO: **Christian Handcraft,** Box 320, Otto, NC 28763.

Wes Handicrafts, Route 1 Box 138, Otto, NC 28763.

PENLAND: **(62) Peter Michael Adams,** Penland School, Penland, NC 28765 (704)765-5500. *One-of-a-kind sculptural furniture.*

RALEIGH: **Arts Decoratifs,** 2509 Shelley Rd., Raleigh, NC 27612 (919)782-0178. *Original designs in Art Deco styles.*

The Outer Limb, Jack B. Blomquist, 8404 Azalea Place, Raleigh, NC 27612 (919)847-3080. *Clocks, desk accessories, limited-edition jewelry chests, unique items for home and office.*

Rolfe's Woodworks, 6905 River Birch Dr., Raleigh, NC 267612 (919)848-8647. *Custom woodcarving of animals, trophies, plaques, insignias, etc.*

ROCKY MOUNT: **Honeycraft,** 1428 Rock Creek Dr., Rocky Mount, NC 27801 (919)446-6885. *Furniture reproductions, adaptations of Queen Anne, Chippendale, Hepplewhite and custom furniture.*

SALUDA: **Chad Voorhees Furniture Design,** HWY 176, Saluda, NC 28773 (704)749-9561. *Contemporary design of commission furniture.*

TRYON: **Bradford Packard,** 299 Warrior Dr., Tryon, NC 28782 (704)859-5435. *Handcrafted one-of-a-kind pieces, cabinets and accessories.*

WALNUT COVE: **(63) Bob Kopf's Wooden Works,** Route 1 Box 140A, Walnut Cove, NC 27052 (919)591-4973. *One-of-a-kind commissions, short production runs. Stools, chairs, tables, etc. No case goods.*

WAYNESVILLE: **Duane Garrett Pieper,** 203 1-2 Meadow St., Waynesville, NC 28786 (704)456-7991. *Small cabinets, stools and accessory items.*

David W. Scott, 309 Shelton St., Waynesville, NC 28786 (704)452-1551. *Stools, chairs, lathe work.*

(63) Wayne Raab Woodworking, 307 S. Richland St., Waynesville, NC 28786 (704)456-9376. *One-of-a-kind furniture and sculpture, commissions, limited editions.*

WEAVERVILLE: **Hans G. Schleicher,** Box 1005, Weaverville, NC 28787 (704)645-5392. *One-of-a-kind boxes, turned and free-shape bowls, wall cabinets, coffee tables, accessories.*

WILMINGTON: **For the Love of Wood,** 1812 W. Lake Shore Dr., Wilmington, NC 28401 (919)343-0301. *Custom-designed fine handmade furniture.*

Davis Strider, Wood Designer, 5741 Verbenia St., Wilmington, NC 28403. *One-of-a-kind, functional sculptures and other custom art objects.*

WINSTON-SALEM: **David Carroll,** 4843 Romara Dr., Winston-Salem, NC 27103 (919)760-0192. *By commission.*

Rudisill Enterprises, 1901 Robinhood Rd., Winston-Salem, NC 27104 (919)725-9724. *Small cabinets, tables, turnings, wall units, boxes.*

WOODLEAF: **Robert Bailey, Cabinetmaker,** Depot Rd., Woodleaf, NC 27054 (704)278-4703. *Hardwood furniture, including period pieces, architectural joinery, restoration.*

North Dakota

BISMARCK: **Don Raveling,** 2038 N. 4th St., Bismarck, ND 58501 ((701)255-1846.

FARGO: **(128) Grey Doffin,** 18 S. 8th St., Fargo, ND 58103 (701)235-2624. *Furniture repair and refinishing. Custom building of looms, rocking chairs, cradles and other furniture.*

GRAND FORKS: **David Bratager,** 1135 So. 12th St., Grand Forks, ND 58201. *Marine carvings.*

Ohio

AKRON: **Worcester Woodworks,** 991 Tweed Dr., Akron, OH 44319 (216)644-4730. *Difficult projects of all kinds requiring master craftsmanship. Furniture reproductions.*

AMESVILLE: **(110) Randall K. Fields Design Studio,** Box 206, Amesville, OH 45711. *Solid-hardwood, original-design furniture made to order. Specialties dining tables, coffee tables, Windsor chairs, stools and custom interiors.*

Stan Schaar, Route 1 Box 103B, Amesville, OH 45711 (614)448-6665. *Solid-hardwood, custom-made items, such as furniture with hand-carved panels.*

ANTWERP: **Finished Woods Shoppe,** Route 1 Rd. 45, Antwerp, OH 45813 (419)258-4145. *Wall cabinets, games, game boards and toys, all hardwood. (Pine when ordered.)*

ARCHBOLD: **Jerry Grieser, Diamond in the Rough,** Route 1 Box 151A, Archbold, OH 43502 (419)445-1802. *China hutch, walnut cradles.*

ATHENS: **Thomas Bennett, Cabinetmaker,** Route 2 Box 37, Athens, OH 45701 (614)592-6301. *Finest quality cabinets, furniture, doors and other architectural elements. Wholesale and retail. Shipping anywhere.*

(99) Mark J. Burhans, 92 N. Congress St., Athens, OH 45701 (614)593-8207. *Limited-production items, individually designed works in wood, often in combination with glass and metal work.*

Connie Campbell-Eaton, Sculptor, 214 W. State St., Athens, OH 45701 (614)592-4984. *Sculptural outdoor installations.*

ATTICA: **J.E. Gutilla, Cabinet Maker,** 10 N. Main, Attica, OH 44807 (419)426-9461. *Fine woodworking to suit your needs.*

BATH: **(130) J. Michael Johnson,** Box 177, Bath, OH 44210. *Clockmaker.*

BEAVERCREEK: **Lowell Converse,** 475 Carthage Dr., Beavercreek, OH 45385 (513)426-2646. *Specialty hardwood items, turnings.*

Richard H. Stoller, 3542 Haven Court, Beavercreek, OH 45432.

BELLEVUE: **Oke Meyer, Jr.,** 149 Robert Ave., Bellevue, OH 44811 (419)483-5326. *Wood turning.*

BURTON: **John A. Vlah,** 14330 Georgia Rd., Burton, OH 44021. *Free edge design and richly grained local hardwoods.*

CANAL FULTON: **Fox-Designer-Craftsmen in Wood,** Box 544-239 N. Canal St., Canal Fulton, OH 44614 (216)854-4605. *Specializes in one-of-a-kind furniture, accessories, library walls, authentic reproductions.*

Village Country Furniture, 5541 Bulterbridge Rd., Canal Fulton, OH 44614. *Stock and custom reproductions of New England, Colonial, Shaker and Queen Anne furniture and accessories.*

CHAGRIN FALLS: **(132) Herbert A. Consor,** 17434 Auburn Rd., Chagrin Falls, OH 44022 (216)543-4870. *Miniatures.*

CINCINNATI: **Michael Lee Brotherton,** 5960 Glenway Ave., Cincinnati, OH 45238 (513)457-6636. *Marquetry, design, custom furniture and architectural woodwork.*

(150) Nicolai Klimaszewski, 7925 Indian Hill Rd., Cincinnati, OH 45243 (513)561-6377. *Designer and maker in wood, glass and metal.*

Richard J. Neubauer, Jr., 8791 Ault Park Ave., Cincinnati, OH 45208 (513)961-6309. *Handcrafted one-of-a-kind hardwood furniture, original relief carvings and sculpture.*

Wayne Siebe, 719 Miles Lane, Cincinnati, OH 45245 (513)752-7693. *Custom-built cabinets, other small containers.*

CLEVELAND: **Dennis M. Dreher,** 1937 Columbus Rd., Cleveland, OH 44113 (216)621-1740. *Furniture (production and custom), furniture service.*

Peter P. Mullen, 10309 Edgewater Dr., Cleveland, OH 44102 (216)651-2121. *Creativity and relaxation.*

David M. Strieter, 18711 Fairville Ave., Cleveland, OH 44135 (216)362-0286.

Wood on Wood Designs, 3206 Clinton Ave., Cleveland, OH 44113 (216)631-3997. *Custom carving, fine woodwork, original designs.*

CLEVELAND HEIGHTS: **APSA-Martin,** 2099 Lamberton Rd., Cleveland Heights, OH 44118 (216)321-8906. *Retail store fixtures, computer furniture, general cabinetry.*

COLUMBIA STATION: **Bob Taylor Woodworking,** 14263 E. River Rd., Columbia Station, OH 44028 (216)236-3117. *Custom-made furniture, wood turning, cabinetry and specialty objects of wood.*

COLUMBUS: **Patrick Pavoni,** Centennial H.S. Shop, 1441 Bethel Rd., Columbus, OH 43220 (614)457-2212.

James V. Rutkowski, 2282 N. High St., Columbus, OH 43201 (614)291-5332. *One-of-a-kind and limited-edition items.*

'Hersh' Westbrook, 3517 Bremen St., Columbus, OH 43224 (614)261-0569. *Hand-carved birds and animals, in-the-round or relief custom carving.*

CUYAHOGA FALLS: **Finley J. Manson,** 2673 Oak Park Blvd., Cuyahoga Falls, OH 44221 (216)928-8794.

DAYTON: **Ray Kunz,** 122 S. Delmar Ave., Dayton, OH 45403 (513)252-0778. *Furniture reproductions, antique restoration, all types of woodcarving. Specialty: wildfowl carving.*

Stat Lamp, 4091 Sunbeam Ave., Dayton, OH 45440 (513)429-2919. *Rheostat lamps.*

DELAWARE: **Larson's House of Wood,** 7 N. Liberty St., Delaware, OH 43015 (614)369-7996. *Primitive and Colonial furniture, carved signs, custom hardwood moldings, and sale of hardwoods.*

DOVER: **W.R. Goehring, Cabinetmaker,** 2701 N. Wooster Avenue, Dover, OH 44622 (216)343-6948. *Designer/maker of fine traditional furniture in native hardwoods.*

DUBLIN: **Charles F. Hicks,** 56 So. Riverview St., Dublin, OH 43017 (614)889-1777. *Decorator and functional items. Also, wood turning.*

GREENFIELD: **Wood Creations,** 12082 Karnes Rd., Greenfield, OH 45123 (513)365-1293. *Walnut, cherry, oak toys and gifts.*

HAMILTON: **The Wood Shop,** 4185 Freeman Ave., Hamilton, OH 45015 (513)863-1396. *Customized walnut cases. Restoration of antique furniture.*

HUBBARD: **John Wilkinson,** 51 Warner Rd., Hubbard, OH 44425 (216)759-8311. *General cabinetry. Shaker cabinets, tables and clocks.*

JACKSON: **Enniskillen Woodworks,** 117 Athens St., Jackson, OH 45640 (614)286-3710. *Montessori educational items and custom woodworking and design.*

KINGSVILLE: **Rob O'Reilly Custom Woodworks,** 4148 Route 193 S., Kingsville, OH 44048 (216)224-0053. *Woodwork done on commission.*

LORAIN: **Robert Ludwig,** 1314 W. 39th St., Lorain, OH 44053.

LOUDONVILLE: **(29) Larry Rogers,** Route 2 Box 219, Loudonville, OH 44842 (419)994-3714. *Inlays. Chests, cabinets, inlayed furniture.*

LYNDHURST: **Nicholas J. Lythos,** 5593 Kilbourne Dr., Lyndhurst, OH 44124.

MEDINA: **Ray J. Rusnak,** 7499 Neff Rd., Medina, OH 44256 (216)483-3945. *Retired wood pattern maker, member NWCA and Parma Wood Carvers Guild.*

MENTOR: **Spectrum Design,** Reynolds Rd., Mentor, OH 44060 (216)255-4355. *Electronic and mechanical design, fabrication and documentation.*

MOUNT VERNON: **Mark Muller,** 302 E. Ohio Ave., Mount Vernon, OH 43050 (614)397-7511.

NEWARK: **(129) J & J Beall Woodworking,** 541 Swans Rd. N.E., Newark, OH 43055 (614)345-5045. *Clocks and large unusual sculptural pieces, simulacra.*

Out of My Tree Woodworks, 1031 Fairbanks Ave., Newark, OH 43055. *Small-item custom design and fabrication.*

NEW CARLISLE: **Ed Ireton, Dulcimer & Harp Builder,** 6865 So. Scarff Rd., New Carlisle, OH 45344 (513)845-8232. *Mountain dulcimers, hammer dulcimers and folk harps.*

NORTH CANTON: **Ralph Z. Neff, Custom Woodworking,** 1616 Greenway Rd. S.E., North Canton, OH 44709 (216)499-4946. *Custom designing and construction of cabinets and furniture, reproductions of antiques.*

OLMSTED FALLS: **(138) Charles M. Ruggles, Pipe Organs,** 24493 Bagley Rd., Olmsted Falls, OH 44138 (216)826-0097. *Designing and building handcrafted organs, utilizing time-honored methods of construction and the finest solid woods.*

OXFORD: **Alan Mills,** 7290 Stillwell Beckett Rd., Oxford, OH 45056 (513)523-7044.

Willis C. Swift, 6060 Fairfield Rd., Oxford, OH 45056 (513)523-8139. *General woodworking.*

ST. PARIS: **Ron Berger,** 210 E. Main St., St. Paris, OH 43072 (513)663-5609. *Custom furniture and cabinets.*

SHAKER HEIGHTS: **Franklin J. Hickman,** 3715 Rolliston Rd., Shaker Heights, OH 44120 (216)283-4591. *Custom furniture and contemporary designs.*

SPRINGFIELD: **Graves Studio,** 1846 Sierra Ave., Springfield, OH 45503 (513)399-0703. *Wood and clay sculptures, ceramics, models in miniature.*

SYLVANIA: **Scott Midgley,** 4561 Vicksburg, Sylvania, OH 43560 (419)886-8662. *Custom design and manufacture of furniture and cabinetry.*

TOLEDO: **David E. Powers,** 6035 Pickard, Toledo, OH 43613 (419)475-4037.

WILLARD: **Leo Dotson,** 4686 Bullhead Rd., Willard, OH 44890 (419)935-0580. *Custom-built furniture, decorator items, quality refinishing.*

WILMINGTON: **Gordon Warren, Handcrafter,** 896 Brown Rd., Wilmington, OH 45177 (513)382-5448. *Turning, especially bowls and trays. Custom woodwork.*

XENIA: **Hank Sunderman,** 1293 Gultice Rd., Xenia, OH 45385 (513)372-1818. *Custom-design and build traditional furniture, cabinets, etc.*

YELLOW SPRINGS: **Generations Woodwork,** Box 307, Yellow Springs, OH 45387 (513)767-9145. *Commissioned furniture, reproductions and restorations, turned objects.*

Oklahoma

ADA: **(171) D.J. Lafon,** 2127 Woodland Dr., Ada, OK 74820 (405)332-6704. *Wood sculpture and sculptured boxes.*

BARTLESVILLE: **George F. Downs,** 1600 Hampden Rd., Bartlesville, OK 74003. *Custom woodwork.*

BROKEN ARROW: **Robert L. Nalbone,** 800 Millwood Rd., Broken Arrow, OK 74012. *Period furniture.*

CORDELL: **Wayne Fleming,** 216 W. 3rd, Cordell, OK 73632 (405)832-3222. *Small turned objects and bandsaw containers.*

DEL CITY: **Chuck Robertson,** 4024 Bismarc, Del City, OK 73115 (405)672-7981. *Original designs.*

EDMOND: **Matthew Heitzke,** 1204 Red Bud Lane, Edmond, OK 73034 (405)340-1356. *Custom furniture and cabinets.*

NORMAN: **Bob Flexner,** 303 E. Main, Norman, OK 73069 (405)360-1042. *Specialties include furniture making and antique restoration.*

(84) James L. Henkle, Designer, 2719 Hollywood, Norman, OK 73069 (405)321-7353. *Design and constructing contemporary furniture prototypes.*

Alan Lacer, 413 W. Himes, Norman, OK 73069 (405)364-9180. *Woodturning.*

OKLAHOMA CITY: **Chris Christensen,** 829 NW 47th St., Oklahoma City, OK 73118 (405)848-5713. *Tables and small cabinets.*

TULSA: **Barry Daniels,** 6217 E. Latimer St., Tulsa, OK 74115 (918)838-1873. *Custom guitar construction and repairs (classic, acoustic and electric). Fretboards are my specialty.*

E.A. Moore Inc., 3112A E. Pine St., Tulsa, OK 74120 (918)834-2801. *Refinishing and restoration of all furniture and woodwork.*

John Paul Shackelford, 1046 E. 34th St., Tulsa, OK 74105 (918)743-3032. *Custom woodcarving and sculpture in wood, clay, stone and metal.*

Stephen Smith Sculptured Designs, 2182 S. 74th E Avenue, Tulsa, OK 74129 (918)663-6244. *I specialize in small functional sculptures, but I also handle small cabinets.*

WELLSTON: **Imel Woodworks, Ben Imel,** Route 3 Box 155, Wellston, OK 74881 (405)356-4005. *Fine furniture and accessories. Each piece is signed and dated.*

Oregon

ALBANY: **Rob Johnston, Builder,** 3310 Idlewood Place, S.E., Albany, OR 97321 (503)926-7245. *Architectural woodwork, speciality cabinets and homes.*

ASHLAND: **Christian Burchard,** 11800 Hwy. 99 S., Ashland, OR 97520 (503)482-9102. *Hand-carved solid furniture of my own design, wood sculpture, carved bowls and boxes.*

The Cabinet Works, Loren Clear and Robert Munroe, 864 A St., Ashland, OR 97520 (503)482-8823. *Fine furniture and furniture-quality cabinetry.*

Dovetail Woodworks, Paul Giancarlo, 219 Meade St., Ashland, OR 97520 (503)482-8789. *Cabinets and furniture. Member of Siskiyou Woodcraft Guild.*

Robet W. Munroe, 769 S. Mountain, Ashland, OR 97520 (503)488-0310. *Custom furniture.*

Michael Schilling, 1146 Beswick Way, Ashland, OR 97520 (503)482-1687. *Furniture built like they used to.*

Woodchuck Cabinet Shop, 84 Garfield St., Ashland, OR 97520 (503)482-1370. *Custom cabinets and furniture with attention to good design and satisfied clients.*

BANDON: **Darwin Knight,** 775 S.W. 8th St., Bandon, OR 97411 (503)347-3814. *Cabinets and one-of-a-kind furniture.*

BEAVERTON: **Bill Gilchrist,** Route 1 Box 525, Beaverton, OR 97007 (503)649-2827. *Classical design, with just a touch of whimsy added.*

Ralph Powell, 13595 S.W. Hazel, Beaverton, OR 97005 (503)646-2655. *Custom furniture.*

Steve Wells, Route 1 Box 468, Beaverton, OR 97007. *Art objects in wood, specializing in lathe-turned bowls and hand-built black powder rifles.*

BEND: **Slaughter 'n Wood,** 61425 Brosterhous Rd., Bend, OR 97702 (503)389-4118. *High-quality functional and aesthetically pleasing furniture that is realistically priced.*

CORNELIUS: **Al Rogers' Clock and Creations,** 410 S. 5th Ave., Cornelius, OR 97113 (503)359-4668. *Jointed hardwood clocks, custom furniture, specialty items.*

CORVALLIS: **(86) Diedrich Dasenbrock, Glass and Woodworking,** 1153 N.W. Taylor, Corvallis, OR 97330 (503)753-4178. *Original designs made in wood and or glass, sculpture, hangings, furniture, windows and doors.*

W. Curtis Johnson, 1265 N.W. Heather Dr., Corvallis, OR 97330 (503)753-6968. *Furniture with clean lines and quality craftsmanship providing simple solution to design problems.*

William Storch Custom Woodworking, 5710 S.W. W. Hills Rd., Corvallis, OR 97333 (503)757-8717. *Functional furniture designed and built to client's wishes, reasonably priced. Also round and oval frames.*

EAGLE POINT: **Woodworking by Daniel Wilkins,** Box 351, Eagle Point, OR 97524 (503)779-4176. *Carefully constructed original furnishings, solid hardwoods using time-proven traditional methods.*

EUGENE: **Gary W. Cook,** 4412 Larkwood St., Eugene, OR 97405 (503)484-9398. *Custom furniture and cabinets, sometimes incorporating stained and etched glass, brass, metals.*

Ken G. Dieringer, 1091 W. 10th, Eugene, OR 97402 (503)345-0942. *Furniture. Chairs, tables, cabinets, banisters, beds.*

Larry Gazley, 2960 Olive St., Eugene, OR 97405 (503)344-4585. *Antique furniture restoration, furniture making, dining room tables, woodcarving, animals, duck and geese decoys.*

Great Western Woodworks, 1852 Charnelton, Eugene, OR 97401 (503)342-8405. *Design, furniture and architectural woodworking.*

John Replinger, 41 W. 35th Ave., Eugene, OR 97405 (503)484-0426.

(127) Del Short, 1324 W. 4th St., Eugene, OR 97402 (503)343-4876. *Wooden furniture repair. Custom lathe work. Wood part duplicating.*

GOLD HILL: **Ted Ballard, Sardine Creek Woodworks,** 3315 Sardine Creek Rd., Gold Hill, OR 97525 (503)855-7332. *Fine cabinetry and millwork. Design and construction.*

Don's Furniture & Cabinet Shoppe, 1191 Foots Creek Rd. Gold Hill, OR 97525 (503)582-0304. *Specializing in oak furniture, kitchen cabinets, video cabinets, gun cabinets and specialty cabinets.*

GRANTS PASS: **Distinctive Wood Designs,** 1168 Soldier Cr. Dr., Grants Pass, OR 95236 (503)479-7687. *Custom furniture, cabinets, display cases.*

Donald M. Steinert, 800 Messinger Rd., Grants Pass, OR 97526 (503)846-6835. *Rolls Royce woodwork restoration. Finishing, specializing in piano-grade lacquer finishes. Furniture, cabinets, antique restoration.*

GRESHAM: **The Master's Craftsmen,** 1335 SW 25th Court, Gresham, OR 97030 (503)665-5442. *Brass inlay, marquetry, traditional furniture design area.*

HALSEY: **Pat D. Weidmann, Luxury in Wood,** Box 112, Halsey, OR 97348 (503)369-2777. *Custom-designed woodworking to fit all tastes.*

HERMISTON: **Bill Neuffer, Woodworking,** Route 3 Box 3452, Hermiston, OR 97838 (503)567-7156. *Original design furniture, jewel boxes and cabinets.*

HILLSBORO: **Shivvers Custom Kitchen Cabinets,** Route 3 Box 249, Hillsboro, OR 97123 (503)647-5828. *Kitchen cabinets, bookcases, hutches, stereo and tv cabinets, made to the customer's dimensions.*

HOOD RIVER: **Mark Mochon,** 1681 Markham Rd., Hood River, OR 97031 (503)386-2549. *Mostly custom furniture, design, construction. California round-over style.*

Edward Norman, 2520 Kingsley Rd., Hood River, OR 97031.

JEFFERSON: **Made In Jefferson,** 3259 Jefferson Scio Dr. SE, Jefferson, OR 97352 (503)327-2543. *All types of furniture.*

JUNCTION CITY: **(99) Elliott Grey, Furniture Maker,** 25494 Hall Rd., Junction City, OR 97448 (503)998-8270. *I work exclusively in fine woods, building everything from household furniture to spiral staircases.*

LA GRANDE: **Osterloh's Hardwood Specialties,** 2004 I Ave., La Grande, OR 97850 (503)963-2034. *Custom hardwood, furniture. Rolltop desks, files, hope chests and dining sets. Custom milling.*

LORANE: **Siuslaw Carpentry Company,** 79567 Fire Rd., Lorane, OR 97451 (503)942-3642. *Custom furniture to fit your needs. Oak frames and kitchen and bathroom remodeling.*

McKENZIE BRIDGE: **(127) Dick Showalter,** McKenzie Bridge, OR 97413. *Wooden toys, art pieces. My designs.*

MILWAUKIE: **(82) Gary Rogowski, Woodworker,** 6614 Needham, Milwaukie, OR 97222. *Custom furniture design.*

MONMOUTH: **Michael Taylor Woodworks,** 9635 Helmick Rd., Monmouth, OR 97361 (503)838-0057. *Commerical and domestic furniture and woodwork.*

MULINO: **Merlin Buser,** Box 815, Mulino, OR 97042 (503)829-6376. *Kitchen cabinets, china, dressers, desks, bedroom furniture.*

NEWPORT: **(158) The Wood Gallery, Kelly O. Barker,** 818 S.W. Bay Blvd., Newport, OR 97365 (503)265-6843. *Inlayed doors, tables and bars for homes and restaurants.*

OREGON CITY: **Earl Marble,** 11186 S. Allen Court, Oregon City, OR 97045 (503)655-3794. *Custom design and furniture building. Also repair and stripping.*

PORTLAND: **A. Knott's Woodcraft,** 16047 E. Burnside No. 29, Portland, OR 97233 (503)253-7647. *Cabinetmaking, sculpture, Appalachian plucked dulcimers.*

Robert F. Burgan, Woodworker, 2055 N.W. 29th 6, Portland, OR 97210 (503)241-8080. *I do original designs in wood. I also do a line of wooden floor lamps.*

(162) Sam Bush, 3125 S.E. Van Water, Portland, OR 97222 (503)653-5229. *Specialty woodwork, design and furniture conservation.*

Pete Clark, 6054 SW 48th, Portland, OR 97221 (503)244-2806.

(22) Doug Courtney, Pro-Forma Designs Inc., 120 N.W. 23rd, Portland, OR 97210 (503)248-9984. *Staircases, entry doors, furniture, fireplace facades, wainscoting, commercial furnishings, antique preservation.*

David J. Crafton, 4219 S.W. Condor, Portland, OR 97201 (503)243-2824. *Custom hardwood furniture and accessories, turning.*

(115) John Economaki, 2834 N.E. 39th, Portland, OR 97212 (503)282-6995. *Desks, dining sets, tables, benches, serving carts, coatracks, silver chests, beds.*

Elana Custom Woodwork & Design, 2764 N.W. Thurman St., Portland, OR 97214 (503)224-0210. *Furniture, music stands, mosaics. Custom work and some production pieces.*

Jeffrey R. Elliott, Luthier, 3748 S.E. Taylor St., Portland, OR 97214 (503)233-0836. *Handmade acoustic guitars, six and eight-string classical, and six and twelve-string steel.*

Stephen J. Feikert, 5633 S.E. 111th St., Portland, OR 97266 (503)761-8207. *Custom woodwork, architectural appointments and custom-crafted hardwood caskets.*

L. Samuel Fort, 5316 S.W. Westwood View, Portland, OR 97201 (503)244-8763. *Creative wood sculpture for architectural wall decoration, doors, newel posts and fireplaces.*

Guyot Arts, 2945 SE 140, Portland, OR 97236 (503)761-9519. *I work alone restoring full-size carousel animals for collectors.*

Harrison Woodworking, 5916 N. Moore Ave., Portland, OR 97217 (503)285-5409. *Anything in wood that doesn't make me feel like a prostitute in wood.*

Bob Harvey, 4628 SW 49th Ave., Portland, OR 97221 (503)246-6283. *Functional artistry of original design or of client's design.*

Laura A. Hinrichs, 16948 N.W. Wapato, Portland, OR 97231 (503)621-3752. *Original furniture and cabinets for the home or office.*

Roger Hockett Woodworking, 3160 NE 35th Place, Portland, OR 97212 (503)288-9943. *Custom furniture, office suites, standard tri-mitre parson's table design in all sizes.*

Kurtsi Johnson, 4115 NE 14th Ave., Portland, OR 97211 (503)288-1301. *Eclectic wooden objects.*

(27) McCaffrey Designs, 1404 S.E. 26th Ave., Portland, OR 97214 (503)239-5367. *I specialize in custom design for residential, commerical and architectural furnishings.*

Multnomah Cabinet Shop, Jim Ziegler Prop., 7634 S.W. Capitol Highway, Portland, OR 97219 (503)246-5457.

The Oregon Bass Co., 10101 SW 55th St., Portland, OR 97219.

(33) Oregon Fine Joinery, 1104 N.E. 28th Ave., Portland, OR 97232 (503)288-9903. *Custom and limited production of commerical and residential furniture. Architectural woodworking, railings, arches and mantels.*

Dale Rush, Box 8475, Portland, OR 97207 (503)284-3113. *Hand-built muzzle-loading rifles.*

(19) Fred Siedow, 5744 E. Burnside St., Portland, OR 97215 (503)236-0336. *Antique furniture restorations (including turning, carving, marquetry inlay, refinishing). Custom-made antique furniture reproductions.*

(140) Per O. Walthinsen, 2926 N.E. 58th Ave., Portland, OR 97213 (503)281-4281. *Harpsichords, clavichords, virginals, custom furniture.*

(10) John Whitehead, 6150 N.E. Davis, Portland, OR 97213 (503)234-5753.

Wind Song Woodworking, 3672 S.E. Lexington St., Portland, OR 97202 (503)771-5221. *Contemporary designs, furniture and cabinets.*

REEDSPORT: **Sheldon K. Smith,** 1321 Ranch Rd., Reedsport, OR 97467 (503)271-3701. *Gun cabinets, architectural doors, jewelry boxes, presentation cases, dollhouses, desk accessories.*

ROSEBURY: **Michael J. Ballis,** 107 Hoover 2, Rosebury, OR 97470 (503)673-6262. *Just your basic shop.*

SALEM: **Anderson Design Woodcrafting,** 2215 Jelden St. N.E., Salem, OR 97303 (503)363-8426. *Contemporary wooden furniture, chairs, tables, desks, case work, accessories.*

Bill Fox's Fine Woodworking, 5591 70th Ave. S.E., Salem, OR 97301 (503)581-0282. *Repair antiques, old house interior and exterior gingerbread, spinning wheels and accessories, specialty custom woodworking.*

Christopher A. Hauth, 4616 Nandale Dr. N.E., Salem, OR 97305 (503)390-7756. *Contemporary furniture, limited editions. Tables, chairs, cabinets, etc. Steambending, laminating and sculpting.*

Jesse Woodworks, Box 15075, Salem, OR 97309 (503)370-9183. *Architectural woodwork, furniture and cabinetry.*

Richard D. Rolf, 2605 State St., Salem, OR 97310. *Special orders of small items like salt and pepper shakers, jewelry boxes, spice racks, lathe workings.*

SHERWOOD: **(31) Mark Newman,** 11220 Tonquin Rd., Sherwood, OR 97140 (503)692-4459. *Original and custom designs in furniture and cabinets. Hairbrushes with exotic hardwood handles.*

SILVERTON: **Ken Altman, Fine Woodwork,** 109 Rock St., Silverton, OR 97381 (503)873-5034. *Limited production and one-of-a-kind custom furniture.*

Joy of Doing, 968 Driftcreek Rd. NE, Silverton, OR 97381 (503)873-4005. *Sculptural inlay in boxes, cradles, mirrors, doors. Sculptural puzzles and panels. Spiral staircases.*

THE DALLES: **Scott A. Bowdish,** Route 3 Box 78A, The Dalles, OR 97058 (503)298-8403.

VENETA: **Wayne Morrow,** 22839 Willow Lane, Veneta, OR 97487. *Very handmade furniture.*

VERNONIA: **Jim Tierney, Leprechaun Industries,** 1209 Bridge St., Vernonia, OR 97064 (503)429-0720. *Custom design and work with solid wood.*

WALDPORT: **Joseph L. Salebra,** 3482 Highway 34, Waldport, OR 97394 (503)563-4817. *Custom-made cabinetmaking. Designed to the person's lifestyle.*

WEST LINN: **Joe Petrovich,** 2306 Tulane, West Linn, OR 97068 (503)655-5394. *Myrtlewood epergnes and candelabras, hurricane lamp bases, also vases of various hardwoods.*

WINSTON: **Dennis D. Danz,** 389 Dawson Dr., Winston, OR 97496 (503)679-9802. *One-of-a-kind, limited-run cabinets and chests, tables and desks, accessories, marquetry.*

YAMHILL: **(12) Lawrence Judd, Woodturner,** Box 282-310 N. Maple St., Yamhill, OR 97148 (503)662-3505. *Bowls, spindles, stairs (parts and assembly). All types of woodturning and general woodworking.*

Pennsylvania

ALIQUIPPA: **Rev. Roy W. Johnsen,** 604 N. Brodhead Rd., Aliquippa, PA 15001 (412)375-7961. *Woodturning.*

Samuel Mitrovich, Jr., 603 Hall St., Aliquippa, PA 15001 (412)378-3089. *Heirloom-quality furniture design and construction.*

ALLENTOWN: **Krud Krafts,** 1127 Emmett St., Allentown, PA 18102 (215)435-4213. *Custom woodworking, specializing in exclusive, one-of-a-kind pieces.*

BANGOR: **Bradley C. Miller,** 580 S. Sixth St., Bangor, PA 18013 (215)588-4881. *General woodworking.*

BARTONSVILLE: **Al Lachman, The Woodworker,** Route 611, Bartonsville, PA 18321 (717)421-4505. *We specialize in one-of-a-kind custom-made pieces of a contemporary mode.*

BEAVER FALLS: **Warsaw Woodworks,** 3304 8th Ave., Beaver Falls, PA 15010 (412)843-3447. *Cabinets and small boxes.*

BETHLEHEM: **Evan's Woodshop,** 3962 Kenrick Dr., Bethlehem, PA 18017 (215)691-6393. *Custom cabinets, bookcases and toys.*

Richard Ng, 2830 W. Blvd., Bethlehem, PA 18017 (215)867-4345.

TZ Design, RD 4 Box 176, Bethlehem, PA 18015 (215)866-8194. *Office and house furnishings. Custom design and construction in wood.*

BLAIRSVILLE: **Quality Woodworks by Randall Overdorff,** Route 1 Box 438, Blairsville, PA 15717 (412)459-5913. *Original designs in cabinetry, seating, furniture.*

BOALSBURG: **Jeff Biddle's Woodworking,** 521 W. Main St., Boalsburg, PA 16827 (814)466-7720. *Eighteenth and early nineteenth-century antique restoration and reproductions.*

BOYERTOWN: **John Kochey,** RD 3 Box 30, Boyertown, PA 19512 (215)367-6180. *Custom handcrafted woodwork.*

BRYN ATHYN: **Glenn H. Bostock,** Box 584, Bryn Athyn, PA 19009 (215)947-1019. *Employed by Odhner and Odhner. Custom millwork, cabinets and furniture.*

Gregory N. Glebe, 785 Fetters Mill Rd., Bryn Athyn, PA 19009 (215)947-1691. *Custom woodworking and furnishings.*

CARLTON: **Folks Furniture, Paul and Suzy Lange,** RD 1, Carlton, PA 16311 (814)425-7578. *Custom building and restoration of all stringed instruments.*

CLARKS SUMMIT: **Raymond S. Wytovich,** 507 Haven Lane, Clarks Summit, PA 18411 (717)961-6171. *Select small unique works such as picture frames, music boxes, etc.*

COLLEGEVILLE: **(20) Raymond A. Kelso,** 720 Black Rock Rd., Collegeville, PA 19426 (215)933-1080. *Contemporary furniture designs in native American hardwoods.*

DREXEL HILL: **Kenneth N. Montgomery,** 925 Childs Ave., Drexel Hill, PA 19026 (215)449-8919. *Dollhouse models 1 in. to 12 in. are available for $65; 2-in. to 12-in. models are available for $75.*

EAST GREENVILLE: **Kurt D. Althouse,** 133 Main St., East Greenville, PA 18041 (215)679-8879. *Fine woodworking.*

ELKINS PARK: **Seymour Lemonick,** 807 W. Church Rd., Elkins Park, PA 19117 (215)887-0757. *Hand-carved vases.*

ELVERSON: **Harvey Beiler,** RD 3 Box 55, Elverson, PA 19520 (215)286-5842.

ERIE: **Gary Cacchione,** 1503 State St., Erie, PA 16501 (814)459-8071. *Custom woodworking, furniture and accessories.*

Neil J. Donovan, 1748 Skyline Dr., Erie, PA 16509 (814)866-2671. *Limited production and one-of-a-kind designs using unusual spalted and burl woods.*

William Sullivan, 1913 Wagner Ave., Erie, PA 16510 (814)899-2773. *Custom furniture.*

(83) Stephen Temple, 2802 Homer Ave., Erie, PA 16506. (814)838-2265.

GREENSBURG: **Gerald Conrath,** 155 Stark Ave., Greensburg, PA 15601 (412)838-1765. *Make Early American chests, beds and benches.*

HAMBURG: **Michael J. Brolly,** 343 W. State St., Hamburg, PA 19526 (215)562-5119. *One-of-a-kind designs.*

HATBORO: **Mark D. Hughes,** 269 E. Montgomery Ave., Hatboro, PA 19040 (215)675-2094. *Design, construction.*

HATFIELD: **Bill Kraynak,** 1334 Koffel Rd., Hatfield, PA 19440 (215)855-0189. *One-of-a-kind items to enhance the beauty of wood.*

HAWLEY: **Fred D. Hatton,** Box 235 Blooming Grove, Hawley, PA 18428 (717)775-9136. *One-of-a-kind pieces. Simple, strong furniture designed with a special home-grown feeling.*

HELLERTOWN: **Mike Panick,** RD 1 Box 125, Hellertown, PA 18055 (215)838-6259.

HOP BOTTOM: **Frank Finan, Cabinetmaker,** RD 1 Box 81-A, Hop Bottom, PA 18824 (717)289-4686. *Kitchen cabinets.*

HOWARD: **E.R. Clair,** RD 2 Box 171, Howard, PA 16841 (814)625-2707. *Custom furniture, design, contemporary and traditional antique restoration.*

INDIANA: **Dave Gindlesberger,** 604 S. 5th St., Indiana, PA 15701 (412)349-9025. *One-of-a-kind furniture and sculpture designs, limited production.*

KENNETT SQUARE: **(75) Peter M. Kenney,** 430 Bartram Rd., Kennett Square, PA 19348 (215)268-8812. *We design and construct contemporary furniture. Commission work.*

Mark Taylor, 404 S. Union St., Kennett Square, PA 19348 (215)444-3158. *Woodturning. Original work as well as reproductions for furniture and restoration.*

KING OF PRUSSIA: **(67) Linda Beck,** 674 N. Henderson Rd., King of Prussia, PA 19406 (215)265-1114. *Custom design, reproductions, antique restoration.*

KNOXVILLE: **Walter A. Bacon, Jr.,** 306 Alba St., Knoxville, PA 16928 (814)326-4255. *Custom woodworking, turnings, carvings, sculpture, antique furniture repair.*

LANCASTER: **David Schaffhauser,** 641 So. Prince St., Lancaster, PA 17602 (717)397-3296. *Art and craft objects, custom woodworking and interior renovations.*

LIGONIER: **(28) Don Burkey, Cabinetmaker,** RD 3 Box 205BB, Ligonier, PA 15658 (412)238-7697. *Design, construct, finish in period and contemporary styles. Traditional joinery in solid hardwoods, woodcarvings.*

LOCK HAVEN: **Tom Svec,** Box 31B Island Route, Lock Haven, PA 17745 (717)748-3946. *Chairs and stools of laminated bentwood construction, dovetailed chests in a variety of design variations.*

MEADVILLE: **Dave Vinch Woodworks,** 883 Thurston Rd., Meadville, PA 16335 (814)333-6597. *Hardwood toys, decoys, furniture.*

MERTZTOWN: **Jerry Madrigale,** Box 103 Park Ave., Mertztown, PA 19539. *Tasteful woodcarving.*

MILFORD: **Barbara Miller,** RR 1 Box 517, Milford, PA 18337 (717) 296 8424. *Living room tables, sculptural furniture, sculpture.*

Sawkill Woodworks, RR 1 Box 441, Milford, PA 18337 (717) 686-2521. *Furniture and sculpture, custom cabinetry, kitchens.*

MOHNTON: **Talarico Hardwoods,** RD 3 Box 303, Mohnton, PA 19540 (215) 775-0400. *Family-run exotic hardwood sales. We take on an occasional commission.*

MOUNT GRETNA: **Max Clox,** 68 Pine St., Mount Gretna, PA 17064 (717) 964-3108. *Original design clocks, furniture, accessories and turnings, crafted with love and respect for the material.*

NATRONA HEIGHTS: **Paul C. Rieger (Pat),** RD 1 Box 366-B Bachman Rd., Natrona Heights, PA 15065 (412) 224-3107. *Small to medium wood products.*

NAZARETH: **(142) Dick Boak's Church of Art,** 14 S. Broad St., Nazareth, PA 18064 (215) 759-7100. *Art, graphics, photography, woodworking, musical instrument design, construction and repair, live concerts, studio recording.*

NEW CUMBERLAND: **Jim Whetstone,** 324 Evergreen St., New Cumberland, PA 17070 (717) 774-6195. *Custom woodworking. Design, draw prints for everything I build.*

NEW HOLLAND: **J.W. Dughi,** 11 Union Ave., New Holland, PA 17557 (717) 354-2338. *Turning, carving, carved turnings.*

NEWTOWN: **Timothy W. Olson,** 111 S. Congress St., Newtown, PA 18940 (215) 968-2819. *Custom cabinetwork.*

NORRISTOWN: **Allen D. Androkites,** 328 Weymouth Rd., Norristown, PA 19401 (215) 279 9344. *Specialize in furniture reproduction and woodturning, Chippendale mirrors, tilt-top tables, bowls and pewter inlays.*

Glenn David Pegon, 113 Farview Ave., Norristown, PA 19403 (215) 539-8521. *Boxes, lathe work.*

PATTON: **The Crow's Nest,** Leonard M. Churella, RD 1 Box 79, State Park Rd., Patton, PA 16668 (814) 674-5579. *Spalted bowls, vases. Nativity mangers, routed signs.*

PENN RUN: **(180) Christopher Weiland,** Box 127A, RD 1, Penn Run, PA 15765 (412) 349-8917. *Designer-craftsman in wood form.*

PHILADELPHIA: **AKC Furnituremaker,** 312 W. Columbia Ave., Philadelphia, PA 19122 (215) 236-3050. *Functional, sculptural hardwood furniture, one-of-a-kind designs.*

Amaranth Gallery and Workshop Inc., 4101 Lauriston St., Philadelphia, PA 19128 (215) 483-5401. *Custom woodturning and woodworking, turning and split turning, architectural design and creations.*

Charles Becker Creative Wood Design, 312-20 W. Columbia Ave., Philadelphia, PA 19122 (215) 235-1631. *Versatility ranges from sculptural furniture to cabinet displays and architectural woodwork.*

Designer-Craftsman in Wood, 7841 Ridge Ave., N. 214A, Philadelphia, PA 19128 (215) 492-3147. *Unique tables with marquetry tops, custom furniture, sculpture and mobiles.*

DiBartolomeo Woodworking, 715 N. 2nd St., Philadelphia, PA 19123 (215) 592-9192. *Furniture making, restoration, bar building, doors, some interiors.*

The Dovetail Joint, Bernard Henderson, 517 Arbutus St., Philadelphia, PA 19119 (215) 844-3310.

Howard J. Goldblatt, 312-20 W. Columbia Ave., Philadelphia, PA 19122 (215) 236-3050. *Custom furniture and design. Short production runs of custom wood products.*

(91) Bob Ingram Furniture Makers, 1102 E. Columbia, Philadelphia, PA 19125 (215) 739-7253. *Furniture.*

Richard Kagan, Woodworker, 326 S. St., Philadelphia, PA 19147 (215) 925-2370. *Domestic and exotic hardwood furniture for residential and corporate interiors. Examples on display in showroom.*

(69) John Kennedy, 312-20 W. Columbia, Philadelphia, PA 19122 (215) 236-3050. *Designers and builders of fine furniture and cabinetry.*

Peter Korn, 4101 Lauriston St., Philadelphia, PA 19128 (215) 487-3287. *Hardwood furniture designed and built.*

Mitchell D. Landy, 312 Columbia Ave., Philadelphia, PA 19122 (215) 235-1631. *Custom furniture from select and rare hardwoods.*

Jack Larimore, Designer and Furniture Craftsman, 325 Gaskill St., Philadelphia, PA 19147 (215) 925-0294. *Commissioned furniture stressing client's needs and featuring historical motifs and various materials.*

Cindy Marotta, 5443 Morris St., Philadelphia, PA 19144 (215) 848-5964.

Mirror-Mirror, 8102 Bustleton Ave., Philadelphia, PA 19152 (215) 745-5167. *Custom mirror, blasted glass, custom-designed glass, mirror and wood furniture and objects of art.*

Frank Slesinski, Richard Kagan Studio, 326 S. St., Philadelphia, PA 19147 (215) 925-2370.

(34) Wendy Stayman, 118 W. Highland Ave., Philadelphia, PA 19118 (215) 242-4983.

(91) Blake C. Tovin, 3 Linden Terrace, Philadelphia, PA 19144 (215) 843-4009. *Custom-made furniture for individuals, interior designers and collectors.*

Joseph A. Vescovich, Woodworker, 331 Claremont Rd., Philadelphia, PA 19120 (215) 224-8697. *Commissions in cabinetry, furniture, architectural, interior design, construction.*

Clifford Wagner, 312 W. Columbia Ave., Philadelphia, PA 19122 (215) 235-1631. *Custom-designed furniture and cabinetry engineered to meet the goals of beauty, durability, utility.*

Paul Wallach, 27 Wiltshire Rd., Philadelphia, PA 19151 (215) 642-3506.

PHOENIXVILLE: **Vixen Hill Mfg.,** RD 2, Phoenixville, PA 19460 (215) 827-7556. *Fine quality pre-fabricated gazebos.*

PITSTON: **Robert Bump,** Box 270-A RD 1, Pitston, PA 18643 (717) 333-5940. *Custom-made furniture and antique restoration and repair.*

PITTSBURGH: **(161) Jerry L. Caplan,** 5812 Fifth Ave., Pittsburgh, PA 15232 (412) 661-0179. *Carved wood, as well as terra cotta sculpture for outdoor use.*

(75) David Carlson, 311 Castle Shannon Blvd., Pittsburgh, PA 15234 (412) 563-3675.

Nelson Heeter, 4621 Baptist Rd., Pittsburgh, PA 15227 (412) 341-9979 or 884-4155. *General woodworking hobby capability.*

(51) Jerry Lilly, 119 N. Homewood Ave., Pittsburgh, PA 15208 (412) 241-1649. *All work done here has a certain grace and elegance.*

William G. Matthews, 811 Rossmore Ave., Pittsburgh, PA 15226 (412) 561-6441. *Fine cabinet work and woodturning.*

(107) Scott C. Smith, Artist Designer and Craftsman, 6824 Thomas Blvd., Pittsburgh, PA 15208 (412) 381-1118. *Custom design and construction of furniture, cabinets and art works.*

Hugh Watkins, 4 Ellsworth Terrace, Pittsburgh, PA 15213 (412) 621-6923. *Electric basses, guitars, wood sculpture, woodcut printmaking, design, graphics, illustration.*

Greg Zymboly, 216 Wilson Dr., Pittsburgh, PA 15235 (412) 243-2291.

PLYMOUTH MEETING: **James Marinell,** 3174 Colony Lane, Plymouth Meeting, PA 19462 (215) 828-1895. *Design, manufacture and repair of clocks and music boxes.*

PORT MATILDA: **Michael J. Mease,** RD 2 Box 513AA, Port Matilda, PA 16870 (814) 692-4225. *Contemporary woodworking and woodcarving.*

REEDERS: **Rafael Keifetz,** Box 188, Reeders, PA 18352 (717) 629-3364. *Custom-built hardwood furniture.*

ROSEMONT: **Frank H. McPherson,** Applegate Lane, Rosemont, PA 19010 (215) 525-7499.

SCHWENKSVILLE: **James S Shott,** 906 Summit Ave., Schwenksville, PA 19473 (215) 287-6385. *Classic contemporary woodworking.*

SELINSGROVE: **Roy Yerger, Jr.,** RD 1 Box 87, Selinsgrove, PA 17870 (717) 374-4583. *Lap desks, jewelry boxes, recipe boxes, wood furniture, dry sinks, hutches, desks, tables.*

SHELOCTA: **Rhett McHenry Zoll,** RD 3 Box 207A, Shelocta, PA 15744 (717) 354-2650. *Mostly small detailed projects with some larger pieces due to lack of space.*

SOLEBURY: **(86) Robert Whitley Studio,** Laurel Rd., Solebury, Bucks County, PA 18963 (215) 297-8452.

STATE COLLEGE: **Chips of Time,** 341 E. Waring Ave., State College, PA 16801 (814) 238-8863. *One-of-a-kind sculptures and furniture done in native American hardwoods.*

STRAFFORD: **Jeffrey W. Prichard, Furniture Designer and Maker,** 755 W. Lancaster Ave., Strafford, PA 19087 (215) 688-0396. *Fine period reproductions, original designs, traditional joinery, hand-carving, hand-turning.*

UNIONDALE: **Thomas J. Noone,** Box 96 RD 1, Uniondale, PA 18470 (717) 222-4334. *Small boxes, utensils and contemporary furniture.*

VOLANT: **(135) Salvatore Palombino, aka Robert H. Chambers,** Box 5, Main St., Volant, PA 16156 (412) 533-4434. *Custom-made violas, basses and wooden objects.*

WASHINGTON CROSSING: **Robert Bittner, Cabinetmaker,** Box 96, Washington Crossing Rd., Washington Crossing, PA 18977 (215) 493-5921. *Custom-designed furniture in Queen Anne and early Georgian styles.*

WAYNESBORO: **Thomas McFarland,** 12664 Polktown Rd., Waynesboro, PA 17268 (717) 762-5975. *Sculpture by commission. Relief, in-the-round, human figures, portraits, wildlife subjects. Specialty: lifelike turtles.*

WEST CONSHOHOCKEN: **Sherman-Gosweiler Woodworking,** 3 Ford Bridge Rd., West Conshohocken, PA 19428 (215) 828-5534.

WORCESTER: **Alvin K. Rothenberger, Jr. Inc.,** Skippack Pike, Worcester, PA 19490 (215) 584-6803. *Custom residental and office furniture, architectural millwork, speciality and short-run production woodwork.*

YARDLEY: **Craftsman in Wood,** Kenneth S. Burton, Jr., 28 Hilltop Rd., Yardley, PA 19067 (215) 493-3133. *Fine hardwood furniture.*

YORK: **Richard G. Diehl,** 1340 Hamilton St., York, PA 17402 (717) 755-3804. *Turnery. Wooden egg collection.*

Walter H. Whiteley, RD 8 Box 228, York, PA 17403 (717) 741-3098.

Rhode Island

BRISTOL: **Working Wood,** Bruce J. Ayres, 18 Mt. Hope Ave., Bristol, RI 02809 (401) 253-4405. *Designing and building fine furniture and interiors.*

CHARLESTON: **(96) Stephen Turino, Designer Maker,** Box 343, Charleston RI 02813. *Furniture and cabinet work.*

CUMBERLAND: **A.C. Tavares,** 495 Hines Rd., Cumberland, RI 02864 (401) 333-4835. *Country-style and Shaker furniture carvings (full and relief).*

NORTH KINGSTOWN: **Craig L. Willey Custom Furnituremaking & Yacht Interiors,** 343 Beacon Dr., North Kingstown, RI 02852 (401) 295-5795.

Howard Rubenstein, 80 Peachtree Rd., North Kingstown, RI 02852 (401) 885-1827. *Commissioned work only.*

NORTH SCITUATE: **Stephen Gaddes,** Hartford Pike, North Scituate, RI 02857 (401) 934-1233. *Custom furniture, repairs, woodturning.*

PAWTUCKET: **Alan Kooris,** 25 Oriole Ave., Pawtucket, RI 02860 (401) 725-8495. *Furniture and cabinets designed and built to specifications from domestic and exotic hardwoods.*

PORTSMOUTH: **Andrew M. Fallon,** 64 Pheasant Dr., Portsmouth, RI 02871 (401) 683-4433. *Designer-craftsman, furniture repair, architectural millwork, customer pieces, one-of-a-kind and limited production.*

PROVIDENCE: **(45) George Gordon,** 433 Wayland Ave., Providence, RI 02906 (401) 351-8432.

(96) John Marcoux, 283 George St., Providence, RI 02906 (401) 351-1398. *Interior design, furniture design, building and sales, residential and business.*

Janice Smith, 387 Charles St., Bldg. 10, Providence, RI 02904 (401) 272-7503. *Handcrafted one-of-a-kind pieces of furniture, works on commission.*

WEST KINGSTON: **(89) John Dunnigan,** RFD Gardner Rd Ext., West Kingston, RI 02892 (401) 539-2595. *Fine furniture.*

South Carolina

AIKEN: **Steve L. Hunter,** 1942 Huckleberry Dr., Aiken, SC 29801. *Five-string banjos for the professional picker.*

CHARLESTON: **Montgomery A. Bentz,** 25 Thomas St. Charleston, SC 29403 (803) 722-1482. *Custom furniture, eighteenth-century reproductions, veneering, carving, furniture refinishing and repairs.*

Brotherwood, 3 Maiden Lane, Charleston, SC 29401 (803) 723-0522. *Hardwood furniture and cabinets, design and construction.*

(108) Robert Scaffe, Cabinetmaker, 2526 Hara Lane Charleston, SC 29407. *Traditional furniture, original and re productions, preferably of the Queen Anne and Chippendale periods.*

Charlie H. Thompson, Cabinetmaker, 443 Wappoo Rd., Charleston, SC 29407 (803) 766-5313. *Custom-designed contemporary furniture.*

DARLINGTON: **F.L. Kosin,** 103 Bennett Dr., Darlington, SC 29532 (803) 393-5936. *Wood turnings, small and special furnishings for home and office.*

GREENVILLE: **Richard H. Lusk,** 37 Quail Hill Dr., Greenville, SC 29607 (803) 288-3028. *Specializing in formal period reproductions.*

(157) Michael P. McDunn, Contemporary Wood Products 115 Eastlan Dr., Greenville, SC 29607 (803) 233-5135. *Custom furnishings and accessories.*

MURRELLS INLET: **Ted Watts,** Wogaw Wheel Farms, Murrells Inlet, SC 29576 (803) 651-6931. *Bar tops, tables and cabinets, wood carving and signs.*

MYRTLE BEACH: **Tom Buckley,** 416 Villa Woods Dr., Myrtle Beach, SC 29577 (803) 293-7227. *Clocks, cutting boards and boxes.*

Horizon Designs, Seaboard Industrial Park, Myrtle Beach, SC 29577 (803) 626-3850. *Laminated furniture, decorative boxes and chests.*

F.M. Lyon, 9-S Palmetto St., Pinelands, Myrtle Beach, SC 29577.

NORTH AUGUSTA: **John P. Piquette,** 2212 Vireo Dr., North Augusta, SC 29841 (803) 279-3309.

PAWLEYS ISLAND: **Curtis Whittington,** Box 1198, Pawley Island, SC 29585 (803) 237-2948. *Custom-made furniture and accessories. Designs with exposed hand-cut dovetails.*

South Dakota

DEADWOOD: **Miguel Apaza,** 51 Sherman St., Box 86, Deadwood, SD 57732 (605) 578-3719. *Custom woodwork and one-of-a-kind furniture.*

RAPID CITY: **Iron Mountain Wood Shop,** 2227 Highway 7 S., Rapid City, SD 57701 (605) 343-1878. *Custom designing and building furniture items. Production line of gift boxes.*

SISSETON: **Jordan Woodworks,** 105 6th Ave. E, Sisseton, SD 57262 (605) 698-7116. *Specializing in wood turning, period furniture, antique restorations and custom cabinetry.*

Tennessee

CHAPMANSBORO: **Fine Woods by Carl F. Struck,** Route Box 133, Chapmansboro, TN 37035 (615) 746-5002. *Unique images in wood. Cabinets, doors, wall designs and small wood objects.*

CHATTANOOGA: **Dean Bendall,** 4904 Willow Lawn Dr Chattanooga, TN 37416 (615) 344-7060. *Small woodcraft.*

HAMPTON: **Hampton Music Shop,** Box 228 U.S. 321, Hampton, TN 37658 (615) 725-3191. *Handcrafted hammered dulcimers from native Appalachian hardwoods.*

JACKSON: **Thomas M. Tate,** 340 Tuckahoe Rd., Jackson, TN 38301 (901) 668-4197. *Mainly custom-build anything made of wood. Make some craft-type items, novelties, useful items, etc.*

KNOXVILLE: **Ernie Gross Designs,** 640 N. Gay St., Knoxville, TN 37917 (615) 523-6840.

(40) Grover W. Floyd II, 6800 Ball Camp Pike, Knoxville, TN 37921 (615) 690-2973. *Shaker and eighteenth-century furniture and restorations, with traditional joinery used exclusively.*

MEMPHIS: **Werner Broeker, Wood Novelties,** 5136 Whitecliff Dr., Memphis, TN 38117 (901) 682-5243. *Cabinetry, turning, veneering. Exotic woods, one-of-a-kind designs, special emphasis on colors and grains.*

(107) Stephen B. Crump, 2127 Young Ave., Memphis, TN 38104 (901) 276-6918. *Contemporary furniture of original design built on commission.*

Hal E. Davis, 1293 Tutwiler, Memphis, TN 38107 (901) 726-6121. *Custom design.*

(115) Justis Reproductions, 4209 Walnut Grove Rd., Memphis, TN 38117 (901) 767-1697. *Antique reproductions of quality workmanship and design. By commission.*

MURFREESBORO: **Larry James,** 202 Juliet Ave., Murfreesboro, TN 37130 (615)893-7433. *Two and three-dimensional, multimedia designs (functional and/or nonfunctional), originals, reproductions and restorations.*

NASHVILLE: **Jan Bell,** 176 McCrory Lane, Nashville, TN 37221 (615)646-5611. *Custom furniture, wall sculpture.*

Bill Kendall, 6033 Jocelyn Hollow Rd., Nashville, TN 37205 (615)352-6558. *Matched end-grain small tables and serving boards of native hardwoods.*

OAK RIDGE: **Richard H. Busey Custom Furniture,** 106 S. Tampa Lane, Oak Ridge, TN 37830 (615)483-5024. *Antique reproductions and custom-designed and built furniture.*

Jerry Spady, 111 Hollywood Circle, Oak Ridge, TN 37830 (615)483-1228.

SEVIERVILLE: **L. Rust Design,** Route 3 Box 521-B, Sevierville, TN 37862 (615)428-1269. *Specializing in audio component cabinetry, instruments, custom-designed furniture and cabinets.*

SMITHVILLE: **M. Pierschalla,** Route 3 Box 347-A1, Smithville, TN 37166 (615)597-6801.

SPARTA: **Russ Jacobsohn,** Route 2 Box 280, Sparta, TN 38583 (615)738-9006. *Small, one-of-a-kind boxes.*

WAYNESBORO: **Harvey Baker, Foggy Hollow Woodshop,** Route 3 Box 265A, Waynesboro, TN 38485 (615)722-9201. *Furniture, cabinetry, architectural work. Quality work made to order.*

WOODBURY: **Alfred Sharp, Cabinetmaker,** Doolittle Rd., Woodbury, TN 37190. *Museum-quality furniture, specializing in eighteenth and nineteenth-century design.*

Texas

ALEDO: **A.K. Echt,** 665 Quail Ridge Rd., Aledo, TX 76008 (817)441-8545. *Original designs in wood.*

AUSTIN: **Michael Allender,** 8300 Cliffview, Austin, TX 78759 (512)250-0512. *Creative individual furniture designs.*

Bill Bergner, Austin, TX 78704 (512)444-4975. *Mostly small remodeling and cabinetmaking, also shelves, stereo cabinets and tables.*

David Amdur Gallery, 307 E. 5th St., Austin, TX 78701 (512)476-8960. *Custom-designed specialties using exotic and unusual woods.*

David McCandless's Enchanted Woods, 2844-B San Gabriel, Austin, TX 78705 (512)478-7630. *Architectural and interior carving, sculpture, relief, statuary, furniture, toys. Ordered by priority of interest.*

Thomas Ehlers, 2006 Montclaire St., Austin, TX 78704 (512)441-1501. *Jewelry, pendulums for divining and dowsing, relics, prototypes and custom furniture.*

(158) Fleetwood, Inc., Joe Mathis & Bill Drawbaugh, 906 E. Fifth St., Austin, TX 78702 (512)472-7465. *Design and limited production of unusual and specific solutions. Media applications. Residential and contract furniture.*

Tyrone D. Gormley, 3005 Val Dr., Austin, TX 78723 (512)926-5658. *Custom-made tables, clocks, hardwood cabinets, chopping blocks, chessboards, special commissions.*

Hamrick Hardwood Furniture, Box 33007, Austin, TX 78764.

Dick Hedgepeth, 611 Park Boulevard, Austin, TX 78751 (512)458-1763. *One-of-a-kind pieces and architectural work. Write for information, design fees.*

Jimmy Hendricks, 2114 Shoalmont Dr., Austin, TX 78756 (512)459-6364. *Sculpture, general hand-tooled carving, specializing in relief-carved panels.*

The Hyde Park Company, 4101 Ave. G, Austin, TX 78751 (512)451-2797. *Architectural millwork.*

Michael O'Neal, Austin, TX 78744. *Design and build handcrafted tables, chairs, case goods and accessory items.*

Ken Picou, Design in Wood, 5510 Montview, Austin, TX 78756 (512)454-3425. *Furnishings and tools of form and function done on a custom or production basis.*

Jim Rodgers, 2201 Barton Springs Rd., Austin, TX 78746.

(12) F.W. Schmidt, 12901 Oak Creek Circle, Austin, TX 78759 (512)478-3769. *Bowls and weed pots from native woods.*

Thunderbolt Graphic Productions, 2041 S. Lamar, Austin, TX 78704 (512)443-0017. *Hand-carved hardwood and redwood graphics. Graphic design, gold-leafing logo and trademark design. Ranch signs and brands.*

Stephen Wise, 707 Aletha Lane, Austin, TX 78745 (512)445-4432. *Acoustic and electric guitars and bass guitars, hammered and fretted dulcimers, mandolins.*

The Wood Pile, Route 5 Box 139, Austin, TX 78748 (512)282-1441. *Custom specialties from spalted woods.*

BASTROP: **Water Street Millworks & Fine Furniture,** 908 Water St., Bastrop, TX 78602 (512)321-5741. *Custom commercial and residential millwork. Doors, windows, cabinets, shutters, restoration work, custom-designed furniture.*

COLLEGE STATION: **Rodney Culver Hill-Sculpture,** 119 Lee Ave., College Station, TX 77840 (713)696-9686. *Custom sculpture, corporate and architectural sculpture, religious sculpture, custom furniture, mantels.*

CORPUS CHRISTI: **Clayton Domier,** 4942 Kosarek, Corpus Christi, TX 78411.

CROSBY: **Richard E. Tuttle,** 15918 Cape Hope, Crosby, TX 77532 (713)328-6223.

DALLAS: **Jerald Goldman,** 4108 Deep Valley, Dallas, TX 75234 (214)247-7799. *Contemporary designs of furniture.*

Douglas Marsden, 3201 Drexel, Dallas, TX 75205 (214)526-8401 or 528-4021.

Randy Murphy, 2948 Marsann, Dallas, TX 76201 (214)247-6681. *Custom furniture, electric instrument repair, custom picture framing and stock. Thickness-planing, ripping to order.*

(24) Mike Norby, Accents N Wood, 3902 Elm St., Dallas, TX 75226 (214)824-3140. *Many people with antique furniture can't find particular pieces. I design and construct them.*

Tremmel Company, 6800 Gaston Ave., Dallas, TX 75214 (214)324-5743. *T-shirt design and manufacturing Wood sculpture.*

Jeff Uhri, Designer-Craftsman, 6108 Velasco, Dallas, TX 75214 (214)823-1769. *Custom furniture, interiors, sculptures.*

T. William Waltrip, 3600 Gaston Ave. Suite 706, Dallas, TX 75246 (214)827-1640.

DAYTON: **Touchstone Wood Creations,** 10 Skylark, Dayton, TX 77535 (713)258-5591. *Clocks, dominoes, chessboards from native Texas woods.*

EL PASO: **(59) Morgan Rey Benson-Woodworkers,** 811 Wyoming, El Paso, TX 79902 (915)532-1077. *Prototype researching and designing. Custom-designed and built furniture and cabinets, small production runs.*

FORT WORTH: **Don Ring, Artisan In Wood,** 5216 Locke Ave., Fort Worth, TX 76107 (817)738-4279. *Woodcarving, period reproductions, pieces designed in period style, contemporary and sculpture.*

FREDERICKSBURG: **Robert F. Stamm,** 216 Crestwood Dr., Fredericksburg, TX 78624 (512)997-3639. *Decorative as well as functional wood items made from domestic and imported woods of contrasting colors.*

FRIONA: **Tommy Carr,** 1012 W. 5th, Friona, TX 79035 (806)247-3525. *Manufacture all types of furniture. Quality hardwoods.*

GREENVILLE: **Danny Hightower,** 901 1-2 Carradine, Greenville, TX 75401 (214)454-6913. *I work for D.A. Steele Cabinet Works. Love working with wood design, antique restoration.*

Woods' Works, 3216 Washington St., Greenville, TX 75401 (214)455-7232. *Specializing in custom-built furniture and antique reproductions.*

HEREFORD: **Bill Bradly Photography, Etc.,** 904 E. Park Ave., Hereford, TX 79045 (806)364-2610. *Slab tables and clocks.*

HOUSTON: **Vincent C. D'Amico,** 6207 Reed Rd., Houston, TX 77087 (713)649-7217. *Lathe turnings, rare wood objects. Colonial furniture reproductions.*

The Dean Luse Company, 909 W. 22nd St. E, Houston, TX 77008 (713)880-2584. *Design and fabrication of residential and commercial furnishings.*

(20) Roger Deatherage, 5200 Nett St., Houston, TX 77007 (713)864-2556. *Hardwood furniture and accessories. By appointment only.*

Brian T. Fuller, 6918 Van Etten, Houston, TX 77021 (713)748-0568. *Cabinetry, residential restoration, carpentry and remodeling.*

Tommy Fullerton, 9102 Country Creek No. 1800, Houston, TX 77036 (713)270-1072. *Custom-built furniture.*

Judaica in Wood, 442 E. Gaywood, Houston, TX 77079 (713)468-4053. *Traditional items of Judaica—Haudalah sets, kiddush cups, seder plates, chalah boards.*

Kodama Woodworks, Wayne Locke, 11450 Bissonnet No. 112, Houston, TX 77099.

Pfluger Cabinet Works, 12843 Westhorpe, Houston, TX 77077 (713)531-6110. *Furniture, doors, fixtures and displays, some renovation work.*

Ron Schumacher, 7435 Elm St., Houston, TX 77023 (713)926-7295. *Wall reliefs combining various hard and exotic woods. Company logos, realistic or abstract pieces for business, church or home installations.*

Wayne Cox Woodworks Inc., 5403 S. Rice Ave., Houston, TX 77081 (713)666-4341. *Production woodworking, architectural woodworking, handmade furniture.*

HUMBLE: **Daniel A. Levy,** 19930 Moonriver Dr., Humble, TX 77338. *Cooperage, antique restoration, reproduction of antique furniture and tools, architectural preservation.*

IRVINE: **Sam Scott,** 806 W. Shady Grove, Irvine, TX 75060 (214)259-6223.

KERRVILLE: **John M. Mosty,** Box 870, Kerrville, TX 78028 (512)367-5562. *Marquetry, carvings, cabinetry, mantels, bar tops carved, inlaid. Originals or reproductions.*

Michael St. Mary, 817 Washington St., Kerrville, TX 78028. *Abstract wood sculpture, representational in origin of design, and organic in form.*

LEANDER: **(29) The Cabinetmakers, Roger Joslin,** 15709 Booth Circle, Leander, TX 78641 (512)258-8125. *Freestanding cabinetry of all kinds. Reproductions, antique repair, contemporary design.*

LUBBOCK: **Doc Gillespie,** 2211 6th St., Lubbock, TX 79401 (806)744-0370. *One-of-a-kind inlaid boxes.*

MANCHACA: **Michael Colca, Summer Tree Woodshop,** Route 1 Box 112, Manchaca, TX 78652 (512)282-0493.

MESQUITE: **C.D. Hughes,** 619 Button Dr., Mesquite, TX 75150 (214)681-1891. *Wooden toys, original designs.*

NEW BRAUNFELS: **John Eric Landry,** 669 Roosevelt, New Braunfels, TX 78130 (512)629-4877.

PANHANDLE: **Crude Creations by Dee Goodman,** 403 Walnut, Panhandle, TX 79068 (806)537-3464. *Woodcarving, Spanish doors, inside and outside, Spanish chairs and furniture, other crude creations.*

PENELOPE: **Randy L. Holub,** Box 143, Penelope, TX 76676 (817)533-2335.

PFLUGERVILLE: **(85) Mark K. Parrish,** Box 773, Main St., Pflugerville, TX 78660 (512)251-4530. *Design and productions of limited-edition pieces and one-of-a-kind commissions for individuals.*

SAN ANGELO: **Chandler L. Hall, Custom Carving,** 106 Tyler Terrace, San Angelo, TX 76901. *Creation and restoration of carved items.*

Bobby Peiser, 102 Tyler Terrace, San Angelo, TX 76901 (915)653 4084. *Office furniture, wall units, tables, doors.*

SAN MARCOS: **Larry Hanson,** 24 Deerwood Dr., San Marcos, TX 78666 (512)392-4462. *One-of-a-kind and antique reproduction and restoration.*

SPRING: **Sutton's Mill,** 6422 Barrygate Dr., Spring, TX 77373 (713)821-1514. *Original designs specializing in cabinetry, framing and photography. Heirloom-quality children's furniture and toys.*

Utah

BRIGHAM CITY: **S.E. Armstrong,** 851 N. Medoland, Brigham City, UT 84302 (801)723-7465. *Custom and one-of-a-kind furniture and cabinets.*

Richard Packer, 538 Holiday Dr., Brigham City, UT 84302 (801)723-7786. *Display-style toys in hardwoods, clocks, breadbox-size projects and smaller. Plans available for many products.*

ELSINORE: **(93) Fred A. Roth,** 40 N. 300 W., Elsinore, UT 84724 (801)527-4626. *Fine handmade household and office furnishings. All pieces signed and dated.*

GLENDALE: **Michael D. Sefcik, Water Canyon Woodworks,** Box 112, Glendale, UT 84729.

LOGAN: **Chris Himmels Woodworking,** 58 1-2 W. 4th N., Logan, UT 84321 (801)752-8561. *Fine hand-built furniture.*

Wood Millers, 58 1-2 W. 4th N., Logan, UT 84321 (801)752-8561. *Custom-design, construct furniture for home and offices.*

MOAB: **Wayne S. Ruth,** 438 Ute Circle, Moab, UT 84532 (801)259-8267. *Small boxes with emphasis on hand joinery, antique reproductions, spoons.*

MURRAY: **Wayne Knuteson,** 3 Regal St., Murray, UT 84107 (801)266-1578. *Commissioned, one-of-a-kind furniture pieces, burl sales, buckeye, walnut, redwood, olive, etc.*

NORTH OGDEN: **(15) The Turning Post,** 3086 N. 150th E., North Ogden, UT 84404 (801)782-5105. *Structural and artistic woodturning.*

OGDEN: **Wood Creations,** 1265-22nd St., Ogden, UT 84401 (801)392-9338. *Custom designs, antique reproductions, repair of high-value items, Chinese-style furniture.*

ROY: **Dee R. Smith,** 4991 S. 2700 W., Roy, UT 84067 (801)825-5132. *Wood lamination, woodcarving, spiral stairways, custom doors and windows and custom furniture.*

SALT LAKE CITY: **Ray Ahone,** 6282 Howey Dr., Salt Lake City, UT 84121 (801)272-3813. *Anything made out of wood. Full and miniature-size furniture.*

Alfano Cabinet Systems, 395 W. Hope Ave., Salt Lake City, UT 84115 (801)486-3756. *Custom cabinets, commercial and residential.*

Stephen A. Goldsmith, 916 W. S. Temple, Salt Lake City, UT 84104 (801)531-0232. *Commissions accepted on a limited basis. All work guaranteed for life of the builder.*

Lange Furniture Gallery, 3651 S. 700 E., Salt Lake City, UT 84106 (801)262-5087. *Designer and builder of handmade art furniture and reproductions.*

Vermont

ARLINGTON: **(111) Dan Mosheim,** Box 2660, Arlington, VT 05250 (802)375-2568. *Custom furniture. Windsor chairs and extraordinary millwork.*

BELMONT: **Zephyr Bowls,** Box 86, Belmont, VT 05730. *Green-turned wooden bowls.*

BETHEL: **Hans Truckenbrod,** Bethel, VT 05032. *Post-and-beam construction, contracting, woodworking of all kinds.*

BRATTLEBORO: **Gemini Woodworking,** Box 521, Brattleboro, VT 05301 (802)254-9463. *Display cabinets and furniture.*

BRISTOL: **(57) James B. Saqui,** Box 4, Bristol, VT 05443 (802)453-2608.

CAMBRIDGE: **Wood Weavers, Linda Milliguay,** Box 990 RD 1, Cambridge, VT 05444 (802)899-2891. *Sweater drawers.*

Wood Weavers, Suzanne Stewart, Box 990 RD 1, Cambridge, VT 05444 (802)899-2891. *Wood and ceramic tile trays and also doors.*

CHESTER: **Stuart Savel, Designer-Craftsman,** Kirk Meadow Rd., Chester, VT 05143 (802)875-3158.

CRAFTSBURY: **Timothy Lee Fritz,** Craftsbury, VT 05827 (802)586-2887.

EAST CALAIS: **(50) David Steckler,** RD 1, East Calais, VT 05650 (802)456-7440. *Custom one-of-a-kind furniture from doors to dressers.*

EAST HAVEN: **Pat Russo,** Star Route, East Haven, VT 05837 (802)467-3463. *Summer months—architectural, custom woodwork. Winter months—viol da gambas.*

ELMORE: **Paul DeCausemacker,** Box 89, Elmore, VT 05657. *Furniture design and construction, architectural woodwork.*

HANCOCK: **(183) Floyd L. Scholz, Woodcarver,** Route 125, Hancock, VT 05748 (802)767-3552. *Creation of realistic wildfowl. Specialty: birds of prey native to Vermont woodlands.*

HUNTINGTON: **Douglas Steward,** Box 148, Huntington, VT 05462 (802)434-3546. *Unique, functional items that are also beautiful.*

MANCHESTER: **Robert M. Gasperetti, Woodworking,** Box 603, Manchester, VT 05254 (802)362-3699. *Reproductions, custom woodworking.*

MARLBORO: **(95) David Holzapfel, Applewood's,** Route 9, Box 66, Marlboro, VT 05344 (802)254-2908. *Functional sculpture made from the burl and spalted hardwoods of Vermont.*

(179) Michelle Holzapfel, Applewood's, Route 9, Box 66, Marlboro, VT 05344 (802)254-2908. *Functional sculpture made from the burl and spalted hardwoods of Vermont.*

MARSHFIELD: **Glenn Russo,** Rural Delivery, Marshfield, VT 05658.

NORTH BENNINGTON: **(53) Thomas Kohn, Kirby Studios,** BCIC Building, Water St., North Bennington, VT 05257 (802)442-3119 (or 425-1/2 Plum St., Red Wing, MN 55066).

(20) Michael Kranz, Kirby Studios, BCIC Building, Water St., North Bennington, VT 05257 (802)442-3119.

Raymond H. Mullineaux, Kirby Studios, North Bennington, VT 05257 (802)442-6980.

(100) Carter Jason Sio, North Bennington, VT 05257 (802)442-3119 or (315)824-1616. *Traditional and/or contemporary.*

NORTHFIELD: **(80) John Wall and Michael Goldfinger, Union Woodworks,** 7 Belknap St., Northfield, VT 05663 (802)485-6261.

POULTNEY: **(53) Michael Coffey,** RD 2, Poultney, VT 05764 (802)287-4091. *Custom furniture making in owner's style. Apprenticeships available.*

PUTNEY: **Dooley Woodworks,** Box 231A RD 3, Putney, VT 05346 (802)387-4325. *Custom design and building of hardwood furniture and accessories.*

Robert F. Olson, Box 451, Putney, VT 05346 (802)387-4288. *Tables, chairs, shelves, chests, cupboards, rockers, beds, stands, oval boxes. Original designs, Shaker adaptations.*

Geoffrey A. Smart, RD Box 395, Putney, VT 05346 (802)387-5365. *Contemporary furniture.*

SHARON: **Lloyd H. Kasper,** Beaver Meadow Rd., Sharon, VT 05065 (802)763-8048. *Sculpture.*

SHELBURNE: **Gail Albert,** Pierson Dr., Shelburne, VT 05482 (802)985-2991. *Native and exotic woodturnings, each unique. Hand mirrors, covered boxes, goblets, plates, bowls, wall mirrors, lamps, rattles.*

SOUTH BURLINGTON: **J.A. Hiltebeitel,** 8 Yandow, South Burlington, VT 05401 (802)658-3961. *Cabinets, small tables, jewelry chests and boxes. Turnings.*

SOUTH DORSET: **Ace Manley,** Route 30, South Dorset, VT 05263 (802)362-1147.

SOUTH RYEGATE: **S.E. Harned Wood Design,** Route 302, South Ryegate, VT 05069 (802)584-3247. *Restore, refinish antiques. Make custom furniture, mainly curly maple and bird's-eye. Also quilted. Some church work.*

TOWNSHEND: **Bellstrom-Moriarty,** Peaked Mountain Rd., Townshend, VT 05353 (802)365-7576. *Furniture, cabinets, bars and architectural woodwork, featuring resawn bookmatched solid American hardwoods.*

WINDHAM: **Alan Perlman,** W. Windham Rd., Windham, VT 05359 (802)874 4427. *Custom-built acoustic guitars. Also do cabinet work.*

WINOOSKI: **Jane Owen,** 64 Weaver St., Winooski, VT 05404. *Sculptured letter boxes with unique designs and original wooden hinge with brass pin.*

WOODBURY: **Jim Wray,** S. Woodbury Village, Woodbury, VT 05681 (802)456-7440. *Custom and limited-production hardwood furniture.*

Virginia

AFTON: **(114) Donald H. Bailey,** RD 2 Box 222B, Afton, VA 22920 (703)456-8215. *Custom-designed furniture along with smaller production pieces for the retail trade.*

ALDIE: **Ebenezer Bros. Inc.,** Route 1 Box 42AA, Aldie, VA 22001 (703)327-4684. *Custom wall systems and original furniture designs in period, traditional and contemporary.*

ALEXANDRIA: **(152) The Harp Woodworks, Thomas Jensen Fannon,** 220 S. Henry St., Alexandria, VA 22314 (703)683-2255. *Furniture design and fine joinery.*

S.B. Swenson, 308 Cambridge Rd., Alexandria, VA 22314 (703)751-4433. *Clocks and barometers.*

George Van Dyke, 3628 Danny's Lane, Alexandria, VA 22311 (703)379-8277. *Turnings and small cabinet work.*

ANNANDALE: **Peter Bach,** 3617 Hummer Rd., Annandale, VA 22003 (703)560-5482.

Stephen LaDrew, 3911 Rose Lane, Annandale, VA 22003 (703)354-5697. *Custom furniture and interiors.*

J. Norris, Mill Creek Woodworks, 4208 Pineridge Dr., Annandale, VA 22003 (703)280-1748. *Custom work. Furniture, small boxes (on request).*

Helmut R. Reinhardt, 7250 Greenfield Rd., Annandale, VA 22003 (703)750-2285. *Custom woodcrafting. Gifts, toys, humorous special request items. No furniture.*

ARLINGTON: **Ron Paci, Fine Woodwork,** 1227 N. Barton St., Arlington, VA 22201 (703)525-5437. *Custom furniture.*

BARBOURSVILLE: **Jaeger & Ernst Inc.,** Route 1 Burnley Station, Barboursville, VA 22923 (804)973-7018. *Custom design and construction of contemporary and traditional hardwood furniture, cabinetry.*

BEDFORD: **(139) Jim Jones,** Route 4 Box 203A, Bedford, VA 24523 (703)297-5457. *Musical instrument construction and repair. Hammer dulcimers, aeolian wind harps, mountain dulcimers, wooden drums and guitars.*

BERRYVILLE: **Warren Hofstra,** Route 2 Box 175, Berryville, VA 22611 (703)955-3153. *Reproductions of eighteenth-century pieces, traditional designs, original contemporary designs.*

BLACKSBURG: **Mark Howe,** Box 413, Blacksburg, VA 24060 (703)951-7926.

CHARLOTTESVILLE: **Stephen A. Clerico,** Route 2 Yule Farm, Charlottesville, VA 22901 (804)295-1401. *Custom furniture, decorative mirrors, hand-carved spoons, kitchenware.*

Hays Woodturning, 116 Blueberry Rd., Charlottesville, VA 29901. *Mainly found woods. Processed green.*

Murray and Wyatt Gaston, Inc., 1313 Belleview Ave., Charlottesville, VA 22901 (804)293-7357. *Custom furniture and architectural millwork to order.*

Ken Swanson, 231 Shamrock Rd., Charlottesville, VA 22905 (804)293-6813. *Hardwood mosiac wall hangings, shadow lights and asymmetrical weed and flower pots.*

CROZET: **William Harrington,** Route 1 Box 407A, Crozet, VA 22932 (804)823-5584. *Woodcarvings, reliefs and metal sculpture.*

DAYTON: **Pierce F. Pitsenbarger,** Route 3 Box 204, Dayton, VA 22821 (703)879-2245. *Battery-operated clocks and small items. Interested in anything different and unusual.*

FREE UNION: **(146) Paul Pyzyna, Shelter Woodworks,** Box 43 Route 601, Free Union, VA 22940 (804)296-7964 or 973-8307. *Custom cabinets, doors, furniture and architectural woodworks.*

GREAT FALLS: **DeSantis Designs Inc.,** 1272 Kenmore Dr., Great Falls, VA 22066 (703)759-2222. *Designing and building, hardwood furniture, tambours, reception areas, mantel pieces, etched glass, gold leaf, hardwood signs.*

HANOVER: **Jamey Hutchinson,** Trilby, Hanover, VA 23069 (804)537-5534. *Custom design.*

KING GEORGE: **Sheild Art & Hobby,** 54 Danube Dr., King George, VA 22485 (703)663-3711. *Original carvings and paintings. Model railroad sales and service.*

LOUDOUN HEIGHTS: **Wood Workshop,** Route 671, Loudoun Heights, VA 22132 (703)668-6259. *Contemporary designs based on traditional themes and done in native American hardwood.*

LOVINGSTON: **Braintree Woodworks, Frederick Wilbur,** Box 425, Lovingston, VA 22949 (804)263-4827. *Routed and carved signs. Hand-carving, architectural and furniture.*

NEWPORT NEWS: **(109) John W. Snead, Joiner,** 208 Ferguson Ave., Newport News, VA 23601 (804)596-7838.

ORANGE: **Henry B. Micks,** 241 E. Main St., Orange, VA 22960 (703)672-4874. *Antique reproductions, silver chests. By commission only.*

PORTSMOUTH: **(85) Reed Cabinetworks,** 740-750 Broad St., Portsmouth, VA 23707 (804)393-6911 or 465-0280. *Custom cabinetry for kitchens, boats, baths, family rooms, store fixtures, furniture repair and restorations.*

PURCELLVILLE: **William Hugh Grubb III,** RFD 1 Box 494, Purcellville, VA 22132 (703)668-6016. *Custom fine furniture and cabinets, architectural woodworking, home restoration and interiors.*

RAPIDAN: **(136) Don Polifka, The Joynery,** Highway 615, Box 104, Rapidan, VA 22733 (703)672-2266. *I presently make guitars, banjos, mandolins, dulcimers, autoharps and fiddles.*

Jim Poole, Highway 615, Box 54, Rapidan, VA 22733 (703)672-2266. *Tables, beds, desks, sofas, floor and wall cabinets, music stands, cradles, stools.*

RICHMOND: **William A. Berry, Jr.,** 318 W. Broad St., Richmond, VA 23220 (804)643-1044. *Repairs, restorations and reproductions.*

George Delk, 3218 A W. Franklin St., Richmond, VA 23221 (804)353-3642.

Michael Funk, 2121 W. Cary, Richmond, VA 23220 (804)257-1477. *Design and fabrication of custom contemporary furniture. Specialty: post-modern design with coloration of wood.*

(97) W. Hammersley, 221 Shafer Court, Richmond, VA 23284 (804)257-1477.

Tres Irby, 2400 Boyle Ave., Richmond, VA 23230 (804)282-3914. *Handmade, original designs with strong emphasis on the finest quality construction and diversification of design.*

Clyde F. Kellogg, 315 W. Marshall St., Richmond, VA 23220 (804)788-1498. *Contemporary furniture, architectural cabinetry, custom interiors, including renovations.*

William N. Koch, Woodesign, 6 W. Cary St., Richmond, VA 23220 (804)644-2803. *Design and construct commissioned pieces and speculative pieces on unique and series basis.*

(111) B. Randolph Wilkinson, 5208-A Brook Rd., Richmond, VA 23227 (804)264-5585. *Windsor chairs in a variety of styles.*

ROANOKE: **Anthony J. Wilkinson,** 916 Winchester Ave. S.W., Roanoke, VA 24015 (703)982-0913. *Custom cabinets.*

SANDSTON: **M.J. Staton,** Sandston, VA 23150 (804)737-1946. *Turning, design, general woodworking.*

STAUNTON: **B.E. Shull, Organbuilder,** Route 1 Box 83, Staunton, VA 24401 (703)886-7515. *Historic keyboard instruments, regals, portatives, positive and continuo organs.*

VIENNA: **Robert T. Bishop,** 9835 Marcliff Court, Vienna, VA 22180 (703)938-1027. *Architectural reproduction and restoration for restored houses.*

VIRGINIA BEACH: **Bertrand Ebbitt,** 2202 Beech St., Virginia Beach, VA 23451 (804)481-1228. *Wooden signs, one-of-a-kind furniture.*

WINCHESTER: **(18) R.L. Heisey, Cabinetmaker Ltd.,** Sunnyside Station, Winchester, VA 22601 (703)667-3095. *Individually designed, meticulously constructed period style and contemporary pieces. Focus: inlay and veneer.*

WOODBRIDGE: **Lee W. Dean,** 4767 Lupino Court, Woodbridge, VA 22193 (703)590-1127. *Fine furniture of domestic and imported hardwoods. Reproductions on request. All projects by appointment only.*

Washington

ALGONA: **Darrell W. Peart,** 135 1st Ave., Algona, WA 98002 (206)939-0507. *Small cabinets, chests and tables, stereo cabinets.*

AUBURN: **Mason Walter Campbell,** 3216 S. 276th St., Auburn, WA 98002 (206)854-2277. *Fine wood furniture.*

Hugh D. Kinkade, 34833 215 Ave. SE, Auburn, WA 98002 (206)886-2251. *Cabinets, tables and custom-designed one-of-a-kind items.*

BAINBRIDGE: **Dr. Harmon F. Adams,** 10043 N.E. S. Beach Dr., Bainbridge Island, WA 98110 (206)842-3630. *A goldsmith specializing in metal and wooden bird sculptures.*

BELLEVUE: **Christopher Associates,** Box 5833, Bellevue, WA 98006. *Small accessories, turned boxes, candlesticks, bandsaw boxes, finishing and refinishing. Antique restoration.*

D'Arcy Nutcrackers, 14230 NE 8th St., Bellevue, WA 98007 (206)747-9424. *Complex projects blending unique, exotic woods, fanciful characters, objects d'art.*

The Normans, 9804 N.E. 14th St., Bellevue, WA 98004 (206)454-3612. *Custom cabinets, furniture. Also do specialty pieces.*

BELLINGHAM: **Greg Aanes,** 5081 Wahl Rd., Bellingham, WA 98226 (206)966-5888. *Solid-wood cabinets and fine furniture. Thoughtful designs in local and imported woods.*

(91) Michael Strong Furniture, 1133 14th St., Bellingham, WA 98225 (206)671-9952. *Furniture design and construction in limited production and custom work. Specializing in seating and tables.*

Rich Murphy, 245 Garden Terrace, Bellingham, WA 98225 (206)671-0215. *Fine woodwork of all types, including architectural.*

Ted Scherrer, 500 Larrabee Ave., Bellingham, WA 98225 (206)733-3411. *Fine woodworking and furniture design. Custom and limited production.*

BRIER: **Grady Mathews Custom Cabinetry,** 23509-29th Ave. W., Brier, WA 98036 (206)483-9377. *Custom-designed and built furniture and architectural cabinetry for residential and commercial applications.*

BRUSH PRAIRIE: **(153) Jim Boesel,** 18702 N.E. Davis Rd., Brush Prairie, WA 98606 (206)256-4228. *Design, building and repair of anything wooden, specializing in chairs, dining tables and carvings.*

J-Juan Cabinets, 16107 NE 94th Ave. Box 279, Brush Prairie, WA 98606 (206)573-4496. *Custom cabinetry, furniture and woodcraft (boxes, frames, etc.,) in contemporary designs.*

CATHLAMET: **William E. Halbom,** 255 Jacobson Rd., Cathlamet, WA 98612 (206)795-3988.

CHENEY: **Harold K. Stevens,** 508 W. Clover St., Cheney, WA 99004 (509)235-6516. *Custom carving, grandfather clocks.*

DAYTON: **Patit Valley Woodworks,** 303 N. First, Dayton, WA 99328 (509)382-3101. *One-of-a-kind furniture, cabinetry, lathe work, signs, turning dreams into reality.*

EASTSOUND: **Tony Howard,** Route 1 Box 1425, Eastsound, WA 98245 (206)376-4471. *Only wood found on Orcas Island used, from tree to finished piece.*

EDMONDS: **John R. Gray,** 23831 111th Place W., Edmonds, WA 98020 (206)542-1760.

ELLENSBURG: **Stephen G. Clausen,** 506 W. 11th, Ellensburg, WA 98926 (509)925-3067. *Exclusively design and construct contemporary furniture.*

(25) Steven Emrick, 710 E. 4th St., Ellensburg, WA 98926 (509)962-6948. *Sculptural designs in wood.*

(25) Thomas C. MacMichael, Capricorn Woodworking, 207 S. Sprague St., Ellensburg, WA 98926 (509)925-2966. *Pushing form to new functions within woodworking.*

FEDERAL WAY: **F.W. Foess and Son, Furniture Makers,** 2134 S.W. 339th St., Federal Way, WA 98003 (206)927-4251. *Fine custom furniture, carving, restorations.*

ISSAQUAH: **Cougar Mountain Custom Woodworking, Bob Adams,** 17426 SE 60th, Issaquah, WA 98027 (206)641-9711. *Custom woodworking and cabinetry.*

KENNEWICK: **Aaron Holloway,** 7919 W. Falls Place, Kennewick, WA 99336.

(123) Joe L. Nevius, 2627 W. 6th Ave., Kennewick, WA 99336 (509)582-3485. *Furniture, sleds and commission work.*

KIRKLAND: **(117) Perfection Woodcrafters Inc.,** 13226 126th Place N.E., Kirkland, WA 98033 (206)821-4277. *Solid-hardwood furniture.*

Jerilyn Petersons, 1125 6th St., Kirkland, WA 98033 (206)827-7077.

LANGLEY: **Flanagan Woodworks,** 5180 S. Nighthawk Rd., Langley, WA 98260 (206)221-3352. *Period reproductions. Custom cabinets.*

(165) John D. Griffith, Northwind, 5034 Inglewood Dr. S., Langley, WA 98260 (206)221-7924. *Fine containers, contemporary furniture and cabinetwork, lapidary work. Design and commission.*

LONGVIEW: **Bowls and Boxes, Leonard R. Bean,** 401 Olson Rd., Longview, WA 98632 (206)425-5797. *Lidded wood turnings and small weed pots.*

MARYSVILLE: **(114) Gert Becker, Woodcarver,** 2632 Mission Beach Heights Rd., Marysville, WA 98270 (206)659-8965. *Historical furniture and sculpture of original design, specializing in German-Austrian Gothic, Renaissance, Baroque.*

MERCER ISLAND: **Gordon Stacey and Son,** 3727 86th Ave. SE, Mercer Island, WA 98040 (206)232-2629.

(148) Wood-You-Like, 2728 63rd Avneue S.E., Mercer Island, WA 98040 (206)236-2409. *Custom designs and limited edition folding screens. All solid wood and carved.*

MOUNT VERNON: **Ray deVries,** 1573 Greenacres Rd., Mount Vernon, WA 98273 (206)424-5398. *Custom-designed wood products built to be functional and to have meaning and symbolism.*

NEWPORT: **(127) Larry Cada,** Route 3 Box 1294, Newport, WA. 99156 (509)447-2303. *Original design and construction of sculptural furniture and other fine architectural objects.*

NORTH BEND: **(168) David Paul Eck, Designer-Craftsman,** 16950 431st Ave. S.E., North Bend, WA 98045 (206)888-3424. *One-of-a-kind pieces, commissions, built-in furniture, limited runs of specific pieces.*

OLYMPIA: **Stuart N. Atwood,** 1240 E. 8th Ave., Olympia, WA 98501. *I build folk harps, hammered dulcimers and Italian harpsichords and virginals.*

(66) Jim Davis, 2406 Delphi Rd., Olympia, WA 98502 (703)866-0457. *Fine tables and lapstrake boats.*

(158) David Knobel, Maker of Fine Furniture, 4826 17th N.W., Olympia, WA 98502 (206)866-0544. *Maker of custom cabinets and fine furniture since 1975. One-man shop, signature-quality work.*

Serendipity Art Works, 1909 Bowman, Olympia, WA 98502 (206)943-5735. *Custom turning and furniture.*

OMAK: **Paul Mannino,** 16 Miller Rd., Omak, WA 98841 (509)826-5984. *Originality with function. Altar furniture. Only commissioned work.*

PORT TOWNSEND: **(98) Discovery Boat Works, James M. McEver, Builder,** 2436 Haines St., Port Townsend, WA 98368 (206)385-5075. *Classic small craft and custom furniture.*

REDMOND: **A & H Cabinets,** 4640 148th Ave. N.E., Redmond, WA 98052 (206)885-5611. *Custom cabinets and woodworking.*

RENTON: **Rob's Woodworks,** 1120 Tacoma Ave. N.E., Renton, WA 98056 (206)226-2275. *Specializing in solid-wood inlay for tables, large tops and floors.*

John West, Box 2364, Renton, WA 98055 (206)271-6113. *Combs and mirrors sets, bookcases, chopsticks, bangles, baby rattles, wind spinners, christmas ornaments. Wholesale/retail.*

RICE: **Olaf Heintz, Designer-Craftsman,** Route 1 Box 28, Rice, WA 99167. *Coopering techniques and variations with joinery.*

RICHLAND: **Oris D. Goodey,** 202 Endress, Richland, WA 99352 (509)946-9438. *Toys, furniture, furniture refinishing, kitchen gadgets.*

SEATTLE: **Amphibian Design, S.C. Addison,** 1220 N.W. 77th St., Seattle, WA 98117. *Architectural and marine. Design/build capabilities in custom construction, historic rehab, solar design, product development.*

(89) Steven Caldwell, 5721 16th Ave. N.E., Seattle, WA 98105 (206)525-4089. *One-of-a-kind and limited-production tables and chairs and desks.*

(56) Jonathan Cohen, Fine Woodwork, 3410 Woodland Park N., Seattle, WA 98103 (206)632-2141. *One-off custom-designed furniture. Bentwood construction.*

(151) Brian Cullen, 325 Harvard Ave. E., Seattle, WA 98102 (206)624-5315 or 324-9391.

(113) Daiku Inc., Lawrence A. Moniz, 9536 48th Ave. N.E., Seattle, WA 98115 (206)527-2522.

(60) Emmett E. Day, 3226 Portage Bay Place E., Seattle, WA 98102 (206)325-9059. *Combinations of precious metals, woods, stone, glass on commission. Furniture, jewelry, sculpture.*

(137) Rion Dudley, Design, 3203 13th Ave. W., Seattle, WA 98119 (206)282-6653. *Custom furniture. Two to six custom mandolins or guitars per year.*

(93) Curtis Erpelding, 110 Union 300, Seattle, WA 98101 (206)625-0754. *Custom furniture and cabinets.*

(93) Don Hennick, Whisperings Wood, 9547 Wallingford N., Seattle, WA 98103 (206)522-5380. *Custom and conventional furniture and cabinets, piano restoration in the home.*

Hank Hoelzer, 2047 26th Ave. E., Seattle, WA 98112 (206)329-7745.

(169) Bliss Kolb, Joinery, 3379 47th N.E., Seattle, WA 98105. *Delicate woodwork with precious materials, jewelry boxes and automata.*

Douglas Krampetz, 814 37th Ave., Seattle, WA 98122 (206)329-4109. *Domestic and architectural woodworking. Yacht interiors and wooden boat construction.*

Scott Lawrence, 204 3rd Ave. S., Seattle, WA 98104 (206)621-9513. *Hardwood furniture, shoji screens, unusual finishes.*

Linde R. Behringer Woodworking, 4333 Phinney No., Seattle, WA 98103 (206)633-2357.

Gregory A. Scott, 4701 21st S.W., Seattle, WA 98106 (206)932-1068. *Custom interiors on yachts and fishing boats, planking, decking, teak trim, handrails. Also furniture and kitchens.*

Tom Simmons, 614B Lake Washington Boulevard E., Seattle, WA 98112 (206)325-3411.

Rene Soulard, N.W. Gallery of Fine Woodwork, 202 1st Ave. S., Seattle, WA 98104 (206)625-0542.

(153) Dennis W. Vidmar, 123 E. Edgar St., Seattle, WA 98102 (206)325-4841. *Monumental woodwork for public and private spaces. Doors, water-bearing fixtures, seating, sculpture, tables and counters.*

(102) The Woodworker, 8512 12th N.W., Seattle, WA 98117 (206)789-0948. *Custom cabinetry, furniture, sculptural pieces and carvings.*

SEAVIEW: **Floyd E. Rank,** Box 127, Seaview, WA 98644 (206)642-2407. *Furniture, clocks and musical instrument reproductions.*

SPOKANE: **Jim Freeman,** 2129 E. Diamond, Spokane, WA 99207 (509)489-5718.

Kit Hanes, E. 2303 S. Crescent, Spokane, WA 99207 (509)535-5782. *Anything in wood, with an emphasis on hand tools.*

The Norseman, 12917 E. 10th, Spokane, WA 99216 (509)924-2082. *Unique furniture design and manufacture.*

TACOMA: **(16) Robert W. Sheedy, Design in Wood,** 8408 33rd W., Tacoma, WA 98466 (206)564-1183. *Turned containers, wooden clocks, unusual furniture.*

Dennis Stroh, Woodworker, 601 Ton-a-Waunda Ave. N.E., Tacoma, WA 98422 (206)927-3964. *One-of-a-kind furniture and sculpture.*

Jerry Timm, 8612 John Dower Rd. SW, Tacoma, WA 98499 (206)582-5172. *Custom designing, rolltop desks and stereo cabinets, bar stools, occasional tables and chairs.*

VANCOUVER: **Tom Dietrich,** 5009 Dubois Dr., Vancouver, WA 98661 (206)695-0339.

Marvin McCoy, Wild Mountain Enterprises, 3112 M St., Vancouver, WA 98663 (206)695-3171. *Purveyor of fine wooden sailing and rowing craft.*

WENATCHEE: **Lynn L. Shirk,** 2409 Riter, Wenatchee, WA 98801 (509)662-8825.

WHITE SALMON: **Steve Wray, White Salmon Woodworks,** W. Spring St., White Salmon, WA 98672 (509)493-3827. *Original one-of-a-kind furniture, presentation and display cases, cabinets, frames for stained glass.*

WINTHROP: **The Niddy Noddy,** 239 Riverside Ave., Winthrop, WA 98863 (509)996-2809. *Yarn, gifts, knitting, spinning and weaving supplies, handmade niddy noddies.*

West Virginia

BECKLEY: **Dr. William Ross Peery,** 210 Berkley St., Beckley, WV 25801 (304)253-6332. *Sawdust.*

BERKELEY SPRINGS: **(153) Bert Lustig,** Route 3 Box 194, Berkeley Springs, WV 25411. *Table lamps, seating furniture, accessories.*

BIG BEND: **(124) Jude Binder,** Route 1 Box 61, Big Bend, WV 26136 (304)354-7874.

CHARLESTON: **Colvin Woodworking,** 1576 Clark Rd., Charleston, WV 25314 (304)345-1277. *Antique reproductions, original commission pieces, specialty clocks (grandfather, wall and shelf).*

CHESTER: **Gary A. Churella,** RD 1 Box 224, State Route 8, Chester, WV 26034 (304)387-2147. *Custom steam-bending, decorative boxes and architectural models.*

CHLOE: **(173) Connie & Tom McColley,** Route 3 Box 325, Chloe, WV 25235. *Contemporary and traditional baskets in hand-split white oak and other natural materials.*

HARPERS FERRY: **(162) Michael Carner,** Route 3 Box 900, Harpers Ferry, WV 25425 (304)725-6282.

MORGANTOWN: **Me & Another Guy Woodworking Inc.,** Route 1 Box 306, Morgantown, WV 26505. *Custom design and construction of furniture made from domestic hardwoods.*

PALESTINE: **Drew Cathell,** 237 Sanoma Rd., Palestine, WV 26160 (304)275-4436. *Furniture and cabinets designed and built with the best of the old and the new.*

PARKERSBURG: **(124) Norm Sartorius,** 1302 Ann St., Parkersburg, WV 26101 (304)485-3394.

ROCK CAVE: **Richard Sink, Cabinetmaker,** Route 1 Box 54-C, Rock Cave, WV 26234 (304)925-8014. *Handmade carvings, wrought-iron work, fifteenth and sixteenth-century designed furniture, contemporary.*

VIENNA: **G.H. Stoltz, Jr.,** 5505 3rd Ave., Vienna, WV 26105 (304)295-7880. *One-of-a-kind turning.*

Wisconsin

ANTIGO: **Ron Retherford,** 1211 Clermont St., Antigo, WI 54409 (715)623-4623. *Clocks, small articles for home and also specialty items.*

APPLETON: **Robert Goldsmith,** 405 N. Drew St., Appleton, WI 54911 (414)739-8903. *One-of-a-kind, limited editions.*

Bruce Petros, Luthier, 603 N. Kensington Dr., Appleton, WI 54915 (414)731-9432. *Steel-string and classical guitars. String instrument repair and restoration. Custom furniture, cabinets and turnings.*

R.A. Schultz Woodworking, 525 N. Durkee St., Appleton, WI 54911 (414)739-4919. *Cabinets, tables, lamps, toys.*

BARRONNETT: **Norsk Woodworks,** Box 66, Barronnett, WI 54813 (715)822-3104.

BAYSIDE: **(121) Bill Stankus, Designs in Wood,** 714 E. Standish Place, Bayside, WI 53217 (414)351-6573. *One-of-a-kind items, custom furniture, prototype development, hand-tool and joinery instruction.*

BEAVER DAM: **Kenneth Strauss,** 142 E. Burnett St., Beaver Dam, WI 53916 (414)887-1160.

BELLEVILLE: **Steve Ruland,** Route 2 Box 137, Belleville, WI 53508 (608)527-5198.

BELOIT: **Linda Sue Eastman,** Beloit, WI 53511. *One-of-a-kind clocks with wooden gearing. Designed by artist or upon commission.*

CEDARBURG: **(87) Autumn Woods Studio,** W63 N653 Washington Ave., Cedarburg, WI 53012 (414)375-1912. *Custom furniture and accents. I also teach fine woodwork classes in my studio.*

CENTURIA: **The Wheelwright Shop,** In basement of home, Centuria, WI 54824 (715)646-2621. *Spinning wheels, clocks, music stands.*

CUDAHY: **Eugene B. Widenski,** 4018 E. Allerton Ave., Cudahy, WI 53110 (414)481-1319. *Wood furniture, lamps, etc.*

DePERE: **James Woods,** c/o 1006 Twilight, DePere, WI 54115 (414)336-7318. *Custom musical instruments and specially designed furniture. Commissioned works.*

EPHRAIM: **Eden North Studio & Gallery,** Shorewood Village, Ephraim, WI 54211 (414)839-2754. *Functional and artistic wood items done primarily in pine and using dowel peg and glue.*

FOND DU LAC: **Lee A. Pickart,** 4406 Lakeshore Dr., Fond du Lac, WI 54935 (414)921-2057. *Turning is shop specialty, but also proficient in cabinet and interior wood furnishings.*

GREEN BAY: **Fred W. Juengst, Jr.,** 846 Cornelius Dr., Green Bay, WI 54301 (414)469-1919. *Scandinavian and contemporary furniture and cabinets.*

GREENFIELD: **Robert J. Michaels,** 7927 W. Bottsford Ave., Greenfield, WI 53220 (414)543-5942.

HUDSON: **John Slight,** 509 S. 11th St., Hudson, WI 54016 (715)386-3239. *Custom-made china hutches to be given as wedding gifts.*

HURLEY: **(156) John Gibbons, Gibbons Sash and Door,** Route 1, Hurley, WI 54534. *Double-spindle shaper specialists. Custom sash and door work, French doors, barred windows and curved moldings.*

LA CROSSE: **(125) Prairie Designs,** 613 S. 8th St., La Crosse, WI. 54601 (608)782-5845. *Woodworking tools and furniture.*

LODI: **Spring Creek Woodworks,** 210 S. Main St., Lodi, WI 53555 (608)592-4039. *Personalized furniture and wall cabinets, wooden signs, entry ways and doors.*

MADISON: **Caldwell Design,** 112 W. Wilson No. 1, Madison, WI 53703 (608)256-2928.

Peter L. Cohen, 1120 Stewart St., Madison, WI 53713 (608)274-2583. *High-quality craftsmanship and custom design, often using classical motifs.*

Peter Flanary, 2829 Perry St., Madison, WI 53713 (608)271-0840.

(106) James Gentry, 303 E. Wilson, Madison, WI 53703 (608)251-2549. *I make and sell solid-wood tables, chairs, writing desks and cabinetry.*

(70) JAK, 409 Powers Ave., Madison, WI 53714 (608)244-5993. *Conceptual furniture and home furnishings. Knock-down multi-functional computer furniture.*

John Michael Linck, 2550 Van Hise Ave., Madison, WI 53705 (608)231-2808. *Wooden toys from fine hardwoods.*

Ken Paulow, 2070 Helena, Madison, WI 53704 (608)255-7283. *Furniture, cabinets, historic restoration, simple musical instruments, carving, toys.*

Gail Prensky, 702 Eugenia Ave., Madison, WI 53705 (608)233-2627.

George A. Sabosik, 515 Maple Ave., Madison, WI 53704 (608)249-9756.

Robert D. St. Clair, 5699 Nutone St., Madison, WI 53711 (608)271-1830. *Quality hand-crafted early American furniture and fine woodwork.*

Steven Spiro, 2829 Perry St., Madison, WI 53713. *Furniture, residential and contract.*

Richard Swanson, 2112 Jefferson St., Madison, WI 53711 (608)256-8991.

(36) Lottie Kwai Lin Wolff, 721 E. Gorham St., Madison, WI 53703.

MARSHALL: **Dean Helwig,** 7628 Deansville Rd., Marshall, WI 53559 (414)623-2135. *Cabinetmaking and novelties.*

MARSHFIELD: **Christopher Claflin, Furniture Maker,** 521 Magee, Marshfield, WI 54449 (715)387-0113. *Design and construction of one-of-a-kind pieces in wood.*

MEQUON: **(71) Contemporary Works,** 11022 N. Cedarburg Rd., Mequon, WI 53092 (414)242-4151. *Custom, fine woodwork. Original furniture and interiors.*

MILWAUKEE: **Bankier-Kaminsky Custom Woodworks,** 2738 N. Stowell Ave., Milwaukee, WI 53211 (414)964-9663. *Custom furniture designs and construction, Japanese shoji, sliding window screens or freestanding panels.*

Judi R. Bartholomew, 3858 S. 57th St., Milwaukee, WI 53220 (414)541-1132. *Bas-relief and three-dimensional carving in hardwoods, ivory, antler. Liturgical and wildlife studies.*

David Erickson Woodworking, 3000 N. Murray Ave., Milwaukee, WI 53211 (414)962-9270. *Commissioned residential furnishings and accessories.*

Designs In Woods, 2804 S. Logan Ave., Milwaukee, WI 53207 (414)483-1475. *Unique wall furnishings.*

Eric's Fine Furniture, 225 E. Bradley Ave., Milwaukee, WI 53207 (414)481-9965. *Contemporary custom hand-crafted furnishings, specializing in walnut, teak and oak.*

Michael Grafwallner, 3554 S. 93rd, Milwaukee, WI 53228 (414)321-6737. *Handmade turned lamps and candleholders, furniture finished with fine wood to your specifications and liking.*

Northwing Studio, 2923 N. Marietta Ave., Milwaukee, WI 53211 (414)963-1415. *Northwing Studio produces wood sculpture, functional sculpture and trade signs on commission.*

(159) Michael R. O'Connor, Woodworker, 1809 N. Cambridge, Milwaukee, WI 53202 (414)272-1170. *Custom-designed commercial and residential furnishings.*

O'Reilly Woodworking and Glass, 504 S. 76th St., Milwaukee, WI 53214 (414)476-1909. *Furniture, stained glass.*

MINERAL POINT: **Joel L. Duncanson,** 200 Clowney St., Mineral Point, WI 53565 (608)987-3085. *Custom furniture, reproduction millwork.*

Russellworks, Rob and Kim Russell, Box 310, Mineral Point, WI 53565 (608)987-3038. *Christmas ornaments, utensils, sculptured nonfunctional bowls.*

John C. Sharp, Jr., Route 3 Box 95A, Mineral Point, WI 53565 (608)987-2526. *Western Americana and wildlife wood sculpture.*

MINOCQUA: **Maureen Neal, Woodworks,** Box 727, Minocqua, WI 54548 (715)356-2390.

MOUNT HOREB: **(166) Sundog Enterprises,** 300 W. Main, Mount Horeb, WI 53592 (608)437-8790. *Tambour closures, contemporary design.*

MUKWONAGO: **Thomas W. Kastern,** Route 5 W297 510761 Phantom Woods Rd., Mukwonago, WI 53149 (414)363-8349.

NEW AUBURN: **(72) Mark Ruddy,** Route 2 Box 230, New Auburn, WI 54757 (715)237-2402. *Contemporary, functional, furniture art.*

OGDENSBURG: **(21) Little Wolf Time Co.,** Box 278A Elm Valley Rd., Ogdensburg, WI 54962 (715)467-2748. *Clocks and fine case work in limited editions of one.*

ONALASKA: **William D. Gautsch,** N4671 Old Hickory Dr., Onalaska, WI 54650 (608)783-7171. *Custom-designed furniture on a commission basis, usually in oak. No production runs.*

OSHKOSH: **Rolf Olson,** 1117 Wisconsin St., Oshkosh, WI 54901 (414)235-6979.

Herbert S. Salzsieder, 4360 N. Shore Dr., Oshkosh, WI 54901 (414)231-5345.

Scott K. Salzsieder, 4360 N. Shore Dr., Oshkosh, WI 54901 (414)231-5345. *Knives, turnings, small boxes, and other things which do not take up much room.*

Walter Yurk, 1725 Indian Point Rd., Oshkosh, WI 54901 (414)231-3910. *Abstracts, ducks, fish, fruit, nuts. Almost any small items made from walnut, cherry, butternut.*

PEWANKEE: **Craig Petros,** W239 N3198 Hwy. F., Pewankee, WI 53072 (414)691-0942. *Furniture, display cabinets and glassworks.*

PHILLIPS: **(11) Dennis A. Dahl,** Hiway 13 S., Phillips, WI 54555 (715)339-3159. *Carving, sculpture, custom furniture, bowls, woodcuts, graphics in wood, design.*

Dawn Johnston, Phillips, WI 54555 (715)339-3159. *Designs in wood. By appointment only.*

PLATTEVILLE: **Heirloom Bowls, David Lory,** RR 2 Box 76, Platteville, WI 53818 (608)348-6344. *Thin bowls from burls and unique wood grains. Finished with epoxy and guaranteed for life.*

PLYMOUTH: **Richard Bronk,** Route 3, Plymouth, WI 53073 (4!4)893-5581. *Chairs of wood with leather upholstery.*

PORT TOWNSEND: **The Interwood Co.,** 1914 Clay, Port Townsend, WI 98368 385-4338. *Traditional and original-design entry doors, hand-built in fine woods. Custom furniture, contemporary and traditional.*

RACINE: **Rod Cronkite,** 2812 Wright Ave., Racine, WI 53405 (414)633-6303. *Turnings. Bowls, boxes, lamps, custom furniture, speaker stands. Kitchenware, fancy cutting boards, picture frames.*

RICHLAND CENTER: **Carlyle Peckham,** Route 3, Richland Center, WI 53581 (608)549-2481. *Small turned objects and cabinetmaking of all types.*

SCHOFIELD: **G.M. Bellas,** 2011 Hemlock Ave., Schofield, WI 54476 (715)359-7805. *Furniture, small functional wooden ware and wood toys.*

SHARON: **Wayne Konkle,** 219 Baldwin St. Box 4, Sharon, WI 53585 (414)736-4887. *Wood turning. Thin burl bowls, lamps, weed pots, hand mirrors, clocks, wall telephones and small cabinetry.*

SHEBOYGAN: **Kevin Wiseman,** 327 Michigan Ave., Sheboygan, WI 53081 (414)452-6324. *Small functional and ornamental objects. Custom work furniture repair.*

SHOREWOOD: **A. Snowdon, Wood Sculptor,** 4321 N. Murray Ave., Shorewood, WI 53211 (414)332-1698. *Wood sculptor, bird carvings, animal carvings, sculptured bowls.*

SOLDIERS GROVE: **Tim Bacon,** Route 2 Box 44, Soldiers Grove, WI 54655 (608)624-5881 or 624-3245. *Chairs, tables, caskets and general furniture built to last.*

SOLON SPRINGS: **Jack Pine Savage Workshops,** Star Route Box 2633, Solon Springs, WI 54873. *Small furniture pieces and cabinets.*

SPARTA: **Mark Kerr,** Route 1 Box 38A, Cinder Dr., Sparta, WI 54656 (608)269-8486. *Custom furniture, cabinets, reproductions. Solid wood. Any species available for use.*

STOUGHTON: **(47) CJON Woodworks,** 3496 Highway 138, Stoughton, WI 53589. *Contemporary design.*

SUN PRAIRIE: **Claude M. Weisensel,** 1655 Calico Court, Sun Prairie, WI 53590 (608)837-7963. *I love woodworking.*

TWO RIVERS: **Peter F. Tegen,** 9601 Highway 42, Two Rivers, WI 54241 (414)794-8812. *Cribbage boards, lamps, butcher-block cutting boards.*

VERONA: **David H. Haessig,** Box 22, Verona, WI 53593 (608)222-4380. *Exotic hardwood creations, clipboards, cutting boards, knife blocks, belt buckles, hand mirrors and lazy Susans.*

VIROQUA: **Daniel Arnold,** Route 3, Viroqua, WI 54665 (608)634-3890. *I design and build furniture cabinets and interiors of native midwestern hardwoods.*

WAUKESHA: **(170) Eccentrics, Tom Rauschke and Kaaren Wiken,** 1609 Delafield St., Waukesha, WI 53186. *Fine art from hand, heart and spirit.*

WAUSAU: **(163) Mark Duginske,** 1010 First Ave. N., Wausau, WI 54401 (715)675-2229. *Frank Lloyd Wright and Prairie School restoration. Functional design.*

WAUWATOSA: **Warren Cartier,** 11400 W. Center St., Wauwatosa, WI 53213 (414)258-9343. *We develop working models of projects selected for student development.*

Norman R. Doll, 1409 N. 67th St., Wauwatosa, WI 53213 (414)257-2878. *Bowls and general woodworking.*

WISCONSIN DELLS: **Jeffrey Dahlquist,** Route 2 Box 65, Wisconsin Dells, WI 53965 (608)254-7820.

WISCONSIN RAPIDS: **Allan Dickman,** 6941 Wazeecha Ave., Wisconsin Rapids, WI 54494 (715)421-3049. *Wooden toys, shoes and furniture.*

Wyoming

CASPER: **John R. Haass,** 420 S. Grant St., Casper, WY 82601 (307)265-9064. *Contemporary wood furnishings and accessories for home and office.*

RIVERTON: **Michael E. Carter, Sculptor & Carver,** 609 E. Jackson, Riverton, WY 82501 (307)856-4989. *Unique hand-crafted wooden items.*

Wind River Woodworks, Route 2, Gardens N. 22, Riverton, WY 82501. *Custom furniture and woodwork, hardwood toys. Hand-carved rockinghorses.*

AUSTRALIA

New South Wales

AUSTRALIAN CAPITAL TERRITORY: **Cuppacumbalong Woodworks, David Upfill-Brown,** Cuppacumbalong, Tharwa, Australian Capital Territory, Australia. *Commissions undertaken in Australian hardwoods—anything from bookends to cathedral doors.*

CHIPPENDALE: **(126) Richard Crosland,** 20A City Rd., Chippendale, NSW 2008, Australia (02)211-5114. *Maker of custom-built furniture, teacher of woodworking at my own school, maker of exhibition pieces (mostly unsaleable).*

(80) Mike Darlow, Woodturning, 20A City Rd., Chippendale, NSW 2008, Australia (02)212-5782. *Bespoke woodturning and cabinetmaking.*

RANDWICK: **James A. Stephany,** 72 Botany St., Randwick, NSW 2031, Australia.

THORNLEIGH: **Leon Sadubin Designs,** 199 Pennant Hills Rd., Thornleigh, NSW 2120, Australia (02)449-2865. *Domestic furniture. We have a range of our own designs, also accept variety of public commissions.*

Queensland

BRISBANE: **(11) Iron Bark, John Jeno Linek,** 3 Pearson Rd., Yatala Via, Brisbane, Queensland 4207, Australia (07)287-3152. *Artistic woodturning, short courses on wood appreciation and turning. Supplier of native woods.*

PORT DOUGLAS: **Black Mountain Woodworks,** Warner St., Port Douglas, Queensland, Australia (07)985-3488. *Custom kitchen tables and boatwork.*

South Australia

SCOTT CREEK: **(139) Kempster Instruments,** Scott Creek Rd., Scott Creek, S. Australia 5153 (08)388-2337. *Musical-instrument building and repair. Almost entirely harps of various sizes and types.*

Victoria

BURWOOD: **Vic Wood, Woodturner,** 31 Wridgway Ave., Burwood, Victoria 3125, Australia (03)288-4441. *Wall plaques, segmented turnings, containers, executive toys and general wood turning.*

ELSTERNWICK: **Andris Stals,** 7 McCombie St., Elsternwick, Victoria 3185, Australia (03)523-5127. *Jewelry boxes, sculptured walking sticks and free-form bowls, slab tables.*

GLEN IRIS: **Innates Woodworking,** 7 Goodwin St., Glen Iris, Victoria 3146, Australia 29 1178. *Principally a chair maker, but interested in making any solid furniture, cabinets, tables, solid doors.*

LYSTERFIELD: **William Presslor,** Lot 1 29 Wellington Rd., Lysterfield, Victoria 3156, Australia (03)758-7827. *Design, sculpture, one-of-a-kind furniture in domestic and exotic hardwoods.*

NORTH MELBOURNE: **(41) Barry Mills,** 42 Courtney St., North Melbourne, Victoria 3051, Australia (03)429-9434. *Sculptural and sculpturally oriented functional pieces.*

RINGWOOD: **(175) Alan Wilson,** 14 Pitt St., Ringwood, Victoria 3134, Australia 011-61-3-870-7533. *Designed one-off furniture and sculptural forms. Lathe-turned objects, including choice pieces of green timber which dictate the final form.*

SURREY HILLS: **(42) Helmut Lueckenhausen,** 10 Suffolk Rd., Surrey Hills, Victoria 3127, Australia (03)836-3447. *Sculptural furniture and functional objects in wood.*

BRAZIL

SÃO PAULO: **Osmar Valente,** Rua Coronel Meirelles, 817 Penha, São Paulo, SP, Brazil.

CANADA

Alberta

CALGARY: **Herm's Turn,** 2816 Grant Cres. S.W., Calgary, AB T3E 4L1, Canada (403)242-4719. *Artistic woodturning.*

CANMORE: **Pielou Woodwork,** Box 823, Canmore, AB T0L 0M0, Canada (403)678-6256. *Designing and building hardwood furniture, cedar-strip canoes, all manner of whimsical woodwork.*

EDMONTON: **(161) Marquetry-Intarsia,** 7950 85th Ave., Edmonton, AB J6C 1G2, Canada (403)469-2619. *Marquetry to my or your designs.*

Randy Patt, 6812-101A Ave., Edmonton, AB T6C 1G3, Canada (403)465-4465. *Custom orders on anything. Majority of work is related to children.*

C.P. Ronden, 6515-145 A St., Edmonton, AB Canada (403)434-4912. *Design and construction of unique pieces of furniture, with emphasis on antique interpretations.*

GRANDE PRAIRIE: **(102) K.M. Cook, Woodworking,** 9307 102nd St., Grande Prairie, AB T8C 2T4, Canada (403)534-5820. *Custom furniture and sculpture, exotic wood, turnings, design services.*

RED DEER: **Treen Fine Furniture and Cabinetry, Chris Bruels and Joe Sybom,** Route 3, Red Deer, AB T4N 5E3, Canada (403)347-0570. *Excellence in design and workmanship. The context is custom furniture.*

STETTLER: **Kempf's Woodwork,** Box 1298, Stettler, AB T0C 2L0, Canada (403)742-6419.

British Columbia

ABBOTSFORD: **Steven M. Daechsel,** 30295 Marshall Extn. Rd., Abbotsford, BC V2S 1M3, Canada (604)853-5878. *Unique furnishings.*

Robt. H. Dueck, The Country Workshop, 1295 Peardonville Rd. RR 1, Abbotsford, BC V2S 1M3, Canada (604)854-5601. *Fine cabinetry.*

(121) Hands and Tools, 2849 Ash St., Abbotsford, BC V2S 4G3, Canada (604)854-6359. *Custom designs in various metals and woods.*

ALDERGROVE: **Wolf Woodworking,** 27618 56th Ave. Route 1, Aldergrove, BC V0X 1A0, Canada (604)856-4269. *Architectural woodwork, kitchen cabinets, custom furniture.*

BURNABY: **Don Shortt,** 4353 Hurst St., Burnaby, BC V5J 1N1, Canada. *Fine guitar repairs and custom building.*

CAMPBELL RIVER: **Dean R. Lemke,** 1991 16th Ave., Campbell River, BC V9W 4L2, Canada (604)287-4128. *Anything your wooden heart desires.*

CLEARBROOK: **Peter Christensen, Woodwright,** Box 2187, Clearbrook, BC V2T 3X8, Canada (604)859-2098. *Quality work of hardwoods, domestic and exotic. Incorporating wooden mechanisms. Enjoy the challenging and unusual.*

DELTA: **Rene Haagerup,** 4959 Kadota Dr., Delta, BC V4M 1X4, Canada (604)943-1370.

DENMAN ISLAND: **PLANE FANCY,** General Delivery, Denman Island, BC V0R 1T0, Canada. *Individually crafted furniture from carefully seasoned local and exotic woods. Emphasis on hand-shaping, carving.*

GRAY CREEK: **Dietrich's Woodcraft,** Box 64, Gray Creek, BC V0B 1S0, Canada. *Spinning wheels.*

HORNBY ISLAND: **Woodwind Furniture,** 1150 Central Rd., Hornby Island, BC V0R 1Z0, Canada (604)335-2663. *Custom-designed, handmade furniture, with each design being a collaboration between client and craftsman.*

LANGLEY: **Domi,** 19625 80th Ave., Langley, BC V3A 4P7, Canada (604)888-2767. *Bathroom and kitchen accessories, custom furniture, mirrors, satirical sculptures. Bandsawn and carved jewelry boxes.*

NARAMATA: **Paul Malakoff,** Route 1, Naramata, BC V0H 1N0, Canada (604)496-5627. *Will consider any type of wood construction project.*

PRINCE GEORGE: **Roch's Guitar Workshop,** 855 2nd Ave., Prince George, BC V2L 3A6, Canada (604)564-9263. *Custom-made electric and acoustic guitars and basses, all types of repairs, custom inlay.*

SURREY: **John G. Stewart,** 2818 Gordon Ave., Surrey, BC V4A 3J4, Canada (604)531-3742. *Custom design and also reproductions.*

VANCOUVER: **Clifton Lee Gass,** 2323 W. 6th, Vancouver, BC V6K 1W1, Canada (604)733-7983. *Sculpture in hardwoods, soapstone, marble and native stone.*

Out of the Woods, 1750 Alberni St., Vancouver, BC V6G 1B2, Canada (604)687-5543. *Custom furniture and kitchens, as well as any other interesting wooden work.*

VICTORIA: **Mad Beaver Woodworks,** 4055 Carey Rd., Victoria, BC, Canada (604)479-2348. *Custom furniture and cabinetry. Fancy interior finishing for house and yacht.*

Geoffrey Munday, Cabinetmaker, 962 Haliburton Rd., Victoria, BC V8Y 1J3, Canada (604)658-1558. *The Sutherland loom (a Swedish-style floor loom), residential and commercial cabinetry, solid-wood furniture.*

Of The Woods, Ken Guenter, 2549 Forbes St., Victoria, BC V8R 4B9, Canada (604)595-2763. *Traditional and contemporary designer furniture.*

(113) Special Editions, 2482 Central Ave., Victoria, BC V8S 2S8, Canada. *Original furniture designs from wall cabinets, tables, desks and frames to seating and storage cabinets.*

Tools 'n Space Woodworking, 338 Catherine St., Victoria, BC V9A 3S8, Canada (604)383-9600. *Custom kitchens, doors, furniture, retail fine hardwoods, finishes, woodworking, books. Teach woodworking courses.*

WHALETOWN: **Timber Wolf Custom Woodworking,** Box 102, Whaletown, BC V0P 1Z0, Canada (604)935-6486. *Custom furniture and cabinets, unique contemporary to antique reproductions, small wooden boats up to 25 ft.*

WHITE ROCK: **Ross Neuman,** 13925 Marine Dr., White Rock, BC V4B 1A3 Canada.

Manitoba

WINNIPEG: **Terry Osnach,** 114 Smithfield Ave., Winnipeg, MB R2V 0B8, Canada (204)338-5176. *Custom furniture, cabinet work, and stairbuilding.*

New Brunswick

HARVEY STATION: **(105) Custom Woodworking,** Route 3, Harvey Station, NB E0H 1H0, Canada (506)366-5794. *All forms of commission work. If it can be done in wood, I'll do it.*

POCOLOGAN: **Idylwyld Studios,** Pocologan, NB E0G 2S0, Canada. *Production items for wholesale. Shaker boxes, bread knives, etc. Furniture (Shaker to contemporary).*

RUTHESAY: **Michael Kippers,** 258 Old Hampton Highway, Ruthesay, NB E0G 2W0, Canada (506)847-4807. *Fine furniture and wooden yacht restoration.*

ST. JOHN: **Seaside Woodworks,** 533 Earle Ave., St. John, NB E2L 1H1, Canada (506)672-8591 or 642-3397. *Furniture, craft items, bandsawn boxes, cutting boards, etc.*

Newfoundland

ST. JOHN'S: **(120) Peter Dawson,** 10 Parliament St., St. John's, Nfld. A1A 2Y7, Canada (709)753-4144. *Designs for publication, one-of-a-kind toys and miniatures.*

Ian H. Stewart, M.S.I.A. (S.A.), 23 Dunfield St., St. John's, Nfld. A1A 1W2, Canada (709)722-7448. *Incised commemorative panels, heraldic achievements in the round, decorated and gilded.*

Nova Scotia

BEDFORD: **Ducharme Fine Wood Turnery,** Box 576, Bedford, NS B4A 2Y2, Canada (902)835-8067. *Bowls and lamps in exotic and local (Canadian) woods.*

DARTMOUTH: **Barry Wheaton,** 353 Waverley Rd., Dartmouth, NS B2X 2E5, Canada (902)435-3460. *Particularly religious art, but have accepted and will accept other challenges.*

HALIFAX: **Thomas Klenck,** Route Jeddore, Halifax, NS B0J 1P0, Canada (902)889-2829. *Contemporary and traditional design and construction.*

John Perkins, The Cat and the Fiddle, 5659 Merkel St., Halifax, NS B3K 2J1, Canada (902)454-8286. *Restoration, conservation of stringed musical instruments and fine furniture. Custom construction.*

Brad Sorrell, 5300 Morris St. 5, Halifax, NS B3J 1B9, Canada (902)422-2156.

Stevenson Wood Products, 2021 Brunswick St., Halifax, NS B3K 2Y5, Canada (902)423-7622. *Design and build furniture for home or office; some antique restoration or conservation.*

HANTSPORT: **M.D. MacKillop, Fundy Woodturning,** Main St., Hantsport, NS B0P 1P0, Canada (902)684-9123. *Small pieces, turned furniture, wine tables, plant stands and general treen ware.*

LUNENBURG CO.: **Jeff Amos, Fine Workings In Wood,** Petite Riviere, Lunenburg Co., NS, Canada. *Furniture by design and craftsmanship to be lifetime investments. Most styles considered. Traditional Windsor chairs.*

PICTOU: **(53) Joseph Wilson,** Route 3, Pictou, NS B0K 1H0, Canada (902)485-4652. *Custom and moderate production furniture and cabinetry. Commercial/residential. Consistent quality in designs and workmanship.*

SYDNEY: **(38) Leo MacNeil,** Route 3, Sydney, NS B1P 6G5, Canada. *Hand woodworking, reproductions and custom pieces designed and built.*

WINDSOR: **Andrew Elliot,** Route 2, Windsor, NS B0N 2T0, Canada (902)798-5625. *String instruments repaired. Guitars and mandolins built. Furniture to order.*

WOLFVILLE: **David Burton,** 168 Main St., Wolfville, NS B0P 1X0, Canada (902)542-5830.

Oldtree Woodworking, Box 941, Wolfville, NS B0P 1X0, Canada (902)538-3271. *Design, construction, and repair of musical instruments, constructions in fine hardwoods.*

Ontario

BARRIE: **(175) Jeffrey Wind,** 458 Blake St., Barrie, ON I4N 1E3, Canada (705)726-4325. *Custom cabinets, furniture and doors.*

BLENHEIM: **The Wood Joint,** 44 Ford Crescent, Blenheim, ON N1P 1A0, Canada (519)676-5821. *One-of-a-kind specialties, limited production furniture, works in the round, solid-wood sculpturing.*

BRACEBRIDGE: **John E. O'Byrne, Designer-Craftsman,** Route 6, Bracebridge, ON P0B 1C0, Canada. *Design ability, ingenuity, curiosity, integrity, happiness, honesty, fairness, love of work, reasonable fees.*

BRAMPTON: **ClassiComfort,** 44 Foster Cres., Brampton, ON L6V 3M7, Canada (416)451-3449. *Home and office improvements, design and decor items, model building and drafting services.*

BURLINGTON: **Daniel Toohy,** 424 Pine Cove Rd., Burlington, ON L7N 1W5, Canada (416)637-0221. *Dragon-head and bird-head walking sticks and staffs.*

CAMBRIDGE: **A & M Wood Specialty Inc.,** 358 Eagle St. N., Cambridge, ON N3H 4S6, Canada (519)653-9322. *Importers and exporters of fine domestic and exotic hardwoods.*

Alex Black, 740 Hamilton St., Cambridge, ON N3H 3E4, Canada (519)653-6172. *Fine cabinetmaking, chair caning.*

(169) Eric Dewdney, 22 Blenheim Rd., Cambridge, ON N1S 1E6, Canada (519)621-2175. *Contemporary furniture.*

(35) Louis Gnida, Fine Furniture, 358 Eagle St. N., Cambridge, ON N3H 4S6, Canada (519)653-9322. *Custom-designed and custom-built furniture.*

CHATSWORTH: **Frederick J. Miller, Custom Woodworks,** Route 1, Chatsworth, ON N0H 1G0, Canada (519)794-3865. *Window sash and custom-built furniture.*

CLARKSBURG: **Wood Works, Robert S. Anderson,** Route 2, Clarksburg, ON N0H 1J0, Canada (519)599-5655. *Interior/exterior design and construction, furniture, cabinets, accessories, reproductions and repairs.*

DEEP RIVER: **Robert Barlow,** 4 Laurier Ave., Box 344, Deep River, ON K0J 1P0, Canada (613)584-3650.

DUNDAS: **(136) Charles Tauber,** 38 Bertram Dr., Dundas, ON L9H 4T3, Canada. *Handmade concert caliber guitars and lutes. Innovative and unique. Also general woodworking and dulcimers.*

H. Vilks, Route 3, 1030 Sulphur Springs Rd., Dundas, ON L9H 5E3, Canada.

ELORA: **The Furniture Gallery,** 439 Union St., Salem, Elora, ON N0B 1S0, Canada (519)846-5945. *Handcrafted custom furniture in domestic and exotic hardwoods.*

FEVERSHAM: **Dennis Klinsky, Artisan,** Route 1, Feversham, ON N0C 1C0, Canada (519)922-2185. *I specialize in design and construction of one-of-a-kind custom furniture.*

GADSHILL: **(130) Barrie Faulkner,** Oakleigh, Route 1, Gadshill, ON N0K 1J0, Canada. *Carvings and clocks of a one-design nature. (No custom work.)*

GUELPH: **Miller Custom Woodworking,** 14 McIlwraith Cr., Guelph, ON N1E 6J3, Canada. *Custom furniture, repair.*

HORNINGS MILLS: **Ted Light, Designer Woodworker,** General Delivery, Hornings Mills, ON L0N 1J0, Canada (519)925-6112.

INGLEWOOD: **(76) Stephen Levitt,** Route 1, Inglewood, ON L6X 1J3, Canada (416)838-3156. *Small runs of executive and office furnishings, as well as custom-designed pieces.*

KAMINISTIQUIA: **(140) Brahm Friedlander,** Route 1, Kaministiquia, ON P0T 1X0, Canada (807)767-2479. *Custom furniture and string instruments.*

KINGSTON: **Dolfin Design Cabinet Works,** Box 1033, Kingston, ON K7L 4Y5, Canada. *Furniture.*

Christopher Laffin, Cabinetmaker, Route 2, Kingston, ON K7L 5H6, Canada (613)548-8898. *Designing and making individual pieces of furniture and woodwork.*

LAKEFIELD: **Alasdair G.B. Wallace,** Box 547, Lakefield, ON, Canada (705)652-8697. *A small shop specializing in the unusual, one-of-a-kind and reproductions.*

LONDON: **Michael Markland,** 1 Ingleside Place, London, ON N6C 1C9, Canada (519)433-8987. *Cabinetmaking.*

LYNDHURST: **The Leeds Cabinetmaker,** Route 1, Lyndhurst, ON K0E 1N0, Canada (613)387-3913. *Traditional Canadian furniture designs, carvings and wooden window sash.*

MARKHAM: **Chase of Toronto,** 90 Nolan Ct., Markham, ON L3R 4L9, Canada (416)474-1915. *Prototypes, artist's easels, cabinets for electronic equipment.*

MISSISSAUGA: **(150) Aleida Ijzerman,** 2134 Haygate Cres. Mississauga, ON, Canada.

(16) Donald Lloyd McKinley, 1460 S. Sheridan Way, Mississauga, ON L5H 1Z7, Canada (416)274-0114. *Individual commissions, designs or prototyes of furniture or accessories. Appointment only.*

Woodlore, 1350 Winding Trail Unit 13, Mississauga, ON L4Y 2T8, Canada (416)624-4207. *Lathe turnings (capacity, 7 ft. 9 in.). Custom work welcome.*

OAKVILLE: **John Robus, Designer/Maker,** 309 Riverside Dr., Oakville, ON L6K 3N3, Canada (416)845-4550. *Custom designing and small-scale cabinet construction.*

OMEMEE: **David Hadley,** Route 4, Omemee, ON K0L 2W0, Canada (705)799-6648. *Wall clocks.*

ORLEANS: **J.W. Design & Woodworking,** 1158 Orleans Blvd., Orleans, ON K1C 2W1, Canada (613)824-2529. *Fine furniture, custom aquariums, craft clocks.*

OTTAWA: **(137) Richard Berg,** 10 Broadway Ave., Ottawa, ON K1S 2V6, Canada (613)233-6063. *Classical guitars, baroque lutes, archlutes, theorobos.*

Fred Halpin, 2777J Innes Rd., Ottawa, ON KIB3J7 Canada (613)824-8798. *Jewelry boxes, spoon racks, instrument cases, gameboards, canes, veneer and marquetry restoration.*

Sculpture by Wayne, 300 Somerset St. W. 10, Ottawa, ON, Canada (613)235-7094. *Unique carved sculptural furniture, architectural carving.*

(129) Adrian Searle Photography, 235 Somerset St. W. 608, Ottawa, ON K2P 0J3, Canada. *Precision-crafted woodwork and design for functional/technical use. Main profession is commercial product photography.*

PETERBOROUGH: **Stewart Bailey,** 621 Harper Rd., Peterborough, ON K9H 6R6, Canada (705)745-0700. *Fine furniture, cabinets, and one-of-a-kind woodturnings in domestic and exotic hardwoods.*

Goodwin Creations, 3455 Parkhill Rd. E., Peterborough, ON K9L 1C4, Canada (705)745-9277. *Modern or traditional custom woodworking, precision turnings and limited-edition design originals.*

RENFREW: **Thomas Lockwood,** 20 Bridge St. W., Renfrew, ON K7V-3R2, Canada (613)432-4809.

ST. CATHARINES: **Architectural Woodcraft,** 12 Grote St. Unit 3, St. Catharines, ON L2N 2E7, Canada (416)937-0344. *Custom cabinetry, staircases, doors, architectural trim details. Tradtional joinery techniques. Renovations, restorations.*

SARNIA: **Dave Watson-Paul Cocarell,** 1018 Briarfield Ave., Sarnia, ON N7V 4A3, Canada (519)542-2889. *Custom cabinets and accessories.*

STONEY CREEK: **Wheelery,** Group 7 Box 5 Route 2, Stoney Creek, ON L8G 3X5, Canada (416)643-2575. *Wheels.*

SUDBURY: **Jacques Berger,** 1479 Laurentian Village, Sudbury, ON P3E 2MS, Canada (705)522-5470. *Anything calling for innovative design.*

TORONTO: **(170) Ken and Pat Bennett,** 1800 Lawrence Ave. W., Toronto, ON M6L 1E2, Canada (416)241-4893.

(167) Peter R. Fleming, 12 S. Dr., Toronto, ON M4W 1R1, Canada (416)922-8386. *Boxes, small objects, commissioned and speculative pieces of furniture.*

(68) Michael Fortune, Designer/Maker, 86 Nelson St., Toronto, ON M5V 1T9, Canada (416)977-3801. *Residential and commercial commissions, steam-bending, laminating, hot pipe bending, surface shaping.*

(67) Douglas Oliver, 86 Nelson St., Toronto, ON M6J 3L6 Canada (416)977-3801. *Custom furniture.*

Owl Woodcrafts, 35 Robina Ave., Toronto, ON M6C 3Y5 Canada (416)654-0482. *Small wooden objects for the home and office.*

Philip Whitcombe Woodworking, 2388 Dundas St. W. 4th floor, Toronto, ON M6P 1W9, Canada (416)535-5096. *Furniture and cabinetry in solid wood and/or veneer. Woodturning.*

(169) Ray Prince, 382 Wellesley St. E., Toronto, ON M4X 1H6, Canada. *Pictorial display of wood, jewelry boxes, etc., enclosed compartmented interiors, handsawn veneers, marquetry. Nonproduction.*

VIRGIL: **Robert Kroeker,** Box 354, Virgil, ON L0S 1T0, Canada (416)468-2811. *Custom-design, period reproductions.*

Prince Edward Island

NORTH WILTSHIRE: **(78) Diane E.H. Gaudreau, Gaudreau Fine Woodwork,** Route 2, Stanchel, North Wiltshire, PEI C0A 1Y0, Canada (902)964-2281. *Designer furniture and accessories.*

Jacques Gaudreau, Gaudreau Fine Woodwork, Route 2, Stanchel, North Wiltshire, PEI C0A 1Y0, Canada (902)964-2281. *Designer furniture and accessories.*

Quebec

ARUNDEL: **(33) Barrie Graham,** Route 1, Arundel, PQ J0T 1A0, Canada (819)687-2375. *Specializing in one-of-a-kind objects and any challenging woodworking project.*

BONAVENTURE: **Ebenisterie La Queue D'Aronde Enr.,** 150 E. Route 3, Co. Bonaventure, PQ G0C 3A0, Canada (418)534-3132. *Custom furniture and woodworking. Restoration of old furniture.*

DALESVILLE: **George Neradilek, Artisan at Dalesville,** Route 327, Dalesville, PQ J0V 1A0, Canada (514)533-4943. *Custom-built furniture modern and antiques, kitchens, one-of-a-kind art objects.*

KIRKLAND: **Robert Duff,** 10 Centennial Cr., Kirkland, PQ H9J 2C8, Canada. *Contemporary creations of decorating accessories and small furniture pieces.*

MONTREAL: **Normand Giroux,** 1 Rue Oakridge, Montreal, PQ H4K 2C5, Canada (514)334-8736. *Contemporary furniture and objects made on commission. Turnings and other samples of my works displayed at the above address and at Le Salon Des Metier D'Art Exposition in Montreal.*

(152) Marc Richardson, Finewoods Designs, 386 Le Moyne, Montreal, PQ H2Y 1Y3, Canada (514)849-1964. *Exclusive, designed furniture from exotic and domestic solid woods.*

PIERREFONDS: **(168) Stefan Smeja,** 4838 Pierre Lauzon, Pierrefonds, PQ H8Y 2C5, Canada (514)684-2849.

STE. FOY: **Oscar Boisjoly,** 2841 rue Legare, Ste. Foy, PQ G1V 2H1, Canada. *Woodturning.*

Denis Marois, 2870 Grondines, Ste. Foy, PQ G1W 1G1, Canada (418)653-5571. *One-design small pieces.*

Jean Rouleau, 987 Bld. Pie XII, Ste. Foy, PQ G1W 4N4, Canada (418)658-2091. *Contemporary furniture.*

ST.-M-des-STS.: **Gilbert Hetu,** 8011 Brassard, CP 314, St.-M-des-Sts., PQ J0K 3B0, Canada. *Bas-relief and carved furniture.*

ST. POLYCARPE: **(11) Francois Lambert,** CP 263, St. Polycarpe, PQ J0P 1X0, Canada. *Woodturning.*

Saskatchewan

SASKATOON: **Mike Hansen,** 313 Campion Crescent, Saskatoon, Sask. S7H 3T8, Canada (306)373-6942. *Canoes, paddles, bowls, exotic boxes, furniture.*

(11) Michael Hosaluk, Woodturner-Furniture Maker, Route 2, Saskatoon, Sask. S7K 3J5, Canada (306)382-2380. *Turned wooden bowls, furniture.*

WILKIE: **Byron's Toy Shop,** Route 2, Wilkie, Sask. S0K 4W0, Canada (30)843-2925. *Replicas of agricultural and industrial equipment and one-of-a-kind showpieces.*

(123) Byron Hansen, Box 95, Wilkie, Sask. S0K 4W0, Canada.

GREAT BRITAIN

England

BRISTOL: **Two's Company Furniture,** 16 Upper Maudlin St., Bristol 2, England 0272 23800. *Handcrafted goods relating to furniture and furnishing.*

CHESHIRE: **W.D. Colgrave,** 24 The Loont, Winsford, Cheshire CW71EV, England 51386. *Individually designed furniture, woodturning.*

DEVON: **Peter Kuh, Endgrain,** Otterton Mill, Otterton, Budleigh Salterton, Devon, England. *Adjustable wood music stands. Most domestic furniture designed and made to order.*

HERTFORDSHIRE: **David R. Burton,** 58 Chapel Lane, Fowlmere-Royston, Hertfordshire, England. *Purpose-designed one-off cabinets.*

LINCOLN: **Peter Willcox,** Rose Cottage, Plough Lane, Fiskerton, Lincoln LN34EY, England. *Specialty: period furniture reproductions.*

LONDON: **(145) Ben Bacon,** Unit 20-72, Dartmouth Park Hill, London, England N19. *Woodcarving and gilding.*

(96) David Shewell, 47 Osbaldeston Rd., Stoke Newington, London, England N16 7DL (01)806-5127. *Commissioned furniture and fittings, both domestic and office, in a variety of hardwoods.*

NORTHANTS: **Jonathan F. Knight,** The Tower, Irthlingborough Rd., Finedon, Northants, England 0933-680807. *Individually designed contemporary furniture in hardwood.*

NORTH YORKSHIRE: **(178) Jon Barnes, Prospect Joinery,** Prospect Rd., Harrogate, North Yorkshire, England 885888. *Designing and making of fine contemporary furniture.*

SHROPSHIRE: **Tony Sibbick, Cabinet Maker,** Grafton House, Montford Bridge, Shrewsbury, Shropshire, England. *Handmade fine furniture.*

Scotland

BANFFSHIRE: **John Wright, Woodworker,** Strath Avon, Ballindalloch, Banffshire AB3 9AS, Scotland. *Hand-built furniture, antique restoration, letter-carving, wood bending, boatbuilding.*

LANARKSHIRE: **(99) John Behm,** 18 Ramsay Rd., Leadhills 258, Lanarkshire MLIZ 6YA, Scotland. *Domestic furniture in native hardwoods, woodcarving, custom hardwood interiors, woodcut prints, music, tools, toys.*

HOLLAND

TEXEL: **Stefan During Houtwerk,** Blazerstraat 4, 1794ap Oosterend, Texel, Holland 02223-879.

IRELAND

DUBLIN: **Woodstock,** The Grange Cottage, Mulhuddart, Dublin, Ireland. *Hand carvings, turnings and individually crafted furniture.*

ISRAEL

HERZLIA: **(118) N. N. Stibbe, Fine Turnery Workshop,** 36 Hamaapilim St., Herzlia 46752, Israel 052-70322. *Production of turned artifacts, including decorative boxes, chess sets, toys and early woodwinds.*

JAPAN

TOKYO: **Satoshi Kushida,** 1-9-10 Nomizu Chotu-shi, Tokyo, Japan. *Original handmade furniture. Cabinets, chests, tables, chairs, desks, etc.*

NEW ZEALAND

RAGLAN: **Whale Bay Woodcrafts,** Whale Bay Rd., Raglan, New Zealand 8678. *One-of-a-kind pieces of furniture, with an emphasis on woodcarving, steam-bending.*

SWEDEN

MALMO: **Max Lund for Margruppen,** Lilla Torg, Malmo, 2433 Sweden. *Together with seven other craftsmen, we sell articles in wood, ceramics, textiles and silver.*

SWITZERLAND

FEUTERSOEY: **Jerry Montgomery,** Neue Post, Feutersoey, 3784 Switzerland. *Intarsia and marquetry, plus small designer articles in solid wood.*

WEST GERMANY

BERLIN: **(103) David Delthony,** Zossenerstr. 10, 1000 Berlin 61, W. Germany. (030)693-4164. *Individual wood sculptures, for relaxation and play, for adults and children.*

KASSEE: **Claus Szypura,** Schachtenstr. 12, 3500 Kassee, W. Germany. *Handcrafted furniture for mental and physical health and almost anything. Own original designs.*